THE
LAST DAYS
OF THE
SPANISH
REPUBLIC

The Coming of the Spanish Civil War
The Triumph of Democracy in Spain
The Politics of Revenge
Franco: A Biography
!Comrades! Portraits from the Spanish Civil War
Doves of War: Four Women of Spain
Juan Carlos: Steering Spain from Dictatorship to Democracy
The Spanish Civil War: Reaction, Revolution and Revenge
We Saw Spain Die: Foreign Correspondents in the Spanish Civil War
The Spanish Holocaust: Inquisition and Extermination in
Twentieth-Century Spain
The Last Stalinist

PAUL PRESTON

THE
LAST DAYS
OF THE
SPANISH
REPUBLIC

WILLIAM
COLLINS

William Collins
An imprint of HarperCollins*Publishers*
1 London Bridge Street
London SE1 9GF
www.WilliamCollinsBooks.com

First published in Great Britain by William Collins in 2016

1 3 5 7 9 8 6 4 2

A catalogue record for this book is
available from the British Library

ISBN 978-0-00-816340-2

Printed and bound in Great Britain by
Clays Ltd, St Ives plc

MIX
Paper from
responsible sources
FSC **FSC**® **C007454**
www.fsc.org

FSC is a non-profit international organisation established to promote
the responsible management of the world's forests. Products carrying the
FSC label are independently certified to assure consumers that they come
from forests that are managed to meet the social, economic and
ecological needs of present or future generations,
and other controlled sources.

Find out more about HarperCollins and the environment at
www.harpercollins.co.uk/green

For Lala Isla.

CONTENTS

Acknowledgements   ix

1   An Avoidable Tragedy   1
2   Resist to Survive   23
3   The Power of Exhaustion   39
4   The Quest for an Honourable Peace   65
5   Casado Sows the Wind   87
6   Negrín Abandoned   117
7   In the Kingdom of the Blind   141
8   On the Eve of Catastrophe   167
9   The Desertion of the Fleet   187
10 The Coup – the Stab in the Back   211
11 Casado's Civil War   237
12 Casado Reaps the Whirlwind   263

Epilogue: Repent at Leisure?   299

Abbreviations   323
Notes   325
Bibliography   359
Illustration Credits   361
Index   377

ACKNOWLEDGEMENTS

In the course of preparing this book, I have had the good fortune to rely on the advice on various issues of the following friends and colleagues. Michael Alpert, Javier Cervera, Robert Coale, Alfonso Domingo, Luis Español Bouché, Xulio García Bilbao, Carmen Gonzalez Martinez, Fernando Hernández Sánchez, Eladi Mainar Cabanas, Ricardo Miralles, Enrique Moradiellos, Óscar Rodríguez Barreiro, Cristina Rodríguez Gutiérrez, Sandra Souto and Julián Vadillo.

I am extremely grateful to the following friends for their help in the location of archival material. Laura Díaz Herrera for her invaluable help in Madrid and Ávila; Ángeles Egido León, José Manuel Vidal Zapater and Luis Vidal Zapater for permitting access to the unpublished memoirs of José Manuel Vidal Zapater; María Jesús González Hernández for help with the Causa General. Aurelio Martín Nájera as so often in the past was immensely generous in helping me with documents held in the Archivo Histórico of the Fundación Pablo Iglesias. Sir George Young and Lady Young kindly granted permission for the use of the papers of Sir George Young. My greatest debt is to Carmen Negrín and Sergio Millares Cantero for their unstinting assistance with both the papers and the photographs held in the Fundación Juan Negrín of Las Palmas.

I also want to put on record my thanks to Jesús Navarro, Juan Carlos Escandell and José Ramón Valero Escandell for an unforgettable day spent exploring 'Posición Yuste' (El Poblet), the houses at 'Posición Dakar' and the airfield (now a vineyard) of El Fondò in Monòver. Professor Valero Escandell also generously provided maps and photographs of the area of the Val de Vinalopó.

The gestation of this book, as with others in the past, was made especially rewarding thanks to my good fortune in being able to discuss many points of fact and of interpretation with my friends Helen Graham, Linda Palfreeman and Ángel Viñas.

1

An Avoidable Tragedy

This is the story of an avoidable humanitarian tragedy that cost many thousands of lives and ruined tens of thousands more. It has many protagonists but centres on three individuals. One, Dr Juan Negrín, the victim of what might be termed a conspiracy of dunces, tried to prevent it. Two bore responsibility for what transpired. One of those, Julián Besteiro, behaved with culpable naivety. The other, Segismundo Casado, behaved with a remarkable combination of cynicism, arrogance and selfishness.

On 5 March 1939, the eternally malcontent Colonel Casado, since May the previous year commander of the Republican Army of the Centre, launched a military coup against the government of Juan Negrín. Ironically, he thereby ensured that the end of the Spanish Civil War was almost identical to its beginning. As General Emilio Mola, the organizer of the military coup of 1936, its future leader General Francisco Franco and the other conspirators had done, Casado led a part of the Republican Army in revolt against the Republican government. He claimed, as they had done, and equally without foundation, that Negrín's government was the puppet of the Spanish Communist Party (Partido Comunista de España, or PCE) and that a coup was imminent to establish a Communist dictatorship. The same accusation was made by the anarchist José García Pradas, who talked of Negrín personally leading a Communist coup.[1] In that regard, it is worth recalling the judgement of the great American war correspondent Herbert Matthews, who knew Negrín well:

Negrín was neither a Communist nor a revolutionary ... I do not believe that Negrín gave the idea of a social revolution any thought before the Civil War ... Negrín retained all his life a certain indifference and blindness to social issues. Paradoxically, this put him in agreement with the Communists in the Civil War. He was equally blind in an ideological sense. He was a prewar Socialist in name only. Russia was the only nation that helped Republican Spain; the Spanish Communists were among the best and most disciplined soldiers; the International Brigade, with its Communist leadership, was invaluable. Therefore, Premier Negrín worked with the Russians, but never succumbed to or took orders from them.[2]

A not unsimilar view was expressed by Negrín's lifelong friend Dr Marcelina Pascua:

Was Negrín a Communist? How ridiculous! Not by a thousand miles. He was congenitally individualistic, utterly disinclined to follow a collective discipline or to put up with tight rules and regulations imposed by a political party or to follow the personal requirements that the instruments of marxism impose on their adherents. As far as any hero worship was concerned, the person that he admired most was Clemenceau (and not his contemporary Lenin) despite being fully aware of his repressive and reactionary policies against the trade unions and his persistent hostility to the French Socialists. I always interpreted Negrín's veneration for 'the Tiger' in terms of his being seduced by the energy and efficacy that he demonstrated during the First World War. This explains the contradiction because what Negrín admired in Clemenceau was exactly the pragmatic determination to win the war that was what he aspired to do in the Spanish conflict.

According to Pascua, Negrín adopted as a private slogan Clemenceau's remark that 'Dans la guerre comme dans la paix le dernier mot est à ceux que ne se rendent jamais.'[3]

Casado claimed that he launched his coup because he was sure that he could put a stop to what was increasingly senseless slaughter and that he could secure the clemency of Franco for all but the Communists. Even if this was genuinely his selfless motive, and there is ample evidence to the contrary, he went about it in the worst way imaginable. In his dealings with Franco, he behaved as if he had nothing to bargain with. He seemed to be oblivious of the fact that Franco was obsessed with capturing Madrid, the very symbol of resistance. The Caudillo had failed to do so in November 1936 and had also been thwarted at the battles of Jarama and Brunete in February and July 1937. Unlike Negrín, who could threaten continued resistance when Franco was being pushed by his German and Italian allies for an early end to the war, Casado took the position that the war was already lost. His only hope therefore was the naive, and rather arrogant, belief that Franco would be susceptible to a vague rhetoric of shared patriotism and the fraternal spirit of the wider military family, as if somehow they were equals.[4] In consequence, his action would actually cause massive loss of life.

It is certainly the case that the defeat of the Spanish Republic was already in sight. What remained possible, however, was to ensure that the war ended in such a way as to secure the evacuation of the most at-risk politicians and soldiers and guarantees for the civilian population to be left behind. As Negrín had commented to Juan-Simeón Vidarte of the executive committee of the Spanish Socialist Party (Partido Socialista Obrero Español, or PSOE): 'A negotiated peace, always; unconditional surrender to let them shoot half a million Spaniards, never.'[5] Ernest Hemingway summed up Negrín's position as follows: 'In a war you can never admit, even to yourself, that it is lost. Because when you will admit it is lost you are beaten. The one who being beaten refuses to admit and fights on the longest wins in all finish fights; unless of course he is killed, starved out, deprived of weapons or betrayed. All of these things happened to the Spanish people. They were killed in vast numbers, starved out, deprived of weapons and betrayed.'[6] With the Spanish Republic exhausted and internationally isolated, Casado's fateful initiative merely precipitated its defeat in the worst imaginable conditions. His revolt against the

Republican government sparked off a mini-civil war in Madrid, ensuring the deaths of 2,000 people, mainly Communists, and undermined the evacuation plans for hundreds of thousands of other Republicans.[7]

It has been suggested that what happened was the consequence of the 'fact' that Casado was a British agent. It is unlikely that he was an 'agent' or even in receipt of payment, but he was certainly in touch with British representatives – the Chargé d'Affaires Ralph Skrine Stevenson and Howard Denys Russell Cowan of the Chetwode Commission, which was trying to arrange prisoner exchanges. Given that the British government had long assumed that the Republic would be defeated, and wished to be free of what was seen as an unnecessary problem, there can be little doubt that Stevenson and Cowan at the very least encouraged Casado in his efforts to end the war. The ex-Communist Francisco-Félix Montiel claimed that 'London was behind Casado.'[8] At the end of February 1939, Casado met some Communist officers at his headquarters on the eastern outskirts of Madrid, given the military codename 'Posición Jaca'. Completely out of context, he assured them that 'the rumours that he was an agent of British intelligence were not true and it was not at his initiative that members of the British Embassy visited him and showered him with attention'.[9] Within Negrín's entourage there was a belief in British involvement in the coup. In 1962, the American journalist Jay Allen wrote to another newspaperman Louis Fischer, both friends of Negrín, 'Who, besides Rafael Méndez, whose address I don't have, could fill me in on the role of the British Intelligence agent who helped pull off the Casado coup?'[10]

Casado was born on 10 October 1893 in Nava de la Asunción in the province of Segovia. He was brought up under the strict discipline imposed by his father, an infantry captain, and became an officer cadet himself at the age of fifteen. He graduated as a first lieutenant in 1920 and made his career as a desk officer, albeit a very competent one. Apart from a brief and relatively tranquil eight-month period in Morocco, he had no battlefield experience. He had no political links, although in January 1935 he was appointed head of the presidential escort of Niceto Alcalá Zamora, whom he admired. After Alcalá had been replaced by Manuel Azaña in May 1936, Casado, who had reached the rank of major, found the post much less agreeable. In August 1936, he resigned from the presidential guard on the grounds that working with Azaña was 'a horrible torture'. Promoted to lieutenant colonel, he then became chief of operations of the general staff when Francisco Largo Caballero became Prime Minister and Minister of Defence. When Vicente Rojo was made chief of staff, a promotion that Casado never forgave since he aspired to the post himself, he became inspector general of the cavalry but deeply resented Rojo and the Communists. His battlefield experiences at Brunete in July and Zaragoza in October 1937 were not crowned with success. Nevertheless, in 1938, by now promoted to full colonel, he was given two important posts, as head of the Army of Andalusia and shortly afterwards as head of the Army of the Centre.[11] He seems to have held an extremely cordial meeting with the PCE top brass in Madrid on 25 July 1938. One of the topics discussed was how, in the event of Republican defeat, a staged evacuation might be mounted. Francisco-Félix Montiel claimed later that the purpose of this meeting was for the PCE to ensure that an incompetent traitor was in place to bring the war to an end in such a way as to absolve the party of responsibility. In fact, it is much more likely that the purpose of the meeting was to ensure the loyalty of Casado and the Army of the Centre just as the Republican army was crossing the Ebro, in the last great push for victory. If the Communists doubted Casado's loyalty, Rojo doubted his competence.[12]

Casado was an irascible officer noted for his rectitude and austerity. In fact, his evil temper and his ascetic way of life were to some extent explained by the painful stomach ulcers from which he suffered. When the vice-president of the Socialist General Union of Workers (Unión General de Trabajadores, or UGT), Edmundo Domínguez Aragonés, was appointed commissar inspector of the Army of the Centre at the end of December 1938, he went to introduce himself to Casado. He found him prostrate on his bed. Casado's unprovoked and gratuitous assertions of loyalty rang alarm bells: 'I am a soldier whose only duty is to respect and obey the Government. You can see just how committed I am to this duty because anyone else in my situation, with an ulcer tearing through his guts, would have ample excuse to abandon it all and look after his health. Not me. Madrid has been entrusted to me and I will defend it or die trying. If I left, they would say that I am a coward.' Domínguez was struck by the way in which, 'emanating self-satisfaction', Casado vehemently asserted that his principal concern was to alleviate the suffering of the women and children of the capital. Far from being convinced, Domínguez's suspicions were aroused that Casado was insincere and trying to hide something.[13]

Fernando Rodríguez Miaja, the nephew and private secretary of General José Miaja, the erstwhile hero of the defence of Madrid, had similar doubts about Casado: 'Intelligent and a technically a good soldier, Casado was ambitious, self-obsessed and histrionic with a bitter and unpleasant character ... He had an uncontrollable desire to be always pre-eminent, in the limelight and centre-stage. He lived and behaved only in the first person singular. These characteristics of his personality had a great bearing on the way the Spanish war ended.'[14]

It is certainly the case that his behaviour during the last months of the Spanish Civil War suggest a self-serving arrogance which fed the ambition to go down in history as the man who ended the war. This was brazenly revealed in the dedication (to M.O.) of the memoir written shortly after his arrival in London in 1939. He wrote sarcastically: 'I left my country because I committed the grave fault of ending a fratricidal struggle, sparing my people much sterile bloodshed.' He went on to comment on the historical transcendence of his actions.[15] While still in Spain he had told Dr Diego Medina Garijo, his personal physician and a member of the Francoist Fifth Column, that it was his intention to astound the world.[16] This rather sustains the judgement of Vicente Rojo that Casado was a vacuous and sinister megalomaniac: 'Casado is all talk. Casado does not serve the people and he never has. He is the most political and most crooked and faint-hearted of the career officers in the Republican ranks.'[17] Even more caustic was the opinion of Dolores Ibárruri, the Communist orator famed as 'Pasionaria': 'It is difficult to conceive of more slippery and cowardly vermin than Colonel Segismundo Casado.'[18]

The bitterness of Pasionaria is comprehensible, given that the Communists would be among the most immediate victims of Casado's coup. Less partisan perhaps is the view of his collaborator, General Miaja, who referred to him in private as 'four-faced' on the grounds that to call him 'two-faced' would barely reflect the reality.[19] More intriguing is the contemptuous judgement of Antonio Bouthelier España, a member of the fascist party Falange Española and one of Casado's contacts with the Fifth Column. He described Casado as 'a soldier who did not feel pride in his profession, who did not understand the word "service", restless and ambitious, envious of politicians in top hat and frock coat, author of long-winded and solemn speeches ... an eternal malcontent who acted only in his own interests'.[20]

In a real sense, there was an inevitability about the eventual defeat of the Republic. The initial military rising took place on the evening of 17 July 1936 in Spain's Moroccan colony and in the peninsula itself the next morning. The plotters were confident that it would all be over in a few days. Their coup was successful in the Catholic small-holding areas which voted for the right – the provincial capitals of rural León and Old Castile, cathedral market towns like Avila, Burgos, Salamanca and Valladolid. However, in the left-wing strongholds of industrial Spain and the great estates of the deep south, the uprising was defeated by the spontaneous action of the working-class organizations. Nevertheless, in major southern towns like Cadiz, Cordoba, Granada and Seville, left-wing resistance was soon savagely crushed.

Within days, the country was split into two war zones. The rebels controlled one-third of Spain in a northern block of Galicia, León, Old Castile, Aragon and part of Extremadura and an Andalusian triangle from Huelva to Seville to Cordoba. They had the great wheat-growing areas, but the main industrial – and food-consuming – centres remained in Republican hands. After vain efforts to reach a compromise with the rebels, a cabinet of moderate Republicans was formed under the chemistry professor José Giral. There was some reason to suppose that the Republic would be able to crush the rising. Giral's moderate Republican cabinet had control of the nation's gold and currency reserves and virtually all of Spain's industrial capacity.

However, it lacked a loyal functioning bureaucratic machinery, especially in the fields of public order and the economy.

There were three major advantages enjoyed by the military rebels that would eventually decide the conflict – the African Army, massive assistance from the fascist powers and the tacit support of the Western democracies. Republican warships were able for only three weeks to prevent the transportation from Morocco to Spain of the rebels' strongest card, the ferocious colonial army under Franco. Moreover, the fact that power in the streets of Spain's major cities lay with the unions and their militia organizations undermined the efforts of Giral's government to secure aid from the Western democracies. Inhibited by internal political divisions and sharing the British fear of revolution and of provoking a general war, the French premier Léon Blum quickly drew back from early promises of aid. In contrast, Franco in North Africa was able to persuade the local representatives of Nazi Germany and Fascist Italy that he was the man to back. By the end of July, Junkers 52 and Savoia-Marchetti 81 transport aircraft were starting to airlift the principal components of the Army of Africa, the bloodthirsty Foreign Legion and the Moroccan mercenaries of the so-called Native Regulars, across the Strait of Gibraltar to Seville. Fifteen thousand men crossed in ten days and a failed coup d'état became a long and bloody civil war. That crucial early aid was soon followed by a regular stream of high-technology assistance. In contrast to the state-of-the-art equipment arriving from Germany and Italy, complete with technicians, spare parts and the correct workshop manuals, the Republic, shunned by the democracies, had to make do with over-priced and obsolete equipment from private arms dealers.

The rebels swiftly undertook two campaigns that dramatically improved their situation. Mola attacked the Basque province of Guipúzcoa, cutting it off from France. Meanwhile, Franco's Army of Africa advanced rapidly northwards to Madrid, leaving an horrific trail of slaughter in their wake, including the massacre at Badajoz where 2,000 prisoners were shot. By 10 August, they had united the two halves of rebel Spain. The rebels consolidated their position throughout August and September as General José Enrique Varela connected Seville, Cordoba, Granada and Cadiz. For the Republicans, there were no spectacular advances, only retreats and two frustrating operations – the siege of the rebel garrison of Toledo in the fortress of the Alcázar and the futile attempt of anarchist militia columns from Barcelona to recapture Zaragoza, which had fallen quickly to the rebels.

The Spanish Republic was fighting not only Franco and his armies but increasingly also the military and economic might of Hitler and Mussolini. Snubbed by France and Britain, the Republican premier, Giral, turned to Moscow. The initial reaction of the Soviet Union was one of deep embarrassment. The Kremlin did not want the events in Spain to undermine its delicately laid plans for an alliance with France. However, by mid-August, the flow of help to the rebels from Hitler and Mussolini threatened an even greater disaster if the Spanish Republic fell. That would severely alter the European balance of power, leaving France with three hostile fascist states on its borders. Stalin's reluctant decision to aid Spain was thus based on raison d'état. Distance and organizational chaos meant that it was mid-September before the transportation of any equipment to Spain. The first shipment of ancient rifles and machine guns arrived on 4 October. Only at the end of September, after the Republic had agreed to send its gold reserves to Russia, was the decision taken to send modern aircraft and tanks – which had to be paid for at inflated prices.

In the meantime, the all-Republican cabinet of Professor Giral had given way to a more representative government of Republicans, Socialists and Communists under the premiership of the veteran trade unionist Francisco Largo Caballero. Although popular among workers, Largo Caballero lacked the energy, determination and vision to direct a successful war effort. He failed to see that an effective war effort required a centralized state apparatus.[21] While the Republic floundered in search of foreign assistance and its disorganized militias fell back on the capital, the rebels tightened up their command structure. On 21 September at an airfield near Salamanca, the leading rebel generals met to choose a commander-in-chief both for obvious military reasons and to facilitate relations with Hitler and Mussolini. Already enjoying good communication with the Führer and the Duce,

Franco was their choice. On the same day, Franco decided to divert his columns, now at the gates of Madrid, to the south-east to Toledo. He thus lost an unrepeatable chance to sweep on to the capital before its defences were ready. However, by relieving the Alcázar, he clinched his own power with an emotional victory and a great media coup. He was also able to slow down the pace of the war in order to carry out a thorough political purge of captured territory. On 28 September, he was confirmed as head of the rebel state. Thereafter, he ruled over a tightly centralized zone. In contrast, the Republic was already severely hampered by intense divisions between the Communists, the middle-class Republicans and moderate Socialists on the one hand, who were rebuilding the state apparatus to make a priority of the war effort, and the anarchists, Trotskyists and left Socialists on the other, who wanted to put the emphasis on social revolution.

On 7 October the Army of Africa resumed its march on a Madrid inundated with refugees and beset by major supply problems. In an effort to rally the population, on 4 November, Largo Caballero added two anarcho-syndicalist ministers to his cabinet in the hope of widen-ing popular support for the beleaguered Republic. Franco's delay permitted the morale of the defenders of Madrid to be boosted by the arrival in early November of aircraft and tanks from the Soviet Union together with the columns of volunteers known as the International Brigades. The siege of Madrid saw heroic efforts by the entire popula-tion. On 6 November, expecting the capital to fall quickly, the govern-ment fled to Valencia. The city was left in the hands of General José Miaja. Backed by the Communist-dominated Junta de Defensa, the unkempt Miaja rallied the population while his brilliant chief of staff, Colonel Vicente Rojo, organized the city's forces. The first units of the International Brigades reached Madrid on 8 November, and consisted of German and Italian anti-fascists, plus some British, French and Polish left-wingers. Sprinkled among the Spanish defenders at the rate of one to four, the brigadiers both boosted their morale and trained them in the use of machine guns, in the conservation of ammunition and in the methods of using cover. They successfully resisted Franco's African columns and, by late November, he had to acknowledge his failure. The besieged capital would hold out for another two and a half years until the fateful sequence of events triggered by Colonel Casado.

The arrival of Russian equipment and international volunteers in the autumn helped save Madrid. However, their presence was also to be used by Franco's sympathizers to justify the intervention of Hitler and Mussolini and inhibit the Western powers. The motivation of both Germany and Italy was principally to undermine the Anglo-French hegemony in international relations, yet both dictators received a sympathetic ear in London when they claimed to be in Spain to combat bolshevism. Besieged, the Republic also had complex internal problems unknown in Franco's brutally militarized zone. The collapse of the bourgeois state in the first days of the war had seen the rapid emergence of revolutionary organs of parallel power – the committees and militias linked to the left-wing unions and parties. A massive popular collectivization of agriculture and industry took place. Exhilarating to participants and foreign observers like George Orwell, the great collectivist experiments of the autumn of 1936 were an obstacle to the creation of a war machine. Opposing beliefs about whether to give priority to war or revolution would lie at the heart of the internal conflict that raged within the Republican zone until mid-1937. The Republican President, Manuel Azaña, and moderate Socialist leaders like the Minister of the Navy and Air Force, Indalecio Prieto, and the Minister of Finance, Juan Negrín, were convinced that a conventional state apparatus, with central control of the economy and the institutional instruments of mass mobilization, was essential for an efficacious war effort. The Communists and the Soviet advisers agreed – it made sense and they hoped that halting the revolutionary activities of Trotskyists and anarchists would reassure the bourgeois democracies being courted by the Soviet Union.

Preoccupied by internal dissensions, and still without a conventional army, the Republic was unable to capitalize on its victory at Madrid. Franco's immediate response was a series of attempts to encircle the capital. At the battles of Boadilla (December 1936), Jarama (February 1937) and Guadalajara (March 1937), his forces were beaten back, but at enormous cost to the Republic. Concentration on the defence of Madrid meant the neglect of other fronts. Málaga in the south fell to newly arrived Italian troops at the beginning of February. The war in central Spain saw no easy victories. At Jarama, the rebel front advanced a few kilometres, but made no strategic gain. The Republicans lost 25,000 men, including some of the best British and American members of the Brigades, and the rebels about 20,000. In March, the rebels made further efforts to encircle Madrid by attacking near Guadalajara, 60 kilometres north-east of Madrid. An army of 50,000, the best-equipped and most heavily armed force yet seen in the war, broke through, but was defeated by a Republican counter-attack. Thereafter, as the Republic organized its People's Army (Ejército Popular de la República), the conflict turned into a more conventional war of large-scale manoeuvre.

Even after being defeated at the battle of Guadalajara, in which a large contingent of Italian troops was involved, the rebels still held the initiative because each reverse for Franco saw the Axis dictators increase their support. This was demonstrated during the rebel campaign in northern Spain in the spring and summer of 1937. In March, Mola led 40,000 troops in an assault on the Basque Country backed by the terror-bombing expertise of the German Condor Legion. In a rehearsal for the Blitzkrieg eventually unleashed on Poland and France, Guernica was annihilated on 26 April 1937 to shatter Basque morale and undermine the defence of the capital, Bilbao, which fell on 19 June. Thereafter, the rebel army, amply supplied with Italian troops and equipment, was able to capture Santander on 26 August. Asturias was quickly overrun during September and October. Northern industry was now at the service of the rebels. This gave them a decisive advantage to add to their numerical superiority in terms of men, tanks and aeroplanes.

The defeats suffered by the Republic during early 1937 would lead eventually on 17 May to the establishment under the premiership of Juan Negrín of a strong government from which the anarcho-syndicalists were dropped. Already, as Minister of Finance and with the help of his under-secretary Francisco Méndez Aspe, Negrín had systematized the Republic's exports of raw materials and its imports of weaponry and food. He had reorganized the Corps of Carabineros (border guards) to put a stop to smuggling and illegal exports. His contribution to the war effort cannot be exaggerated.[22] Now, as Prime Minister, Negrín put his faith in the brilliant strategist Colonel Vicente Rojo, who tried to halt the rebels' inexorable process by a series of diversionary offensives. At the village of Brunete, west of Madrid, on 6 July, 50,000 troops smashed through enemy lines, but the rebels had enough reinforcements to plug the gap. For ten days, in one of the bloodiest encounters of the war, the Republicans were pounded by air and artillery attacks. At enormous cost, the Republic slightly delayed the eventual collapse of the north. Brunete was razed to the ground. Then, in August, Rojo launched a bold pincer movement against Zaragoza. At the small town of Belchite in mid-September, the offensive ground to a halt. As at Brunete, the Republicans gained an initial advantage, but lacked sufficient force for the killer blow. In December, Rojo launched a further pre-emptive attack against Teruel, in the hope of diverting Franco's latest assault on Madrid. The plan worked. In the most intense cold, the Republicans captured Teruel on 8 January 1938 – the only time that they managed to capture a provincial capital that had been in rebel hands. However, the triumph was short-lived. The Republican forces were dislodged after six weeks of heavy battering by artillery and bombers. After another costly defence of a small advance, the Republicans had to retreat on 21 February, when Teruel was on the point of being encircled. The casualties on both sides had been alarmingly high.

The Republicans were exhausted, short of guns and ammunition and demoralized after the defeat at Teruel. Franco now seized the initiative with a well-resourced offensive through Aragon and Castellon towards the sea. A total of 100,000 troops, 200 tanks and nearly 1,000 German and Italian aircraft began their advance on 7 March 1938. By early April, the rebels had reached Lérida and then moved down the Ebro valley, cutting off Catalonia from the rest of the Republic. By 15 April, they had reached the Mediterranean. In consequence, there was no shortage of senior figures on the Republican side who considered that the war could not now be won. Among them could be found both the chief of staff, Colonel Rojo, the head of the air force, Colonel Ignacio Hidalgo de Cisneros, and that eternal pessimist Indalecio Prieto. Negrín, however, refused to acknowledge the possibility because he was aware of the dangers of defeatism.[23] He remained confident in continued Russian logistical support. However, Russian deliveries were few after June 1938. Already, by the late summer of 1937, attacks on neutral shipping by rebel warships and Italian submarines had closed the Mediterranean as a supply route for the Republic. Russian supplies now came from Murmansk or the Baltic ports and were unloaded in Le Havre or Cherbourg and then transported to the French–Spanish border.[24] To get them across France, Negrín had to spend valuable foreign currency bribing local officials. As the the Minister of Agriculture, the senior Communist Vicente Uribe, later commented: 'To get the necessary mechanisms working in France, it was necessary to grease them copiously, according to Negrín, with the funds of the Republic.'[25] In June 1938, the frontier was closed by the French Prime Minister Edouard Daladier and remained closed until late January 1939. The situation was most desperate in Catalonia, where the difficulties of supply of weaponry and food grew ever more acute. Daladier opened the frontier reluctantly only after Negrín told the recently appointed French Ambassador Jules Henry that Republican defeat in Catalonia and the arrival of German and Italian forces at the Pyrenees would constitute a threat to the security of France.[26]

That being the case, Franco could have been tempted to adopt a more attacking strategy. However, he was more interested in the total destruction of the Republican forces than in a quick victory, and he ignored the opportunity to turn against a poorly defended Barcelona. Instead, in July 1938, he launched a major attack on Valencia. The Republicans' determination in defence ensured that progress was slow and exhausting but, by 23 July, Valencia was under direct threat, with the rebels less than 40 kilometres away. In response, Vicente Rojo now launched another spectacular diversion in the form of a daring push across the River Ebro to restore contact between Catalonia and the central zone, separated since the Francoists had reached the Mediterranean in April. In the most hard-fought battle of the entire war, the Republican army of 80,000 men crossed the river and broke through the rebel lines, although at great cost to the International Brigades.

For some time, Negrín had pinned his hopes on an escalation of European tension that would alert the Western democracies to the dangers facing them from the Axis. The outbreak of a general European war would, he hoped, see the Republic aligned with France, Britain and Russia against Germany and Italy. Any such hopes were dashed when the Republic was virtually sentenced to death by the British reaction to the Czechoslovakian crisis. British foreign policy had long been orientated in favour of a Francoist victory. Rather than risk war with Hitler, Chamberlain effectively surrendered Czechoslovakia to the Nazis when he signed the Munich Agreement of 29 September 1938. It was a devastating blow to the Spanish Republic which, since July, had been engaged in its last great battle, at the Ebro. Even before the betrayal by the Western powers, Stalin had ordered the withdrawal of the International Brigades from Spain.[27]

The more immediate military objective for which the huge Army of the Ebro was created had been to divert the rebel attack on Valencia. Given the Republic's lack of armaments, it was an immensely risky venture. By 1 August, the Republicans had reached Gandesa 40 kilometres from their starting point, but there they were bogged down when Franco ordered massive reinforcements, including the Condor Legion, to be rushed in to check the advance. With inadequate artillery and air cover, the Republicans were subjected to three months of fierce artillery bombardment and sweltering heat.[28] Despite its strategic irrelevance, Franco was determined to recover the lost ground irrespective of the cost and relished the opportunity to catch the Republicans in a trap, encircle and destroy them. He could simply have contained the Republican advance and driven forward against a near-helpless Barcelona. Instead, he preferred, irrespective of the human cost, to turn Gandesa into the graveyard of the Republican army. With nearly 900,000 men now under arms, he could afford to be careless of their lives. At stake in this desperate and ultimately meaningless battle was the international credibility of the Republic. Munich had undermined the already dwindling faith in the possibility of victory among both the civilian population and the officer corps. Overwhelming logistical superiority in terms of air cover, artillery and troop numbers would see Franco score a decisive victory. In a sense, the Ebro operation, initially a tactical success, was a strategic disaster for the Republic since it used up vast quantities of equipment and left the way open for the rebel conquest of Catalonia.[29]

Ten days before the signing of the Munich Agreement, Vicente Rojo had drawn up a detailed report on the Republic's military situation in the context of the Czechoslovak crisis. It was his hope that the democracies would resist Hitler's demands and provoke a general war in which the Spanish Republic would be allied with Britain and France.[30] Nevertheless, he also analysed the likely consequences should the democracies give in to Hitler. Rojo's conclusion was that such a capitulation would give Italy and Germany an even freer hand to help Franco than hitherto: 'our war would enter, in such a case, a period of acute crisis because of the greater difficulties that we would have to overcome in order to sustain the struggle against an ever more powerful enemy'. Nevertheless, Rojo was still optimistic that 'a favourable resolution of our conflict' could be achieved. For this to happen, supplies of food and war matériel would have to be secured and the army's morale kept high and its organization improved. These two conditions he described as 'doable. They are problems for the Government'. To this end, he called for an effort to obtain greater foreign help and for a centrally controlled war effort such as that enjoyed by Franco – more efficient rationing, measures to be taken against those who evaded conscription, a single command for all the armed forces, central control of transport facilities and of industry, and an end to the proliferation of political parties and of competing newspapers.[31]

What Rojo was suggesting was as necessary as it was impossible. To achieve the fully centralized war effort to which Negrín and the Communist Party had aspired since the beginning of the conflict had already provoked opposition from anarchists, Trotskyists and sections of the Socialist Party. To go further, as Rojo now suggested, would generate even greater resentment. In any case, given the scale of the myriad problems faced by Negrín, the enormous reorganization required was simply out of the question. What Negrín did manage to do, along with his secret peace initiatives, was to intensify his efforts to secure military supplies from Russia. He successfully negotiated the supply of aircraft, tanks, artillery and machine guns. While what was agreed was less than he had hoped for, these armaments could have made a huge difference if, after their arrival in France in mid-January, they had been transported to the Catalan border. However, the continuing obstacles placed in the way by the French government ensured that they did not arrive in time.[32] Another aspect of Rojo's report would also have disappointing results. He added an appendix on military plans in which he talked of the relief that could be given to the Republican forces on the Ebro by the launching of offensives in the centre-south zone.[33] The four armies that made up what was called the Group of Armies of the Centre (Grupo de Ejércitos Republicanos del Centro) – Extremadura, Andalusia, the Levante and the Centre – were under the overall command of General Miaja, with General Manuel Matallana Gómez as his chief of staff. The Army of the Centre was commanded by Colonel Casado. Since all three were reluctant to continue the fight, Rojo's orders to this effect were never properly implemented.

The decisive Nationalist counter-offensive on the Ebro was launched on 30 October 1938. Concentrated air and artillery attacks on selected areas followed by infantry attacks gradually smashed the Republican forces.[34] By mid-November, at horrendous cost in casualties, the Francoists had pushed the Republicans out of the territory captured in July. The remnants of the Republican army abandoned the right bank of the Ebro at Flix late at night on 15 November. As they retreated back across the river, they left behind them many dead and much precious matériel. It had taken Franco four months to recover the territory gained by the Republic in one week in July. As we have seen, he had in July rejected the more adventurous strategy of holding the Republicans near Gandesa and pushing on to Barcelona from Lérida. By so doing, Franco demonstrated his preference for attrition and for the physical annihilation of the Republican army. He thereby ensured that there would be no armistice, no negotiation of peace conditions.

It was Munich that turned the battle into a resounding defeat, especially for the Communist Party which had invested energy, resources and prestige in the Ebro initiative.[35] Before, during and after the battle, this last throw of the dice contributed massively to civilian and military demoralization. After the defeat at Teruel in February and during the great Francoist advance through Aragon to the coast, the Republic had already suffered massive losses. In order to create the Army of the Ebro, the government had been obliged to call up a further nine years' worth of conscripts (the *reemplazos* of 1923 to 1929, and of 1940 and 1941). The need to train, and rely on, both older and younger men had a negative impact on the Catalan economy and society at large. Labour was in short supply and families were outraged that, during the battle of the Ebro, many Republican soldiers were seventeen-year-old adolescents. During the battle itself, army requisitioning, effectively the troops scavenging off the land, exacerbated the growing discontent. Further tension was caused by the Republican military intelligence service (Servicio de Inteligencia Militar, or SIM) which was pursuing those who had evaded conscription and those who had deserted.[36] Approximately 13,250 Spaniards and foreigners were killed, 6,100 (46 per cent) of them Francoists and 7,150 (54 per cent) Republicans. In roughly similar proportions, about 110,000 suffered wounds or mutilation. The richly fertile Terra Alta became a vast cemetery – tens of thousands of men were buried quickly, many were left where they lay and others drowned in the river. To the dismay of the local peasantry, and to the detriment of the Republican war effort, the fighting ruined the harvest of wheat and barley in July, of almonds in August, of grapes in September and of olives in November.

Negrín was fully aware of the significance of Munich. He knew that Republican victory was impossible. In late September 1938, the deputy secretary of the PSOE executive, Juan-Simeón Vidarte, told him that the committee's members remained convinced that the unconditional surrender demanded by Franco was out of the question. Commenting that no one forgot what had happened in Andalusia, Extremadura, the Basque Country and Asturias, he remarked: 'We can't hand over half of Spain and an army of a million men so that they can exterminate them as they like.' Negrín replied with resigned realism: 'Guarantees for an honourable peace is all that I want.'[37] To this effect, he consulted the Republic's legal adviser Felipe

Sánchez Román, who drafted the minimal conditions which Negrín accepted as the basis for negotiations with Franco, including a promise not to take reprisals against the supporters of the Republican government and a guarantee to maintain public order.[38]

Another close friend of Negrín, the cardiologist Dr Rafael Méndez Martínez, at the time Director General of the border guards, the Carabineros, wrote later of how the spirit of victory had been tranformed into the spirit of resistance that would last until such time as it was possible to achieve 'the second of his aims, a satisfactory peace'. In this regard, he believed that only an effective and well-ordered resistance that prolonged the war might persuade the democracies to help negotiate such a settlement. 'Once Negrín had accepted that victory was impossible, the nub of his policy was resistance to the end and the mobilization of international support to achieve a peace settlement that would prevent the extermination of thousands and thousands of Republicans.' His peace initiatives included a secret meeting with the German Ambassador in Paris.[39]

Over the next two months, their success at the Ebro would see Franco's forces sweep through Catalonia. Confident that, after Munich, the Republic would not find salvation in a European war, Franco gathered over 30,000 fresh troops. He granted substantial mining concessions to the Third Reich in return for sizeable deliveries of German equipment.[40] With the French frontier closed and help from the Soviet Union reduced to a trickle, Franco had every possible advantage for his final push. Months of Italian bombing raids had taken their toll on morale. An immense army was gathered along a line surrounding Catalonia from the Mediterranean in the east to the Ebro in the west and to the Pyrenees to the north. Originally planned for 10 December, the offensive was postponed until the 15th. Further delays were caused by a period of torrential rain and it was eventually launched on 23 December.[41] The scale of war-weariness, resentment of the conflict's human and economic costs and defeatism in the wake of Munich made a successful defence seem the remotest possibility. Nevertheless, despite the overwhelming superiority of the attacking forces in terms of air cover, artillery and sheer numbers, the Republican retreat never turned into a rout. Franco could rotate his troops every forty-eight hours while the Republicans had had no leave for seven weeks.

The forces of Enrique Líster managed to hold up the Nationalist advance for nearly two weeks at Borjas Blancas on the road from Lérida to Tarragona. Nevertheless, the advance was inexorable. On New Year's Eve, a ferocious Italian bombing raid on Barcelona brought to the city what Negrín, in a broadcast to the United States, called 'sorrow and mourning'. His Minister of Foreign Affairs, Julio Álvarez del Vayo, commented: 'Perhaps this is "Happy New Year" in the Italian language.' Herbert Matthews, who had helped Negrín polish his English for the broadcast, wrote later: 'I had never seen him so moved.' On 4 January 1939, the Francoists broke through at Borjas Blancas and the end was nigh for Catalonia. Without adequate armaments and with the troops drained after their superhuman efforts, the road was open to Tarragona and then on to Barcelona. The bespectacled Lieutenant Colonel Manuel Tagüeña, a tall, thin mathematician who had risen through the ranks of the militias to command an army corps, mounted a determined defence but had only a fraction of the necessary weaponry.[42]

In the wake of the Munich Agreement and the consequent conviction in Moscow that Russia had been betrayed by the democracies, a concern for security saw Stalin start to make tentative overtures to Nazi Germany. Engaged in a war with Japan in China, with serious preocupations in Eastern Europe, and with obstacles in the way of transport to Spain, Russia had to cut back on aid in the last six months of the Civil War just as Germany and Italy significantly increased their assistance to Franco. The consequence was, in the words of Herbert Matthews, that:

> the last year of fighting was a miracle of dogged, hopeless courage, made possible solely by the tenacity and indomitable spirit of Negrín. However, this astonishing display of leadership was the most bitterly criticized feature among Spaniards of Dr Negrín's career. The fight was hopeless, his critics said, and all that 'unnecessary' destruction, all those extra lives lost, all the intensified hatred of Spaniard for Spaniard, could have been

avoided. It is certain, on the other hand, that the Loyalists could have held out longer had it not been for treachery, and that World War II could have saved Republican Spain … Don Juan's aims were consistent, patriotic and honorable. He stood for a fight to the finish, first to save the Second Republic and – when that became impossible – to get the best terms for those who had remained loyal. In the process, he had to rely heavily on Stalinist Russia and then almost exclusively on the Spanish Communists.[43]

2

Resist to Survive

While Negrín continued desperately trying to maintain a war effort in the hope, not of victory, but of an honourable peace settlement, Casado worked to consolidate his links with both the Francoist espionage networks and the Fifth Column in Madrid. Without them, it would have been much more difficult for him to pull together the various elements of his coup. He was also seconded in what he did by the distinguished Socialist intellectual Julián Besteiro, Professor of Logic in the University of Madrid. On the night of 5 March, the two, together with disillusioned anarchist leaders such as Cipriano Mera and the Socialist trade union leader Wenceslao Carrillo, announced an anti-Negrín National Defence Junta (Consejo Nacional de Defensa) under the presidency of General José Miaja. The enterprise was driven by the hope that Casado's contacts with the Francoist secret service and Besteiro's links with the Fifth Column in Madrid would facilitate negotiation with Franco in Burgos. They may also have hoped that, by inspiring a military uprising 'to save Spain from Communism', they would somehow endear themselves to Franco.

Casado justified his action on the grounds that he was preventing a Moscow-inspired Communist take-over. Although such intentions on the part of the Communists were demonstrably non-existent, the fiction was believed by those in the Republican zone desperate for an end to the war, many of whom had already acquired a deep hostility to the Communists.[1] Casado's later justification was founded on his outrage that Negrín and the Communists had talked of resistance to the bitter end when shortages of food and equipment made that impossible. In denouncing Juan Negrín's commitment to continued resistance, he was ignoring the Prime Minister's Herculean efforts to secure by diplomacy a negotiated peace with adequate guarantees against a justifiably feared Francoist repression. According to Prieto, Negrín's efforts had even extended to the Third Reich. It should be noted that Negrín's diplomacy remained secret lest it trigger defeatism.[2] Similarly, Casado seemed unaware of the extent to which Negrín's rhetoric of resistance was a necessary bargaining chip to be used to secure a reasonable peace settlement with Franco.

Although Casado had never joined the Communist Party, as had many other career officers on the Republican side, his ferocious anti-communism was of recent vintage. He was a freemason with a pedigree as a Republican. When the military coup took place in July 1936, he was still commander of Manuel Azaña's presidential guard. He took part in the defence of Madrid from the attacks through the sierra to the north of the capital. According to his own account, in October 1936 he was dismissed as head of operations of the general staff for his criticism of the way in which priority was being given to the Communist Fifth Regiment (Quinto Regimiento) in the distribution of Soviet weaponry. In fact, the decision had been made by Vicente Rojo, who thought him incompetent. Antonio Cordón, the under-secretary of the Ministry of Defence, had a higher opinion of Casado than Rojo had, regarding him as intelligent and professional. However, Cordón believed that Casado's positive qualities were neutralized by his 'overweening pride and uncontrolled ambition'. Believing himself to be the man who could win the war, Casado was eaten up with resentment that he had not been promoted to positions commensurate with his own estimates of his worth. His bitterness was focused on Rojo. Nevertheless, over the following months, he was given important postings. Indalecio Prieto made him commander of the Army of Andalusia and, in May 1938, Negrín appointed him commander of the Army of the Centre.[3] This last appointment was interpreted by the ex-Communist Francisco-Félix Montiel in terms of a bizarre conspiracy theory that Casado had been chosen by the Russians for his incompetence as part of a long-term plan to bring the war to an end without blame for the Communist Party.[4] It is more plausibly an indication that the Communists were not as committed, as Casado later claimed that they were, to total domination of the Republic's armed forces.

The reasons for Besteiro's involvement went back much further. His experiences during the repression which followed the Socialist-led general strike of 1917 intensified his repugnance for violence. He became aware of the futility of Spain's weak Socialist movement undertaking a frontal assault on the state. He opposed the PSOE's affiliation to the Moscow-based Communist International (Comintern), and a period in England on a scholarship to do research on the Workers' Educational Association in 1924 confirmed his reformism. He had argued from his position as president of both the PSOE and the UGT that, in order to build up working-class strength, the Socialist movement should accept the offer that it collaborate with the dictatorship of General Miguel Primo de Rivera. Yet, in mid-1930, he argued against Socialist collaboration in the broad opposition front established by the Pact of San Sebastián and eventually in the future government of the Republic. Finding himself in a minority, in February 1931, he felt obliged to resign as president of both the party and the union.[5] Thus began a process of marginalization from his erstwhile comrades. Moreover, his theoretical abstractions about the nature of the historical process through which Spain was passing seem to have given him a sense of knowing better than they did. Indeed, as President of the Cortes between 1931 and 1933, he had manifested some hostility towards the deputies of his own party.

With the bulk of the PSOE and the UGT eager to use the apparatus of the state to introduce basic social reforms, Besteiro's abstentionist views fell on deaf ears. In fact, the rank and file of the Socialist movement was moving rapidly away from the positions advocated by Besteiro. Right-wing intransigence radicalized the grass-roots militants. The conclusion drawn by an influential section of the leadership led by Largo Caballero was that the Socialists should meet the needs of the rank and file by seeking more rather than less responsibility in the government. Besteiro's belief that socialism would come if only socialists were well behaved underlay a disturbing complacency regarding fascism. He opposed the growing radicalization of the Socialist movement.[6] Thus he had opposed its participation in the revolutionary insurrection of October 1934 which had followed the inclusion of the right-wing CEDA in the government.[7] His failure to understand the real threat of fascism prefigured some of his misplaced optimism about Franco at the end of the Spanish Civil War.[8]

In the course of that Civil War, Besteiro had behaved in a way which confirmed the suspicion of many within the PSOE that he did not fully understand the great political struggles of the day. Outside of political circles, he reinforced his popularity by refusing numerous opportunities to seek a safe exile.[9] He continued to work in the university, being elected Dean of the Faculty of Philosophy and Letters in October 1936. At the same time, he assiduously fulfilled his duties as a parliamentary deputy, as councillor of the Ayuntamiento de Madrid, to which he had been elected on 12 April 1931, and as president of the Committee for the Reconstruction of the Capital. His friends tried frantically to persuade him to leave Madrid. Yet, despite, indeed because of, his view that the war would end disastrously for the Republic, he steadfastly refused. From the beginning, Besteiro made no secret of his, at the time, inopportune commitment to a peace settlement. As Spain's representative at the coronation of George VI in London on 12 May 1937, he had tried to seek mediation by the British government, but it was a bad moment for such an initiative. The rebels were in the ascendant – in the north, the fall of Bilbao was expected from one day to the next. At the same time, the Republican government was facing significant internal difficulties. In Barcelona, from 3 to 10 May, the forces of the government and the anarcho-syndicalist National Confederation of Labour (Confederación Nacional del Trabajo, or CNT) were locked in a bloody struggle for control of the city. Besteiro's mission was doomed to failure. In his absence, the Largo Caballero cabinet fell. The resolution of the crisis with the appointment of Juan Negrín as Prime Minister of the so-called 'Government of Victory' on 17 May seemed to bring to an end the political infighting that had characterized the previous history of the Republic at war. Negrín, with the remarkable organizational ability that he had demonstrated in the Ministry of Finance, was regarded as the man who could create a centralized war effort.

This seemed possible because May 1937 had seen the defeat of the revolutionary elements within the Republic – the FAI (Federación Anarquista Ibérica), the extremist wing of the anarchist movement, and the anti-Stalinist POUM (Partido Obrero de Unificación Marxista) – and the marginalization of the rhetorically revolutionary wing of the PSOE under Largo Caballero. However, that did not mean that any of these groups accepted their fate with docility. As military defeats mounted – the loss of the north, and of Teruel, and the division of the Republic in two – their resentments would grow and be focused increasingly on Negrín and the Communists. As far as Besteiro was concerned, his desire to be the man who brought peace was shattered on the rock of Negrín's determination to fight on to victory. Since Negrín believed, rightly, that only a major military triumph by the Republic would bring Franco to the negotiating table, he had no interest in fostering Besteiro's ambitions. The highly touchy Besteiro, however, perceived an insult in Negrín's understandable failure to follow up on his London trip.[10] Disappointed that his inflated sense of the importance of his own mission was not matched by Negrín, Besteiro began to harbour a fierce grudge against the new Prime Minister. The fall of the Largo Caballero government in mid-May 1937 opened up the post of ambassador in France. Besteiro aspired to the Spanish Embassy in Paris in order to seek French mediation in the war, but Negrín's commitment to resistance to the last against Franco made such an appointment impossible.

In the wake of the failure of his peace mission, Besteiro returned to his university post and his position in the Madrid Ayuntamiento. As a city councillor, he worked hard on the problems of the besieged capital to the detriment of his health. He was tortured by the idea that mistakes made in the early 1930s, particularly Socialist participation in government, had been responsible for the war. He was also appalled by the violence of the conflict and especially by the sound of firing squads and gunshots in the night – which he took to be the sounds of political assassinations.[11] In contrast, in the last months of the war, he seemed oblivious to reports of the Francoist repression in captured areas.[12]

Initially, Besteiro's stance as a silent but critical spectator of the Republican government had puzzled many rank-and-file Socialists, although as the war progressed, his stock began to rise again. The departure from government of Largo Caballero in May 1937 had provoked considerable anti-Communist sentiment within the PSOE in Madrid and much of the UGT. Similarly, the removal in April 1938 of the ever pessimistic Prieto from his post as Minister of Defence had intensified anti-Communism within Socialist ranks. This was unfair. The Communists had certainly wanted to see a more positive and dynamic person as Minister of Defence, but they had been keen to see Prieto kept in the government. They feared, as actually was to happen, that his spleen would quickly be directed against them. As it turned out, it was Prieto who refused a different ministry in the cabinet formed on 5 April. Fomented even further by Prieto's embittered and tendentious interpretations of what had happened, the growing resentment of the Communists would undermine the principal bulwark of the Republican war effort.[13]

Besteiro, like Prieto, conveniently ignored the immense contribution of the Communist Party to the survival of the Republic. A key component of the People's Army, the party had lost thousands of militants either killed, seriously wounded or captured as territory fell to the Francoists. By the end of 1937, some 60 per cent of the PCE's militants were in the People's Army. It was calculated that around 50,000 had been captured by the rebels after the fall of Málaga, Santander and the Asturias. Another 20,000 had been lost in the course of the battle of the Ebro and the last-ditch defence of Catalonia.[14] On 18 February 1939, General Rojo sent Negrín an analysis of the possibilities of maintaining resistance in the centre-south zone. In his covering letter, he wrote of the PCE:

I don't need to tell you that of all the political parties, it has been and remains the only one with which I sympathize. I believe that they are making a big mistake, even in assuming the general responsibility for the field commanders and the overall leadership of this phase of the struggle, because they are going to ensure that the efforts of the enemy and from all countries will be concentrated on them even further. They will end up ensuring the definitive destruction of their party, the only one that is relatively healthy within our political organization.[15]

In general, the anarchists resented the Communist pre-eminence in the armed forces. This was largely to do with the fact that, in endeavouring to create a centralized and effective war effort, the revolutionary ambitions of the anarchists had been reined in, sometimes brutally. This was perceived by all sectors of the libertarian movement as simply a desire on the part of the Communists to attain a monopoly of power, and the underlying military necessity was utterly ignored. On the other hand, there were numerous complaints of anarchists being murdered. It was certainly the case that there was considerable hostility between Communists and anarchists within the army, in part because of the harsh discipline imposed by Communist commanders. Summary executions of deserters and of commanders deemed to be ineffective were not uncommon. The anarchists alleged that a Communist terror was carried out in front-line units, complaining that there were 'thousands and thousands of comrades who confess that they feel more fear of being assassinated by the adversary alongside them than of being killed in battle by the enemies opposite'. In a spirit of revenge, in the Levante, lists were drawn up of the names of Communists within military units. Those listed would become targets after the Casado coup. In fact, Communist influence within the armed forces was considerably less than that alleged by the anarchists.[16]

Forgetting or perhaps unconcerned by the need for the Republic to be defended militarily, after his return from London Besteiro had become even more anti-Communist and commensurately less hostile to the Francoists. The main target of his obsession was Negrín, whom he frequently accused of being a Communist. This view was increasingly shared by many within the Socialist Party. Largo Caballero, for instance, was outraged when Julián Zugazagoitia, then Negrín's Minister of the Interior, had prohibited a meeting in Alicante at which, it was feared, he planned to denounce the Prime Minister and thereby undermine the war effort.[17] Thus the followers of Largo

Caballero, Prieto and Besteiro were converging in their anti-Communism and could count on the growing sympathy of the President, Manuel Azaña. Negrín, overwhelmed by his efforts, as premier, to improve the international situation of the Republic and, as Minister of Defence, to run the war effort, did not have the time to combat the corrosive effect of the growing anti-Communism which, in some cases, overcame the higher priority of the defence of the Republic and thus contributed to division, despair and defeatism.[18]

Besteiro's hostility to the Communists masked his more generalized lack of enthusiasm for the Republican cause. At his later trial at the hands of the Francoists, it was revealed by his defence lawyer that in the course of 1937 he had used his position as Dean of the Faculty of Philosophy and Letters to protect several Falangists in the university. Through some of these colleagues, Professors Julio Palacios (the Vice-Rector), Antonio Luna García, Luis de Sosa y Pérez and Julio Martínez Santa Olalla, he had established contact with the clandestine Fifth Column in Madrid. In fact, since September 1937, Luna García had run an important section of the Fifth Column in Madrid, known as the 'Organización Antonio', which had been created at the end of the previous year by Captain José López Palazón.[19] In his statement on Besteiro's behalf to the military tribunal, Luna García spoke of his surprise at the vehemence with which Besteiro had criticized the Republican government.

His report at the time to Burgos identified Besteiro as a potential target for the Fifth Column. In April 1938, Luna was instructed by the clandestine organization of the Falange to try to persuade Besteiro to move beyond refusal to work with the government and to try actively to bring the war to an end. This initiative coincided with the division of Republican territory by the successful Francoist offensive through Aragon to the Mediterranean coast. With the Republic's central zone cut off from the government in Valencia, Besteiro agreed. From the summer of 1938, he started to lobby energetically to be permitted to form a cabinet as a preliminary step to peace negotiations.[20]

Besteiro's position was converging with that of Segismundo Casado. Already in the summer of 1938, shortly after Casado's promotion to the command of the Army of the Centre, a prominent member of the Madrid Fifth Column, the Falangist Antonio Bouthelier España, had approached him. Bouthelier was able to get near to Casado because he was secretary to the prominent CNT member Manuel Salgado, who worked in the security services of the Army of the Centre. He had used this position to help Francoists cross the lines. Bouthelier also had a short-wave radio with which he passed information to rebel headquarters. For various reasons, the Francoist espionage service was aware of Casado's anti-communism. His brother Lieutenant Colonel César Casado was a member of the Fifth Column, and Segismundo Casado was doing everything in this power to protect him. Given Bouthelier's closeness to Casado, he was instructed to propose to him that he act as a spy for the rebels. He was emboldened to do so because he knew of the sympathies for the rebel cause of both Casado's wife María Condado y Condado and his brother César. Casado did not immediately accept the proposal but, significantly, did not report the contact to the Republic's security service, the Servicio de Inteligencia Militar, in order to open an investigation into Bouthelier. César Casado was only one of several pro-Francoist officers that Segismundo was protecting by giving them posts within his general staff. In fact, aware of these contacts, the SIM was already carrying out surveillance of Casado and his family. However, since the Socialist Ángel Pedrero García, the head of the Servicio de Inteligencia Militar in the Army of the Centre, sympathized with Casado, no action seems to have been taken against him.[21]

One of the members of the Organización Antonio was a major in the army medical corps, Casado's doctor Diego Medina Garijo. Another was a retired major of the medical corps, Dr Ricardo Bertoloty Ramírez. He was one of the team that had saved Franco's life in 1916 when he was seriously wounded at El Biutz in Morocco. In 1931, Dr Bertoloty had taken advantage of Azaña's reforms to leave the army, but he remained a close friend of Franco.[22] Contacts with pro-rebel sympathizers in the Republican Army were monitored through the Servicio de Información y Policia Militar (SIPM), run within Franco's general staff by Colonel José Ungría Jiménez. A key figure in the SIPM in close contact with the Organización Antonio was Lieutenant Colonel José Centaño de la Paz, Casado's adjutant, who belonged to another fifth-column organization called 'La Ciudad Clandestina'. Centaño was in constant radio contact with Franco's headquarters in Burgos. In late January 1939, Antonio Luna's group brought Besteiro and Casado together in order to discuss plans to overthrow Negrín. However, Ángel Pedrero García had already brokered a prior meeting with Besteiro at the end of October 1938, though it is unlikely that they discussed anything as dramatic as an anti-Negrín coup d'état. Not until 5 February did Centaño reveal to Casado his role in the SIPM.[23]

That the SIPM regarded Casado as potentially useful was hardly surprising. They were aware that, on 8 December 1938, Casado had met the British Chargé d'Affaires Ralph Stevenson in Madrid and discussed with him London's desire to end the Spanish conflict.[24] That together with the way in which Casado had run the Army of the Centre must have delighted them. He had imposed rigidly traditional military discipline and completely emasculated the corps of political commissars, which had been created shortly after the conflict began in response to the fact that war had been triggered by a rebellion of professional officers against the constitutional authority of the Republic. The commissariat existed in parallel with the traditional military structure. Commissars were essentially evangelists of the Republican cause. They worked to maintain morale and to explain the political purpose of the war effort, and provided a link between the rank and file, the officers and the Republican government. They held the same rank as the commander of the unit in which they served, even where that unit was the army as a whole. Inevitably, most career officers resented the authority enjoyed by commissars to question major military decisions. By early 1939, as the commissars worked to maintain the spirit of resistance, this resentment intensified in proportion to the growing defeatism of the professional officers, especially so in the case of Casado.[25]

The consequence was that new conscripts were left with little idea of what they fighting for. This fostered the spread of demoralization and desertions. At the same time, Casado showed no inclination to use his forces in battle, something for which Vicente Rojo would never forgive him. Casado was far from being the only or indeed the most senior defeatist in the Republican ranks. In late November, to take pressure off the retreating Army of the Ebro, Rojo had ordered three diversionary attacks by the armies of the centre-south zone under General Miaja, the commander of the Republican armies of the south and centre. With his chief of staff, General Manuel Matallana Gómez, Miaja was supposed to organize a major offensive westwards into Extremadura and a landing at Motril in Granada. Colonel Casado, commander of the Army of the Centre, was to carry out an advance on the Madrid front at Brunete. All three simply failed to carry out their orders. Many of the officers in the Army of Catalonia were committed Communists like Colonel Antonio Cordón, or had risen through the ranks of the militia like Juan Modesto and Enrique Líster. In contrast, the senior officers of the Army of the Centre were professional officers who had made their careers in Africa. If, like Miaja, they had sought membership of the Communist Party, it was out of convenience rather than conviction.

The various offensives should have begun on 11 December 1938 but were inexplicably delayed until 5 January 1939, by which time the Francoist drive into Catalonia was virtually unstoppable. The lack of commitment by the southern army commanders was seen in Negrín's immediate circle as the result of 'treachery, sabotage and defeatism'.[26] The failure to launch the operations owed much to the fact that the chief of operations of the Army of the Centre, Lieutenant Colonel Francisco García Viñals, was a close collaborator of the SIPM. He did everything possible to ensure that the Republican forces in the centre zone remained inactive.[27] The landing at Motril never took place. Several commanders, the Communists Enrique Castro Delgado and Juan Modesto Guilloto, the moderate Republican (and anti-Communist) Juan Perea Capulino and the commissar general of the Group of Armies of the Centre (Grupo de Ejércitos Republicanos del Centro), the Communist Jesús Hernández, bitterly criticized Miaja in their respective memoirs. They alleged that Miaja had failed to use the troops at his disposal for the attack in Extremadura, preferring to keep them in defensive positions when he could have exploited the local numerical superiority occasioned by Franco's concentration on the Catalan campaign.

Hernández denounced Miaja's delays in launching the Extremadura offensive. Modesto declared that the decision to disobey Rojo's orders and simply not launch the attack on Motril was an act of sabotage by Miaja, Matallana and the commander of the Republican navy, Rear Admiral Miguel Buiza Fernández-Palacios. He also alleged that Miaja deliberately exhausted and demoralized the troops at his disposal by long route marches of 150 kilometres to north and south: 'The delay of the offensive in Extremadura, the unnecessary troop movements, a dozen days of forced marches from north to south, from south to north and again from north to south, as well as exasperating and exhausting the soldiers, provoked insecurity, doubts, indignation and discontent among the troops and their officers.' When on the verge of success, Miaja inexplicably called a halt, failed to to seize the opportunity to attack Cordoba and thus allowed the Francoists to regroup.

The third offensive, on the Madrid front at Brunete, was a disaster and Modesto alleged that Casado had allowed his battle plans to be seen by the Francoists. In fact, Burgos had received the plans from more than one source. Casado had assured his staff that the attack would be a walk-over. It was to be a surprise attack, launched against a weak sector of the rebel front, with considerable logistical superiority. In fact, Casado failed to attack at the point that Rojo had chosen. Instead, he launched the Army of the Centre against a well-fortified – and well-informed – sector and thereby guaranteed the failure of the operation. Edmundo Domínguez Aragonés, the recently appointed commissar inspector of the Army of the Centre, who followed the operation from Casado's headquarters, was appalled when he went ahead even after it became obvious that the enemy was expecting it. Casado knowingly sent hundreds of men to certain death against positions well defended with banks of machine guns. Modesto dubbed the calamitous Brunete offensive 'the ante-room to the Casado uprising', an operation that deliberately set out to weaken the best units of the Republic. Franco's own staff was in any case fully informed of most of the Republic's military plans in the last six months of the war.[28]

The accusations made by Modesto, Castro Delgado, Hernández and Perea were seen to have considerable substance when General

Matallana was court-martialled after the Civil War. Before the trial took place, Palmiro Togliatti, the Comintern delegate and the effective leader of the PCE, wrote that, in 1937, Matallana 'had been suspected of contacts with the enemy but nothing concrete was ever proven'.[29] In fact, he had many contacts with the Fifth Column, including with the Organización Antonio, confiding in Captain López Palazón his hatred of reds and his distress that the beginning of the war had found him in Republican Madrid. He had also used the funds of the general staff to support pro-Franco officers who were in hiding.[30] At his trial, Matallana asserted that he had been serving the rebels since early in the war, passing information to the Fifth Column through his brother Alberto about the strength of the International Brigades, the residences of Russian pilots, the location in Albacete where tanks were assembled and the times of the arrival in Cartagena of ships carrying war matériel. Regarding the latter period of the war, he claimed to have sabotaged numerous operations including the Brunete offensive and facilitated rebel operations by failing to send reinforcements. His advice to Miaja was always to stabilize the fronts and to avoid attacks. At his trial, he said that in the archives of the Republican forces there were many projects that he had managed to get postponed indefinitely on different pretexts. He ensured that the various general staffs to which he had belonged never produced battle plans or directives on their own initiative. During the battle of the Ebro, he had placed obstacles in the way of requests for diversionary attacks in the centre zone.

To this end, he said, with the help of his second-in-command Lieutenant Colonel Antonio Garijo Hernández and the head of his own general staff Lieutenant Colonel Félix Muedra Miñón, he controlled the easily manipulated Miaja. By dint of flattery and by encouraging his desire for the limelight, they gained his confidence. They exploited his festering envy of Rojo and fomented rumblings of discontent. Taking advantage of Miaja's resentments, they managed to delay the fulfilment of orders from Rojo. Matallana later claimed that, to undermine offensives, he ensured that troops were moved by rail instead of with trucks since the railway was slow and had limited capacity. The consequent delays allowed the Francoists to work out the Republican battle plans. Moreover, the removal of trains from civilian use led to the collapse of the food-distribution network and provoked demonstrations by women protesting about lack of food. Negrín was obliged to intervene to guarantee supplies and to reconcile the needs of the capital with military requirements.[31]

There was a vast distance between the reputation of Miaja as the heroic saviour of Madrid assiduously fabricated by Republican propaganda to boost popular morale and the reality. Miaja was a fairly mediocre soldier who was always averse to taking risks. According to the Francoists Antonio Bouthelier and José López Mora, he was 'grotesque, sensual and bloated, always completely oblivious to what was going on around him'. Togliatti wrote later of Miaja that he was 'totally brutalized by drink and drugs'.[32]

Having received huge deliveries of German and Italian war matériel, Franco was poised for a major assault on Catalonia. Yet, in order to do so, he had left his southern fronts relatively undefended. Herbert Matthews, the extremely well-informed correspondent of the *New York Times*, who was close to Negrín, wrote later: 'Naturally, we thought that the Madrid zone would save the day. Miaja, by that time, was approaching a breakdown, from accounts that I received afterwards. He was drinking too much and had lost what nerve he had once possessed. The picture of the loyal, dogged, courageous defender of the Republic – a picture built up from the first days of the siege of Madrid – was a myth. He was weak, unintelligent, unprincipled, and, in that period, his courage could seriously be questioned.'[33] The reasonable hopes of both Negrín and the head of the army general staff, Vicente Rojo, were to be dashed by the failures, if not outright treachery, of the commanders in the centre zone – Miaja, Matallana and Casado.

The issue was not just the treachery of the high command of the armies of the centre-south zone. There was also the issue of ever greater logistical differentials between the two sides. The superiority of the Francoists in tanks, artillery, air cover, machine guns and even functioning rifles was overwhelming. At the end of January 1939, the President of the Cortes, Diego Martínez Barrio, arranged a meeting between Negrín and President Azaña, who since the 22nd of that month had been established in the castle of Perelada near Figueras. Relations between the two had deteriorated significantly over the last months. Martínez Barrio described them as 'fire and water'. Azaña disliked Negrín's dynamism and brutal realism; Negrín saw Azaña as an intellectual wallowing in unrealistic ethical conundrums. Azaña complained to Martínez Barrio: 'he treats me worse than a servant'. Negrín arrived at the meeting utterly exhausted after two days without sleep. He told the others that thousands of tons of war matériel – tanks, artillery, aircraft, machine guns and ammunition – were on their way across France from Le Havre to Port Bou. In fact, the French government had put every possible obstacle in the way of their transport across the country. If the supplies had arrived two weeks earlier, Negrín claimed, the situation in Catalonia could have been saved. When Martínez Barrio asked him if anything could be done, he replied: 'I'm afraid not.' It was decided that Azaña should move to La Bajol, a mere 3 kilometres from the French frontier.[34] Negrín made a similar point to the standing committee of the Cortes on 31 March 1939 when he claimed that, if this matériel had arrived four months earlier, the Republic could have won the battle of the Ebro and if it had arrived even two months earlier, Catalonia would not have been lost.[35]

Shortly after his meeting with Azaña on 30 January, Negrín requested from Miaja a report on the military situation in the centre zone. Miaja's depressing response centred on the collapse of morale and the lack of rations, clothing and usable weaponry, particularly artillery, after the unsuccessful initiatives in Extremadura and Andalusia. In fact, shortly afterwards, Miaja successfully requested the French Consul in Valencia to put a visa on his diplomatic passport that would permit him entry into France or Algiers.[36] Barcelona suffered sustained bombing raids on 21, 22 and 23 January. The starving population attacked food warehouses but, according to Colonel Juan Perea, commander of the Army of the East, vast quantities of food and equipment were left in the Catalan capital and fell into the hands of the Francoists when they entered the city in the afternoon of 26 January.[37] The military retreat, now swelled by 450,000 civilians, continued to the French frontier and on to the unhealthy internment camps of France's windswept southern beaches. Among the Republican authorities that fled before the advancing Francoists, only Negrín and his ministers and the Communists had the courage to return to the remaining Republican territory. There too, from the Republic's eastern frontier in Badajoz to the Mediterranean coast in Valencia and Murcia, there were shortages of basic necessities and weaponry, intense demoralization and dread of what was seen as inevitable defeat. The loss of Catalonia and the consequent isolation of the central zone provoked widespread fear. This was reflected in bitter divisions between the Communists and other parties and within the Socialist Party.[38]

3

The Power of Exhaustion

As has already been noted, there have been claims that the Communists were plotting to end the war long before the fall of Catalonia.[1] In fact, as late as 26 January 1939, the Comintern was urging the Communist leadership in Britain, France and the USA to organize demonstrations to push their respective governments into lifting the blockade on arms for Spain and to make arrangements for the accommodation of refugees. The French party was told to recruit volunteers for Spain and to send a delegation to Catalonia to counteract capitulationism in the Republican and Socialist parties. A message was sent via the French urging the Spanish Communists to hold on. Even after news had reached Moscow of the fall of Barcelona, the head of the Communist International, Georgi Dimitrov, stood by his instructions to the Spanish Communists to fight on. On 7 February, Dimitrov sent a further message to the PCE: 'the course of resistance must be maintained … the front in Levante must be activated; capitulation by the Spanish government must be prevented, through replacing adherents of capitulation in the government with staunch adherents of resistance'. On the same day, he ordered Maurice Thorez, leader of the Parti Communiste Français (PCF), to organize demonstrations to pressurize the French government into permitting the dispatch of the Army of Catalonia back to the central zone. The PCF was instructed to organize the supply of arms and food to Valencia and to look after the welfare and morale of the Spanish refugees in France.[2]

Meanwhile, in Madrid, all these efforts were undermined by the activities of an ever more active rebel Fifth Column. Its success derived from the ease with which it was able to feed on the growing anti-communism. This was a reflection of the fact that the PCE was totally identified with government policy and therefore held responsible for the widespread hardship in the beleaguered city. The Fifth Column was also able to exploit the bitter resentment of the victims of PCE security policy since late 1936. In their efforts to impose a centralized war effort, the Communists had been ruthless in their suppression of anarchists and Trotskyists who had wanted to pursue a revolutionary line.[3] Defeatism was rife. The intense anti-Communist hostility from the leadership of the CNT was matched within much of the Socialist Party. Relations between career officers and the Communist hierarchy had cooled. In an effort to improve the situation, at some point in October the leader of the Communist youth movement (Juventudes Socialistas Unificadas, or JSU), Santiago Carrillo, had lunch at Casado's headquarters. Casado had a reputation as a thoroughly humourless and sour individual, his constant irritability the consequence of the acute stomach pains he suffered as a result of ulcers. Knowing this and fully apprised of the rumours about Casado's conspiratorial activities, Carrillo was surprised at the lunch by the effusiveness of Casado's assertion that he shared Negrín's determination to maintain resistance. Carrillo had been informed that his father, Wenceslao, a life-long friend of Largo Caballero, was actively engaged in seeking support within the PSOE for an anti-Negrín peace initiative. Shortly afterwards, in an acrimonious meeting, Santiago tried in vain to convince his father that such an action would leave tens of thousands of Republicans at the mercy of Francoist terror.[4]

The isolation of the central zone signified a logistical nightmare. There was no fuel for domestic heating or cooking, and no hot water. Medicines and surgical dressings were in dangerously short supply. The exiguous scale of rations in Madrid was insufficient, according to a report by the Quaker International Commission for the Assistance of Child Refugees, to sustain life for more than two or three months. The standard ration consisted of 2 ounces (55 grams) of lentils, beans or rice with occasional additions of sugar or salted cod. It was said that more than 400 people died of inanition each week in Madrid. A growing food crisis intensified a popular sense that Negrín's government, located in Barcelona, had simply abandoned the centre to its fate. This was unfair, since the food situation in the Catalan capital was little better. In the central zone, Negrín's rhetoric of resistance was increasingly out of tune with popular feeling.[5] In November, when the Francoists bombed Madrid with loaves of fresh white bread, JSU militants denounced this as an insulting gesture and burned the loaves in street bonfires. Álvaro Delgado, a student at the time, told the British historian Ronald Fraser: 'It came down in sacks with propaganda wrapped round it saying: "This bread is being sent you by your nationalist brothers." It was beautiful, fine white bread. Some came through a broken skylight at the Fine Arts school, and when no one was around I and other students ate so much we felt sick.' On the streets, others trampled the bread in a fury. Despite their hunger, people were shouting: 'Don't pick it up.' Even Casado recalled later that women with children launched themselves on to some men who were seen picking up the bread. They then collected the loaves and took them to the Dirección General de Seguridad, the national police headquarters, whence it was transported to the battlefront and handed back to the Francoists.[6]

Discontent was stoked up by the Fifth Column which talked of the plentiful food in the Francoist-held areas and also of the likely mercy of Franco for those who were not Communists. War-weariness boosted the growth of the Fifth Column. David Jato, a significant Falangist militia leader, told Ronald Fraser: 'I wouldn't say we had people inside Casado's general staff; I'd say the majority of the staff was willing to help us. So many doctors joined that Madrid's health services were virtually in our hands. The recruiting centres were infiltrated by our men. Even some Communist organizations like Socorro Rojo ended up in fifth column hands.'[7] The Socorro Rojo Internacional (International Red Aid) was a social welfare body.

In the wake of the Francoist advance through Aragon, dissident elements of the PSOE and the UGT had met with members of the CNT to discuss their discontent with Communist policy as early as April 1938. In mid-November 1938, anti-Negrinista Socialist officials in Alicante, Elche and Novelda and CNT elements in Madrid and Guadalajara had participated in a rehearsal of their efforts to oust

Negrín. These initiatives were nipped in the bud by the SIM.[8] The JSU organizations of Valencia, Alicante, Albacete, Murcia, Jaen and Ciudad Real were in favour of breaking Communist domination of the organization and re-establishing the Socialist Youth Federation (Federación de Juventudes Socialistas, or FJS) as it was before the unification with the Communist youth movement in 1936. The knee-jerk, and futile, response of the JSU secretary general, Santiago Carrillo, was to denounce the dissidents as Trotskyists. His alarm was understandable since JSU members made up a high proportion of the Republican armed forces.[9]

A combination of the Republic's worsening situation, the consequent divisions within the Socialist Party and his conversations with Luna García convinced Besteiro that he was far from alone in his anti-communism. Aware of his own popularity, he had reached the conclusion that the time had come to emerge from his self-imposed obscurity in Madrid. At the PSOE executive committee meeting held in Barcelona on 15 November, Besteiro's speech, which at time strayed into rhetoric indistinguishable from that emanating from the Franco zone, discussed the likely consequences of the Communists being removed from power.

> The war has been inspired, directed and fomented by the Communists. If they ceased to intervene, it would be virtually impossible to continue the war. The enemy, having other international support, would find itself in a situation of superiority … I see the situation as follows: if the war were to be won, Spain would be Communist. The rest of the democracies would be against us and we would have only Russia with us. And if we are defeated, the future will be terrible.[10]

It was a virtuoso performance of pessimism, defeatism and irresponsibility. He had recognized the inevitability of cooperation with the Communists yet had remained aloof, determined to keep his hands clean. Now, he denounced collaboration without offering any alternative other than division, defeat and the tender mercies of General Franco.

The underlying naivety of Besteiro's words reflected his belief that the PCE, 'the party of war', was the only obstacle to peace and reconciliation. Indeed Besteiro would seemingly be coming to believe the Francoist propaganda line that, by handing over the PCE, the Republicans could 'purify' themselves and establish a basis for postwar reconciliation 'between Spaniards' (although obviously not Spaniards who were Communists). In the course of his speech, Besteiro returned to what had become an obsessional theme, declaring that Negrín was a Communist who had entered the Socialist Party as a Trojan horse. The next day, he reported to Negrín himself what he had said: 'Before they tell you anything, I want you to hear from me what I said in the executive committee. I regard you as an agent of the Communists.' He told Azaña and others that Negrín was a 'Karamazov', 'a crazed visionary' – presumably a reference to the violent sensualist Dmitri Fyodorovich Karamazov in Dostoevsky's *The Brothers Karamazov*. He later gave the British Chargé d'Affaires a bitter account of his meetings with Azaña and Negrín.[11]

Accordingly, while in Barcelona, Besteiro discussed with Azaña the formation of a government whose principal task would be to seek peace. He told Julián Zugazagoitia, the editor of *El Socialista*, that 'we Spaniards are murdering one another in a stupid way, for even more stupid and criminal reasons'.[12] Deeply concerned about the consequences for the bulk of the population of inevitable Republican defeat, he was ever more hostile to Negrín because he believed him to be unnecessarily prolonging the war. Misplaced rumours about a peace cabinet saw Besteiro subjected to virulent attack by the Communist press.[13]

Before going to Barcelona, Besteiro had confided his anxieties to Ángel Pedrero García, the head of the Servicio de Inteligencia Militar in the Army of the Centre, and a close collaborator of Colonel Casado. Apparently, Casado had already intimated to Pedrero that he would like to get in touch with Besteiro. Accordingly, in October 1938, when Besteiro had expressed a similar wish, Pedrero arranged a meeting in his own house. Besteiro shared with Casado his conviction that an early peace treaty was necessary and that the military high command should pressure Negrín's government to negotiate. From this time, there were regular contacts between Casado and General Manuel Matallana Gómez, of the general staff, and Casado's close collaborator Colonel José López Otero, a general staff officer with anarchist sympathies. They also made tentative efforts to bring Miaja aboard. Their caution was related to Miaja's membership, formally at least, of the Communist Party. In December, Casado had a meeting with Ralph Stevenson, the British Chargé d'Affaires, in the hope of ascertaining if he could rely on support from London. Casado was also in touch with the diplomats of France and several Latin American countries. Stevenson followed up the meeting by seeking out Besteiro to find out more about the peace plans.[14]

On his return to Madrid, a deeply disillusioned Besteiro reported his conversations in Barcelona to his acquaintances in the Fifth Column. He was resigned to the fact that Azaña would not be commissioning him to form a peace government and that, even if the President did so, he would be unable to find sufficient political support. However, Antonio Luna García set about persuading him that, if he was unable to fulfil his hopes of forming a peace government with wide political support, he should consider doing so with military backing.

It is astonishing that Besteiro could have been unaware of Franco's determination to maintain the hatreds of the war long after the end of hostilities. If he was left in doubt after the savage repression unleashed in each of the provinces as they fell, an interview that the Caudillo gave on 7 November 1938 to the vice-president of the United Press, James Miller, should surely have made it clear. Franco declared unequivocally: 'There will be no mediation. There will be no mediation because the delinquents and their victims cannot live side by side.' He went on threateningly, 'We have in our archive more than two million names catalogued with the proofs of their crimes.'[15] Having dismissed any possibility of an amnesty for the Republicans, he confirmed his commitment to a policy of institutionalized revenge. The mass of political files and documentation captured as each town had fallen to the Nationalists was being gathered in Salamanca. Carefully sifted, it provided the basis for a massive card index of members of political parties, trade unions and masonic lodges which in turn would provide information for a policy of sweeping reprisals.[16]

That Besteiro had preoccupations other than the fate of defeated Republicans was revealed to Tomás Bilbao Hospitalet, Minister without Portfolio in Negrín's government. A member of the minor Basque party Acción Nacionalista Vasca, Tomás Bilbao had joined the cabinet in August 1938 to replace Manuel Irujo, who had resigned in solidarity with Artemi Aiguader i Miró of Esquerra Republicana de Catalunya, who had himself resigned in protest at the limits imposed on the powers of the Catalan regional government, the Generalitat. Contrary to expectations, Bilbao had shown himself to be a shrewd and loyal member of Negrín's team.[17] In late 1938, he visited first Casado and then Besteiro, whom he found irritated and harshly critical of the government for not having pursued the peace policies that he had recommended. Bilbao informed Negrín of his fear that Besteiro, in conjunction with Casado, might do something dangerous. Negrín was sufficiently confident about Casado not to take the warnings seriously.[18]

However, as things got worse for the Republican cause, both Casado and Besteiro were readying themselves for action. With the knowledge of Luna García's group, the two met on 25 January 1939, just as Franco's forces were on the point of entering Barcelona. The next day, Lieutenant Colonel Centaño sent a message to Burgos: 'Besteiro is beginning to work with Casado and everything is under our control.' At the end of January, Ungría's SIPM had instructed Julio Palacios of the Organización Antonio to inform Casado of the guarantees offered by the Caudillo to those professional army officers who laid down their arms and did not have common crimes on their conscience. The text had been transmitted orally to Palacios and then written up to be passed on to Casado. The wording contrasted starkly with many of Franco's public declarations, but the concessions seemingly offered to senior officers would have been attractive to Casado personally since he would soon reveal his intention of leaving Spain after the war.

For senior and other officers who voluntarily lay down their arms, without having been responsible for the deaths of comrades or guilty of other crimes, in addition to their lives being spared, there will be greater benevolence according to how important or effective are the services that they render to the Cause of Spain in these last moments or how insignificant and without malice has been their role in the war. Those who surrender their weapons and thereby prevent pointless sacrifices and are not guilty of murders or other serious crimes will be able to obtain a safe-conduct that will enable them to leave our territory and, in the meanwhile, enjoy total personal safety. Simply having served on the red side or having been active in political groups opposed to the National Movement will not be considered reason for criminal charges.

The message was passed from Palacios to Ricardo Bertoloty, who in turn passed it to Casado's personal physician and close friend, Diego Medina. When Casado expressed doubts that these 'guarantees' really came from Franco, it was arranged that Radio Nacional would broadcast a coded message drafted by Casado himself. Not entirely convinced, Casado replied on 1 February, 'Understood, agreed and the sooner it is broadcast the better.' He demanded a further guarantee in the form of a letter from his friend Fernando Barrón y Ortiz, one of Franco's most trusted generals. Casado also told Medina that it was his fervent hope 'to end the war with a magnificent deed that would astound the world, without the loss of a single life or the firing of a single bullet'. The requested letter from Barrón would eventually reach Casado on 15 February.[19]

Unaware of the extent of Casado's contacts with Burgos, on 2 February, encouraged by the clandestine organization of the Falange, Besteiro had again used his acquaintance with Ángel Pedrero to request an urgent interview with Casado. When they met at Besteiro's house, Casado told him about his by now much more advanced plans for peace which were moving towards the idea of a coup d'état. According to reports received in Burgos from the Fifth Column, the two remained in close contact throughout February.[20]

An inadvertent but crucial step towards the Casado coup had been Negrín's declaration of martial law on 23 January 1939 as Franco's forces approached Barcelona. No previous Republican government had wished to take this step both because it would put an end to democratic liberties and because of lingering suspicion of military loyalties.[21] It was a desperate, perhaps inevitable and certainly fatal initiative, aimed at forcibly uniting all forces within the centre-south zone under military authority. The decree handed power to the military – and specifically to General Miaja, chief of the centre-south army group, and to General Matallana, chief of his general staff, both of whom hoped for an early end to the war. It downgraded the authority of civil governors, handing their authority over censorship and the holding of public meetings to the military governors in each province.

According to Vicente Uribe, 'the majority of [the military governors] were real fossils who had demonstrated their inability to command and to make war. The upshot was that a measure introduced to strengthen the fight against the enemy and reinforce discipline among civilians was used by these fossils against the Communists in particular, by putting obstacles in the way of our activities and our work.'[22] It thus facilitated Casado's conspiracy. There were many other features of the situation which encouraged Casado. After the fall of Barcelona, the Republic's senior authorities had joined the exodus to the French frontier. Neither President Azaña nor General Vicente Rojo, chief of staff and effectively commander-in-chief of the Republican armed forces, returned to Spanish territory. Indeed, after the fall of Barcelona, the Communists had noted a change in the attitude of General Rojo. In a manuscript written as a contribution to the official Communist Party history of the war, Vicente Uribe asserted: 'in the last days of the campaign in Catalonia, he no longer showed any confidence in the cause of the Republic nor any desire to continue the fight'.[23] Negrín, on the other hand, would do both.

In the wake of the Francoist promises, Casado had lunch in Valencia with Generals Matallana, Miaja and Leopoldo Menéndez (commander of the Army of the Levante). The exact date is not known but it was probably on 2 or 3 February, certainly before Negrín returned from France. Nor is it known if it was before or after Casado's meeting with Besteiro. In his later account, Casado claimed that he and the three generals had agreed that, in the event of Negrín returning to the central zone, they would create a National Defence Junta (Consejo Nacional de Defensa) to overthrow the Prime Minister. 'The three generals, without argument, regarded themselves as committed to this course of action, with all its consequences.' However, Miaja's secretary, his nephew Lieutenant Fernando Rodríguez Miaja, who was present at the lunch at his uncle's residence, gives a very different account. The four main protagonists were accompanied by their adjutants and there were twelve people around the table.

> What became obvious during the meal was Colonel Casado's profound discontent with Dr Negrín, against whom he let loose a stream of insults. He ate nothing and drank only milk because the gastric ulcer which exacerbated his evil temper, already bitter and disagreeable by nature, had worsened in recent weeks. Obviously, in front of that audience, even though it was quite small, he did not reveal any intention of organizing a coup against the government … The other guests also expressed their dissatisfaction with the way the war was being run but not in the extremely violent terms used by Casado.[24]

In Negrín's continued absence at the French–Catalan border, Casado was increasingly indiscreet about his determination to bring an end to the war. This was revealed at a meeting held in the afternoon and evening of either 7 or 8 February at Los Llanos in Albacete, the headquarters of the air force in the centre-south zone. The property of the Marqués de Larios, Los Llanos was a country house previously used as a hunting lodge but converted into a hospital for wounded airmen. The estate surrounding the house was used as an aerodrome.[25] The proceedings of this gathering can be reconstructed thanks to a memoir by José Manuel Vidal Zapater, at the time a young airman who was charged with taking the minutes. The meeting was convened by Jesús Hernández in his capacity as commissar general of the Group of Armies of the Centre and was an attempt to get the top brass in the central zone to commit to continued resistance. Among the approximately ten senior officers present were Casado, Matallana, Miaja, Colonels Domingo Moriones Larraga and Antonio Escobar Huertas (respectively commanders of the armies of Andalusia and of Extremadura), Colonel Antonio Camacho Benítez, commander of the air force in the centre-south zone, and the commander of the fleet, Admiral Buiza.

With the Army of Catalonia in the process of crossing into France, Hernández was effectively the senior civilian authority in the army (after Negrín as Minister of Defence and Prime Minister). The officers present (mainly career officers whose service pre-dated 1936) intensely resented commissars in general and Hernández in particular. The first item of business was the launch by Hernández of a dramatic manifesto to the nation, calling for last-ditch resistance and the mobilization of the remaining drafts of conscripts. His presentation was repeatedly and rudely interrupted by Casado, whose hostile reaction effectively revealed what he was up to. Rather more politely, the other officers present supported Casado's remarks about the impossibility of continuing the war. Buiza stressed the precarious situation of the Republican navy and Colonel Camacho spoke in deeply pessimistic terms of the massive superiority of the Francoist air force, with nearly 1,500 aircraft opposed to the Republic's barely 100 usable machines. The only officer who did not oppose Hernández was Miaja who, after a heavy lunch, gave the impression of being asleep. He woke once, pointing at Vidal Zapater and asking Matallana who he was. When Matallana replied that he was a stenographer, Miaja, being rather deaf, asked again, and Matallana shouted, 'A stenographer!' Miaja then returned to his siesta. Vidal Zapater suspected that this was a pantomime on Miaja's part to save him from having to take sides openly. In contrast, Casado's recklessness may well have been part of his efforts to secure allies within the high command.[26]

That Casado should have proceeded with his anti-Negrín plans after the ratification a few days later, on 9 February, of Franco's Law of Political Responsibilities was a measure of the vehement anti-communism that he shared with the Caudillo. Retroactive to October 1934 and published on 13 February, the law aimed to 'punish the guilt of those who contributed by acts or omissions to foment red subversion, to keep it alive for more than two years and thereby undermine the providential and historically inevitable triumph of the National Movement'. The law deemed all Republicans to be guilty of the crime of military rebellion.[27] The arrogance and egoism that underlay Casado's actions persuaded him that the law could not possibly be applied to him. Even before he got the requested letter from Barrón, on 10 February, Colonel Ungría had received a message from one of his agents which read: 'Casado in agreement with Besteiro, he requests that the lives of decent officers be respected.' This extremely limited, not to say selfish, request suggests that Casado and his closest collaborators believed that some sort of esprit de corps united professional officers on both sides of the lines and exempted them from Franco's vengeful plans. It is clear that he was happy to pay for Franco's mercy in Communist blood. As he later revealed to his contacts in the Fifth Column, Casado's intention was to escape. At the same time, his rhetoric was about astounding the world with an historic achievement, the bloodless end to the Civil War. Presumably, he could have escaped at any time but to have done so would have covered him in shame, whereas, he believed, his plan would allow him to escape covered in glory.

Whether he realized it or not, Casado was about to sacrifice thousands of civilian lives. Even if Franco's promises of immunity for professional soldiers were to be believed, his entire conduct of the war, his recent declarations and the publication of the Law of Political Responsibilities should have shown Casado that the surrender that he was contemplating would have bloody consequences for the Republican population. Franco had turned away from several opportunities to end the conflict quickly, preferring instead a slow war of attrition aimed at annihilating the Republic's mass support. As his declarations to the United Press in early November 1938 had made clear, there would be no amnesty for the Republicans.

Negrín, in contrast, had long since been tortured by a sense of responsibility towards the Republican population. In July 1938, when a senior Republican figure, almost certainly Azaña, suggested that an agreement with the rebels was an inevitable necessity, he responded: 'Make a pact? And what about the poor soldier of Medellín?' At the time, Medellín, near Don Benito, was the furthermost point on the Extremadura front and about to fall. Since Franco demanded total surrender, Negrín knew that, at best, a mediated peace might secure the escape of several hundred, maybe some thousands, of political figures but that the army and the great majority of ordinary Republicans would be at the mercy of the Francoists, who would be pitiless.[28] Knowing that Franco would not consider an armistice, Negrín refused to contemplate unconditional surrender. On 7 August, he had said to his friend Juan Simeón Vidarte: 'I will not hand over hundreds of defenceless Spaniards who are fighting heroically for the Republic so that Franco can have the pleasure of shooting them as he has done in his own Galicia, in Andalusia, in the Basque country and all those places where the hoofs of Attila's horse have left their mark.'[29]

In his determination to see the war end with the least suffering for the Republican population, Negrín was unable to rely on the support of the President Manuel Azaña. At their meeting on 30 January, he had tried to persuade Azaña that, after he had crossed into France, he should return to Madrid immediately, but Azaña refused on the grounds that to do so would constitute support for Negrín's plans for resistance. The scale of Azaña's panic was such that Negrín had him placed under surveillance lest he head for France without warning. When it was apparent that he could not be persuaded to stay, Negrín offered to put an aircraft at his disposal to fly to Paris, but Azaña refused for fear that he would be taken back to the centre-south zone in Spain against his will. Martínez Barrio told Álvarez del Vayo that before going into the meeting Azaña had said: 'Negrín can tie me up, he can gag me and put me on an aeroplane. That's the only way he's going to get me to the centre-south zone, but as soon as I get off the plane and they remove the gag, I will scream until they either kill me or let me go.'[30]

In the meeting, he declared that, once he had crossed the frontier into France, he would not return under any circumstances and would devote himself only to seeking a peace treaty. Negrín was finally obliged to accept that the President could not be persuaded to return immediately. When Azaña said that he planned to go to the house of his brother-in-law, Cipriano Rivas Cherif, in Collonges-sous-Salève, Negrín told him that he must take up residence in the Spanish Embassy in Paris. Azaña agreed to go to the Embassy but insisted that he would not return to Spain. Accordingly, Negrín told Azaña that this meant he should therefore withdraw his confidence from his Prime Minister and name a substitute who could negotiate surrender with Franco. Azaña did not respond. This left Negrín with the option only of resignation. And to resign, knowing as he did what could be expected of Franco's 'justice', would have seemed to him a betrayal of the Republican masses. To mitigate the damaging consequences of Azaña's cowardice, Negrín said that the government would announce that the circumstances obliged the President to take up temporary residence in the Spanish Embassy in Paris. Azaña replied that, if such an announcement was made, he would not contradict it but that he still had no intention of returning. After the meeting, Negrín told Julio Álvarez del Vayo that he was sure that Azaña was reacting emotionally and that he would eventually see that he had to return to Spain.[31] In consequence, both Negrín and Azaña would have different recollections of what had been agreed at the meeting. In a letter to his friend Ángel Ossorio y Gallardo, Azaña wrote five months later that he had told Negrín that, irrespective of any such announcement, he would not return to Spain. However, when Negrín reached Paris on 7 March 1939 after the Casado coup, he told Marcelino Pascua, the Spanish Ambassador to France, that the agreement had been for Azaña to reside in France merely provisionally until the government had re-established itself in Madrid. This accounts for the cold tone of Negrín's subsequent telegrams to Azaña requesting his return to Spain.[32]

When Pascua received the news of the President's imminent arrival, he was appalled. He thought, and told Azaña, that his presence in Paris would cause immense damage to the Republic, effectively announcing to the British and French authorities that he considered the war lost and thereby undermining the basis of Negrín's policy of using the rhetoric of resistance as a negotiating card. Pascua was soon irritated by what he described as Azaña's carefree routine of 'la dolce far niente'. It consisted largely of a daily touristic excursion around Paris in an Embassy car accompanied by his inseparable friend and brother-in-law Cipriano Rivas Cherif followed by an evening gathering (tertulia) with his friends in the French capital. Resentful of what they believed to be a betrayal of the Republic, the domestic staff of the Paris Embassy even refused to serve him.[33] In fact, Azaña was more concerned with the preservation of the artistic treasures of the Prado than with the impact of his decision to flee. He had said to Álvarez del Vayo: 'A hundred years from now, few people will know who Franco or I were but everyone will always know who Velázquez and Goya are.'[34] He was also concerned to go on collecting his salary.[35]

The tensions deriving from Azaña's presence in Paris were exacerbated by the closeness of his relationship with Cipriano Rivas Cherif. Rivas Cherif was regarded as a frivolous lightweight by Pascua, by Álvarez del Vayo and by Negrín. He had made damaging mistakes as Consul in Geneva and, merely to please Azaña, he had been given the virtually meaningless title of Introductor de Embajadores, effectively head of protocol for the President. However, in Paris, he was Azaña's liaison with the Quai d'Orsay and behaved as if he was at the service of the French government rather than the Spanish Republic. To the French Foreign Minister Georges Bonnet he parroted Azaña's view that the Republic was finished and that the rhetoric of resistance by Negrín and Álvarez del Vayo was merely a device to gain time. His conversations with Bonnet convinced the French that the Spanish government was adrift and in conflict with the exiled head of state who, unlike Negrín and Del Vayo, had the good sense to see that the only answer was an immediate peace settlement.[36]

Negrín knew that the war was effectively lost, but he was not prepared simply to walk away. As he told the standing committee of the Cortes on 31 March 1939: 'The Government, in the first few days after reaching Figueras, after leaving Barcelona, realized that we were facing a real catastrophe, a catastrophe infinitely bigger than the catastrophe that we have suffered with the retreat of the civilian population and the army. It was fully aware that there was very little chance of saving the situation, but the Government knew that it was its duty to look for a way, if there was one.'[37] When Negrín said 'the Government', he was referring to himself.

On the morning of Sunday 5 February, Azaña achieved the exile he had longed for. He described the pathetic manner of his entry into France some months later in a letter to his friend Ángel Ossorio y Gallardo. He and his entourage left at dawn in a small convoy of police cars. As a courtesy, Negrín accompanied them across the frontier. The President of the Cortes, Diego Martínez Barrio, travelled ahead in a separate car. This vehicle broke down. Negrín and others in the party tried unsuccessfully to push it out of the way. The party was obliged to cross the hazardously icy border on foot, thereby fulfilling a gloomy prophecy made by Azaña at the beginning of the Civil War. He had said to his wife, Dolores Rivas Cherif: 'We will end up leaving Spain on foot.'[38] When taking his leave, before walking back into Spain, Negrín kissed the hand of Dolores Rivas and said: 'Until we meet again soon in Madrid.'[39]

As Julián Zugazagoitia commented, Negrín and Azaña were incompatible, the one energetic, dynamic and fearless; the other sedentary and timorous. By this stage 'They felt mutual contempt. At that moment, they hated each other.' On his return to Spain, Negrín remarked to Zugazagoitia: 'You have to feel sorry for poor Azaña! He is fearfulness incarnate. His fear gives him a greenish-yellow colour and makes him look like a decomposing corpse.' As he was approaching the frontier, Negrín encountered Lluís Companys, the Catalan President, José Antonio Aguire, the Basque President, and Manuel Irujo, who had been Minister of Justice in his own government. They had proposed accompanying Azaña into France, but he had refused their offer because to have crossed together would have implied that they were on the same level. They now offered to go back into Spain with Negrín, but he politely declined, allegedly muttering to himself, 'That's one less thing to worry about.'[40]

The cabinet had been installed in the castle of Figueras on a hill overlooking the town. With a drawbridge, thick outer and inner walls, it seemed impregnable but was an entirely inappropriate location for a government. According to the British Chargé d'Affaires, Ralph Stevenson, it was:

a large fortress-like barracks on the outskirts of the town. At the best of times, it must have been an uncomfortable place, cold, dank and dirty. But with the débris of the Spanish Government heaped into it pell-mell it was an unforgettable sight. Luckily the weather was bad and there was no great likelihood of aerial bombardment for the place was a veritable death-trap, with only one narrow road, serving for both ingress and egress, along certain stretches of which only one vehicle could pass at a time.[41]

When the weather permitted, the town was subject to frequent rebel bombing raids. Around the courtyard, various ministries were installed in rooms with the words 'foreign ministry', 'ministry of the interior', 'cabinet office' and so on roughly chalked on the wall next to the door. The town square, where the office of press and propaganda had been installed in a requisitioned house, was heaving with refugees. There was little by way of furniture and even less food for the staff. In the words of Herbert Matthews, 'It was a madhouse of bewildered officials and soldiers, struggling desperately, not only with their own work, but with those thousands of swarming refugees who filled every house and doorway and covered almost every inch of the streets where men, women and children slept through the bitterly cold nights with almost no food and certainly no place to go.'[42] Negrín worked ceaselessly to try to limit the catastrophic humanitarian consequences of the defeat in Catalonia and to keep alive the idea of resistance as the best way to achieve a peace settlement that would prevent a vengeful mass slaughter at the hands of the Francoists. To this end, he maintained 'the mask of resistance come what may'. With a colossal weight on his shoulders, he tried to conceal his exhaustion and despair from his ministerial colleagues. Zugazagoitia related that 'one evening, he appeared in the castle, exhausted, almost unable to breathe. He asked if we had anything to eat, sat down at the table and, on the verge of tears, was plunged into a crisis of melancholy.'[43]

Negrín spoke to the last meeting of the Republican Cortes held in the stables of the castle at midnight on 1 February. It was so cold that many of the deputies sat in overcoats. According to the correspondent of the London *Daily Herald* who was present:

Empty chairs were stacked along the walls. Over 106 failed to answer the toll call: many of them were in France, others were holding the dispirited troops together, others had already fallen into Franco's hands. Four times during the session the unshaded swaying lights registered the bombardment which was hitting the town. Negrín, immaculate in a brown suit, was so calm he might have been addressing his students in the quiet prewar days of Madrid.

In his exhaustion, he had to pause frequently to gather breath.[44]

In the dark, echoing stone chamber, the proceedings appeared to Zugazagoitia like 'an intimate religious ceremony celebrated by a persecuted sect'. Negrín was, in many senses, virtually alone, deserted by many, supported by a small group of faithful friends. Yet he assumed the responsibility of fighting on, of doing the best for the Republican population that faced defeat and the 'mercy' of Franco. Bone-tired, he delivered his speech with what Zugazagoitia termed 'unutterable anguish'. The main burden of his words was the need for international mediation to secure guarantees that there would be no reprisals at the end of the war. He presented a plan to bring the war to an end in return for Franco observing certain conditions, the principal one being that there should be no bloodbath. He suggested that the exodus of 450,000 refugees after the fall of Barcelona constituted a plebiscite against the Francoist invaders.[45] The assembled deputies gave Negrín a unanimous vote of confidence, although, as they left, there were embittered mutterings against the Communists. All the deputies went into France, some to seek ways of returning to the central zone, others to stay and secure their own safety. Among those who stayed in France, especially the anarchists and the Socialist supporters of Largo Caballero, there were absurd accusations that Negrín and the Communists were responsible for the defeat of the Republic. As Zugazagoitia commented, they reflected a desire to avoid recognizing the real causes of Republican defeat.[46]

According to Herbert Matthews, 'No one could call it an oratorical masterpiece: it was disjointed, and badly delivered, by a man so exhausted that he could hardly stand, yet it should take its place with the great documents of Spanish history.'[47] In contrast, for Stevenson, Negrín's speech 'did not carry as much conviction as was usual with his pronouncements. He spoke valiantly about continued resistance and ultimate triumph, but his words came from his lips and not from his heart.' The following day, Stevenson and his military attaché had an hour-long meeting with Negrín and the Minister of Foreign Affairs, Julio Álvarez del Vayo, 'in a dark, meagrely furnished room'. Stevenson reported to London that 'Dr Negrín appeared to be as combative as ever. He showed at times flashes of humour, when his face would light up. At other times, it would set in savage determination. He was obviously very tired. He reiterated to me his fixed intention to resist as long as possible in Catalonia and thereafter, if necessary.' Negrín stated that a victory for Franco would be disastrous for the democratic powers, which Stevenson countered by saying this had been duly considered in both London and Paris. They then moved on to discussion of the three points that Negrín regarded as the sine qua non of any peace treaty – that Spain would be independent, that the Spanish people would be free to choose their own form of government and that there would be no reprisals. Negrín said that if these were guaranteed the Republican forces would lay down their arms. In his view, the request for these guarantees had to come jointly from the British, French and United States governments, since to request them himself would be disastrous for the Republic. Stevenson merely asked permission to forward this point to London.[48]

On the same morning, the French Ambassador, Jules Henry, had also gone to Figueras and urged surrender on Negrín, who refused categorically. Henry described the encounter in Figueras to Georges Bonnet: 'it is there that Negrín hides like a tiger trapped in the last refuge of the jungle, and it is from there that he hopes to direct what could be the last act of the Spanish tragedy ... Negrín with a smile on his lips has assured me once more of his confidence in the final success of the cause that he defends ... This time I am not convinced.'[49] In fact, with Franco about to gain control of the entire frontier between Spain and France, it was absolutely essential for Paris to have some sort of diplomatic relations with him. To this end, the government had already sent the Senator Léon Bérard to Burgos to negotiate arrangements for the return to Spain of the refugees already on French territory and of those expected to arrive, as well as for formal representation at Franco's headquarters. Although the French government was anxious to send an ambassador to Franco, it could not do so as long as Negrín remained in power since it could not have two Spanish ambassadors in Paris. In the meantime, until formal diplomatic relations were established, Paris hoped to establish some sort of representation at Franco's headquarters similar to that constituted by the British diplomatic agent Sir Robert Hodgson. The fear was that Franco under Italian pressure would refuse and insist on having a fully fledged ambassador.[50] This being the case, it was hardly likely that Negrín could expect much support from Paris. Indeed, when Bérard met Franco's Foreign Minister, the Conde de Jordana, he broached the subject of a guarantee of no reprisals as a prerequisite of recognition of Franco's government. Jordana told him brusquely: 'The Generalísimo has amply demonstrated his humanitarian feelings but at this moment the only possibility is the unconditional surrender of the enemy which must trust in his generosity and that of his Government.'[51]

Two days after his meeting with Negrín, Ralph Stevenson received 'a secret and personal message' from President Azaña stating that 'he was at complete variance with Dr Negrín's policy of continued resistance. He claimed that his efforts to contact the French Ambassador had been blocked by Negrín. Stevenson immediately informed Jules Henry, who visited Azaña later the same afternoon. The President's message to both diplomats was that their two countries should press Negrín's government to seek an immediate cessation of hostilities. If Negrín did not accede to pressure from the two governments, Azaña told both ambassadors, it was his intention to resign as President.[52]

The British and French governments meanwhile decided to press Negrín to agree to the cessation of hostilities 'on the understanding that General Franco would guarantee the peaceful occupation of the remainder of the country with no political reprisals and the removal of foreign troops from Spain'. In the afternoon of 6 February, Stevenson and Henry met Álvarez del Vayo at Le Perthus. They informed him that the British and French governments were seeking guarantees from Franco and asked if the Republican government would agree to a cessation of hostilities if they were forthcoming. Since there was no response from Franco, Álvarez del Vayo could undertake only to discuss the matter with Negrín. The next day, Negrín received the British and French representatives at the house in the village of La Vajol where he was staying. He conceded that defeat in Catalonia could not be avoided but expressed his view that a European war was inevitable and that resistance could be sustained in the centre-south zone of the Republic. In this regard, he hoped that the equipment being taken into France by the retreating Republican forces could be repatriated. In fact, Georges Bonnet had already informed Franco's envoy in Paris, José María Quiñones de León, that his government would not permit the return of Spanish Republican troops and equipment to the centre-south zone.[53] Unaware of this, Negrín repeated to the British and French diplomats that he would agree to a cessation of hostilities if Franco made a declaration accepting his three conditions of Spanish independence, free elections and no reprisals. To this third point, he added that he wanted an undertaking that at-risk Republican political and military leaders could be evacuated from the centre-south zone under international supervision. It was agreed that this message would be passed on to London and Paris.

After the meeting, Stevenson met with the US Counsellor, Walter Thurston, who commented that Franco would almost certainly reject the demand for Spaniards to be able to choose their own destiny and probably the other two conditions as well. Stevenson replied that the key point was that Negrín had offered capitulation and since the offer had been made, 'the working out of terms will be a mere formality'. This suggested that the British, like the French, were not likely to be overly concerned about ensuring that Franco would not carry out reprisals. The American Ambassador Claude Bowers believed that 'Negrin's purpose is to force a formal official rejection of the terms for the sake of the record or their acceptance'. Bonnet discussed Henry's report with the US Ambassador in Paris, William Bullitt, on 8 February and said that the British were transmitting Negrín's terms to Franco, adding that he thought Franco would reject them and propose unconditional surrender.[54]

The British and French response, Negrín reported later, was that 'it was impossible to reach a satisfactory agreement with the so-called Burgos government because totalitarian governments do not understand humanitarian sentiments nor are they interested in pacification or magnanimity and, what is more, the rebels had claimed that they would only punish common crimes'. To this, Negrín's understandable reaction was: 'In a war like ours, a pitiless and savage civil war, either all crimes are common crimes or none are.' Accordingly, he offered himself as an expiatory victim, letting it be known through the British and French representatives that he would hand himself over if Franco would accept his symbolic execution in exchange for the lives of the mass of innocent Republican civilians. He did not reveal this offer to the majority of his own cabinet. Zugazagoitia knew about it, but Negrín did not make it public until after the Second World War.[55]

Negrín commented to Vidarte after the session: 'People want peace! Me too. But wanting peace is not the same as facilitating defeat. As long as I am prime minister, I will not accept the unconditional surrender of our glorious army, nor a deal that might save several hundred of the most at-risk individuals but allow them to shoot half a million Spaniards. Rather than that, I would shoot myself.'[56] Negrín's offer to hand himself over as the sacrificial scapegoat was ignored by Franco. The government remained in Spain at the Castillo de Figueras until the last units of the Republican army had crossed the frontier on 9 February.

The situation was summed up succinctly by the correspondent of *The Times* of London, Lawrence Fernsworth. A conservative and Roman Catholic, he sympathized with the plight of the defeated Republicans. He wrote: 'At all points where the Pyrenees here slanted away toward the sea, fleeing hordes of Spaniards, each one the embodiment of an individual tragedy, spilled over the mountainous borders, immense avalanches of human debris.' Negrín planned to hold out, as Fernsworth put it, to 'protect the escape from Madrid of thousands who would otherwise fall victims of Franco's reprisals'. Casado opposed Negrín by launching the falsehood that resistance was merely a cover for the establishment of a Communist dictatorship.[57] This notion obviously was already axiomatic for the Francoists, but it also appealed to the anarchists and Socialists who had resented the arrogance and harshness of Communist policies during the war. Assuming, as Casado and the anarchists did, that the PCE was a puppet of the Kremlin, a Communist dictatorship in Spain would have made little sense. Nothing could have been less in accord with the USSR's needs throughout both 1938 and 1939. In 1938, Soviet priorities were for collective security via alliance with France and Britain against Nazi Germany. After the Munich Agreement, the USSR – now moving towards the Molotov–Ribbentrop Pact of August 1939 – was not prepared to alienate Hitler.[58]

On the night of 8 February, one of the few colleagues who remained in Spain with Negrín, his friend Dr Rafael Méndez, said to Álvarez del Vayo: 'I have no idea what we are doing here. I rather fear that tonight we'll be awakened by the rifle-butts of the Carlist *requetés* [militia].' Hearing this, Negrín called Méndez aside and said: 'We won't leave here until the last soldier has crossed the frontier.'[59] Yet again at the forefront of his mind was the determination to see these Republicans safe from the reprisals of Franco. The Carlists, an extreme right-wing monarchist faction, had shown elsewhere that they were all too ready to carry out mass executions. As Negrín wrote later to Prieto: 'From the last house on the Spanish side of the frontier which the rebels occupied an hour later, I stood for eighteen hours watching the file of the last forces that were retreating into France. I managed not to lose my head, and simply by dint of doing my duty, it was possible to save those half a million Spaniards who are now awaiting our help.'[60]

Only after General Rojo had arrived to announce that the final Republican troops in Catalonia had crossed the frontier on the morning of 9 February did Negrín enter France. His most loyal ministers wept. At the Spanish Consulate in Perpignan, an improvised cabinet meeting was held. Negrín announced that he would travel on to Toulouse and from there fly to Spain. Some ministers thought that he was mad, but as he himself later explained: 'If I hadn't done that then, today I would die of shame; I probably would not have been able to survive my disgust with myself. Was the Government going to leave those still fighting in the Central zone without leadership or support?

Was it the Government of Resistance that would flee and surrender them?'[61]

Shortly after Negrín had reached Perpignan on Thursday 9 February, an emissary from General Miaja reached the Spanish Consulate. Captain Antonio López Fernández, Miaja's fiercely anti-Communist secretary, came with the mission of persuading Negrín to remain in France and for President Azaña to grant Miaja permission to negotiate peace with the rebels. Prior to leaving Alicante on the plane for Toulouse, he had telephoned General Rojo, who had asked him to come to the Spanish Embassy in Paris to meet both himself and Azaña on 10 February. On reaching the Consulate in Perpignan late on Thursday evening, Captain López was received by Negrín, Álvarez del Vayo and the Minister of Finance, Francisco Méndez Aspe. He gave them a detailed report on the situation in the central zone, the thrust of which was that there was no possibility of further resistance and that the only possible solution was to entrust Miaja with the task of negotiating surrender on the best terms possible. Negrín listened in silence until López concluded with the words: 'Prime Minister, at this moment, the Centre-South zone is like an aircraft in flight whose engines have stopped. The salvation of those on board depends on the skill of the pilot. In the view of all the senior officers in the zone, that pilot is General Miaja.' When Negrín asked what was needed for resistance to continue, López replied: 'There is no possibility of resisting; there are no weapons, no food, no fuel and our armament is so worn out, with no possibility of replacement or repair, that to oblige the Army to resist is self-evidently senseless and criminal.' When Álvarez del Vayo pressed him further, López replied that resistance would be possible only if huge deliveries of arms and aircraft could arrive immediately. Negrín told López that he would consider his report and that, the next morning, he and Vayo would go to the central zone and discuss future prospects with Miaja.[62]

López then went to Paris and had a meeting with Azaña and Generals Rojo and Hernández Saravia and Lieutenant Colonel Enrique Jurado. There he found a more receptive audience for his pessimistic report. He asked Azaña to return to the central zone to oblige Negrín to resign and to give constitutional legitimacy to negotiations with the Francoists. López's message from Miaja was as hopelessly naive as the beliefs of Casado. It echoed the conclusions of the lunch shared by Miaja a week before with Casado, Matallana and Menéndez in Valencia. He told the President that it was necessary to form a government of professional soldiers who would be able to secure a reasonable peace treaty with Franco. Azaña allegedly replied: 'I have decided to wash my hands of the problems of Spain. Whisper to General Miaja that he should do whatever he thinks best and what he considers to be his duty as a soldier and a Spaniard.' Rojo then gave López letters for Miaja, Matallana and Negrín. López later claimed implausibly that the letter to Negrín urged him to resign and leave Spain while those to Miaja and Matalla instructed them to execute Negrín if he refused to leave. No such letters have been found subsequently.[63]

According to Vicente Uribe, 'The majority of the Ministers had no desire to go to Madrid, morale was extremely low. No one dared say no and preparations to leave were made in accordance with Negrín's orders.' Negrín issued instructions to the soldiers and civilians who had accompanied him, some to return to the centre-south zone and others to remain in France to deal with the refugees and other issues regarding the evacuation. From Toulouse, he flew that night to Alicante, arriving on the morning of the next day. He was accompanied by Julio Álvarez del Vayo, his Foreign Minister, and Santiago Garcés Arroyo, the head of the Republic's security apparatus, the Servicio de Inteligencia Militar. They flew under assumed names, paying their passage on a scheduled Air France flight.[64]

Before leaving, Negrín and Méndez Aspe had a meeting with Trifón Gómez, the quartermaster general of the Republican army. Gómez claimed later that they had discussed the question of food supplies for the centre zone. Negrín allegedly told him to continue sending food but to be careful not to build up stocks. Méndez Aspe allegedly went even further, saying that the war would probably last only another couple of weeks, and that, if there were enough supplies for that time, he was opposed to Gómez sending more. General Rojo made a similar point in his memoir of the period: 'The supply services in the other zone were being dismantled: nothing could be sent, neither men, nor arms, nor matériel, nor munitions, nor raw materials; on the other hand, the political authorities were concentrating on bringing things to an end.'[65]

Assuming this to be true, it shows two things: first, that Negrín was returning to make peace and thus using the rhetoric of resistance as a bargaining chip and, second, that he and Méndez Aspe wanted to conserve resources for the inevitable exodus and subsequent exile. After overseeing the passage of the last Republican troops over the French frontier, Zugazagoitia remembered Negrín saying: 'Let's see if we can do the second part. That's going to be more difficult.' Zugazagoitia went on: 'We were bringing things to an end and when he contemplated returning to the Centre-South zone, Negrín had only one thing on his mind, the end, with as little damage as possible, of a war that was lost.' This coincides with the testimony of Negrín's secretary Benigno Rodríguez, to whom he said that he was returning to Spain 'to save as much as we can'.[66]

4

The Quest for an Honourable Peace

It was assumed by many of the politicians, army officers and functionaries who had crossed into France in early February 1939 that the government would not be returning to Spain. Even some cabinet ministers had their doubts. In cafés where exiles gathered and even in a meeting of senior members of the CNT, there was much venomous gossip about Negrín ranging from blaming him for the fall of Catalonia to accusing him of abandoning the Republic.[1] Of course, Negrín did no such thing but went back in the hope of being able to negotiate a reasonable settlement. He arrived totally exhausted and drained emotionally and physically. Since becoming Prime Minister nearly two years earlier, the stress that he endured had increased exponentially. As well as exercising the basic duties of president of the council of ministers, hc had continued to work hard to build on his achievements as Minister of Finance in ensuring the Republic's economic survival. In April 1938, he had also become Minister of Defence with an intensely active involvement in the role. Throughout, he had carried out a notable diplomatic effort in a vain quest for international mediation to bring the war to an end without reprisals on the part of the Francoists. In addition, he had to deal with the petty squabbles and more than petty jealousies both within the wider coalition of Republican entities, the Popular Front, and within the Socialist Party. Inevitably, all of this took its toll. Just before midnight on Saturday 28 January, Azaña met Rojo and Negrín to discuss the situation in the wake of the loss of Barcelona. Azaña was shocked to see the 'utter dejection' of a Negrín who was 'beaten and on his knees'. After the fall of Catalonia, and the Prime Minister's long vigil at the frontier, his closest collaborators were alarmed at the visible deterioration in a man of once boundless energies.[2]

The full horror of the defeat in Catalonia, the subsequent exodus and the suffering of those condemned to the makeshift camps in southern France was never fully reported in the centre-south zone. Nevertheless, there was no shortage of rumours, together with some reliable information and considerable exaggeration. It all fed the fears of the already exhausted, starving and demoralized population. The sense that a similar fate awaited them led to a widespread hope that someone in authority would appeal to the other side for a negotiated peace. For some at least, in the eloquent phrase of Ángel Bahamonde, 'The psychology of defeat led to an acceptance of blame, the confession of sin and the payment of repentance, sieved through the imagined forgiveness of our brothers on the other side.'[3] In fact, many hundreds of thousands of Republicans expected nothing of 'brothers on the other side'. They knew only too well what Franco's clemency and justice meant. They were those who would flee en masse to the coast at the end of March 1939 in the vain hope of evacuation. Yet they too longed for an end to the war. In fact, for two reasons, there would be virtually no more fighting in the centre zone. On the one hand, Franco needed time to reorganize his forces after the titanic effort involved in the Catalan campaign. On the other, he had confidence that the treachery of Casado, Matallana and other pro-rebel officers would bring down the Republic without further military effort on his part.

Palmiro Togliatti, the senior Comintern representative in Spain, later reported to Moscow on the situation after the loss of Catalonia: 'The great majority of political and military leaders had lost all confidence in the possibility of continued resistance. There was a general conviction that the army of the central zone could not repel an enemy attack because of their overwhelming numerical superiority and because of our lack of weaponry, aircraft and transport, and its organic weakness.' Many professional officers, including the Communist ones, with the sole exception of Francisco Ciutat, believed that prolonged resistance was impossible. Colonel Antonio Cordón, the under-secretary of the Ministry of Defence, the recently promoted General Ignacio Hidalgo de Cisneros, the chief of the air force, and Colonel Carlos Núñez Maza, the under-secretary of air, all career officers but also members of the Communist Party, told Togliatti 'openly' that they did not believe resistance was possible in the centre zone unless the men and weapons taken into France could be returned to Spain. In his report to Moscow, Togliatti wrote: 'I also believe that the conviction that further resistance was impossible was also quite widespread among the officers who had risen from the ranks of the militia. The same belief was also unanimous among the cadres of the Anarchists and of the Republican and Socialist parties, and in the police and state apparatus. Accordingly, the problem was no longer how to organize resistance, but how to end the war "with honour and dignity". There were divergent opinions on how to do this. However, the one point on which there was widespread agreement was that the Communists were the 'sole obstacle' to ending the war. By smearing the Communists as 'the enemies of peace', the defeatists had found a way of channelling the war-weariness and fear of the masses. Togliatti saw this slogan as the 'cement' that united the disparate elements of the non-Communist left. At least retrospectively, he believed that Negrín himself had 'no faith in the possibility of further resistance'.[4]

The most visceral hostility to the Republican government was to be found in the anarchist movement. This derived in part from the bitter resentment of many anarchists about the way in which the libertarian desire for a revolutionary war had been crushed in the first half of 1937 in the interests of a more realistic centralized war effort. However, the anarchists had also been on the receiving end of extremely harsh treatment by the Communist-dominated security services because of the ease with which the CNT–FAI could be infiltrated by the Fifth Column. The Republican press, Communist, Socialist and Left Republican, frequently published accusations about Fifth Column networks that functioned on the basis of using CNT membership cards.[5] The crack security units known as the Brigadas Especiales were focused on the detention, interrogation and, sometimes, elimination of suspicious elements. This meant not only Francoists but also members of the Madrid CNT. The Communist

José Cazorla, who in December 1936 succeeded Santiago Carrillo as the Counsellor for Public Order in the Junta de Defensa de Madrid, believed the CNT to be out of control and infiltrated by agents provocateurs of the Fifth Column.[6] The Communist press demanded strong measures against these uncontrolled elements and those who protected them, calling for the annihilation of the agents provocateurs who were described as 'new dynamiters', a term intended to invoke echoes of anarchist terrorists of earlier times.[7] The presence of Fifth Columnists was perhaps to be expected in an officer corps of the armed forces largely made up of career officers who sympathized with their erstwhile comrades of the other side. However, infiltration of one-time militia units could also be found. Cazorla investigated Fifth Columnist infiltration of the ineffective secret services (Servicios Secretos de Guerra) run in the Ministry of Defence by the CNT's Manuel Salgado Moreira. Shortly before the dissolution of the Junta de Defensa by Largo Caballero, on 14 April 1937, José Cazorla announced that an important spy-ring in the Republican Army had been dismantled. Among those arrested was Alfonso López de Letona, a Fifth Columnist who had reached a high rank in the general staff of the 14th Division of the People's Army, commanded by the anarchist Cipriano Mera. López de Letona had become a senior member of Manuel Salgado's staff on the basis of a recommendation by Mera's chief of staff, Antonio Verardini Díez de Ferreti.[8]

The belief that the anarchist movement was infested with Fifth Columnists was not confined to the Communists. Largo Caballero told PSOE executive committee member Juan-Simeón Vidarte that 'the FAI has been infiltrated by so many agents provocateurs and police informers that it is impossible to have dealings with them'. That view was shared by the Socialist Director General de Seguridad, Largo Caballero's friend Wenceslao Carrillo. One of José García Pradas's collaborators in the CNT–FAI newspaper Frente Libertario was the prominent Fifth Columnist Antonio Bouthelier España, who also held the position of secretary to Manuel Salgado.[9] The easy acquisition of CNT membership cards provided the Fifth Column with access to information, an instrument for acts of provocation and relative ease of movement. Once equipped with CNT accreditation,

Fifth Columnists could also get identity cards for the Republican security services.[10]

While Negrín was still in Catalonia, the anarchist movement initiated contacts with the generals who were also being sounded out by Casado. On 1 February 1939 the secretaries of the three principal anarchist organizations, the CNT, the FAI and the anarchist youth movement, the Federación de Juventudes Libertarias, jointly sent an obsequious letter to General Miaja. They suggested that they create for him an organization uniting all anti-fascist forces in the centre-south zone, insinuating that it exclude the Communists. Over the next three days, the anarchists held meetings with Miaja, Matallana and Menéndez. Since all three generals were already conspiring with Casado, it is reasonable to suppose that areas of mutual interest were sketched out. According to the anarchist chronicler José Peirats, in the meeting with the anarchists Miaja declared that the Communists intended to impose a one-party government led by Vicente Uribe. There was no truth in the claim – it merely reflected what Casado had told Miaja earlier on the same day.[11]

In the wake of these anarchist initiatives, three senior figures of the libertarian movement of the centre-south zone were sent on a mission to try to secure a coordinated response of the CNT and FAI to the deteriorating military situation. Juan López Sánchez, who had been Minister of Commerce in the government of Largo Caballero, Manuel Amil, secretary of the CNT's Federación Nacional del Transporte, and Eduardo Val Bescós, seen as the most powerful figure in the anarchist movement in Madrid, had left for Catalonia in the early morning of Sunday 5 February, ten days after the Francoist capture of Barcelona. Their purpose was to make contact with the CNT's National Committee to discuss the situation after the expected loss of Catalonia. Their aircraft, unable to land in Catalonia, where Figueras was about to fall, took them to Toulouse. In contrast to the silent Val, the tall and brawny Manuel Amil was a loquacious raconteur. They were trapped in France for several days, visiting the consulates in Toulouse and Perpignan in search of the CNT's National Committee before finding the CNT headquarters set up in Paris. What they learned and their subsequent reports would play a significant part in the anarchists' participation in the Casado coup. Throughout the delegation's sojourn in France, Val's main contribution had been to mutter imprecations against Negrín.[12]

On 8 February, they took part in a meeting in Paris with senior members of the CNT, including Juan García Oliver, the head of the National Committee Mariano Vázquez and the minister Segundo Blanco. García Oliver said that it was necessary to remove Negrín and form a government to bring the war to an end. Val then shocked the group by declaring that he had proof that Negrín was not planning resistance but meant to end the war. He then persuaded them that it was not the moment to think in terms of surrendering. His optimistic view of the possibilities of lengthy resistance did not prevail. However, since the main objection to Negrín was, bizarrely, that he was defeatist, the group finally agreed that it was necessary to remove him and form a government capable of resisting long enough to achieve an acceptable peace settlement. The general consensus was that 'the more resistance we are capable of mounting, the better the peace conditions we can secure'. Ignoring the military reality, Mariano Vázquez declared simplistically, 'Whoever can strike hard is in a position to make themselves feared.' They then had immense problems getting back to the centre-south zone, which they finally managed to do in the early hours of the morning of Monday 20 February.[13]

Underlying the anarchist initiatives was both a visceral anti-communism and a belief that Negrín was incapable of continuing the war effort. In fact, Negrín harboured vain hopes that, after the collapse of the Catalan front, it would be possible to secure the return to Spain both of the evacuated army and of the equipment that they had taken over the border. He had also believed that the supplies from friendly nations, especially the Soviet Union, that had accumulated in France could be delivered to the central-southern zone. Given his commitment to holding out until a peace settlement could be made that would secure the evacuation of those at risk, these hopes sustained his rhetorical commitment to the possibility of continuing the war. While the anarchists simply did not want to believe him, his rhetoric also exposed him to the criticism of many, most notably Azaña and Rojo.[14]

Just before the fall of Catalonia, the internationally famous journalist Martha Gellhorn wrote a letter to Eleanor Roosevelt,

I find myself thinking about Negrín all the time. I suppose he will fly to Madrid when it is ended in Catalonia and carry on there. Negrín is a really great man, I believe (and he can't stop being now), and it's so strange and moving to think of that man who surely never wanted to be prime minister of anything being pushed by events and history into a position which he has heroically filled, doing better all the time, all the time being finer against greater odds. He used to be a brilliant gay lazy man with strong beliefs and perhaps too much sense of humour. He was it seems never afraid and loved his friends and his ideas about Spain and drinking and eating and just being alive. Now he has grown all the time until you get an impression he's made of some special indestructible kind of stone: he has a twenty hour working day and in Spain you get the idea that he manages alone, that with his two hands every mornng he puts every single thing into place and brings order. Of course, he cannot hold a front. I hope he gets to Madrid. If they are going to be defeated, I still hope they don't surrender.[15]

In contrast, some months after the end of the war, Rojo produced a devastating criticism of Negrín:

It would appear that the view that we should continue a policy of resistance was imposed in the hope that it might provoke a change in the international situation. The same hope that had sustained our sacrifices but now without any basis. What do sacrifices matter! Resistance! A sublime formula for heroism when it is nurtured by hope and sustained by an ideal; but when the will that flies the banner of that ideal collapses and hope becomes a denial of reality, then resistance is no longer an heroic military battle-cry but an absurdity. What were we to resist with? Why were we going to resist? Two questions for which no one had a positive answer.

Rojo's diatribe reflected the distress caused him by the plight of the exiles, but, safe in France, he failed to take into consideration the appalling consequences of a swift unconditional surrender. He followed up his comments on the futility of continued resistance with a disturbing rhetorical question:

> Should I have embarked on an undertaking proposed in such a confusing manner? If it was true that the war in the central zone was going to be continued seriously, why were the stocks of food, raw materials and armaments accumulated in France sold off? This was too obvious and significant not to be disconcerting: on the one hand, the conflict was being wound up economically by the sale of these stocks; on the other hand the order to resist was given without the means to carry it out, even in terms of food. It was clear to me that I should not take part in or support from my technical post what was an incomprehensible action.[16]

It was certainly the case that Francisco Méndez Aspe had been ordered to shore up the Republic's financial resources by selling material that was either in France or had been ordered but not yet delivered. This was part of Negrín's plans to pay for the exiles in France and for the evacuation of Republicans. Clearly, it would have been difficult to do both that and mount a full-scale resistance. Effectively, Negrín seems to have been concentrating on the former while maintaining the fiction of resistance both to gain time and in the hope of securing concessions from Franco.[17]

Only with the greatest reluctance had Azaña agreed to take up residence in the Spanish Embassy in Paris, preferring to be further from the influence of Negrín's Ambassador in France, Marcelino Pascua. He had arrived on 9 February and wasted little time in publicly expressing his support for British and French proposals for mediation, which effectively meant early surrender. His presence in France and its implication that there was no proper government in Spain were necessarily damaging to Negrín's efforts to secure guarantees from Franco. As Negrín later repeated to Marcelino Pascua, he had expected Azaña to return to Spain once the members of the government were back in Madrid. To this end, after the first cabinet meeting on 13 February, the Foreign Minister Julio Álvarez del Vayo sent a telegram to Pascua instructing him to inform Azaña that the government required his presence in Spain. Azaña did not reply and, the next day, Álvarez del Vayo arrived in Paris to underline personally the urgency of the President's return. Azaña merely listened and said that he would inform Negrín of his views. This he did the following day, disingenuously asking Negrín to give reasons why there should be any change to what had been agreed before he left Spain.[18] Negrín was taken aback by Azaña's continued prevarication and claimed that, at their meeting on 30 January in the presence of Martínez Barrio, it had been agreed that he would reside in Paris only until the cabinet needed him. In fact, at that meeting, the issue had not been resolved. Although Azaña had insisted that he would not return, Negrín had been confident that the overwhelming needs of the Republic would oblige him to relent. Negrín now reiterated the obvious reasons why the President's absence was undermining the work of the government. Despite frequent prompts from Pascua, Azaña did not reply to Negrín's message. He did, however, ask for financial help and was given 150,000 francs (the equivalent today of US$85,000).[19]

The situation faced by the refugees was appalling. Within days of Negrín leaving, the Consul in Perpignan, Antonio Zorita, was replaced. He had shown virtually no readiness to help the refugees. Indeed, his wife had tried to prevent Colonel Tagüeña and other senior military personnel from staying in the Consulate on the grounds that they upset the routine of the household. Both Tagüeña and Rafael Méndez were helped immensely by the feminist Margarita Nelken, who acted as Méndez's liaison with the French authorities and gave Tagüeña and his comrades French currency with which to buy food. Álvarez del Vayo told Méndez that Negrín wanted him to replace Zorita as Consul.[20] Many prominent officers, including General Sebastián Pozas, once commander of the Army of the East and most recently the military governor of Figueras, and Colonel Eleuterio Díaz Tendero Merchán, the head of personnel classification in the Ministry of Defence, chose to remain in France.[21]

There has been some controversy regarding the decision of General Rojo not to return to Spain. According to both Julián Zugazagoitia, now secretary of the Ministry of Defence, and Mariano Ansó, a Republican friend of Negrín who had been Minister of Justice in the first months of 1938, General Vicente Rojo and Lieutenant Colonel Enrique Jurado, the commander of the Army of Catalonia, refused to obey the instruction sent by Negrín on 14 February that they should return to the centre-south zone. When Pascua handed them the telegram, the two generals argued that the war was effectively over and that their duty was to look after the soldiers who were now refugees in France. They were not alone in their decision. The bulk of the officers of the command structure of the Armies of the East and of Catalonia, including Generals Pozas, Masquelet, Riquelme, Asensio, Gámir, Hernández Saravia and Perea, also decided that the war was lost and that they were under no obligation to continue the fight.[22] It is probable that their decision was influenced both by the palpable defeatism of the high command of the navy and by events in the Balearic Islands. On the same day that the Republican Army had crossed the frontier into France, Menorca was also lost.

On 22 January, four days before leaving Barcelona, Negrín had faced the almost insuperable problem of finding a replacement for the head of the fleet, Luis González Ubieta. In general, most naval officers were right-wing, in most cases defeatist and, in some, actively sympathetic to the Francoist cause. The chosen successor, acting Rear Admiral Miguel Buiza Fernández-Palacios, was an exception to the general tendencies of the aristocratic officer corps. He was the black sheep of a rich right-wing family in Seville and a Republican who was popular with his men. His family and his fellow officers shunned him because of his marriage to Maravilla, a woman whose brother was a stoker and so considered to be of unacceptably inferior social class. The laconic and diffident Buiza was hardly a sea-going warrior and was far from fulfilling the needs of the Republican war effort, but Negrín had little choice. In January 1936, Buiza had been head of the personnel section within the naval general staff. His loyalty to the Republic was no more than geographic, having been based in Cartagena when the war started. Throughout the war, his role had been at best passive and at worst advantageous for the Francoist fleet, commanded as it was by many of his friends. He had protected Fifth Columnists among his officers and had long been suspected of defeatism. Despite Negrín's doubts, Buiza was appointed three days before his forty-first birthday. In addition to being profoundly defeatist, he was deeply affected by a personal tragedy. On 26 January, as Franco's forces entered Barcelona, his wife, suffering from post-natal depression, and convinced that her husband had been captured, committed suicide. Perhaps to help keep his mind off these circumstances, he accepted the new post, saying that he owed it to the rank-and-file crewmen.[23] Given that so much depended on the loyalty and efficacy of the fleet, Buiza was hardly suitable as overall commander.

González Ubieta was transferred to take command of Menorca. In the days following, aircraft from Francoist-held Mallorca bombed the base at Mahón and dropped thousands of leaflets demanding surrender. This was the first part of a plan to seize Menorca hatched by Captain Fernando Sartorius, Conde de San Luís. Sartorius, the liaison officer between the Francoist air force and navy in Mallorca, arranged with Alan Hillgarth, London's Consul in Palma de Mallorca, for a British cruiser, HMS *Devonshire*, to take him to Mahón. The ship would then provide a neutral base for a negotiation between Sartorius and González Ubieta. The ship's captain Gerald Muirhead-Gould, like Hillgarth, had a pedigree in the Naval Intelligence Department, was a protégé of Winston Churchill and a Franco sympathizer. Arriving on 7 February, Muirhead-Gould persuaded González Ubieta to meet Sartorius, who threatened González Ubieta that, if he did not surrender, there would be a full-scale aerial bombardment of Mahón. González Ubieta refused and a full-scale pro-Franco rebellion broke out in Ciudadela on the night of 7 February.

Francoist reinforcements arrived from Palma, González Ubieta's pleas for help from Miaja went unanswered and Muirhead-Gould pressed him to discuss surrender with San Luís. While awaiting a resolution, HMS *Devonshire*, anchored in the harbour of Mahón, was attacked by Italian aircraft. A deal was finally reached. On 9 February, around 300 Republican loyalists under the command of González

Ubieta, 100 women and 50 children, and what Sartorius described as 'some really repugnant types', were taken to Marseilles. Menorca was of secondary importance in the war but the significance of what Sartorius and Muirhead-Gould achieved was that it sent a misleading message to the Republican officer corps that a bloodless surrender would be possible.[24]

The decision of Rojo not to return to Spain was deeply damaging to Negrín's hopes of securing the full backing of the forces of the centre-south zone for his plan to use the threat of last-ditch resistance to help secure reasonable peace terms from Franco. In fact, Rojo's stance was more disastrous even than it seemed at the time given that his most likely replacement, Manuel Matallana, was already working in favour of the rebel cause. According to Zugazagoitia, Rojo refused to return to Spain with the words, 'The only reason for obeying the order to return is the duty of obedience but you surely realize that just because a superior officer orders us to jump out of a window we do not have to do so.' He told Zugazagoitia and the Consul in Perpignan, Rafael Méndez Martínez, that 'he was not prepared to preside over an even bigger disaster than the one in Catalonia'. When he was informed of this, Negrín had Méndez draw up a document, witnessed by Zugazagoitia, registering both his instructions to Rojo and Jurado and their reasons for disobeying them. Zugazagoitia was deeply shocked by Rojo's comments. Although he could not believe that they reflected cowardice on his part, he later wondered if Rojo knew what was being planned by Casado and was passively complicit. For Togliatti, Rojo was simply a deserter.[25]

After the retreat into France, Uribe was commissioned by the PCE leadership to speak to Rojo and:

> try to show him that his views were mistaken and to convince him of the need to continue the war, explaining the possibilities that we still had. I was also instructed to make him see his responsibilities which he should fulfil before going to the central zone with the Government. Our conversation lasted three hours. I could get nothing out of him. He was unshakeable in his judgement that, from a military point of view, the Republic

could do nothing, the war was over and the best that could be done was to seek a way of ending it on the best possible terms. As far as he was concerned personally, he had made his decision on the basis of the military situation and nothing would make him change his mind. None of the arguments used in the conversation, including discipline and honour, had the slightest effect. Rojo had decided not to go the central zone and he did not go.[26]

The Republican Ambassador in Paris, Marcelino Pascua, sent telegrams to Negrín that were highly critical of Rojo. Even more critical comments were passed between Zugazagoitia and Pascua in their private correspondence. Recalling Rojo's remarks about the limits of obedience, Zugazagoitia wrote: 'the fact is the General's statements were among the most shocking that I heard in the entire war'. He questioned Rojo's role in the fall of Barcelona, asking why he had sacked General Hernández Saravia, who had arrived in the city with the intention of organizing a last-ditch resistance such as that which had saved Madrid in 1936. Above all, both Zugazagoitia and Pascua were outraged by the way in which, in his book ¡Alerta los pueblos! written immediately after the war, Rojo fudged the issue of his personal responsibility. In it, he denied that he had received orders to return to Spain. In fact, Negrín sent a telegram to Marcelino Pascua on 16 February instructing him to tell General Rojo and Colonel Jurado again that they must return to Spain. Pascua gave the telegram to Rojo. Similar telegrams were sent to the Republican consuls in Toulouse and Perpignan for delivery to him.[27]

Juan López, who was in France as part of the stranded CNT–FAI delegation, was in the Republican Consulate in Toulouse when he overheard a telephone conversation between the Consul and Rojo, who was in Perpignan. He heard the Consul say: 'I have received a telegram from the prime minister instructing me to let you know that you must come here to Toulouse to arrange your return to Spain.'[28] The publication of Zugazagoitia's book with its account of Negrín's call for Méndez to notarize the refusal of Rojo and Jurado to return to Spain ensured for him Rojo's enduring resentment.[29]

In *¡Alerta los pueblos!*, Rojo claimed that he and Negrín had parted amicably and that he had remained in France 'to finish my task'. His vain hope had been to see the French implement promises to allow the refugee troops and their equipment to return to Spain. He went on to describe the calamitous situation of the thousands of Republican soldiers now in improvised, overcrowded and insanitary concentration camps on the beaches of southern France. The Republicans herded there lacked adequate shelter, food, clean water and basic medical provision. His distress at what he saw impelled him to write to Negrín on 12 February a bitter letter of complaint and protest. In it, he expressed his disgust that, while plans had been made for the evacuation of President Azaña, the President of the Cortes, the Basque and Catalan governments, parliamentary deputies and large numbers of functionaries, nothing had been done to plan for the evacuation of ordinary citizens. He was appalled by the camps, 'where today hundreds of thousands of civilian refugees and tens of thousands of soldiers, including middle- and high-ranking officers, are perishing'. He was outraged by evidence that Republican functionaries were simply not doing their job – a point reiterated in many of the memoirs of the period.[30]

Rojo's letter of 12 February reflected his obsession with the plight of the refugees in the camps and the way the French authorities pursued and humiliated those who had managed to avoid internment. He reproached Negrín for not having accepted his advice to surrender in Catalonia before the present situation arose. The letter underlined his refusal to return to Spain and his determination to continue working on behalf of the exiled troops: 'I have not returned because I have no wish to be part of the second disaster to which the Government will almost certainly condemn our army and our people. I have stayed here believing that it is necessary that someone look out for the fate of our men. I was right to fear that we would be abandoned.' He went on to make several demands of the Prime Minister. He began by asking that Negrín accept 'the total and absolute renunciation of my post'. He went on to make suggestions that he believed would avoid a humanitarian catastrophe: that a government minister be sent to take charge of the refugee situation; that, in the interim, the

Ambassador Marcelino Pascua be required to come to Perpignan; and that more funds be made available. Finally, he threatened that, if these demands were not met, he would deal directly with Franco to arrange the repatriation of the refugees and would publicize the situation, threatening to take 'serious decisions if something was not done to improve the state of affairs'. He did not implement his threat, he said in the book, so as not to make things worse. The letter bore an olive branch for Negrín: 'Perhaps among those whom I accuse of being responsible for this dereliction of duty, you are not the only exception because I am aware of your constant preoccupation, your sleepless nights, your integrity and I know how you have had to fight, along with a handful of ministers, against the insuperable fear that had invaded every level of the higher reaches of the State.'[31]

General Rojo wrote with some pride of the retreat: the army 'had carried out a methodical withdrawal ... it had held off the enemy, continuing to fight throughout, without letting the weakening of morale open the way to collective indiscipline or panic, without the demoralization spreading through its rearguard, and crossing into the neighbouring country in good order led by its officers'. The Minister of Culture in the Catalan Generalitat, Carles Pi Sunyer, wrote: 'It is only fair to underline in honour of both Negrín and the army that it retreated in good order and with strict discipline without the epic grandeur of the withdrawal being stained by any explosion of vengeful violence.'[32]

Just before he entered France on 9 February, Negrín had said to the faithful group that accompanied him: 'Let us hope that we achieve the same success with the second part of the task.' The 'first part' was the evacuation of Catalonia; the 'second part' would be the evacuation of the centre-south zone. As Zugazagoitia commented, although Negrín's public declarations spoke of resistance, 'nobody knew better than he did how meaningless the slogan was'.[33] In this regard, his arrangements to transfer the financial resources of the Republic to France were a crucial part of his plans for evacuation. Rojo's accusation that no plans had been made was unjust, although it was certainly true that the scale and speed of the final debacle had not been, indeed could hardly have been, anticipated. After the defeat at the Ebro,

Negrín had already begun to prepare for the likely Francoist triumph and the need to organize the evacuation, and subsequent support, of many thousands of Republicans. He had instructed the Minister of Finance, Francisco Méndez Aspe, and the most trusted officials of his Ministry, Jerónimo Bugeda, José Prat and Rafael Méndez, to draw up lists of the assets still in the hands of the government. He instructed Méndez Aspe to recover where possible the assets that the Republic had deposited in its offices in Czechoslovakia, the USA, Mexico, France and Britain to pay for arms, munitions, food, medical supplies and raw materials. His task included arranging for goods that had been bought but still not delivered to be converted into cash. Most of the jewels, gold and silver plate, stock and bond holdings of wealthy persons who had left Spain during the war, together with many art works belonging to the Church, had been confiscated by the Caja de Reparaciones and used to buy arms and supplies for the Republic. Since the autumn of 1938, truckloads of the remaining valuables had been brought to Figueras and nearby frontier towns.[34]

While still in Figueras, Negrín ordered that what remained should be packed and transported to France. He arranged with the French authorities that two sealed trucks laden with 110 boxes of these valuables be permitted to cross the frontier without examination by customs. The trucks went first to the Republican Embassy in Paris and then on to Le Havre where they would be loaded on to a vessel. This was a yacht, originally named *Giralda*, that had been bought by the Republican government via intermediaries from the former king Alfonso XIII and renamed *Vita*. In March, with the permission of the French Minister of the Interior Albert Sarrault, the Servicio de Evacuación de los Refugiados Españoles (SERE) was created in Paris, under the protection of the Mexican Embassy and the chairmanship of Pablo Azcárate. The valuables which were intended to constitute its funds were embarked for Mexico on the *Vita* on or about 10 March. There, in complicated circumstances, they fell into the hands of Indalecio Prieto. The subsequent fate of these funds would be a toxic issue within exile politics.[35]

Enrique Castro Delgado recounted a meeting with Rojo at this time. Allegedly, Rojo told him that Negrín had ordered him to return to Spain. When Castro asked him if he would go, Rojo replied: 'No, there are hundreds of thousands of men here needing our help.' When a shocked Castro asked if there were not also hundreds of thousands inside Spain who needed help, Rojo replied, 'There's nothing to be done there ... it's the inevitable death agony that will be followed by the terrible death of an era, the death of a regime, the death of the hope of millions of people.'[36] So committed was Rojo to remaining in France that, in his book, he revealed his indignation that Tagüeña, Líster and the chief of his general staff, López Iglesias, the under-secretary of the Ministry of Defence, Colonel Antonio Cordón, the chief of the Republican air force Ignacio Hidalgo de Cisneros and other Communist officers and commissars had returned to Spain without seeking his permission.[37]

The armies defeated in Catalonia had a strong element of Communists and officers and men who had come through the militias. In contrast, the armies of the centre-south zone had a far higher proportion of career officers, a significant minority of whom were of doubtful loyalty to the Republic. Themselves often under surveillance, they had sought desk jobs behind the lines in training schools and the general staff. They had often provided money, safe-conducts and other documentation and protection for Francoist comrades who had refused to serve the Republic and were in hiding. Franco's espionage services were especially interested in the beliefs of members of the Republican officer corps in order to ascertain whom among them they could use. As defeat followed defeat, the nostalgia of career officers for the pre-war army provided fertile soil for the recruiters of the Francoist Servicio de Información y Policia Militar (SIPM). These disgruntled professionals had long since felt a certain mistrust of, if not contempt for, the officers who had come through the militias. They harboured the vain hope that there could be a peace settlement arranged with Francoist officers with whom they had been educated in military academies and with whom they had served before 1936. Among the most typical of such officers, and one of the most powerful, was Segismundo Casado.[38]

Accordingly, such officers in the centre-south zone had no desire to see the return of Líster, Modesto and other Communist commanders who were committed to continuing the fight. These commanders, after doing what they could to improve the conditions of their men, returned to Spain over the next few days. Tagüeña states that he, Líster, Francisco Romero Marín and several other officers from the Army of the Ebro returned on 19 February. There is some confusion over the date of this flight – in two books of memoirs, Líster dated it both five and six days earlier on 13 and 14 February. However, they coincide in lamenting that numerous leading figures of the Communist Party, including Antonio Mije, Francisco Antón, Santiago Álvarez and Santiago Carrillo, did not return on the grounds that the PCE did not want them exposed to danger. Líster recalled that the thirty-three-seat aircraft in which he had travelled had twenty empty seats. Hidalgo de Cisneros told Burnett Bolloten, a United Press correspondent who, by his own account, was a Communist sympathizer at the time, that the last six aircraft that flew from France to Republican Spain were 'nearly empty'.[39] That Negrín had his doubts about those who would or wouldn't return was reported later by Francisco Romero Marín, who had returned with Hidalgo de Cisneros. When they entered Negrín's office in the Presidencia building in the Castellana, the Prime Minister exclaimed: 'Here come another group of lunatics.'[40]

Cordón met Rojo on 18 February in Perpignan. The new Spanish Consul Rafael Méndez informed them that he had received a cable from Negrín ordering all senior officers and officials of the Ministry of Defence to return to the central zone. A visibly annoyed Rojo said: 'Well, I will not regard myself as having received that order until the Minister of Defence gives it to me personally.' Méndez told him to do what he liked and remarked that he thought that soldiers did not need to receive orders to rejoin the army in time of war. Rojo replied that he knew better than anyone where his duty lay and that he was fully occupied in attending to those who were arriving in France and in trying to organize the matériel brought by the army into France. When Méndez replied that there were people doing that already, Rojo walked away without a word. Three days later, Cordón had dinner at the Toulouse railway station with Rojo and Jurado. Equipped with splendid new leather luggage, the two men were on their way to Paris to seek more money at the Embassy for their work with the exiled officers. They had already spent the 4.5 million francs originally given them for this purpose. When Cordón asked if they planned to return to Spain, Rojo again stated that he had not received a direct order to do so and that, in any case, he would go only if he could do something concrete by way of negotiating peace. Cordón reminded them that orders had been issued for their return and that, if they didn't obey, measures would be taken against them. Jurado replied threateningly that, in such a case, they might make damaging revelations – presumably a reference to the failures of the Republican authorities to prepare for the evacuation and subsequent care of the refugees. Rojo would later make the implausible claim in his book that he had been preparing to return when the Casado coup intervened and made it impossible.[41]

In fact, Rojo's absence from Negrín's side was to contribute substantially to the success of the Casado coup. As Vicente Uribe, wrote in his memoir of the period:

It saw the Government lose a valuable collaborator who would have been immensely useful because of his reputation, and the influence that he wielded over the career officers and the subversives who were already plotting received a major boost from Rojo's desertion. They knew all about his views and his refusal. Rojo himself had made sure to let them know. In any case, it was evident that he had not accompanied the Government back to Spain. In contrast, the Communist officers had returned to what remained of Republican territory to do their duty.[42]

Hidalgo de Cisneros stayed on for several days vainly negotiating with the French authorities for his men to fly back to Spain in their own aircraft. At the Paris Embassy, he met both Rojo and Enrique Jurado. Azaña asked for all three to meet him and explain the military situation in the wake of the fall of Catalonia. All three gave bleak reports, of which the most pessimistic was that by Jurado. When Azaña asked them to put their thoughts in writing, Hidalgo suspected that the President was simply looking for a justification for his resignation. After consulting with the Ambassador, Marcelino Pascua, Hidalgo refused, stating that such a report should come from the Minister of Defence, that is to say Negrín. Rojo and Jurado used the same excuse. Azaña was greatly displeased. When Hidalgo returned to Madrid, he recounted this to a furious Negrín, who immediately sent a telegram to Azaña saying that he would hold him responsible for the consequences of behaviour that he regarded as tantamount to treachery. In fact, Rojo had already given Azaña a deeply gloomy oral assessment of the situation which almost certainly reinforced the President's already firm determination not to return to Spain. Indeed, Azaña would later claim that this was the case.[43] Negrín was understandably annoyed and so Rojo wrote a letter to him explaining that he had been virtually ambushed by Azaña during what he had assumed would be merely a formal visit in accordance with protocol. Along with his letter, Rojo enclosed a detailed report on the economic, human and military reasons why continued resistance in the centre-south zone was futile. It seems that he was unaware of the extent to which the rhetoric of resistance was a ploy by Negrín to enhance his diplomacy. Before receiving the letter, Negrín sent, via Marcelino Pascua, a firm instruction to Rojo to make reports to Azaña only via the Minister of Defence, that is to say, Negrín himself. Rojo then wrote another letter reiterating that he had fallen into a trap set by Azaña. The letter also contained a detailed report on the condition of the refugees. Rojo sent copies of these various reports to Matallana, which meant that their gloomy conclusions were known both to other members of Casado's conspiracy and, of course, to the Francoist SIPM.[44]

Rojo subsequently claimed that he had stayed on in France because his orders were to remain and do everything possible to ameliorate the situation of the thousands of Republican soldiers now in exile. It is true that he distributed funds to officers for them to buy food, but he also ignored the multiple orders from Negrín to return.[45] Rojo declared later that 'there was no shortage of heavy hints that I should also return'. This was an utterly disingenuous reference to explicit instructions issued by Negrín, not to mention the conversations recounted in their memoirs by Cordón, Tagüeña and Zugazagoitia.[46]

According to Martínez Barrio, the President of the Cortes, who saw Azaña every day in the Paris Embassy, the text of the telegram sent to the President by Negrín in mid-February was cold, formal and rather threatening. Azaña, who regarded the war as effectively over, had reacted furiously: 'A fine programme he's offering me! To enter Madrid, accompanied by Negrín and Uribe, with Pasionaria and Pepe Díaz on the running board of the car.' (José Díaz was secretary-general of the PCE.) Martínez Barrio pointed out to Azaña that, if he refused to accept Negrín's insistence that he return to Spain, it was his constitutional duty either to resign as President or else to appoint a new prime minister. Had Azaña resigned then, Martínez Barrio felt that, as his automatic successor, he could have helped Negrín seek a reasonable peace. As it was, Azaña was sunk in lethargy and did not respond. Some days later, Negrín sent another 'even ruder and more humiliating' telegram 'in the name of the Spanish people' accusing the President of failing in his constitutional duty and demanding his immediate return. Azaña replied on 25 February denying that his absence from Spain had in any way weakened the government or encouraged any of the Great Powers to hasten their recognition of Franco. Before Negrín could reply, Azaña had left the Embassy. He attended a concert at the Opéra Comique with Cipriano Rivas; returning to the Embassy merely to collect their luggage, the two men left together for the Gare de Lyon. Their departure eagerly recorded by an army of journalists and photographers, they took the night train to Collonges-sous-Salève near the Swiss border. As Azaña had done on previous occasions in his political career, he fled from the pressures besetting him, and his flight would be severely damaging to the Republic.[47] The Minister of Justice, Ramón González Peña, declared that Azaña's behaviour was high treason. Negrín even toyed with the unrealistic idea of having Azaña put on trial.[48]

5

Casado Sows the Wind

Meanwhile, the hostility between the Communists and Casado was becoming ever more public. In fact, Casado had long been attempting to foment dissent between the Communists and the other component groups of the Popular Front. A fruitful opportunity had arisen when the PCE harshly criticized Largo Caballero, who after crossing into France on 29 January 1939 had decided to remain in Paris. As he had abandoned Madrid once before, on 6 November 1936, claims that he had sent his papers and household linen and silver in an ambulance two days before crossing the frontier with his family fuelled accusations of cowardice.[1] On 2 February, the PCE issued a manifesto severely censuring his absence at a time when his presence in Madrid might have contributed to raising morale:

> The Politburo denounced before the working class and the Spanish people the shameful flight from our national territory of Sr Largo Caballero who, aided by a small group of enemies of the unity of the Spanish people and its organizations, has done everything in his power to sabotage the work of the Government and break the unity and resistance of our people and now crowns his previous criminal activity with this desertion.

In addition to banning the distribution of the manifesto, Casado held a meeting of the Madrid Popular Front at which he deliberately fuelled Socialist hostility towards the Communists by making a theatrical show of stressing his indignation at the way in which Largo Caballero had been depicted. He claimed, falsely, that the manifesto had called the veteran leader 'a thief and a murderer'.[2]

With the more realistic and prudent Palmiro Togliatti still in France – after the loss of Catalonia – PCE leaders in Madrid made unrestrained and belligerent declarations about last-ditch resistance. The Comintern adviser present, the Bulgarian Stoyan Minev, alias 'Boris Stepanov', was also talking in terms of sidelining Negrín and establishing a revolutionary war council to put an end to capitulationism. Stepanov was doing no more than articulating the party leadership's visceral resentment of the way they were being blamed for the course of the war. This was made clear in the course of a meeting of the PCE provincial committee held in Madrid between 9 and 11 February. In an unrestrained speech, Dolores Ibárruri attacked Largo Caballero, Casado and Miaja. She referred to the two officers as 'distinguished mummies'. Vicente Uribe went further, denouncing the cowardice of those who were doing the job of the enemy by spreading the notion that peace without reprisals was possible. His proposal that the Communist Party take power to purge such defeatists and strengthen the war effort was a symptom of impotence, an empty threat designed to inhibit the conspirators. The inevitable effect of its threatening tone was further to isolate the PCE and make Casado readier to act. His initial response was to attempt to censor *Mundo Obrero*'s report on the the speeches, but his orders were ignored.[3]

The proceedings of this meeting further intensified Casado's hostility towards the Communists. He had tried to prevent it taking place, which was a dictatorial abuse of the powers associated with the state of martial law decreed in late January. Deeply irritated by the Communist leadership's references to the failure of the Brunete offensive and the strong possibility of disloyalty within the military, Casado was all the more furious because Dolores Ibárruri had called him a 'mummy'. He shouted: 'I should have no hesitation!… They had better look out! I have foreseen all the consequences. In case anything happens to me, I have a list of all my enemies and at least thirty of them will die!' Edmundo Domínguez was convinced that Casado's bluster reflected fear of his machinations being discovered.[4]

On his return from France on 10 February, Negrín was furious. He viewed the PCE's calls for an exclusively Communist-led resistance as disloyalty. On the 15th, Líster reported to Negrín in Madrid. The Prime Minister received him in his bathroom where he was shaving. There was nothing unusual in that. On a regular basis, while shaving and or even while soaking in the bath, Negrín would conduct business. He was not bothered by the niceties of protocol and, with so many responsibilities and so little time, he would listen to reports or take advice where he thought it was useful, and one such place was in his bathroom. The American journalist Louis Fischer, who advised him on the foreign press, described how Negrín would invite him to his quarters to talk and he would often find him in the bathroom shaving, clad only in his pyjama bottoms. He would then take a bath while Fischer sat on a stool or leaned against the wall chatting with him: 'Occasionally a secretary would come in with a telegram, bend over the bath-tub and hold it while Negrín read it. Negrín was very natural and simple about all this.'[5]

Now, on 15 February, after expressing his appreciation that Líster had returned to the central zone, they talked about the prospects of further resistance. Saying that the pair of them were likely to end up being shot, Negrín gave Líster a gloomy outline of situation. 'He told me that a whole series of senior military commanders and political and trade union leaders – anarchists, Socialists and Republicans – were ready to capitulate. Wherever they looked, all they saw were difficulties and, instead of working to strengthen the discipline and morale of the troops and of the civilian population, they spent their time spreading defeatism and conspiring.' Negrín confided in Líster that Rojo had written him a letter presenting his resignation and threatening to make a public statement if he (Negrín) did not put an end to the war and provide more money for the troops exiled in France. Significantly, Negrín added that Rojo had sent a copy of his letter to Matallana. Regarding the situation within the government, Negrín 'bitterly criticized some of his ministers, saying that they were cowards and did little but squabble among themselves about petty issues. He added that those who continued to behave with dignity were Uribe, José Moix Regàs, the Minister of Labour, and Vayo.'[6]

The following day, 16 February, according to a report by Togliatti, Negrín spoke on the telephone to Uribe saying, 'I am told that the

Communists in the Popular Front have declared that whether they respect or not the orders of the government depends what the Party decides.' He said angrily: 'I will shoot all the Communists.' According to a similar account of this confrontation given by Stepanov, Negrín rang Uribe and asked him if it was true that the PCE politburo had decided that government measures would be accepted only with its approval. Before Uribe could reply, Negrín said that, if it was true, he would have the entire politburo arrested and put on trial. Shortly after this conversation with Uribe had taken place, Togliatti returned from France and he was able to smooth things over with Negrín.[7]

During the three and a half weeks that Negrín spent in Spain after his return to the centre-south zone, he seemed to be afflicted with a degree of uncertainty. The man appointed on 24 February to be head of the corps of political commissars, Bibiano Fernández Osorio Tafall, although a member of Azaña's Left Republican party Izquierda Republicana, was a supporter of the policy of resistance.[8] He confided in Cordón his concern that Negrín was wasting time reorganizing government departments instead of creating a general staff of loyal officers. Cordón saw this as the Prime Minister suffering one of his occasional bouts of indecision. Indeed, he concluded that Negrín had returned to Spain 'not with a sense of being a resolute leader firmly determined to take the reins and steer events, but with the rather heroic attitude of a decent man who accepts a sacrifice, even though he is sure of its futility, in the more or less vague hope that it will not be rendered pointless at the last minute'. In an earlier version of his memoirs, Cordón speculated that Negrín had returned to ease his conscience. Cordón's concern about what he saw as Negrín's indecision derived from a conviction that, although the situation was desperate, resistance was still possible and indeed the only way to save thousands of lives.[9] After the end of the war, the senior PCE politburo member, the organization secretary Pedro Checa, told Burnett Bolloten (then engaged in writing a pro-Communist history of the Spanish Civil War) that Negrín did not really believe in the possibility of resistance.[10] Checa was probably right, but, as Zugazagoitia pointed out, Negrín did believe that a rhetoric of resistance could help bring about a better peace settlement.

A letter from Negrín to Prieto dated 23 June 1939 substantiates the comments of both Ossorio Tafall and Cordón. 'Once I reached the centre-south zone I endeavoured to raise morale, reorganize services so as to meet the new circumstances, gather the elements necessary for an effective resistance. The measures adopted … would have allowed us to keep fighting until now. Keep fighting, I say, because, even if we could not win, there was no other way to save what we could or at least save our self-respect.'[11] This had been confirmed even before that. Álvarez del Vayo had written to Marcelino Pascua on 25 February stressing the importance of giving the British government the sense that the Republic had the capacity for a lengthy resistance in the centre-south zone so that London would put pressure on Franco to agree to no reprisals as the basis of a peace settlement.[12] When, after Casado's coup, Fernando de los Ríos, the Republican Ambassador in Washington, recognized his Consejo Nacional de Defensa as a legitimate authority, Negrín sent him an angry telegram in which he reminded him that the whole point of the rhetoric of resistance was to gain time for a coordinated evacuation and some guarantees against reprisals.[13]

Prieto's reply to Negrín's letter on 3 July quoted a report written after Casado's 5 March coup by a close collaborator of Besteiro, Trifón Gómez, quartermaster general of the Republican army and president of the Railwaymen's Union. He supported the coup but had taken little part other than to try to negotiate refuge in Mexico for the Republicans who had to flee. His efforts in Paris to this end were rendered futile by Besteiro's refusal to allow any government resources to be used to pay for the passage of those who had to flee. Besteiro believed that the national wealth was needed in Spain for post-war reconstruction and that Franco would treat those who stayed behind in Spain all the better for having thus safeguarded resources. That short-sightedness seemed not to diminish the loyalty to Besteiro of Trifón Gómez. Through the visceral anti-communism of his report can be discerned the impotence of Negrín's government after his return from Catalonia.

Only men blinded by vanity and arrogance could fail to see that everyone was against them when they returned to the centre-south zone; everyone except the gang of Communists who continued to manipulate Negrín, driving a wedge between him and the Socialists and forcing him to oppose the will of the rest of the Spaniards … Negrín's government was a phantom. Not one Ministry worked; none of the Ministers had the slightest desire to establish themselves; their one obsession was to secure for themselves a way of getting out of Spain … The government had no will to lead and, what is worse, no one thought that they had to obey it.[14]

Unlike Trifón Gómez, the Communist Jesús Hernández believed that resistance was possible, yet he described Negrín's government in similar terms as 'a kind of mute paralytic phantom that neither governed nor spoke and that lacked both an apparatus of state and a fixed seat of government'.[15]

On 8 February, while still in France, Negrín had made three appointments that he would soon regret. The unreliable General José Miaja was promoted from commander of the group of armies of the Centre to supreme commander of the Republican army, navy and air force, which was really only a promotion in name. The pro-Francoist General Manuel Matallana Gómez was promoted from chief of the general staff of the armies of the Centre to commander thereof. Matallana's previous post went to the equally pro-Francoist Colonel Félix Muedra Miñón. Already, there were rumours, which Miaja hastened to deny, that his general staff was in contact with Franco's headquarters. He called it 'an absurd fabrication' (una patraña absurda) but it was in fact the case.[16]

These postings were, in part, Negrín's considered response to a series of suggestions made to him on 2 February, almost certainly by Colonel Cordón. The doubt arises because the document containing the recommendations is unsigned. However, the overall drift suggests the thinking of the Communists and, therefore, in the context of Figueras on 2 February, of Cordón. The first suggestion, which was acted on, was the most intriguing. It was that, given the accumulation of tasks falling to Miaja since the declaration of martial law, operational responsibility for the Army Group of the Centre should be passed to General Matallana. If, as the other recommendations imply, the document's author was Cordón, it would show that, at this stage, neither the Communists nor Negrín had any substantial suspicion of Matallana's loyalty.

The next two proposals, however, point to a degree of suspicion and therefore to Cordón's authorship of the document. They called for the Communist ex-minister Jesús Hernández to be left as commissar to Miaja and that another Communist hard-liner, Luis Cabo Giorla, be appointed as commissar to Matallana. The next suggestion was that Casado be relieved of command of the Army of the Centre and be appointed Director of the Higher War College, where he had been a professor before the war. The idea was that Casado would be replaced by Colonel Juan Modesto. Equally interesting were the following recommendations which called for José Cazorla, the coldly efficient Civil Governor of Guadalajara, to be made overall chief of the Republican security service, the Servicio de Investigación Militar (SIM), in the centre-south zone and for Ángel Pedrero to be replaced as head of the SIM in Madrid by a Republican, Juan Hervás Soler. Apart from a series of proposals for improving the efficiency of the Army of Catalonia, the most significant of the other suggestions was that the highly talented Communist Civil Governor of Cuenca, Jesús Monzón Reparaz, be made Director General de Seguridad.[17]

Dolores Ibárruri recalled in her memoirs that the PCE leadership had informed Negrín of its belief that Miaja and Casado should be replaced. This reinforces the likelihood of the document having been drawn up by Cordón. She claimed that Negrín had refused to dismiss either man 'lest it provoke acts of indiscpline that could undermine resistance'.[18] Had Casado been replaced by Modesto and Pedrero by Hervás, the planned coup would probably have been dismantled before it could be implemented. Of course, the Francoist high command had other sympathizers to whom it could turn – above all Matallana, but also numerous key elements in the general staff, notably Colonel José López Otero, the head of Casado's general staff.

Nonetheless, the SIPM had focused its plans on Casado. There remained the existence of the anarchists' fierce opposition to Negrín and the Communists. The IV Army Corps led by Cipriano Mera was to be an essential element of Casado's project. However, it might be speculated that without Casado and with Cazorla, Monzón and Hervás in control of the security services, anarchist subversion might have been forestalled. Shortly after his return to Spain, on 11 February, Negrín had ordered that Pedrero be dimissed. When Santiago Garcés, the overall head of the SIM, asked him to resign, Pedrero replied that he could do so only if ordered by the Minister of the Interior. He added that, if he was sacked, Casado would resign as commander of the Army of the Centre. When Negrín met Casado the next day, he confirmed that he would indeed resign if Pedrero was removed.[19] In the event, the only elements of the suggested reorganization of military and security forces that were implemented were those relating to Miaja and Matallana.

It will be recalled that, while Negrín was mulling over Cordón's suggestions, on 2 or 3 February, Casado had met Generals Miaja, Matallana and Menéndez. According to Casado's memoirs, they had agreed that, if Negrín returned to the central zone, they would create a Consejo Nacional de Defensa and remove him as Prime Minister. Similarly, on 7 or 8 February, three of the four, Casado, Miaja and Matallana, had taken part in the meeting at the Los Llanos airbase in Albacete. It was convened by the commissar general Jesús Hernández to discuss the further conduct of the war. In addition to Miaja and Matallana, those present included acting Rear Admiral Miguel Buiza, commander of the fleet, and Colonel Antonio Camacho, head of the air force in the centre-south zone. Following so soon after his lunch in Valencia with Miaja, Matallana and Menéndez, it is likely that Casado used the opportunity to sound out further support for his plans. With the exception of Hernández, who argued vehemently in favour of further resistance, the others were uniformly pessimistic in their interventions, aggressively so in the case of Buiza.[20]

The following day, Casado made a first, and successful, attempt to recruit for his schemes the anarchist commander of the IV Army Corps of the centre, Cipriano Mera. It is clear from Mera's recollection of the encounter that Casado made no mention of his links with the Fifth Column. Rather, he gave the impression that, with Negrín out of contact, his preoccupation was with the effective management of the war effort to facilitate an eventual evacuation. Mera suggested that the Army of the Centre make an advance into Extremadura in order to occupy Franco's forces while preparations were made for a full-scale guerrilla war. Casado dismissed the idea and claimed that he had agreed with the commanders of the rest of the Army Group of the Centre that the best strategy would be to concentrate a force of 80,000 well-chosen men near Cartagena, both to secure the fleet and to resist until the outbreak of a wider European conflict. If indeed Casado had discussed such an idea, it would have to have been during the previous day's meeting at Los Llanos. However, there is no mention of such a proposal in the memoir by Vidal Zapater. Moreover, such an idea was at odds with the general tenor of that gathering, which was deeply hostile to the notion of resistance, let alone one that was similar to the views of Negrín. It is more likely that Casado used the fact that he had indeed just met the other commanders at Los Llanos to give credence to his claims to Mera, claims made to obscure his links with the Fifth Column. Having consolidated the trust of Mera, there would follow frequent conversations as Casado quickly incorporated Mera into the planning for his coup.[21]

On 10 February, as soon as he reached the aerodrome of Alicante, Negrín had gone to the offices of the Civil Government and telephoned Miaja, Matallana, the commanders of the three armies of Andalusia, Extremadura and the centre zone and the commander of the fleet, Rear Admiral Buiza. He was taken aback by their reaction: 'From the tone of the conversations on the phone I realized that the arrival of the Prime Minister there had produced real unease and even considerable distress, as if it had spoiled something that they had planned. As I say, I was really struck by the cold and curt tone in which they spoke to me.'[22]

On that same day, after his telephone conversation with Negrín, Buiza had held a meeting on board the flagship *Miguel de Cervantes* with the commissar general of the fleet (Bruno Alonso), the naval general staff and the captains of the main warships to inform them of the Prime Minister's return. He spoke in virulent terms that left little doubt as to his position:

> Despite the arrival of Negrín, bearing in mind that he has not kept any of the promises that he made and, on the contrary, carried out a policy of deceit and distortion of the truth, the commanders of the fleet (the admiral and the political commissar) are going to meet him to demand that he make clear what he intends to do to make the best of the critical situation that has been created and to insist on proof that he will fulfil his promises because both the people and the forces are fed up with his empty speeches. Negrín is, in the view of his own subordinates, a dangerous impostor who must be challenged aggressively. He does not inspire confidence. Surrounded by Communists, the only people prepared to stay with him, any attempt to resolve the state of collapse using these immediate collaborators will be seen as a challenge. He takes the shameful obedience of the military commanders as respect. Only the head of the fleet opposes him openly and tells him what he feels, sacrificing subordination to loyalty. Anger undermines Negrín's judgement. Buiza says publicly and honourably what, cynically, Casado and Matallana pretend to condemn and disapprove, although they are morally ready to overthrow Negrín.[23]

Late at night on 10 February, Miguel Buiza and Bruno Alonso arrived in Valencia for a meeting with Negrín intending to transmit what had been announced to the naval staff in Cartagena. Since Negrín was understandably too exhausted to see them, Buiza returned to Cartagena. The following morning, 11 February, in Valencia Negrín and Álvarez del Vayo met Miaja. Before the meeting, a Francoist air raid saw Alonso and Miaja accompany Negrín and Vayo, both still in their pyjamas, to an underground shelter. At the subsequent meeting in Miaja's office, when Alonso spoke about the situation in the fleet, he was brutally outspoken in stating that further resistance was pointless and complaining about the pre-eminence of the Communists. Negrín was furious. Alonso then left for Cartagena and on the way crossed with Buiza who was returning for the postponed meeting with Negrín, Miaja, Matallana and Casado. When all four finally met Negrín, none of them mentioned the meeting three days earlier in Los Llanos at which they had agreed that further resistance was impossible. Buiza gave a report on morale in the fleet that was every bit as depressing as that given by Alonso. He threatened aggressively to sail the fleet away from Cartagena because of the incessant Francoist bombing raids. Casado and Matallana cynically reprimanded Buiza for his disrespectful tone. Negrín asked Buiza if this was his personal opinion or reflected a widely shared view, to which the admiral replied that it represented the views of the entire fleet. Negrín then stated categorically that the fleet could not be taken from Cartagena 'because every soldier considered the fleet as a guarantee for when evacuation becomes necessary and, in any case, we have to keep the fleet ready in order to be able to import the things we need to maintain the struggle'. When Negrín left, Casado and Matallana congratulated Buiza on his statement, saying that they had not felt able to support him during the meeting because it had been convened at such short notice that they had been unable to consult with their staff. Whether that was true or not, the encounter certainly saw the consolidation of the conspiratorial links between Casado, Matallana and Buiza.[24]

Along with Vayo, Negrín was deeply shocked by the defeatism expressed by those present. Vayo wrote later:

Although outwardly we were greeted with every sign of loyalty and respect, I felt that we were being considered as two unexpected guests whose arrival had upset a programme drawn up carefully and in secret. Our words of encouragement found no echo in their hearts, which were dead to all vigorous reaction, and longing only for an early end to hostilities. The one obsession of these men – scarcely veiled by the conventional language of discipline – was to put an end to the war, no matter how. Before we parted that night, Dr Negrín said to me: 'Did you see that? The rebels don't need motorized divisions against people with such a morale. A few bicycles would be enough to break up the front.'

Negrín and Vayo were unaware both of the depth and frequency of Casado's contacts with the Francoist secret services and of his explicit conversations with Miaja, Matallana, Buiza and Mera about overthrowing the government.[25] The reaction of Buiza must have been especially disconcerting for Negrín. His hopes for an evacuation of those at risk depended on the protection that the fleet could provide for merchant vessels. Buiza was confirming what Negrín already knew. He had, of course, long been aware that he did not have in the navy, as he did in the army, a core of reliable officers. In fact, the naval officer corps was riddled with Francoist collaborators. This explains why the fleet had done so little to protect shipping that was bringing supplies to the Republic by impeding the Italian warships that were attacking such vessels.[26]

Uribe also visited Miaja at his headquarters along with other ministers and was treated even more dismissively: 'He was in his pyjamas when we arrived and remained like that for the entire time. It showed that, for him, the Government was less than nothing, since to receive anyone in your pyjamas is a lack of consideration and respect, for a soldier to receive his superiors like that was the height of contempt.'[27] For Negrín to conduct business while still in his pyjamas reflected his determination to deal with the overwhelming scale of his responsibilities. In contrast, for Miaja, it was a symptom of the habitual slackness of a man whose reputation had been built on the back of the 1936 propaganda campaign which had presented him as the hero of the defence of Madrid.

At midday on 12 February, barely thirty-six hours after his return to Madrid, Negrín began a long four-hour meeting with Casado of which the only accounts are those given in the two versions of the latter's memoirs. In the first book, written in English in 1939, the meeting is dated 25 February. Both accounts portray Casado as bravely and honestly standing up to Negrín. However, it is also clear from both those sources that, with his plans for a coup already well advanced, Casado was far from honest with Negrín. After the Prime Minister had recounted to him the last days of the war in Catalonia, Casado launched (or so he claimed) into the gloomiest of reports about the situation in the central zone. He asserted that the loss of

Catalan war industries had halved the Republic's capacity to produce weaponry. That, together with the shortage of raw materials, meant that it was impossible to produce the indispensable minimum required to permit the war effort to be sustained. Casado gave a depressing list of mortars, tanks, anti-tank guns, artillery and automatic weapons that were in such short supply that enemy units had three times the fire power of equivalent Republican units. Food and clothing for the troops were alarmingly deficient. In appalling winter conditions, troops in the sierras had to wear rope-soled sandals (*alpargatas*) because boots were not available. His survey of aircraft resources was even more depressing and he stated that, such was the numerical and technological superiority of the Francoist air force, to send Republican pilots into combat was to condemn them to death. He then gave an alarming picture of starvation conditions endured by the civilian population in Madrid. Rations were 150 grams of bread per day and 100 grams of other food. Lack of fuel meant that cooked food had become a rarity. He claimed that he insinuated to Negrín that the deafening popular demand for peace made surrender necessary: 'The civilian population of Madrid, which for thirty months has squandered bravery, self-denial and a spirit of sacrifice, is not afraid to say out loud that it is tired of war and wants peace.' He contrasted this bleak vision with an account of the concentration of enemy forces massing for a final decisive assault on Madrid. 'In such conditions, the fall of Madrid is inevitable with enormous loss of lives that will be sacrificed in vain and with the likelihood that, for fear of reprisals, the population and the troops will turn Madrid into a heap of rubble given the huge quantities of available explosives in the capital.'

Whether this meeting took place on 12 or 25 February or indeed at all is thrown into question by a letter that he sent to Negrín. Dated 15 February, the first half of the letter consisted of a diatribe against the politicization of the armed forces as a result of the war. 'This lamentable fact has produced the consequence that our brave and self-denying army has suffered the disease of political ambitions to the extent that virtually all its component elements are political fiefs in which life is rendered impossible for those who do not share each one's prevailing ideology.' The second half of the letter, drafted in obsequious terms, broadly coincides with the accounts in Casado's memoirs. However, there is a crucial difference. Without going into the detail of which he boasted in his later accounts, he stated baldly: 'The people, with its acute intuition, has lost faith in us. It does not want the war and lives, with a defeatist spirit, in ever worsening hunger. The troops have low morale, are badly fed and worse clothed.' He claimed that a huge enemy offensive was imminent and that there were food reserves for only two days. Rather than suggesting surrender, he actually proposed something that was not very different from Negrín's own objective. He wrote that 'The painful moment has arrived for our beloved people to suspend the fighting if the enemy guarantees the departure from Spain of all foreigners and a general amnesty based on humanitarian principles.' By suggesting that such exigent demands be made of Franco, Casado was trying to divert Negrín's suspicions of his basically capitulationist intentions.

Understandably, neither in his accounts of the meeting nor in the letter did Casado mention his own contacts with the Fifth Column. Negrín told him that the British and French had not supported his proposals for a capitulation without reprisals. Accordingly, he said, the only option was resistance until such time as Franco could be persuaded to agree to refrain from mass reprisals. He told Casado that he was optimistic about being able to get back from France the enormous quantities of war matériel taken across the frontier in the retreat from Catalonia. Casado disagreed, pointing out that it was highly unlikely that the French would allow the return of the matériel and, that even if they did, the logistics of getting it back to Spain would be intractable. He also reminded Negrín that Britain and France were anxious to recognize Franco as soon as possible and had diplomatic agents in Burgos. Accordingly, he recommended that Negrín arrange a conference with the senior commanders of the army, air force and navy so that they could give him their opinion as to what should be done. Negrín almost certainly already had it in mind to call such a meeting and he did so three days later. Now, he allegedly said to Casado: 'I agree with your view but I cannot renounce the rallying-cry of resistance.' Casado later claimed that he took this as proof that Negrín was obeying Soviet orders, a bizarre claim made in his self-serving 1968 account but not present in his earlier 1939 account nor indeed one that was consistent with the letter he wrote to Negrín on 15 February. That letter was not incompatible with Negrín's view, not at all related to any Soviet orders, that the threat of continued resistance was the only bargaining chip available in any negotiations with Franco.[28] The meeting with Casado, taken with those on previous days with Miaja, Matallana and Buiza, can have left Negrín with little doubt about the extent of defeatism within the higher reaches of the armed forces and particularly his own general staff.

According to Edmundo Domínguez who, as commissar inspector to the Army of the Centre, saw him frequently, Casado manifested considerable anxiety after this encounter. He had come away from the meeting convinced that Negrín did not trust him and feared that he would be dismissed or even that his life might be in danger. He had heard the rumours that he was to be replaced by Modesto. His fears were expressed in terms of aggressive bravado and threats of what he would do in the event of action against him: 'I have taken precautions against any action against me!' He boasted: 'I have considerable prestige in Madrid and throughout Spain and I have the confidence of the people, the true people that suffer silently, and I will do what they want!' It was almost as if he were talking to himself, trying to calm his inner fears about the consequences of what he was up to.[29]

It will be recalled that, in the days preceding this meeting with Negrín, Casado had been awaiting confirmation of the generous terms that the representatives of the Fifth Column had assured him would be forthcoming from Franco. On 15 February, three days after he delivered to Negrín the missive with his own hard-line terms for an armistice, he received the anxiously awaited letter from his friend General Fernando Barrón y Ortiz confirming the Caudillo's benevolence. In an oblique reference to Casado's unhappiness with Negrín's policy, Barrón asked about his poor health and advised him to have 'blind faith in the treatment that would cure his illness'. Casado replied via his Fifth Column contact Professor Julio Palacios that everything was 'ready for the assault on the last communist redoubts with the battle-cry of "Long live Spain and death to Russia!"' Fully satisfied, Casado then passed on the message to Miaja and others. It is astonishing that Casado should believe the statement from the SIPM, since so many officers, not to mention tens of thousands of civilians, had already been executed by the Francoists on the strange grounds of 'military rebellion', that is to say failure to join the National Movement. Perhaps Casado was seduced by being told that Franco would negotiate with no one other than him.[30]

Its text would certainly have been seen, if not actually dictated, by Franco himself. The phrase 'blind faith' (*fe ciega*) was one of his favourite expressions. Casado had long since been targeted by Franco's intelligence services. He was the obvious candidate, deeply conservative and with influential friends in Franco's peripatetic field headquarters known as 'Terminus'. He was the commander of the Republican forces in the area where the next major assault would be launched. During the battle of the Ebro and the assault on Catalonia, he had demonstrated covert sympathy for the rebels by putting de-cisive obstacles in the way of Rojo's diversionary operations.[31] With a degree of self-aggrandizement, Casado managed to convince himself that the end of the war would be something negotiated between himself and Franco. Even more unrealistically, he came to believe – or at least he told others whom he was trying to recruit for his schemes – that Franco would incorporate officers who had served the Republic into the post-war armed forces.

After Casado had received Barrón's letter, the Organización Antonio reported to Ungría's headquarters in Burgos on 16 February that Casado had said:

I am playing cleanly. I guarantee that in my sector [a reference to the Army of the Centre] there will be no offensive and if one were attempted elsewhere, I would thwart it within three days, as has been agreed with, among others, several ministers [a reference to those he was planning to include in his coup]. I am expecting the constitution of a cabinet presided over by Besteiro, in which I will be Minister of War. If that appointment were not to materialize, it wouldn't matter. I would sweep the others aside. I think that Nationalist forces should enter Madrid within no more than two weeks.

As for the specifics of how the surrender would take place, Casado told his personal physician Diego Medina that he had a perfect plan clear in his mind. He was confident that he could arrange for Franco's forces to enter Madrid without a shot being fired. He was also confident that, thanks to him, their unopposed victory parade would be universally admired and go down in history. His demands for recompense for this astonishing offer were limited in the extreme. He requested only mercy for his own staff. He lamented that it would not be possible to prevent the flight of some prominent Republicans and other 'ringleaders'. However, he promised that many would remain in Madrid and that they would be arrested.[32]

In the first two days after his return, Negrín held cabinet meetings. At the first, near Valencia, he announced that Madrid would once more be the seat of government.[33] The decision was fundamentally a symbolic one aimed at boosting the morale of the population. Madrid was hardly safe. The battle-front in the Casa de Campo was barely a 3-kilometre tram ride from the offices of the Prime Minister in the Castellana. Togliatti was convinced that it was a grave error on Negrín's part to declare Madrid once more to be the capital of Republican Spain. His reasoning was that ministers could not work in Madrid and that, as soon as there was a major enemy advance, they would have to be evacuated to Albacete or Cartagena. In fact, within a week, efforts were in place to set up ministries in safer areas of the centre-south zone, in the Levante.[34] (All his ministers had followed him back to Spain, save the Minister without Portfolio, José Giral, who remained with Azaña, and the Minister of Finance, Francisco Méndez Aspe, who was on crucial government business in Paris.)

The day after the second cabinet meeting, held in Madrid on 12 February, Negrín made a prophetic broadcast in which he urged the population to fight on:

Either we are all saved or else we all succumb to extermination and shame … Only if each and every one of you, the Army, men, women, trade unions, political parties, the press, everyone, throw themselves into a common effort and give everything will it be possible for the government to lead the resistance until it can achieve the ends for which the Spanish people have been fighting. Those ends are none other than to guarantee the independence of Spain and to avoid our country sinking into a sea of blood, hatred and persecutions that will ensure that for many generations the Spanish fatherland will be unified only by violence, terror and foreign domination.[35]

Once in Spain, Negrín began the enormous task of reorganizing both the networks of food distribution and the military forces of the centre to facilitate resistance either until a European war started or at least until he could arrange a massive evacuation and ensure the lowest number of Republican deaths possible. Knowing that Franco was determined to impose an unconditional surrender and was committed to a policy of *depuración* (purification), and harbouring only slight hope of changes in the European situation that would have helped the Republic, Negrín's sole option was to use what resources he had at his disposal to pressure Franco into a public undertaking not to take reprisals against the defeated population. Negrín believed rightly that capitulation would simply open the floodgates to mass slaughter. Resistance in the centre-south zone was not about fighting to the death but rather about creating the conditions for a controlled retreat, maintaining Republican control of air facilities, of the roads to the south-eastern coast and of the key Mediterranean ports from which massive evacuation of those Republicans in most danger could take place.[36]

Essentially, Negrín believed that he had to strengthen the position of the Republic in order to persuade Franco that it was in his interests to make peace, and to do so with a guarantee of no reprisals against civilians. The centre-south zone consisted of ten provinces, ten million inhabitants, many important cities, including the capital, and four major ports at Alicante, Valencia, Almería and Cartagena. The various armies of the Group of Armies of the Centre numbered half a million men. The Republican fleet under the command of Rear Admiral Buiza consisted of three cruisers, thirteen destroyers, seven submarines, five torpedo boats and two gunboats. Where there was considerable weakness was in terms of aircraft. Nevertheless, the overall military strength of the Republic hardly suggested that Negrín should immediately offer unconditional surrender. Accordingly, both he and his ambassadors in London and Paris (Pablo de Azcárate and Marcelino Pascua) worked to get British and French support to press Franco to accept his three points.[37]

Despite the Republic's substantial remaining assets, Negrín's hopes were at best flimsy because, as the last Republican forces were crossing into France, London had already decided to recognize Franco. A decision effectively to recognize Franco as soon as hostilities ceased, and without demanding specific conditions, had been taken by the British cabinet on 8 February. The Foreign Secretary Lord Halifax had stated that 'He thought it was clear that General Franco was going to win the war, and he thought that the sooner this country got on terms with General Franco and made up lost ground the better.' The point was raised that recognition of Franco would mean that the government troops were regarded as rebels and so such a policy could not be adopted while substantial resistance continued. In reply, the Foreign Secretary said that he was afraid that Spain might drift into a position in which guerrilla warfare continued for a considerable time without any marked change in the situation. Nevertheless, he and the Prime Minister expressed their view that they would be happy to proceed to recognition as soon as circumstances permitted. However, no decision was made as to when to implement and announce the decision.[38] Alarmingly, it was not the intention of HM Government to require a commitment that Franco would refrain from reprisals. The government of Neville Chamberlain was anxious to see the Spanish war concluded as soon as possible since its continuation threatened his policy of appeasement. Believing that, so long as the war continued, Franco would remain beholden to Germany and Italy, Chamberlain and his cabinet hoped that once hostilities ceased Franco would be obliged to turn to Britain and France for the capital needed to rebuild Spain's shattered economy. The under-secretary at the Foreign Office told the US Chargé d'Affaires on 14 February that 'although no final decision has yet been reached, [the cabinet's] present view is that recognition: (1) should be given quickly, and (2) should not be contingent upon conditions of performance on the part of General Franco. He went on to say that the decision was imminent and would be taken in the conviction that there was more chance of influencing Franco after recognition than before.'[39]

The British cabinet on 15 February decided:

(l) That it was desirable that His Majesty's Government should recognise General Franco's Government in the near future.

(2) That, if possible, recognition should follow surrender by the Spanish Government forces but that if the Spanish Government Authorities proved obdurate and negotiations were prolonged, it might be necessary that recognition of General Franco's Government should precede the cessation of hostilities.

(3) To authorise the Secretary of State for Foreign Affairs, in consultation with the Prime Minister, to despatch the necessary telegrams to give effect to these decisions.

(4) To authorise the Prime Minister and the Foreign Secretary, if events should make it necessary, that General Franco should be recognised before the next weekly meeting of the Cabinet, to take the necessary action without further reference to the Cabinet.[40]

On 14 February, the Republican Ambassador to London, Pablo de Azcárate, visited Lord Halifax. He pointed out that the Republic had the capacity to continue resistance but was prepared to contemplate a negotiated peace on the basis of Negrín's three points. It was agreed that the British government would act merely as a 'channel of communication' and not put any pressure on Franco. They met again two days later and Halifax showed Azcárate a telegram to be sent to

Franco via the British diplomatic agent in Burgos, Sir Robert Hodgson, calling for a commitment to allow senior Republicans to leave Spain and to refrain from reprisals. Ignoring the first two of the three points in Negrín's proposal for peace, that Spain would be independent and that the Spanish people would be free to choose their own form of government, Halifax required acceptance from Negrín that surrender could be arranged on this basis. As it happened, given the control over telephonic and telegraphic communications exercised by Casado, Azcárate was unable to discuss this with Negrín until after Halifax's deadline had passed. It hardly mattered since Chamberlain had already taken the decision to recognize Franco.[41]

The British Embassy in Washington sent an aide-memoire to the Department of State on 18 February which revealed that the only reason for delay in announcing recognition was the desire of the French government to get assurances from Franco, to which end it had sent Senator Bérard back to Burgos. London's toothless approach to Franco was summed up in the mealy-mouthed comment, in relation to HMG's request to Burgos for a commitment that senior Republicans be allowed to leave Spain and that there be no reprisals, that 'whilst His Majesty's Government recognize his [Franco's] right to decide what, if any, response to make to this communication they feel its consideration might afford an opening for bringing about a pacific solution'. Bonnet was informed that 'His Majesty's Government would prefer full recognition without conditions'. Sir Robert Hodgson in Burgos was authorized to tell Franco that recognition 'would be facilitated if General Franco were able to accept the terms contained in the Spanish Government's communication regarding the cessation of hostilities and if he would be willing to state publicly that when the fighting is finished he would not permit anything in the way of unauthorized or general political reprisals'.

On 21 February, the British government received a telegram from Hodgson containing the utterly mendacious response from Franco's Foreign Minister, the Conde de Jordana. It declared:

Nationalist Spain has won the war and the defeated side has no choice but to surrender unconditionally. The patriotism, the chivalry and the generosity of the Caudillo, of which he has given so many examples in the liberated regions, as well as the spirit of equity and justice that inspires every act of the national-ist government, together constitute a firm guarantee for all Spaniards who are not criminals. The courts of justice will confine themselves to trying and judging those who have committed crimes, applying the laws and procedures existent before 16 July 1936 within the limits imposed by them. If by prolonging a criminal resistance, the red leaders continue to sacrifice lives and shed more blood exclusively in their own interests, given that the nationalist government and the Caudillo are free of all spirit of revenge, the only thing that they will achieve is the continuation of this lunatic resistance and thereby increase their own criminal responsibilities.

In the light of this, Halifax told the cabinet that he thought that 'the right course was to accept the message as the best assurance that we were likely to receive, and to recognise General Franco without further delay'.[42]

Thanks to Azcárate, Negrín was fully apprised of the British government's urgent desire to bring the Civil War to a rapid end. At the same time, he quickly became aware of the scale of war-weariness and defeatism within Spain's civilian population and even among some senior officers. Casado was making every effort to put obstacles in the way of the political commissars doing their job of raising morale among the troops. Negrín knew too about the growing success of Fifth Column activities. Nevertheless, his visits to various parts of the front convinced him that morale was still high within the ranks of the forces: 'Unlike what was going on in other sectors, the combat troops, when they looked at things realistically, rejected all appeasement and were determined to go on fighting to the end.' He believed at the time that there were sufficient stockpiles of weaponry and food to continue resistance for six months. Moreover, he was confident of substantial deliveries of arms from abroad, particularly of fighter planes and anti-aircraft guns. However, he was convinced, in retrospect, that the defeatists had done everything possible to undermine the distribution of both food and equipment. In that regard, defeatism had led to hoarding. Negrín was not only hampered by British machinations and official French hostility but also by internal divisions within what remained of the Popular Front. Moreover, it would soon be starkly clear that the hoped-for deliveries of weaponry would not materialize and that there were food supplies for barely one month.[43]

Despite a widely held view that resistance was impossible. Negrín was not alone in his optimism that the Republic could hold out. On the eve of defeat in Catalonia, Lieutenant Colonel Henri Morel, the French military attaché in Madrid, reported to the Ministry of Defence in Paris as follows: 'It seems highly unlikely that Republican forces can mount a victorious resistance against the Nationalist army, but the Army of the Centre, even if Madrid were lost, can transform the vast spaces that it still controls into an immense Rif and hold on. Will it want to fight to the death? Will it want to hold on? That is the question.' Morel was referring to the area of Spanish Morocco where rebel tribesmen had for years fought a guerrilla war against the colonial occupiers.[44]

On the morning of 16 February 1939, as agreed with Casado, Negrín held a five-hour meeting of the high command of the three branches of the armed forces at Los Llanos near Albacete. Those present were Generals Miaja, Matallana Gómez, Leopoldo Menéndez (the Army of the Levante), Carlos Bernal García (commander of the naval base at Cartagena), Colonels Casado (Army of the Centre), Domingo Moriones Larraga (Army of Andalusia) and Antonio Escobar Huertas (Army of Extremadura), Lieutenant Colonel Antonio Camacho Benítez (head of the air force of the central zone) and the commander of the Republican navy, Rear Admiral Miguel Buiza Fernández-Palacios. In the wake of the collapse of the Catalan front, Negrín informed them of his unsuccessful efforts to get the British and French governments to mediate a peace without reprisals. In the light of this failure and the possibility that the international situation might change, he argued that continued resistance in order to secure a peace with guarantees was the only option. The meeting then broke up for lunch.

When it resumed at 3.00 p.m., Negrín, having concluded that the morale of the ordinary soldier seemed high, was surprised by the vehemence with which Matallana argued, in the same terms as Casado four days earlier, that further resistance was impossible and that it was necessary to end the war as soon as possible. Bernal said that the mood in the base at Cartagena was unremittingly defeatist. The grimmest account, and the one most pleasing to Casado, was given by Admiral Buiza. He declared that the fleet would leave Spanish territorial waters if peace was not made quickly. He alleged that a committee of the crews had informed him that they were not prepared to tolerate the daily Francoist bombing attacks against which they lacked anti-aircraft defences. In contrast, General Menéndez and Colonels Escobar and Moriones all said that, despite shortages of equipment, their armies could probably hold out for another four or five months, although they did not see the point of doing so. When those present asked Negrín why he did not call for an immediate peace treaty, he replied, 'Because to sue for peace is to provoke a catastrophe.' To the intense annoyance of Casado, Miaja spoke in favour of continued resistance.[45] Casado was disconcerted by this because of his meeting, in Valencia on 2 February, with Miaja, Matallana and Menéndez at which, he believed (or later claimed), all four had agreed on the need to overthrow Negrín. His recollection of that lunch was not shared by other guests.[46]

According to both Álvarez del Vayo and Mariano Ansó, all of the officers, except Admiral Buiza, orally at least, gave the impression of accepting that 'what the Government had been trying for weeks to obtain was the very minimum that could be asked in exchange for a surrender of arms'.[47] Buiza went beyond what he had said at the earlier meeting in Valencia and threatened that he would remove the fleet from Spanish waters if Negrín did not engage in serious peace negotiations. Buiza was responding to signs of disaffection among his senior officers who, like the rank-and-file crews, were complaining that the fleet, lacking adequate air cover, was vulnerable to constant bombardments while in its base in Cartagena. Colonel Camacho spoke of the shortage of aircraft. Buiza was supported by Bernal, the commander of the Cartagena naval base. Given that so many naval officers were of like mind, Negrín did not think it prudent to rebuke Buiza for his insubordination. He did not have trustworthy replacements and was concerned that a strong reaction might provoke a naval revolt. Instead, he made a speech praising the heroism of the armed forces which received a standing ovation from the officers present. However, as soon as the Prime Minister had left the meeting, Matallana and Casado approached Buiza to congratulate him and to reassure him that they approved of his firm stance with Negrín.[48] Casado regarded Buiza as a key element in his plans, but it seems he failed to realize the danger that lay behind the threats of a man rendered so volatile by his appalling personal situation after the suicide of his wife.

Álvarez del Vayo and Francisco Méndez Aspe did not arrive in time for the meeting at Los Llanos but they attended the dinner that followed. Álvarez del Vayo was struck by the attitudes ranging from hostility to cool reserve emanating from the officers present. Jesús Hernández concluded that a damaging consequence of the meeting at Los Llanos had been to allow the defeatists among the general staff to see how widely their views were shared. Uribe deduced from conversations with Negrín that the Prime Minister seemed not to appreciate fully the extent to which the anti-communism of the officers at the Los Llanos meeting was also anti-Negrinismo.[49] In the wake of the depressing encounter, despite his optimism regarding the morale of the fighting troops, Negrín realized that he faced near-insuperable problems. That sense was intensified by the receipt of another bitter letter from Vicente Rojo written in the wake of the meeting at which Zugazagoitia and Méndez had passed on Negrín's orders that he and Jurado return to Spain.

> We are told that our presence in the central zone is indispensable to give the world the impression of a fully organized State and to collaborate with you in the last phase of the war for which the slogan of resistance has been given. Yet, at the same time, we are told that it is really a question of organizing the departure

from that zone of all those who are at risk, that the order to resist and the firm commitment to the war has no other objective than to be able to negotiate with France and England a dignified way out. That is to say it is a political device but with the contradiction that the objective is the evacuation of the greatest possible number of people from the zone yet the orders are that priority be given to the greatest possible number of officers and commissars.[50]

The ambiguity of Rojo's position could be deduced from a letter that he sent to Miaja on 19 February. Rojo congratulated Miaja on his promotion to supreme commander of the Republican army, navy and air force. He also referred to the trip to France made ten days earlier by Miaja's secretary Captain Antonio López Fernández. In the Spanish Consulate in Perpignan, López had attempted to persuade Negrín to remain in France and for President Azaña to grant Miaja permission to negotiate peace with the rebels. In his letter, Rojo mentioned the oral report on the military situation that he had given López with instructions that he pass it on to Miaja. He also stated that he assumed that Matallana would have kept him informed regarding the information that he (Rojo) was sending him. The letter ended with the ambiguous statement: 'I am telling Matallana that as soon as you and he need our presence there [presumably of Rojo and Jurado] for anything, just say so because our bags are packed and we are ready to leave as soon as you say even though it be for us to commit suicide together.'[51]

Rojo knew that Matallana was a defeatist and that he was in contact with the Fifth Column. However, it is difficult to believe that he knew that Matallana had reached the point of declaring that he was at the orders of the SIPM.[52] Matallana handed over maps and a detailed account of the position of the principal Republican units in the centre-south zone. At the end of the war, Matallana would surrender at his Valencia headquarters and was court-martialled in August 1939. The Francoist prosecutor called for the death sentence, but he was given thirty years' imprisonment of which he served only a short period. On 12 July 1940, the sentence was commuted to twelve years as a reward 'for services rendered to the Nationalists'. On 12 May the following year, his sentence was reduced to one of *prisión atenuada* which conceded the freedom to leave the prison during the day, and on 30 May it was further reduced to one of conditional liberty. Such moderate punishment, in comparison with that given to other officers, such as Escobar, who was executed, is hardly surprising given the scale of his collaboration with the enemy.

At Matallana's trial, numerous well-known members of the Fifth Column, including Colonel Félix Muedra, Lieutenant Colonel Antonio Garijo Hernández, Diego Medina, José Centaño de la Paz and Manuel Guitián, spoke on his behalf. Matallana himself claimed that his commitment to the rebel side could be confirmed by important Francoist figures such as the Caudillo's cousin and aide-de-camp Francisco Franco Salgado-Araujo and General Luis Orgaz. Two favourable reports from the SIPM attested that his commitment to the Nationalist cause was 'total'. Diego Medina testified that Matallana was in frequent contact with José Centaño de la Paz and Manuel Guitián and had passed useful information to them. In a fulsome testimony, José Centaño stated that Matallana had been in touch with the SIPM through Captain Julián Suárez Inclán, passing on details of troop movements and of the overall strength of Republican army groups. He asserted that 'if Matallana had not been in the position that he was, putting obstacles in the way of Republican operations, the final conflicts would have been much more difficult'.[53]

Negrín was demoralized by the desertion of Rojo and he continued trying to get him to return to Spain. On 27 February, he sent him a telegram via Marcelino Pascua urging him to resume his duties as chief of the general staff.[54] It is inconceivable that Negrín was unaware of the generalized conviction among his closest collaborators that lengthy resistance was impossible. Accordingly, eventually he understood and was able to forgive Rojo's stance despite the fact that his own quest for a just peace obliged him to maintain the fiction of continued resistance. When Rojo left for exile in Argentina, he was given $10,000 by Negrín and was considered by Azaña (a view conveyed to Giral) to be one of 'Negrín's protégés'.[55] In a speech made in London on 14 April 1942, presumably seeing no point in opening old wounds, Negrín stated that Rojo had been commissioned to stay in France and try to secure the return to Spain of the men and equipment taken into exile. He paid tribute to Rojo's courage and ability in terms that left no doubt of his admiration and respect for him.

> The day will come when it is necessary to emphasize the role of the Chief of the General Staff. Because of his seriousness and modesty, his achievements in our war have not been recognized in due proportion to his merits. His specific military qualities (imperturbable serenity in the most difficult moments, his remarkable bravery, without show, and an extraordinary competence as a military technician revealed in battle) ... were not the only reasons for his appointment. In the Chief of the General Staff there came together an amazing capacity for work, formidable organizational skills, the ability to get the best out of his collaborators ... and above all an absolute discretion that was fundamental given his responsibilities. There were also private reasons for the opinion that I had of him: his inflexible sense of duty, his critical spirit, as severe with himself as he was understanding and benevolent with others, his absolute integrity, his irreproachable chivalry, his enlightened patriotism, and above all the noble and generous heart of a good man. All these qualities, and not least the last one, made General Rojo an admired collaborator with whom it was easy to share the troubles of the most bitter and difficult moments.

Having voiced this hymn of praise, however, Negrín went on to lament that Rojo had not returned to Spain.

> Although the presence of the Chief of the General Staff in France was considered indispensable, his stay there was supposed to be short. There was every reason to think that it was essential for the future conduct of the war that he should return immediately to Spain. Perhaps his decision to remain in France was a grave mistake because the government would not have found itself, as it did, deprived of advice and capable and loyal technical help.

Moreover, it is possible that the Chief of Staff's own prestige and his knowledge of the military staff would have prevented or stifled the intrigues that then took place ... That mistake is one of the great responsibilities incurred by him who committed it but whoever takes any action must know that they risk making a mistake. May this thought mitigate what happened.[56]

Because of these comments by Negrín and because the subsequent official history produced by the Spanish Communist Party did not criticize Rojo, Burnett Bolloten suggested that 'neither Negrín nor the PCE wished to lock horns with the man whom they had elevated to the top military post ... To have condemned his defeatism and defection openly would have provided ammunition to their opponents and undermined the legend that has been fostered for half a century that the loss of the war was due entirely to "traitors and capitulators". It was not true that Rojo had reached his eminence thanks to Communist influence. Bolloten's somewhat malicious accusation might have some substance when it came to the PCE's official history but is less plausible in terms of Negrín's 1942 speech. While there may have been an element of political calculation in that Negrín always did everything possible to avoid deepening the divisions among the exiles, his words also reflect a genuine admiration and gratitude for Rojo's services for the Republican cause.[57]

6

Negrín Abandoned

In the second half of February 1939, however, beset with doubts as to which military and political allies were reliable, Negrín spent much of his time in frenetic visits to the front. According to Ángel Pedrero García, the head of the Republican counter-intelligence organization, the Servicio de Inteligencia Militar, for the Army of the Centre, after the meeting at Los Llanos Negrín was so dejected that his behaviour was that of a madman. 'Abandoned by everyone including even his own ministers he would wander around Madrid as if unhinged. Often, leaving his car at the door of the premier's office, he would depart the building by a back door and disappear to the Bar Chicote to spend time drinking whisky. At other times, he would take lengthy walks alone through the streets, standing on the pavement for long periods listening to a blind man playing the violin.'[1] Casado claimed that the Director General de Seguridad, Vicente Girauta, had reported that Negrín picked up a prostitute.[2] Even if these reports were true, they reveal a Negrín who was under inhuman pressure and reveal even more about the malice of his accusers.

Pedrero's less than objective view was echoed from the other end of the political spectrum by Communists who also described Negrín's isolation. Uribe alleged later that Negrín held only two or three cabinet meetings during his last month in Spain. He complained that the Prime Minister disappeared for days on end and was incommunicado. Dolores Ibárruri's secretary, Irene Falcón, a long-time acquaintance of Negrín through their mutual links with the celebrated pathologist Santiago Ramón y Cajal, believed that the Prime Minister was absent abroad seeking support for the Republic.[3] In fact, Negrín had relatively little telephone access to his ministers and had to rely on the telegraph for contact with his ambassadors. That traffic had to pass through the headquarters of Casado, who took advantage of this to undermine Negrín's peace negotiations, simply by blocking or delaying communications between the Prime Minister and his embassies in London and Paris.[4] For Negrín, travel from one part of Republican Spain to another was a precarious enterprise.

As for isolation, it is certainly the case that, except for Álvarez del Vayo, Méndez Aspe and the Communist ministers Uribe and Moix, most of Negrín's cabinet had little faith in his resistance policy. The doubters included two of the Socialists, the Minister of Justice and president of the PSOE, Ramón González Peña, and the Minister of the Interior, Paulino Gómez Saez, both of whom were close to Prieto. In a letter to Negrín on 3 July 1939, Prieto quoted González Peña's comments on the situation in mid-February:

> It goes without saying that the atmosphere here, both in military and civilian circles, is all about bringing things to an end, although some try to obscure the fact with talk of resistance. Even the most optimistic is worried about how things will turn out ... In my view, and it is a personal opinion, the influential people in our party and in the workers' movement should be sounding out the French and British governments as to their views on how the war might end. Because I at least fear that they are waiting until the rebels begin another offensive so that, after results that I fear will be similar to those in Catalonia, they can call for our unconditional surrender.[5]

According to the Comintern delegate Stoyan Minev ('Boris Stepanov'), some of Negrín's ministers were conspiring against him. The main object of his criticisms was Paulino Gómez Sáez, who had replaced Julián Zugazagoitia as Minister of the Interior in April 1938. In Stepanov's exaggerated account, Gómez was preoccupied both with arranging the escape from Spain of Prietista Socialists and with pursuing anti-Communist policies. It is certainly the case that Gómez had good reason to feel hostile towards the PCE which, in October 1938, had broken his ban on reporting of the trial of the POUM leadership by issuing virulent accusations of Trotskyist treachery against the accused. Stepanov alleged that, shortly after Negrín's return from France, at a dinner that he hosted for his cabinet colleagues, tempers were raised to the point of chairs being thrown.[6] In contrast, Zugazagoitia praised Gómez for his heroic disregard for his own personal safety in the fulfilment of his duties: 'he lives ethically and courageously, he thinks of everything except his own personal safety. He rates his conduct higher than his very life, as always'.[7]

Since Pedrero was one of Casado's men and the remarks quoted above were made to his Francoist interrogators, there may well have been an element of exaggeration of the dark side of Negrín's psyche. Nevertheless, it is hardly remarkable that the meeting at Los Llanos should have depressed him. Already one year earlier, on Saturday 22 April 1938, Negrín had met Azaña and the President had told him bluntly that the war was virtually lost and mocked his hopes that further resistance would enable him to broker international mediation for a reasonable peace settlement. Negrín responded with a revealing insight into his own humanity. He told Azaña of his fears of catching a bullet and of other terrors, yet insisted on the need to keep resisting. Ten days later on Wednesday 3 May, they met again and Azaña reiterated his conviction that resistance was pointless. Negrín spoke of what it cost him to keep resisting: 'he spoke of his fear and of the fact that he often cries and suffers attacks of angina pectoris. And that he doesn't care what people think of him.' Apparently, he always carried trinitroglycerin tablets as an immediate response to angina, and also sleeping tablets.[8] The sheer weight of responsibility that he bore, together with his insomnia and other health problems, would more than explain his depressive state.

Stepanov claims that, after the dinner at which chairs were thrown, Negrín furiously set off for the battlefront, remarking to his adjutant that, with luck, an enemy bullet would hit him and therefore resolve the difficult questions facing him. This hardly constitutes the suicidal tendencies reported by some, although it does fit in with his readiness to offer himself as sacrificial victim to Franco. The incident described by Stepanov was also related by the anarchist Joan Llarch, who claimed that Negrín oscillated between depression and euphoria:

Once when he was in Madrid, Negrín suddenly disappeared and no one knew where he had gone. In his dreadful state of depression, he had headed for the front at the Ciudad Universitaria in the hope that an enemy bullet might free him from his anguish by taking his life in a way that would mask what was really suicide. When he reached that sector of the front, although he carried false documentation, he was recognized by the soldiers and the word rapidly went round that the premier was with them in the trenches. Cheers of 'Long live President Negrín!' went up, enthusiastically echoed. Dr Negrín was moved, his anxieties replaced by gratitude towards his soldiers, the weight of his responsibilities lightened by joy.[9]

His journeys around the central-southern zone gave his loyal Communist officers the impression that he was being indecisive, which again is not really surprising. They thought that he should create a new and reliable general staff, as if this were a simple task that could be achieved rapidly. It is likely that he feared that to build a staff consisting exclusively of Communists, the only officers he could really trust, might push the defeatists into action. It is possible that this was his reasoning in promoting Brigadier Vicente Rojo to lieutenant general and Lieutenant Colonel Enrique Jurado to brigadier despite their mutinous refusal to return to Spain. As soon as he read the news in the press, Rojo sent Negrín an indignant telegram, refusing the promotion.[10]

On 24 February, Casado, pretending fulsome loyalty to Negrín, told Colonel Cordón that he was outraged by the two promotions of what he called two deserters who had been responsible for the loss of Catalonia. He said, 'Rojo is what he has always been, inept and a traitor. He is to blame for the present situation.' Referring to Jurado's promotion, he said, 'Jurado is an ass. While he was in the central zone, he did nothing but idiotic things and he pretended to be sick so he could get away as soon as possible. His promotion has caused widespread discontent. I must admit that I believe that I deserve it far more than him, so much so that I am prepared to overcome my reluctance to raise the issue with the Minister [of War, that is Negrín].' In fact, Casado's own promotion to general was already drafted and would be announced the next day. Casado was equally savage in his opinion of Azaña: 'I now see that those who called this scoundrel a queer were right.' He then went on to mention a meeting that he had had with Besteiro, claiming that they had met merely to discuss the reconstruction of Madrid, and denied any suggestion that they were plotting to form a government. After talking vehemently (and mendaciously) of his own commitment to resistance, he went on to say that he knew that Franco would not take reprisals and would recognize the ranks of Republican officers in his post-war armed forces. He also told Cordón that he had had conversations with British officials about arranging the evacuation of 20,000 people. When Cordón spoke to Negrín about this conversation, the Prime Minister remarked that Casado had said the same things to him and he advised Cordón not to pay him any attention. There is little reason to suppose that the British government was much concerned about the likely fate of defeated Spanish Republicans.[11]

Indeed, barely two weeks later, on 8 March, the British cabinet would debate whether help should be given for mass evacuation and Lord Halifax's comments revealed how little sympathy there was. He declared: 'we should have to make certain, before evacuating refugees, that they were not criminals whom no one ought to wish to save from their proper fate'. He thought it was 'impossible for us to make ourselves responsible for the mass evacuation of whoever wished to leave Spain for whatever reason'. Chamberlain agreed and the Home Secretary, Sir Samuel Hoare, said that 'we were already experiencing trouble with undesirables getting into this country; but he assumed that we should, if need be, have to allow Dr. Negrin and a few other leaders to enter the country'.[12]

It is certainly the case that, some days before his conversation with Cordón, Casado had spoken to a British representative, Denys Cowan, a member of the Chetwode Commission which was attempting to broker prisoner exchanges. Cowan spoke reasonably good Spanish, having previously been Consul in Havana. The subsequent report by Cowan provides insight both into the attitude of British officialdom towards Casado and into Casado's attempt to secure British support:

I had an hour's conversation last night [Monday 20 February] with Casado, Commander-in-Chief Central Armies including Madrid area. He said he anticipated a Nationalist offensive in Jerrama [*sic*] and Guadalajara fronts within a few days. If this materialised, he and his army, out of loyalty to the constituted Government, would have no option but to resist thus entailing further devastation of life and property at a moment when indiscriminate shelling of civilian quarters had reduced Madrid to semi panic and everyone is longing for peace. Negrín is the one obstacle. The only hope is that Azaña will dismiss him and call upon Besteiro to form a government. I saw the latter on Friday [18 February]. If appointed he would at once negotiate peace. It would help such negotiations and reduce the final panic if Franco could be induced to state in more specific terms the scope of his promises of clemency, e.g. whether the Government supporters who have merely followed their polit-ical ideals are 'criminally responsible' and so on. Casado said he could guarantee public order if there were a peaceful entry but that he would not be answerable for the consequences in case of an offensive or if Italians and Germans or Moors entered the city.[13]

In his 1939 memoirs, a book riddled with untruths, Casado claimed that he had no contact with British representatives until after the coup. He had clearly forgotten meetings that he had held with both Cordón and the head of the air force Hidalgo de Cisneros at which he assured them that he had been given guarantees by British agents that Franco would be obliged to refrain from reprisals and also to recog-nize the ranks of Republican officers.[14]

Casado had attended the meeting at Los Llanos aware that his own general staff was already preparing to hand over the central zone to the Francoists. Indeed, such was Negrín's vulnerability that Casado was later criticized by a Francoist officer for not arresting Negrín before he left the meeting; 'That is how to carry out a coup d'état.'[15] On 17 February, SIPM headquarters in Burgos received a report that a member of Casado's senior staff, Lieutenant Colonel Antonio Garijo Hernández, had requested a safe-conduct enabling him to go to the rebel zone in order to finalize arrangements for the surrender. Franco was already extremely optimistic that the end was nigh as a result of the report received by Ungría on 16 February about the imminent creation by Casado and Besteiro of a government of surrender. This seemed to be confirmed by the developments at Los Llanos, about which Franco was fully informed. The unanimity of the top brass of the armed forces had led Garijo and other members of the general staff of the Army of the Centre to postpone such a meeting in Burgos because they were convinced that events were moving so fast as to make it unnecessary. Nevertheless, evidence of Negrín's determination to raise morale for further resistance diminished the optimism in Franco's headquarters.[16]

Accordingly, Lieutenant Colonel Centaño was instructed to urge Casado to accelerate his plans for a coup and remove Negrín from power. Together with another member of the SIPM, Manuel Guitián, Centaño visited Casado on 20 February at the bunker where he had his headquarters. Codenamed 'Posición Jaca', it was located in the El Capricho gardens of the Alameda de Osuna on the eastern outskirts of Madrid. Centaño told him bluntly that Franco wanted no more delays. Guitián's subsequent report to Burgos spoke of the 'extraordinary warmth' with which Casado received them at 3.30 p.m. Before they could say anything, he poured forth affirmations of 'his desire to prove that he is an implacable enemy of the vile procedures followed by the Soviet leaders and the cruel and unjust masses who have followed them'. He presented himself as a liberal, a fervent Republican, a fierce adversary of Azaña, of Álvarez del Vayo, and above all, of the Communists whom he called 'poisonous'. He referred to Azaña as 'an abominable monster'. He boasted that he had removed the most dangerous Communists from his forces.

Centaño and Guitián pressed Casado not to delay his coup. Casado replied that if he was too precipitate, there could be 'horrific bloodshed'. In total contrast to what he had told Negrín at Los Llanos, he claimed that 'the armies of the central zone are not like the one in Catalonia. They are capable of resisting until they are annihilated.' As for the Republic's political leaders, Casado said that it would be best to let them leave Spain: 'The more, the better. In this way, afterwards, there will be less bloodshed and less bitterness.' Guitián went on to report that Casado preferred not to undertake their pursuit and arrest. 'Moreover, he intends to leave the country.' They gave him a document containing a final list of the concessions that Franco was prepared to make to those officers who surrendered. Casado read it carefully and expressed his delight: 'Magnificent, magnificent!' he crowed, appearing moved and enthusiastic. The two SIPM agents then urged Casado to give them a definite date for the surrender of the Republican army. Casado replied that it could be carried out 'in about two weeks' and that he would shortly be going to Valencia to discuss it with his senior military staff there.[17]

The document containing Franco's offer of concessions was substantially more limited than might have been suggested by Casado's effusive response. In fact, the contents can have come as no surprise to him since, in part at least, they repeated, with minor differences, what Bertoloty had transmitted to him at the end of January. The document also offered dramatically less than Casado later claimed to Cordón and Hidalgo de Cisneros. The text ran:

> The war is completely lost for you. Further resistance would be criminal. NATIONALIST SPAIN demands surrender. NATIONALIST SPAIN stands by those offers of pardon that have been made in declarations and on the radio and will be generous towards those, who without having committed crimes, were deceived and dragged into fighting. For those who voluntarily lay down their arms, and are not guilty of the death of their comrades nor responsible for other crimes, apart from sparing their lives, our benevolence will be all the greater according to how important or effective are the services that they render to the Cause of Spain in these last moments or how little their intervention and ill-will has been during the war. Those who surrender their weapons and thereby prevent point-

less sacrifices and are not guilty of murders or other serious crimes will be able to obtain a safe-conduct that will enable them to leave our territory and, in the meantime, enjoy total personal safety. Simply having served on the red side or having been active in political groups opposed to the National Movement will not be considered reason for criminal charges. Crimes committed during the period when the reds were in control will be a matter for the courts of justice. Punishment for civil crimes will take into account the conditions of the families of the guilty. NATIONALIST SPAIN has established the redemption of sentences by work with part of the day wage earned to go to the families. Nobody will be deprived of freedom for criminal activities for any longer than the time necessary for their correction and re-education. The new regime guarantees work for all Spaniards without forgetting the pain they might have caused. Those exiled Spaniards who reform their lives will receive protection and help. Any delay in surrender and criminal and pointless resistance against our advance will lead to blood being uselessly spilled and thus be subject to the most severe punishment.[18]

According to Casado, these conditions were soon broadcast by Francoist radio stations. There were two principal differences between this document and what Casado had been told in late January. The first was that the wording in the earlier text offered mercy only to 'senior and other officers', but this later one widened the offer to all those who laid down their arms. The second difference was the highly expurgated account of what Francoist 'justice' offered. Casado's enthusiasm may well have been fuelled by a sense that this document would be easier to sell to the population. Interestingly, the version that he published later, an amalgam of both documents, used the words 'senior and other officers' from the earlier version.[19] They may well have found a ready reception within a population on the verge of desperation after years of deprivation and defeat. However, in the light of what had happened when Francoist forces had captured Republican territory, the self-proclaimed generosity of the document was barely credible. As soon as the war was over, it would soon be revealed as utterly mendacious. All trials would be conducted in military courts with all those tried accused of military rebellion as well as more specific 'crimes', real or invented. In most cases, 'the time necessary for correction and re-education' involved sentences of thirty years or life imprisonment. The system of redemption of sentences by work was the basis for virtual slave labour by prisoners.[20]

Two days later, before Casado made his promised trip to Valencia, Manuel Guitián came to see him again. On 21 February, Guitián had visited Valencia. Whatever it was that he learned there had impelled him to seek this second interview with Casado. According to the report sent by Guitián to Burgos, he had again urged Casado to set a definite date for the coup being prepared. Casado replied that he would 'bring the matter to a conclusion' at the end of the month. He requested that the Nationalists delay their offensive, which was almost completely ready, 'because he cannot take responsibility for the bloody outrages that would occur in Madrid and because, if the offensive were launched, "he will have to act as a Republican officer who fulfils his duty as such to the end"'. Casado ended by asking for time and requesting that he be trusted so that 'not one more drop of blood will be shed'. The report on the interview is as optimistic as the previous one. 'We have the impression', it said, 'that Casado CAN REALIZE HIS PLAN WITH COMPLETE SUCCESS AND TOTAL SECURITY!'[21]

Shortly after the meeting at Los Llanos, Negrín had learned from the commissar inspector of the Army of the Centre, Edmundo Domínguez, the extent of Casado's conspiracy against him. A surprised Negrín replied: 'I thought that he was just unhappy because I haven't made him a general. The decree with his promotion is already signed.' That Negrín should think this is understandable because he knew that, a couple of days earlier, Casado had complained to Cordón about not having been promoted. Domínguez deflated Negrín's optimism, declaring that 'it might already be too late. I suspect that this will not divert him from his commitments and his plans.' 'Commitments?' asked a puzzled Negrín. Domínguez replied, 'Yes, commitments. This will come as a surprise to you. Even as we speak, his agents are in negotiation with rebel officers and other agents of Franco.' Domínguez told Negrín about Casado's connections with elements of the CNT, especially Cipriano Mera, the ascetic commander of the fourth of Madrid's army corps, with Besteiro, with Wenceslao Carrillo and with Ángel Pedrero, and with numerous army officers and also about his dealings with the British diplomat Denys Cowan.[22]

Normally, some of these activities would have triggered an investigation by the Servicio de Inteligencia Militar. This was impossible because the head of the SIM for the central zone was Ángel Pedrero, who had been working closely with Casado since November 1938. In late January 1939, Negrín had ordered Pedrero to be dimissed but, when Casado threatened to resign, he relented.[23] After his return from France, the order was repeated but Casado simply ignored it. Pedrero remained in his post as chief of the SIM for the Army of the Centre, now more deeply resentful of Negrín then ever and a crucial element in the coup being prepared.[24] In response to Domínguez, Negrín let slip an insight into the terrible burden that he was carrying: 'I would like nothing better than for what is happening to release me from being chained to my post! It would relieve me of so many responsibilities!' Shortly afterwards, Domínguez asked Santiago Garcés, the overall head of the SIM, to investigate the connections between Colonel José López Otero and the Francoists and his activities, on behalf of Casado, in relation to the military commanders of Albacete and Murcia. Garcés revealed his impotence when he responded that Pedrero's position rendered this virtually impossible.[25]

In an effort to pursue his strategy without exacerbating existing civilian and military discontent within what was left of Republican territory, Negrín had relied on professional officers, unaware that some of them had already committed themselves to Casado. Casado's hostility to the Communists became ever more unrestrained, particularly as a way of ingratiating himself with Franco. It facilitated his unlikely alliance with the radical anarchists, like Val and García Pradas, whose visceral hatred of the Communist Party was even greater than his own. He told Edmundo Domínguez that he had a list of Communists he planned to have eliminated. At the same time, he was building support by using the control of the censorship that he exercised as commander of the Army of the Centre to present an image of Negrín as a lunatic determined to go down in flames and take the Republic with him. A subsidiary part of this propaganda offensive was the idea, shared by Besteiro and greatly inflated in his post-war writings, that the Communists were planning their own take-over to facilitate war to the death. It is clear that neither the Spanish leadership of the PCE nor their Comintern advisers would have contemplated such a thing. Casado found the final justification, of many, for his own coup in Negrín's decision in early March 1939 to rely on Communist officers to secure the Cartagena naval base and other key points of his evacuation strategy.[26]

The warmth of Casado's relations with the anarchists, if at first sight remarkable, is entirely explicable. It is especially comprehensible in the case of Lieutenant Colonel Cipriano Mera, an ex-bricklayer who had risen through the ranks of the militias and, by sheer application, become a highly competent officer. Although an anarchist, he imposed strict discipline on the forces under his command.[27] Despite their starkly different backgrounds, Mera, whose deeply lined face reflected the hardship of his working-class origins, shared with Casado both personal austerity and an obsession with military discipline. Moreover, Casado needed Mera, whose control of the IV Army Corps in the centre zone offered the military force without which he had little hope of crushing Communist resistance.[28] In the very different case of Eduardo Val Bescós, Casado's readiness to collaborate is explicable not only in terms of the ferocity of their shared hatred of the Communists but also because, given Val's decisive influence over the anarchist organization, Casado needed him as much as he needed Mera. Val was a seemingly anonymous figure who, as the head of the Madrid CNT–FAI Regional Defence Committee (Comité Regional de Defensa, or CRD) set up in the first days of the war, was behind the murders of many rightists in the capital and also of numerous Communists. A tall, taciturn, thirty-year-old ex-waiter from Jaca in Huesca, he had overall control in the capital of the anarchist militias and the vigilante units and detention centres known as *checas*. Before the Civil War, the intelligent and elusive Val had run the CNT–FAI 'action groups' in Madrid; in the words of a comrade, 'a man of deeds, not words, he slips from one place to another as silent as a shadow. In clandestinity, he moves like a fish in water.'[29] Gregorio Gallego, the leader of the regional organization of the Federación de Juventudes Libertarias (the anarchist youth movement), wrote of him: 'nobody suspected that behind his gentle, slightly ironic smile lurked the man who pulled the secret strings of the terrorist groups. By nature, he was mysterious, elusive and little given to revealing anything ... Upon this man, fiercely private, secretive, more violent and daring than anyone could imagine, rested the security of the Castilian CNT.'[30]

Ricardo Sanz, who came to Madrid in November 1936 with the anarchist leader Buenaventura Durruti, described Val as the brains behind the Comité Regional de Defensa: 'Everything is centred on him. Nothing, not the slightest detail, escapes his powerful mind. Any problem put before him is immediately solved. His capacity is inexhaustible.'[31] Juan García Oliver wrote of Val, 'he was really smart and turned out to be a good organizer. The entire weight of the Comité de Defensa fell on his shoulders but he was mainly concerned with the combative side of the CNT.'[32] It is inconceivable that Casado did not know of Val's record, but the vehemence of his anti-communism permitted him to ignore it.[33]

The other members of the Comité de Defensa who would play key roles in Casado's junta were José García Pradas and Manuel Salgado Moreira, both, like Val, members of the FAI. The three were the key figures in the CRD which they had turned into the all-powerful general staff of the libertarian movement in the centre-south zone. In general terms, the CNT–FAI was hobbled by a labyrinthine network of national and regional committees and sub-committees. What the Val–Salgado–García Pradas troika did was to take over the executive functions of the Regional Committee of which, in theory, the CRD was merely a sub-section.[34] Val was the operational leader while Salgado ran its intelligence services and García Pradas its propaganda. The CRD constituted the real power of the anarchist movement in the centre-south zone. García Pradas was editor of the newspapers *CNT* and *Frente Libertario*, the mouthpieces of the

Comité de Defensa. All three were violently anti-Communist but García Pradas's hatred was unbridled and virulent.[35] Bitter hostility had been generated by the Communists' belief that anarchist opposition to a centralized war effort constituted sabotage. The members of the CRD thirsted for revenge both for the repression carried out by the Communist security forces against perceived subversion and for the defeat of the CNT when it rose against the government in the May Days of 1937 in Barcelona. There was also seething resentment of the fact that the Communists justified action against the CNT with the claim that some of the anarchist violence that had discredited the Republic internationally and spread demoralization was perpetrated by agents provocateurs embedded within the anarchist movement. That was certainly a more than plausible claim given the links between Salgado and the Falangist Antonio Bouthelier España. In June 1937, Salgado was replaced as head of the Special Services Bureau of the general staff of the Army of the Centre by another one of Casado's future collaborators, Ángel Pedrero.[36]

It appears that the anarchists in general and Salgado and Val in particular were innocents abroad when it came to the Fifth Column. In 1961, Professor Julio Palacios, Besteiro's university colleague and, along with Antonio Luna, a key link between him and Casado, wrote an article in the Madrid daily *ABC* in which he, or whoever composed the heading, wrote of having 'suffered persecution'. This provoked an indignant letter to Palacios from Manuel Salgado, then in exile in west London. He stated that Palacios had never suffered any kind of persecution and 'was always protected by the Defence Committee of the CNT which gave him a job as a teacher in the school that it had established'. Salgado took a reference by Palacios to 'individuals with appalling records' in Casado's Consejo de Defensa to mean Manuel González Marín and Eduardo Val. He responded by pointing out that 'it was Eduardo Val who went to most trouble to get you appointed in the school'. With regard to Palacio's mention of Antonio Bouthelier, Salgado wrote that 'Bouthelier lived in my house and he was treated there like a son until the very last days of the war. Whether in the Ministry of Defence or the newspaper *Frente Libertario* or the 14th Division, I never saw any sign of disloyalty in him and I am still convinced that he never betrayed me. I never suspected that he was in contact with the enemies of the legitimate government.'[37]

As to why the anarchists were prepared to collaborate with Casado, their participation in the coup fed off both war-weariness and a long-standing and bloodstained hatred of the Communists. Resentment of the Republican government's imposition of a centralized war effort, with its necessary repression of the anarchists' revolutionary aspirations as well as the movement's perceived subversion, embraced Negrín as well as the Communists. Ever since the capitulation of the anarchists in the crisis of May 1937, the influence of the CNT and the FAI had been in precipitate decline. This had been symbolized by the proceedings of a national plenum of the FAI in Valencia in the first week of July 1937. The meeting had seen the birth of the Movimiento Libertario Español (Spanish Libertarian Movement) which united the CNT, the FAI and the Juventudes Libertarias. The MLE was altogether more bureaucratic and hierarchical than its three component organizations had been hitherto.[38] The action groups of Madrid, dominated by Val, Salgado and García Pradas, resented the consequent stultification of the MLE. The exile in early February 1939 of the high command of Catalan anarchism increased the influence of the Madrid-based troika and opened the way to their collaboration with Casado.

The anarchists in general blamed the PCE for the military debacle in Catalonia, indeed for every military problem from the time of the Ebro retreat onwards. In doing so, knowingly or otherwise, they ignored the international situation, the difficulties of securing weaponry and the extent to which the war effort had been undermined by the incompetence or deliberate sabotage of professional officers and indeed by much of the behaviour of the anarchists themselves. They complained that the war effort was being criminally badly run, especially in the wake of Negrín's return to Spain, and, at the same time, held the almost paranoiac view that the Communists were all-powerful. An indication of this was an FAI report of June 1938 that presented a detailed, and erroneous, account of Communist domination of the armed forces. In terms of its judgements on specific officers, the report was often wildly inaccurate and profuse in accusations of incompetence. For instance, General Juan Hernández Saravia, a loyal follower of President Azaña, was presented as 'a faithful instrument in the hands of the Communists'. Leopoldo Menéndez, Hernández Saravia's successor as commander of the Army of the Levante, a man who would be a key element in the coup of March 1939, was said to be 'like General Saravia, a Communist who deserves to be shot'. Miaja was described as a spineless puppet of the Communists. Revealingly, Casado was commended for having a good relationship with the CNT–FAI.[39]

In fact, the anarchists had good reason to believe that Casado was as committed as they were to an effective war effort. On 23 January 1939, when the decree of martial law was issued, Casado had issued an edict in the centre-south zone:

Citizens: The Government of the Republic has decided to declare martial law in the entire national territory. My humanitarian sentiments do not exclude, indeed they reinforce, my determination to fulfil my duty and, in consequence, demand that all of the inhabitants of the territory under my command do the same. Let no one interpret this determination as a puerile threat but rather see it as an honest warning since I assure you that I will be inexorable with those who commit acts whose punishment is foreseen within the decree. I will not tolerate any faltering, any vacillations, nor lack of enthusiasm nor betrayals. Today more than ever, we must maintain firmly our faith in the victory of the forces of the Republic in the service of Spain and of freedom. Citizens, long live our national independence.[40]

In the wake of this rousing call for the fight to go on, on 2 or 3 February, as has been seen, Casado met Generals Miaja, Matallana and Menéndez to discuss an early peace settlement. On 7 February, he went to Los Llanos for the meeting convened by the commissar general Jesús Hernández to discuss the further conduct of the war. Hernández had been alone in arguing for a strengthened war effort against the defeatist rhetoric of Casado, Miaja, Matallana, Admiral Buiza and Colonel Antonio Camacho, head of the air force in the centre-south zone. Before setting off to Valencia to recruit support for his plans, Casado issued a communiqué in Madrid calling for a firm response to the reverses in Catalonia:

All anti-fascists have understood that their morale must be reinforced in proportion to the demands of adversity. This has been the case since the beginning of the war when we were abandoned by the rest of the world ... Our people know that the only way to save themselves and fulfil a universal duty is with the following slogan: the greater the adversities, the stronger the determination, the greater the will to fight on ... The authorities and the people are at their posts. And in our post we will stay, faithful to the totality of our duty and convinced that the epic that Spain began to write on 18 July 1936 will not have one single page unworthy of the spiritual grandeur of its heroism.

That communiqué was published in the Madrid press the following day when Casado made his first approach to recruit Cipriano Mera. Needless to say, he spoke to Mera in the same belligerent terms as the communiqué, rather than making reference to his defeatist talks with Matallana, Miaja, Menéndez and Buiza or to his conversations with the Fifth Column.[41]

Herein lay a never fully exposed contradiction in the alliance between Casado and the anarchists. Casado was interested in an early peace settlement with Franco in whose generosity he trusted with culpable naivety, blinded perhaps by his own selfish arrogance. In contrast, Mera and the anarchists had plans to fight on in order to secure the evacuation of those at risk. In that sense, their hatred of the Communists apart, their aspirations were not wildly dissimilar to those of Negrín. Their complaints that Negrín was not really running the war effort in any meaningful way failed to take into account the unavoidable truth that, on his return from France, he was basically leading a divided cabinet of no fixed abode and trying to deal virtually single-handed with insuperable problems in terms of arming and feeding the Republic. His task was rendered impossible in a context in which he had to combat the defeatism expressed by the senior officers present at the Los Llanos meeting. He could do so only by turning to the Communists which, in turn, intensified the hostility of those ranged against him.

However, it seems clear that the anarchists knew little about Besteiro's links with the Fifth Column and nothing of Casado's promises to the Francoist secret services to leave 'reds' to be captured. The CNT's participation in the Consejo Nacional de Defensa, unlike that of Casado, was made on the basis of neither wanting nor anticipating early Republican capitulation. Where they agreed – and what held them together – was Casado's rhetoric about Negrín being the prisoner or stooge of the PCE and his claim that only by breaking that stranglehold could the Republic's 'genuinely Spanish and patriotic' elements have any chance of winning concessions in peace negotiations with Franco. At a popular level, where near-starvation and intense war-weariness had taken their toll, the Fifth Column was stoking all this by insidious gossip to the effect that only the Communists stood in the way of a reasonable peace settlement.

Mera had already been sounded out by Casado about a possible coup. They had discussed it at their meeting on 8 or 9 February. Immediately after this encounter, the first of several to elaborate on arrangements for the coup, Mera had gone to the offices of the Comité Regional de Defensa to brief Eduardo Val. On being informed that Val was still in France with Amil and López, Mera told Salgado about the meeting with Casado. In mid-February, Mera was reprimanded by the liaison committee of the Movimiento Libertario Español for his involvement in Casado's plans, which suggests that they were hardly a closely guarded secret. Mera's furious response had been to denounce the extent to which the movement was hobbled by its slow-moving committees. He went on to suggest that the members of the liaison committee should be shot for failing to take decisive action.[42]

Mera's frustration was shared by the troika that ran the Comité Regional de Defensa and they decided to take matters into their own hands. Their hostility to the Communists and, by extension, to Negrín took operational form at a meeting held in the last week of February. After the Val–Amil–López delegation had returned from France in the early hours of the morning of 22 February, Cipriano Mera,

Eduardo Val, Manuel Salgado and José García Pradas convened what they called a restricted plenary meeting. The purpose of the gathering was to lay the ground for the anarchist participation in the coup being prepared. The carefully selected militants who were convened were told that important decisions would be taken regarding the war and the policy of Dr Negrín. At 11.00 a.m. on 24 February in the meeting hall of the showbusiness union, the Sindicato de Espectáculos Públicos, in Madrid's calle de Miguel Ángel, there was a gathering of about one hundred prominent members of the regional and local committees of the CNT, the FAI and the Libertarian Youth Movement (Juventudes Libertarias), the editors and journalists of the three main anarchist newspapers *CNT*, *Castilla Libre* and *Frente Libertario* and various military figures led by Cipriano Mera. A seven-hour discussion of the situation in the central zone hinged on the choice to be made between war to the death, 'the suicide of an entire people' and 'an honourable peace which some of us had begun to contemplate'.

Manuel Amil reported on what the delegation had seen in France in terms of the 'privileged' situation of the Socialists. He then made a statement that ran though the delegates 'like an electric shock'. He alleged that, on the plane back from Toulouse to Albacete, he had overheard two Communists saying that Negrín 'planned to carry out a coup d'état and dismiss the army officers who were not his supporters'. According to Gregorio Gallego of the Juventudes Libertarias and now an army officer: 'although Manuel Amil was notorious for his passion for intrigue, no one questioned what he said he had heard'. Amil's unsubstantiated tittle-tattle was taken as proof of the immediate intentions of the PCE. In fact, the anarchist movement in general and this audience in particular were disposed to believe anything critical of the Communists.

A powerful intervention was made by Manuel Salgado, who had been head of the secret service of the Ministry of Defence which was infiltrated by the Fifth Column. He would be an important link between the libertarian movement and the senior officers involved in the Casado coup. His speech to the meeting was a diatribe against the supposed dictatorial ambitions of Negrín. He claimed that the majority of the Republicans and Socialists shared with the anarchists the desire to see the end of 'the power of a man incapable of leading the war effort and of respecting the democratic principles of the Republic'. He stated mysteriously, 'I have good reason to know that if we have the courage to oppose him, many officers of the Army and Navy who still believe in an honourable peace will be on our side.' The 'good reason' for Salgado's confident assertion could well have been information from Mera or from Antonio Bouthelier España.

Salgado's words provoked a fierce debate. A representative of the FAI declared indignantly: 'An honourable peace is synonymous with treachery or vacillation and I believe that we should have no truck with it. Moreover, if Dr Negrín and the Communists are crazy enough to launch a dictatorship, rather than an honourable peace, we will be thinking in terms of an honourable death because the whole thing will collapse.' Before he had finished speaking, the FAI delegate was loudly interrupted by García Pradas, who launched into a frenzied anti-Communist harangue. In the crudest terms, he declared that the war was already lost and warned that if the Communists seized power, as he was sure they intended to do, they would carry out the bloodiest massacre in history against the anarchist movement. García Pradas's shocking words provoked another delegate to interrupt, shouting: 'It won't be as bad as the one the fascists will organize if we get entangled in internecine struggles.' There followed a noisy argument over whether the Communists or the fascists were worse. García Pradas ploughed on, drunk with heroic rhetoric, denouncing both but concluding that 'it was the duty of anarchists, as the torch-bearers of libertarian principles, first to destroy the dictatorial ambitions of the Communists and then to damage Franco's sword with our own necks'.

Finally, the meeting agreed, by a massive majority, to oppose any effort to impose a dictatorship. In García Pradas's later account, there was agreement that it was crucial to avoid 'the chaos, the enraged clamour of the abandoned or betrayed masses, the horror of a military catastrophe followed by the dislocation of our rearguard that, in a matter of hours, would be driven insane by panic and despair as had happened in Málaga, in Santander, in Asturias and in Catalonia'. The three principal committees of the Libertarian Movement were authorized to make agreements and forge alliances with those anti-fascist forces that were still faithful to democratic principles.

Immediately afterwards, the military participants in the mass meeting were called to the offices of the Comité Regional de Defensa in the calle Serrano to get concrete instructions. Twenty anarchist officers met in Eduardo Val's office. He convinced them of the need to set up a defence committee for the entire centre-south zone to avoid total collapse. They agreed that the CRD should have full power over all aspects of the organization, particularly military, political police, propaganda and transport sections. The committee consisted of Eduardo Val, Benigno Mancebo, Melchor Baztán, Manuel González Marín, Manuel Salgado Moreira, Manuel Amil and José García Pradas.[43] This would be the operational basis for the anarchist participation in Casado's coup. They were all fierce anti-Communists and none more so than García Pradas, who was noted for his vitriolic prose as editor of the CRD's principal newspapers. Some had blood on their hands from the ruthless repression of right-wingers in Madrid during the early months of the war. Benigno Mancebo, for instance, had run the notorious Checa de Fomento and had subsequently been one of the CNT–FAI representatives on the anarchist-dominated Comité Provincial de Investigación Pública. Mancebo and his comrades acquired notoriety for their role in the so-called *sacas* – the removal and subsequent assassination of prisoners.[44] While Manuel Salgado was running the CNT–FAI's investigation units, which were eventually incorporated into the Ministry of Defence as the Special Services Bureau of the general staff of the Army of the Centre, prisoners disappeared in suspicious circumstances. Overall, his operation had been ineffectual in part because of sheer inefficiency but largely because of its infiltration by Fifth Columnists.

Val gave those present a tendentious account of what he claimed were Negrín's intentions and of his own meetings with the senior military officers and 'authorities of the centre-south zone', which clearly included Casado. He reported that both the military and political figures were in agreement that the limits of resistance had been reached. He went on to say that he regarded both last-ditch defence and surrender as equally stupid. Accordingly, the most important thing was to maintain the unity of the anti-fascist forces. However, 'if Negrín goes the whole hog and hands over power to the Communist officers who lost the battle in Catalonia', boasted Val, 'he will get the response he deserves, even if we all live to regret it'. Val's other remarks left little doubt that he believed that Negrín was planning a dictatorship. He also left no doubt that an anti-Negrín coup was being planned when he instructed his comrades to listen each night to the war report on Unión Radio at midnight. When they heard the signal, they should be ready to take control of their units and proceed to arrest the supporters of Negrín.[45]

Even before the plenary meeting, Val and Salgado had agreed with Mera on the need for a deal with Casado. To this end, Val, Salgado and García Pradas pushed the liaison committee of the Movimiento Libertario to demand that Casado be made chief of the general staff, a move which would have helped the projected coup. Ironically, that promotion would go to General Matallana, who was already working with the Francoist secret service and in collaboration with Casado.[46] Links between the anarchists and Casado were facilitated by Ángel Pedrero, Salgado's successor in the security services of the Ministry of Defence. Like Mancebo, Pedrero had also been involved in one of the most notorious *checas*, in his case the Brigada García Atadell, and had subsequently served in Salgado's secret service.[47] Another link to Casado was a forty-five-year-old anarchist from Seville, Melchor Rodríguez García. A one-time bullfighter, Melchor Rodríguez was credited with limiting the repression behind the Republican lines and saving thousands of lives. He was head of a group known as 'Los Libertos de la FAI' and had used the Palacio de Viana in Madrid to give refuge to many rightists, priests and monks, military officers and Falangists. Indeed, his humanitarian activities eventually earned him the nickname of 'the red angel' (*el ángel rojo*) and gave him a wide network of contacts in the Fifth Column. They had also created friction with the CRD and Val who was outraged by Melchor's interference in what he saw as his necessary extermination of rightists.

In mid-February, Casado had sent his secretary Rafael Sánchez Guerra to make contact with Melchor. Sánchez Guerra visited him several times at his home, and on 27 February the photographer Alfonso Sánchez García was present and recorded the occasion. In the course of these visits, Sánchez Guerra told Melchor what was afoot and that Casado had the support of both Miaja and Matallana. When Casado, who was bedridden with severe stomach pains, saw Melchor, he told him that his name headed a black-list of those to be murdered by the Communists. In the hope of encouraging Melchor to join the conspiracy, he revealed that he had already met with Eduardo Val, Manuel Salgado, González Marín and Cipriano Mera. This had the reverse effect, since Melchor said that he had no wish to be associated with Eduardo Val and Gónzalez Marin, whom he regarded as killers. Nevertheless, Melchor did believe Casado's warnings about the need for protection from the Communists and, for that reason and because of his friendship with Cipriano Mera, did agree to collaborate with the planned junta.[48]

As Melchor was leaving his meeting with Casado, he bumped into José Rodríguez Vega, the secretary general of the UGT, who had just returned from France. He was astonished by the level of deference that he saw being shown the anarchist by Casado's staff. It confirmed for him reports that he had received from a journalist friend in the Febus news agency that frequent visits by anarchists to Casado at the headquarters of the Army of the Centre were related to an anti-government plot. In the wake of these initial contacts with Casado, on 26 February Melchor was invited to meet Julián Besteiro and the Director General de Seguridad, Vicente Girauta, at Casado's office. Now it was suggested by Casado that Melchor Rodríguez might be president of the projected Consejo de Defensa Nacional. Nothing came of that particular proposal. At the end of March, as interim Alcalde (mayor) of Madrid, he would formally hand over the capital to the Francoist forces.[49]

Almost immediately after this meeting, someone called 'Señor Milanes' contacted Abbington Gooden, the British Consul in Valencia, and informed him about what had been discussed at Casado's meeting with Melchor Rodríguez. It is probable that 'Señor Milanes' was a locally recruited consular official who was in touch with Casado and may indeed have been the basis of Casado's claims that he had important contacts with British officials. The next day, 28 February, Gooden sent a telegram to the Foreign Office in London:

I have just learned from Sr. Milanes that Colonel Casado and Senor Bestero [*sic*] are to form in Madrid nucleus of new Republican Government which is to include Senor Melchior Rodriguez [*sic*]. Colonel Casado would have support of army. They intend to conclude an early armistice with General Franco's government. Sr. Milanes has been promised that question of Italian prisoners would receive favourable and rapid attention as soon as the change takes place. The welfare of the refugees in the various missions has been assured. Doctor Negrín has presumably not been consulted in this matter so that the proposed change is in the nature of a coup d'état.

This information that a coup d'état was being prepared in Madrid was immediately passed on to the British agent in Burgos, Sir Robert Hodgson, to Ralph Stevenson and to the British Embassy in Paris. It was not, however, passed on to Juan Negrín.[50]

7

In the Kingdom of the Blind

Even before he had been in touch with the anarchists, after the fall of Catalonia, Casado had made contact with the stronghold of anti-Communist sentiment within the PSOE, the Madrid Socialist Group (Agrupación Socialista Madrileña, or ASM), the most powerful organization of the Socialist Party and one dominated by influential followers of Largo Caballero. These contacts were intensified in the immediate aftermath of Azaña's resignation as President of the Republic on 27 February 1939. Wenceslao Carrillo, a friend and collaborator of Largo Caballero, was given by a Socialist comrade, Orencio Labrador, a message from Casado requesting that he visit him.[1] When he arrived, Casado told him that major offensives were about to be launched by Franco and that something had to be done before this happened to save thousands of those at risk. Of course, Franco had no plans nor indeed any need to launch offensives. Indeed, he had halted his advance against the Republicans in the central-south zone in the confidence that Casado's plans made it easier simply to await the internal collapse of Republican resistance. In support of his criticisms of Negrín, Casado gave Carrillo a detailed account of the meeting at Los Llanos. He asked his opinion about a project to set up a Consejo Nacional de Defensa with all parties except the PCE. Inevitably, the already fiercely anti-Communist Carrillo liked the idea and said that he would consult with other senior members of the ASM. After they had authorized him to continue talks with Casado, meetings took place in the offices of the ASM involving Wenceslao Carrillo, Julián Besteiro, Cipriano Mera, Ángel Pedrero and Carlos Rubiera of the Federación de Juventudes Socialistas (Socialist Youth).[2]

Not all senior Socialists shared the hostility to Negrín expressed by Wenceslao Carrillo and Besteiro. News of the Los Llanos meeting inevitably intensified existing divisions in the Socialist movement as a whole. José Rodríguez Vega, a supporter of Negrín, attended a meeting of the union's executive committee a few days after the gathering of the military top brass at Los Llanos. In the light of what was known of the opinions expressed there by the various commanders, about which Wenceslao Carrillo had been fully informed by Casado, another supporter of Largo Caballero, Ricardo Zabalza, raised the issue of surrender. Zabalza was head of one of the most important sections of the UGT, the landworkers' union, the Federación Nacional de Trabajadores de la Tierra, as well as parliamentary deputy for the Socialist Party. The proponents of capitulation were defeated in the meeting. Nevertheless, two or three days later, Zabalza and Rodríguez Vega went together to see Negrín in Madrid. Their encounter was soured by the vehemence with which Zabalza argued in favour of surrender. Rodríguez Vega assured Negrín that Zabalza's views were not the official views of the UGT executive. Negrín listened carefully to both and then reaffirmed his determination to organize and continue resistance. To this end, Negrín urged Rodríguez Vega to try to revive the Popular Front organization in Madrid. One of the fruits of Rodríguez Vega's efforts was a telegram from the Popular Front to Azaña vainly urging him to return to Spain.[3]

Even before Negrín had been alerted to Casado's machinations by both Antonio Cordón and Edmundo Domínguez, his suspicions had been aroused by the discovery that Casado had used his control of the censorship to block reports of his speeches. Casado also pressured Negrín to take up residence in a house under his control in the Paseo de Ronda in Madrid and to accept a group of specially selected bodyguards. When Negrín refused, Casado had him followed not only in Madrid but when he visited other army bases elsewhere in the central zone. Casado came to visit him frequently, addressing him always in the most obsequious terms and even calling him 'the saviour of Spain'. At the same time, he complained to government ministers and the Communist officers that Negrín did not trust him. Rightly fearing that Casado was planning to keep him where he could be easily arrested, Negrín stayed only a few days in Madrid, moving his head-quarters around the Levante before, on or about 25 February, estab-lishing his headquarters in Petrer near Elda in the province of Alicante. In fact, on 27 or 28 February, Casado informed his Fifth Column contacts that he planned to imprison Negrín when he next came to Madrid.[4]

So peripatetic was Negrín's cabinet that, according to the venom-ous hyperbole of García Pradas, he held important meetings at road-sides. With a slightly closer relationship to the truth, one Communist functionary described him as 'a wandering shadow'.[5] On 20 February, Negrín met Líster, who urged him to make more use of the officers returning from Catalonia via France. The Minister of Agriculture, Vicente Uribe, also lamented that he had similarly begged Negrín to do this but he had done nothing. To Líster, Negrín replied that he was thinking about replacing the existing commanders, although Líster was anything but convinced. Nevertheless, Negrín did ask him to draw up an assessment of the officers in the Army of the Levante. Líster visited various senior officers and got the firm impression that they were displeased by the return of the Communist officers from France. Miaja, concerned about any possible challenge to his author-ity and the prospect of the war being continued, expressed outraged incredulity that Líster had returned from France. Since it was Líster's duty to do so, Miaja's reaction was as surprising as it was revealing. Matallana was more cautious, demonstrating considerable know-ledge of the military situation. In the course of the conversation with Líster, Matallana let slip that he had received the letter from Rojo announcing his resignation as chief of the general staff. Líster also visited Leopoldo Menéndez, the commander of the Army of the Levante, and found a defeatist atmosphere at his headquarters.[6]

On 23 or 24 February, Negrín went to Guadalajara to meet Casado's ally, Lieutenant Colonel Mera, the commander of the IV Army Corps of the centre. He was responding to a request from Mera. Negrín was accompanied by Casado, but Mera refused to allow the Prime Minister's aide de camp, Major Julián Soley Conde, into his office on the grounds that he was a Communist. It is astonishing that this act of disrespect was tolerated by Negrín, who was then subjected by

Mera to a long rant about the behaviour of the Communist Party. Mera also expressed his indignation that some of those who made speeches about resistance were already making arrangements to tranfer money into foreign bank accounts and get their families out of Spain. He protested that it was useless to continue to speak about resisting when the Republic lacked the means to do so and was already effectively defeated. In support of this assertion, he stressed the loss of Catalonia and its industry, the fact that so many men and so much equipment were now in France and the lack of armaments and food in the centre zone. He went on to talk of possible military strategies, including infiltrating Francoist territory with guerrilla units.

Mera's principal point was that negotiations should be opened with Franco with a view to saving lives. Nonetheless, it was clear that he believed that effective negotiation required some threat of continued military action. Negrín explained patiently that he had already tried in vain to get British mediation. In the light of British indifference, he concluded that continued resistance was the only possible option.[7] Negrín's forbearance with Mera now, as had been the case with the Admiral of the Fleet Miguel Buiza and the commissar Bruno Alonso on 11 February, and indeed with all of the top brass at Los Llanos on 16 February, is easily explicable. He was patiently trying to convince them all that his intention was to use the threat of continued resistance as the centrepiece of his plans to negotiate a peace settlement with a reasonable level of protection from reprisals of those who were at risk.

All of this was taking place within a hostile international context. It will be recalled that in mid-February, Sir Robert Hodgson, the British dipomatic agent in Burgos, had been instructed by London to tell the Conde de Jordana that recognition of Franco would be facilitated if he accepted the Republic's offer to cease hostilities in return for guarantee of no widespread political reprisals. While Negrín was trying to secure the cooperation of the senor commanders in the centre-south zone for his ploy of resistance, London had communicated to the US government the gist of Jordana's message with Franco's highly sugared response to the message transmitted by Hodgson:

As the war has been won by the Nationalists the Spanish Government must surrender unconditionally. As already proved, the motives inspiring the Nationalist Government constitute a sure guarantee for all Spain's other fugitives. The tribunals are restricted to dealing with criminals whose cases fall within the framework of the laws promulgated before July 1936. Spain will not accept foreign intervention calculated to impair her dignity or infringe her sovereignty. Reprisals being alien to the Nationalist Government, the only effect of prolonged resistance will be to postpone the termination of insane resistance and increase the responsibility of their leaders.

London's cynical, or at best naive, interpretation of Franco's words was: 'This announcement appears to His Majesty's Government to be as satisfactory as they could hope for regarding reprisals, which were their chief concern in connexion with their proposed recognition of General Franco.'[8]

The British decision in principle to recognize Franco without guarantees on his part had actually been taken already on 8 February. The public announcement was delayed and Neville Chamberlain had lied in response to parliamentary questions from Clement Attlee on 14 and 23 February asking if a decision had been taken.[9] Sir Alexander Cadogan, the permanent under-secretary at the Foreign Office, for instance, revealed the central objective of British policy towards Spain when he wrote in his diary on 15 February that he approved of the effort to seek guarantees against Francoist reprisals 'so long as it doesn't delay recognition'.[10] It is clear that London had informed the French government of the decision since, on 24 February, Edouard Daladier revealed that his cabinet had received advice from the British government that the hour had come to recognize General Franco and that Paris should wait no longer. After considerable prevarication by Neville Chamberlain, and only in response to persistent questions from the parliamentary Labour Party, the decision was announced in the House of Commons on 27 February. Franco was informed by Sir Robert Hodgson.[11]

Chamberlain claimed that the area of Spain controlled by the Republic was very small and very weak and that there was no effective government in Republican Spain. It was, he said, 'impossible to regard the Spanish Republican Government, scattered as it is and no longer exercising settled authority, as the Sovereign Government of Spain'. He said that Burgos had been informed. No undertaking was required of Franco regarding reprisals against civilians since, he said, 'His Majesty's Government have noted with satisfaction the public statements of General Franco concerning the determination of himself and his Government to secure the traditional independence of Spain and to take proceedings only in the case of those against whom criminal charges are laid.'[12] On 28 February, the Conde de Jordana was asked to receive Sir Robert Hodgson as Chargé d'Affaires pending the appointment of an ambassador. At the same time, Pablo de Azcárate vacated the Spanish Embassy in London, which was taken over by the Duque de Alba. Franco requested that the British government receive Alba as Spanish Chargé d'Affaires.[13] Since he was also the Duke of Berwick on Tweed and a close friend of Winston Churchill, Alba was seen in Whitehall as highly desirable.

Speaking in parliament the following day, Clement Attlee mocked the behaviour of the Prime Minister. He lamented that the government had concealed a decision clearly taken some time before and that Chamberlain had previously refused to answer questions on the subject: 'When the Prime Minister said he was not going to be cross-examined, he might have been a dictator addressing the Fascist Grand Council.' He referred to Chamberlain's justification of recognition as 'a tissue of half truths, which are worse than lies'. Attlee put forward a motion:

That, in the opinion of this House, the decision of His Majesty's Government to grant unconditional recognition to Spanish insurgent forces dependent upon foreign intervention constitutes a deliberate affront to the legitimate Government of a friendly Power, is a gross breach of international traditions, and marks a further stage in a policy which is steadily destroying in all democratic countries confidence in the good faith of Great Britain.

His speech ended with a devasting condemnation of Chamberlain's policy:

It is crystal clear that the policy of the Government all through has been to back General Franco to win and to do everything they could to help him. The sham of non-intervention has been really a device to prevent the Spanish Government exercising the rights that it has under international law. They have allowed every kind of breach of international law to be committed and have thrown aside doctrines of maritime law that every states-man in this country for generations has upheld. The Right Hon. Gentleman is the first Prime Minister to show himself perfectly indifferent to those laws of the sea which were created and upheld by statesmen of this country. He connived at the starving of women and children, he connived at the bombing of open towns and the slaying of men, women and children and non-combatants, and now he is scrambling with indecent haste to try to make friends with the perpetrators. This is not in the interests of democracy. It is not in the interests of the safety of the British Empire. He is thinking all the time of the interests of British capital. What does it matter if Gibraltar is endangered if Rio Tinto Mines pay a dividend? What does it matter about women and children if Spain is made a place safe for autocracy?

Attlee was referring inter alia to the Italian sinking of British ships in the Mediterranean and the Francoist blockades of the Basque coast in 1937 and of the Levant coast in 1939. In his feeble response, Chamberlain sidestepped these charges and simply referred to Azaña's absence from Spain in justification of the recognition:

The President is no longer in Spain: indeed, he has resigned. Some of the ministers are in France, some are in Spain, and many, I believe, of Dr. Negrín's own ministers and military advisers are urging upon him a cessation of hostilities. It is doubtful whether the Government can be considered a legal Power. What is the authority of the Cabinet in the absence of the President and in the impossibility of calling together the Cortes? The Diplomatic Corps is accredited to the head of the State, and where the head of the State legally resides that is where they should perform their mission. How can they perform their mission when the head of the State is no longer in Spain?

He justified his policy by saying: 'We know perfectly well that it is quite impossible for us to exact such conditions unless we are prepared to go to war to enforce them.'

Nevertheless, Chamberlain implicitly acknowledged sympathy for Franco's declared desire for revenge: 'It would not be reasonable to ask General Franco to grant beforehand a complete amnesty which would include the men who had been guilty of such horrible crimes.' Chamberlain then proudly read out the telegram received from Jordana in response to Hodgson's request for clarification of the issue of reprisals:

The telegram is dated the 22nd of this month, and it reads: 'National Spain has won the war, and it is therefore incumbent on the vanquished to surrender unconditionally. The patriotism, chivalry and generosity of the Caudillo, of which he has given so many examples in the liberated regions, and likewise the spirit of equity and justice that inspires all the National Government's actions, constitute a firm guarantee for all Spaniards who are not criminals. The courts of justice, applying the established laws and procedure promulgated before 16th July, 1936, are restricted to bringing to judgment, within the framework of those laws, the authors of crime. Spain is not disposed to accept any foreign intervention which may impair her dignity or infringe her sovereignty.'[14]

Chamberlain survived the motion of censure. Sir Alexander Cadogan saw him afterwards and noted with delight the Prime Minister's remark that he had 'got away with it'.[15]

It is perfectly clear that, having long connived at a Francoist victory, neither the Conservative government nor the Foreign Office regarded Negrín's humanitarian concerns as a priority. When informed of the imminent recognition of Franco, Azcárate had made a last desperate attempt to persuade the Foreign Secretary Lord Halifax to use the influence of the British government to ensure that the promises contained in the telegram from Jordana would be fulfilled. Although Halifax was clearly distressed, it was to no avail.[16] Already at the beginning of February, Abbington Gooden, the acting Consul in Valencia, had requested permission to arrange for Republican officials at risk of imprisonment or execution to be evacuated on British ships. The reply from London was that such measures could be implemented only for those individuals already named in existing exchange agreements with Franco. Despite estimating that 50,000 lives were in danger in southern Spain alone and knowing that there would be little mercy for civilians, the Foreign Office instructed Gooden not to give the impression that there would be British help to facilitate evacuations lest it encourage Negrín's government to fight on.[17] At the first meeting of his cabinet after the announcement of the recognition, Chamberlain revealed his views when he said: 'it was to be hoped that General Franco would now be careful to avoid action which might offend the opinion of the civilised world. At the same time it had to be remembered that there were a number of very dangerous criminals who had committed acts of great brutality, and it was, therefore, too much to expect General Franco to proclaim a general amnesty.'[18]

Meanwhile, in Madrid, Casado had been pressed on 22 February by Manuel Guitián of the SIPM to set a definite date for his coup. Having promised that he would 'bring the matter to a conclusion' by the end of the month, Casado now tried to get more support within the Republican high command. A meeting that he had with Antonio Cordón on 24 February has to be seen in this context. After making insulting remarks about Azaña similar to those he had made to Guitián, he assured Cordón of his own passionate commitment to resistance and dismissed rumours about his contacts with Besteiro and others. This could be read as a subterfuge to divert any suspicions that Cordón might have of his machinations and thus neutralize him. However, it could just as well be seen as a way of securing Cordón's trust prior to a tentative proposition about surrender. Casado was effectively referring to his meetings with Centaño and Guitián. He then went on to tell Cordón of his conviction that Franco would make concessions, not just in terms of reprisals but also in terms of recognition of the ranks of Republican officers in a post-war army. He also told Cordón that he had had several meetings with 'utterly trustworthy British agents'. He claimed that they had assured him that the British government had enough ships ready for the evacuation of 20,000 people. Even more implausibly, he claimed that these 'agents' had told him that the British government would impose the conditions of no reprisals and the recognition of Republican military ranks.[19]

The claims made by Casado to Cordón were almost certainly a wildly exaggerated account of meetings that he had held with a British official, either Denys Cowan or the consular employee 'Sr Milanes', shortly after the announcement of the Anglo-French recognition of Franco. This was reflected in the fact that Abbington Gooden in Valencia sent a telegram to the Foreign Office reporting that Casado and Besteiro had informed the British official in question that it was their intention to overthrow Negrín. They had gone on to request that the British government undertake to help in the evacuation of between five and ten thousand Republican military officers and political leaders.[20]

In fact, the statements of the British Prime Minister Neville Chamberlain and the Foreign Secretary Lord Halifax both in parliament and in private cabinet meetings make it clear that there was no possibility of the British government doing what Casado was promising. Certainly, the British were anxious to hasten the end of the war. If Denys Cowan made such assurances to Casado, it could only have been as a result of his anxiety to fulfil instructions to encourage Casado to make peace. The only way that there would have been the remotest possibility of Casado being able to negotiate a less intransigent line from Franco would have been if he could have offered to hand over both Negrín and the Communist leadership. In the event, their flight on 6 March made this impossible, but the fact that Casado left hundreds of Communists in jail would suggest that he was prepared to pay for Franco's clemency in Communist blood.

Casado's meeting with Cordón was a reflection of the fact that Franco was becoming impatient with the lack of progress in the negotiations with him. On 25 February, the Generalísimo went back on the minimal offer made five days earlier. He informed his staff that, since the Nationalist army had more than ample means to occupy Madrid 'by force, when and how it pleases, the surrender must be without conditions'. Franco's view was that any negotiated surrender, even without conditions, favoured the defeated. His statement to his staff continued with the words: 'if the officer in charge in Madrid hands over the city, we will not fight; if not, we will take it by force, something that does not bother us'. He went on to say that if Casado could not arrange the surrender of the entire central zone, it would be of interest for him to facilitate the surrounding of the Army of the Centre by permitting passage through the Jarama and Guadalajara fronts. This message was passed on to Casado by agents of the SIPM. It would appear that Casado showed this message to Matallana, who began to prepare detailed maps of the fronts mentioned by Franco, highlighting the weak sectors most vulnerable to a Nationalist motorized attack. He then sent them to the Francoist high command with a note that they could be used 'in the unlikely event of Casado's plans not prospering'. The information from Matallana did not reach Burgos until 5 March.[21]

Franco's message made it clear that if Casado was to derive benefit from his machinations he had to fix the date for his coup and the surrender of the Republican forces before Franco launched an attack. Shortly afterwards, Casado was given a portable radio with which he could contact the SIPM agent Francisco Bonel Huici on the Toledo front. By this means, Casado sent a message on Monday 27 February stating that the Junta that would arrange the surrender would be announced the following day. He thus requested permission for Besteiro and Colonel Ruiz Fornells of the general staff to fly to Burgos to negotiate the surrender. The reply from Burgos was brutal: 'We must emphasize that Nationalist Spain will not accept anything but unconditional surrender subject to the generosity indicated in previous telegrams. One or two professional officers from the red zone of proven reliability may come here, but only in order to be informed of the procedure for the surrender to be carried out. The presence of Besteiro or other civilians is unacceptable.'[22]

It was arranged that a military-only delegation would fly from Madrid to Burgos on 2 March to arrange the surrender terms. However, Franco's chief of staff, General Juan Vigón, waited in vain at the local airport of Gamonal. The reason was that plans for Casado's take-over were not progressing smoothly. Indeed, Matallana's treacherous communication of maps of the front suggested considerable nervousness about the delay. While Vigón loitered at Gamonal, on 2 March, the SIPM in Madrid informed Burgos that Casado had received Franco's ultimatum but was inhibited by doubts among the politicians. The proposed Junta was 'slipping away from Casado at least for the moment because the politicians hoped to obtain what they call an honourable capitulation, which would allow the free departure of those who wish to leave'. The sticking point was that Casado had wanted Besteiro to be allowed to go to Burgos and negotiate with Franco so as to be able to announce a high-level agreement permitting the flight of all those who wish to leave irrespective of their 'guilt'. Two days later, the SIPM reported further on the delays: 'Everything hinges on the flight abroad of the leaders so that Casado does not appear to be a traitor.'[23]

Some days earlier, Negrín had established his base in the farmhouse of El Poblet, a densely wooded estate on the northern outskirts of Petrer, a small town to the east of, and nowadays contiguous with, Elda. In Elda-Petrer, Negrín was accompanied by his military adjutant Major Julián Soley Conde, his secretary Benigno Rodríguez and the under-secretary of the Ministry of Propaganda, Manuel Sánchez Arcas. All three were members of the PCE. In addition, there was a small administrative staff of twelve. The building had been requisitioned some weeks earlier by the head of the SIM, Santiago Garcés. It had been chosen in part because it had the advantage of the nearby airstrip at Monóvar known as El Fondó. The headquarters at El Poblet was referred to in military code as 'Posición Yuste' and subsequently in most memoir literature simply as 'Elda'.[24] Negrín's decision to move to 'a place far from any major urban centre' was later criticized by Líster as 'the best way to give the conspirators a free hand and to choose to isolate himself from the people and the military forces'.[25] Uribe similarly complained later that El Poblet lacked the facilities necessary for a government to function properly. He claimed that the choice had been determined by the knowledge that 'there were two airfields nearby with planes ready to take off at short notice. In my view, this was no coincidence. It formed part of Negrín's plans in the light of how he expected his role as head of the Government to end.'[26]

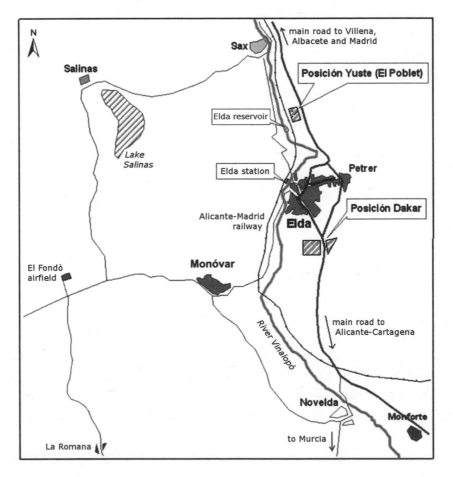

The retrospective comments by Líster and Uribe about the absurdity of the choice of Petrer for the Prime Minister's headquarters were at best disingenuous and at worst a way of throwing blame on Negrín for the later lack of resistance against Casado. They neatly ignored the fact that there was no government apparatus that could have functioned properly and that the Levante was a good place to try to create one. Madrid and Valencia were dangerously near battlefronts whereas Elda-Petrer was in a more central position within the remaining Republican territory. On the main road and rail links between Madrid and Alicante, it also had excellent communications with Valencia, Albacete, Murcia and Cartagena.[27] Similarly, later comments by other Communists about Negrín's alleged inactivity overlooked the exhausting and frenetic activity at El Poblet. For instance, Stanislav Vaupshasov, the senior Russian adviser to Domingo Ungría, commander of the XIV Guerrilla Army Corps created by Negrín in October 1937, wrote in similar terms to those expressed by Líster: 'Premier Negrín established his base in Elda but shied away from work. He had no desire to meet anyone, he did nothing. His depression played into the hands of the defeatists and conspirators.'[28]

Lieutenant Colonel Francisco Ciutat de Miguel, the operations chief of Menéndez's Army of the Levante, wrote in a later report to the PCE central committee of 'the inactivity of Negrín and therefore of the Government, of Negrín's irregular life and his inopportune frivolity'. Such comments to some extent reflect only total ignorance of the round-the-clock – and necessarily chaotic – activity carried out by Negrín, his endless meetings with military officers and politicians and his tireless efforts to maintain the international credibility of the Republic despite the sabotage of Azaña and others. In fact, what the Ciutat report makes clear is that when the Communists spoke of inactivity, they meant the failure to replace Casado.[29]

Moreover, on the basis of warnings from Edmundo Domínguez, José Rodríguez Vega, Cordón and others, Negrín knew, as indeed they did, of the scale of the conspiracy being hatched. Negrín's thinking in choosing El Poblet as a strategic point from which to conduct the resistance and, even more so, the future evacuation was confirmed in some notes jotted down after a conversation with Ramón González

Peña: 'A dignified end that would be approved by the UGT and the Socialist Party. To protect the evacuation. Analyse how best to carry out the evacuation. Dignified end means guaranteeing, in winding up the war, the departure of those politically significant figures who have no chance of surviving under the rebels. That there are no persecutions or reprisals.'[30] The Communist top brass was working on plans for a staged retreat to the ports of Alicante and Cartagena. Accordingly, it may be deduced that Negrín's decision was not just prudent but, at the time, clearly enjoyed the approval of the Communist Party. Indeed, the politburo would shortly follow and move from its headquarters in Murcia and take over a group of houses south of Elda, known by its military codename as 'Posición Dakar'.[31]

The anarchists also made bitter, and absurd, criticisms of the fact that, in El Poblet, Negrín had not created a full-scale government apparatus. In addition to this, in the particularly malicious account by García Pradas, who never visited El Poblet, the *guerrilleros* who guarded the house were described as bandits (*bandoleros*) protecting Negrín while he indulged himself in orgies with prostitutes while gorging on partridges, swilling good champagne and smoking Havana cigars.[32] The reality was that the house at El Poblet was guarded by a unit of one hundred hardened Communist guerrilla fighters from Ungría's XIV Guerrilla Army Corps. They were posted with machine guns among the trees that surrounded the house and there were guards in the house itself. The XIV Army Corps was advised by a number of officers of Soviet Military Intelligence (Glavnoe Razvedupravlenie – GRU), including Stanislav Vaupshasov.[33]

One of the visitors to Negrín's new headquarters was the UGT secretary general José Rodríguez Vega, whose account suggests that he arrived on 3 March. Far from interrupting an alcohol-fuelled orgy, he found the Prime Minister in conversation with a number of people whose role in the continuation of the war he deemed to be crucial. Among them were Juan Ignacio Mantecón of Izquierda Republicana, who had been Governor General of Aragón until its capture by Franco in the spring of 1938 and was about to be named commissar of the Army of the Levante; 'Augusto', a popular radio personality in Madrid; the quartermaster general Trifón Gómez; the commander of the Army of Andalusia, Domingo Moriones, and other senior officers. Vega Rodríguez informed Negrín of the meeting with Casado at which he had been surprised to see Melchor Rodríguez and of the proposal of the anarchists for the creation of a Junta de Defensa. Negrín replied that the government, by which he meant himself and Álvarez del Vayo, was engaged in efforts to secure the mediation of Britain and France for a peace settlement. Referring to the various anti-government initiatives reported by Rodríguez Vega, he said: 'If they are foolish, they will ruin everything.' In an emotionally charged voice, he added: 'There is no way that we can make a pact without an acceptance of the three points established by the Cortes in Figueras.'[34]

Earlier on 2 March, the same day that Casado had hoped to send a delegation to Burgos, at around 1.00 p.m., Negrín had held a meeting with Miaja, Matallana, Casado and Buiza and told them that on 6 March he would be broadcasting a speech whose theme would be that continued resistance was the only way in which a tolerable peace could be secured. Casado responded with a doom-laden and entirely fallacious claim that Franco was about to launch an irresistible assault on Madrid. Despite having assured Burgos that it was his intention to leave Spain, he declared in a faux-heroic tone, 'I will stay until the end in Madrid and I will die there.' He outlined his intention to prevent anyone, 'especially politicians', from leaving the capital. This was perhaps an unintended hint of his imminent intention to arrest the supporters of Negrín. The Prime Minister quickly pointed out that, while Casado could issue such orders to soldiers under his immediate command, politicians and other civilians were subject to the authority of the government. They went on to discuss the general situation, of which Casado gave the bleakest possible vision.

Buiza then inadvertently revealed what all four had been planning when he suggested that 'perhaps the military could do something by dealing directly with the military on the other side'. Negrín still did not fully suspect Miaja and Matallana but, after this meeting, he could have had no doubt that Buiza and Casado were not to be trusted. Accordingly, he told Casado that his appointment as head of the general staff would be announced the following day and, in brusque terms, he ordered Buiza not to take the fleet out to sea. In response to what he had learned in this meeting, Negrín now decided to control Buiza by replacing General Carlos Bernal in Cartagena with the Communist Lieutenant Colonel Francisco Galán Rodríguez.[35] Buiza's reaction to the meeting and to Negrín's orders was, on his return to Cartagena, to assemble the senior officers and commissars of the fleet. He announced that the ultimatum he had given Negrín at Los Llanos to make peace was running out. He went much further and revealed that senior army officers and prominent political figures were preparing to create a Consejo Nacional de Defensa to replace Negrín's government. As the first step in the plot, the fleet would go out to sea and then radio Negrín that he had twenty-four hours to make peace. To arrange this would take at least until 4 March.[36]

Even if Negrín had considered replacing Casado with Modesto, no such posting was ever made. Rather, it was the firmness of Negrín's stance with Buiza and Casado that, in the view of Zugazagoitia, precipitated the conspirators' decision to act. On 1 March, the promotion of Modesto to the rank of general had been announced. Later on the same day, at Posición Yuste, Modesto had suggested to Negrín that he give him command of the Army of the Centre. Negrín merely told him that he was thinking about it and would reach a decision in a few days.[37] The trigger for an already well-advanced plot was not, as Casado later claimed, any decision by Negrín to replace him with Modesto. The possible posting of Modesto to command the Army of the Centre was never announced or implemented. Nevertheless, it was later cited mendaciously by Casado as proof that Negrín and the Communists were planning a coup. The invention of a plan by the Communists to establish their dictatorship – without any suggestion by Casado as to their purpose in doing so – was merely a ploy to justify his own coup. In his three untrustworthy accounts, Casado claims that, after the meeting with Negrín on 2 March, he and Matallana went to Valencia to see Menéndez and Miaja. This is clearly inaccurate in so far as Miaja was already with them. In fact, his accounts had elements of surrealism. Having decided to proceed without delay to his coup against Negrín, his decision was confirmed by a minor miracle. On returning to his headquarters, 'that very night, as if raining down from heaven, I received Dr Negrín's complete plan to make the Communist coup d'état that he had planned' for 1 March. Unfortunately, Casado did not clarify the nature of this divine intervention. He went on to claim that, knowing that there would be opposition, Negrín's plan had been postponed until he could make the postings that would turn the army into a blind instrument in the hands of himself and the Communist Party.[38]

Meanwhile, despite fervent efforts by Negrín to persuade him to return to Spain, Azaña was adamant in his refusal.[39] On Sunday 25 February, knowing that recognition of Franco by Britain and France was imminent, Azaña had left the Republican Embassy in Paris and boarded a train for Collanges-sous-Salève near the Swiss border, where he had rented a house. Pascua was obliged to send a messenger after him with Negrín's most recent desperate telegram urging him to return to Spain.[40] Two days later when the recognition of Franco was formally announced, without bothering to inform Negrín of his intention Azaña sent a letter announcing his resignation from the presidency of the Republic to the President of the Cortes, Diego Martínez Barrio. This left the Republic without an internationally recognized figurehead.

Azaña's letter claimed that he had been motivated to leave Spain and work for peace because General Rojo had told him on 30 January that the war was lost. Now, he said, the recognition of the Burgos government by the Great Powers deprived him of the international juridical representation necessary to transmit to foreign governments 'not only that which is dictated by my conscience as a Spaniard but that which is also the profound wish of the immense majority of our people'. The disappearance of the apparatus of the state, of the parliament, of the executive bodies of the political parties left him unable to fulfil his presidential functions. 'Under these circumstances, it is impossible to retain, even in name, this office which I did not renounce on the day that I left Spain because I had hoped to see the time used to bring about peace.' Julián Zugazagoitia saw a photograph of Azaña taken at the press conference at which he announced his resignation and commented that he was beaming, clearly delighted to be able to return to his books.[41]

General Rojo, on the other hand, was outraged and sent a telegram to Martínez Barrio denouncing Azaña's 'lamentably erroneous remarks'.[42] He also wrote a furious letter to the French press denying that he could have made the remarks attributed to him by Azaña. Then he went to pay his respects to Diego Martínez Barrio, the acting President, who gave him yet another telegram from Negrín asking him to return to the centre-south zone. In his book, ¡Alerta los pueblos!, he stated that he told Martínez Barrio that this was the first formal order that he had received. In that version, he agreed and began to make preparations for his journey. Just as he was about to leave, he said, the Casado coup intervened. Nevertheless, according to his biographer, his willingness to return went a long way towards repairing the rift with Negrín.[43] In fact, several telegrams and the notarized statement drawn up for Negrín by Zugazagoitia and Rafael Méndez relating what had happened on 14 February undermined this statement. In a letter to Zugazagoitia, Pascua wrote of Rojo's 'outrageous mendacity', adding that in his book 'he tries to confuse, to blur, and to obscure what really happened with half-sentences, vague expressions and some obvious falsehoods stated even more brazenly. I get the impression that he is writing confident that no one will point out what really happened. If they did, the obvious implications would have serious consequences for his military reputation.'[44]

The twin blows of Anglo-French recognition of Franco and Azaña's resignation were utterly devastating to Negrín. It would be difficult not to see a degree of betrayal and mendacity in the bleak text of Azaña's letter. His declaration that the war was lost did nothing to induce Franco to contemplate a merciful generosity. It also completely undermined Negrín's efforts to play the card of resistance in order to press for reasonable terms of surrender. The stress that Azaña placed on the recognition of Franco by Britain and France deliberately disregarded the fact that the Republic had fought for thirty months while Franco was already effectively enjoying the tacit assistance given him by the farce of non-intervention. Azaña conveniently forgot that the Republic still enjoyed the recognition of the Soviet Union and Mexico as well as the United States and numerous smaller countries. It was not entirely true that the apparatus of the state, the parliament and the leadership of the various Republican parties had disappeared. Although many individuals within all of these had remained in France, the political parties still functioned and Negrín was working desperately to reconstruct the sinews of state. The letter also neatly ignored the fact that Azaña had effectively deserted the Republic when he crossed into France with no intention of returning to Spain.[45]

In fact, in strict legal terms, if it was to be valid Azaña's resignation had to be accepted by a higher authority, which effectively meant the Cortes of the Republic. Apart from the fact that many deputies elected in the last elections in 1936 were either in the Francoist zone or else had been murdered by one side or other during the war, there was a much greater difficulty. The French government had prohibited all political activities by the Spanish exiles, a prohibition now more strictly applied since the recognition of Franco. Accordingly, Martínez Barrio took the risky decision to call a clandestine meeting of the standing committee of the Cortes for 3 March in Paris. Negrín believed that the President of the Cortes would automatically become President of the Republic and was anxious for Martínez Barrio to accept the post so that he could come to Spain and reinforce his authority. Martínez Barrio, in contrast, was determined to respect the constitutional prerequisite of election by the Cortes or at least by its standing committee. He was anything but keen to accept the presidency without certain guarantees, and there was an interchange of telegrams with Negrín in the three days prior to the meeting.

On Friday 3 March, the sixteen members of the standing committee convened in an elegant Paris restaurant to discuss the consequences of Azaña's resignation. Once the resignation had been unanimously accepted, the deputies agreed to the elevation of Martínez Barrio to the interim presidency with the condition that he 'work exclusively, by way of humanitarian service, to bring to an end the present situation in Spain with the least damage and fewest sacrifices possible'. Fully aware of Azaña's reference to the lack of an apparatus of state, Martínez Barrio reluctantly agreed to accept the post. He told the assembled deputies that he would take on the responsibility if he had full authority to put an end to the war. For this, he needed the agreement of Negrín: 'I refuse to go to Spain to be a new banner of discord.' He then sent a telegram to Negrín stating that he would return to Spain only on the understanding that he was doing so in order to negotiate peace. He made it clear that, if this condition were not accepted, he would refuse to become interim President.[46]

The government received and debated Martínez Barrio's telegram. A unanimously agreed and positive reply to the conditions was sent to the effect that the government 'of course accepted the agreements [of the standing committee] regarding the need to proceed swiftly to make peace with the enemy as long as there were no persecutions or reprisals, which was in fact the policy that the government had been pursuing openly in recent times, to which it was committed and which it was ready to continue carrying out. However, at the same time, the government was at the disposal of the President of the Republic to facilitate any changes either of policy or of government that he thought appropriate.' Although Negrín had sent his agreement to Martínez Barrio's terms, the President of the Cortes never received it. As Negrín told the standing committee of the Cortes on 31 March, his reply was 'probably another of the telegrams that were sabotaged'.[47]

It was more than likely that the conspirators had used their control of the communications network to block transmission of the telegram. As Stepanov reported later, 'coded telegraphic communications for abroad passed through Casado's general staff ... until the very last moment, all telephonic communication from Elda to Valencia and then from Valencia to Madrid passed through the apparatus of Miaja and Matallana. Then, all telephonic communication between Valencia and Madrid and beyond passed through control of Casado's general staff.'[48] After all, Casado had already intercepted communications between Negrín and his Ambassador in London, Pablo de Azcárate.[49]

Now Casado almost certainly blocked transmission of Negrín's telegram accepting Martínez Barrio's determination to pursue a peace policy. That he should do so undermines his later claim that his coup was meant only to prevent unnecessary slaughter. If that was the case, he could have cooperated with Negrín. However, that would have undermined his relationship with the Francoist espionage service and the Fifth Column. Anticipating, naively, that his collaboration would bring him glory, he had revealed to the Fifth Column his intention 'to astound the world'. And later, in exile, he would refer to his actions as his attempt to be the 'redeemer'.[50] It is hardly surprising then that he blocked transmission of Martínez Barrio's telegram to Negrín and accelerated his own plans. His assertions to Cordón on 24 February and some days later to Hidalgo de Cisneros, chief of the air force, had shown that he harboured hopes of his military rank being recognized in Franco's post-war army. Accordingly, a peace treaty on Negrín's terms would deprive him of his place in the sun. As Negrín later alleged to the standing committee of the Cortes, it was when Casado realized that the Prime Minister planned to make peace that he accelerated his plans for a coup because he did not want to be left without a cause.[51]

The announcement of a new President who, in collaboration with the government, would seek a peace settlement conditional on a Francoist undertaking to refrain from reprisals would have undermined the entire raison d'être of Casado's coup. Negrín had already told Casado on 2 March that he would be making a speech about possible peace negotiations, for which it would be necessary to have continued resistance as a bargaining chip. That he was about to make a speech was announced in the press on the same day. As early as 25 February, his secretary Benigno Rodríguez had drafted a preliminary version which had been approved by Negrín's intimate friend and one-time medical student Blas Cabrera Sánchez. Moreover, it was widely known that Negrín was going to broadcast the speech at 10.00 p.m. on 6 March. It had been announced in the provinces, and loud-speakers were being set up at the front and throughout the rearguard. What is not known is what Negrín planned to say, but his agreeing to Martínez Barrio's conditions for accepting the presidency suggests that it would have been about resistance as the basis for possible negotiations.[52]

Meanwhile, Martínez Barrio waited in vain for the telegram that never arrived and, annoyed that Negrín had not made the necessary financial provisions for him to travel to Spain, he turned to General Rojo to make the arrangements. Rojo responded with a bleak outline of the difficulties. The Republican airline, Líneas Aéreas Postales de

Española, now functioned only within the central zone since any of its aircraft landing in France would be sequestrated. An Air France flight or a boat from Marseilles to Oran would still leave the problem of how to get to a Republican port other perhaps than on a French warship. Those difficulties, together with the fact that he had not received a reply from Negrín agreeing to the conditions outlined in his telegram, saw him declare to the standing committee of the Cortes that he could not accept nomination as President. In any event, Martínez Barrio would have been saved from having to make a difficult journey by news of Casado's coup.[53]

Azaña's resignation coming immediately after British and French recognition totally undermined Negrín's public rhetoric of resistance masking a private determination to secure the best conditions for an evacuation. Zugazagoitia wrote later:

> Resist? For what? It is the unanimous question. Not a single soldier believes in victory. The fall of Barcelona, the loss of Catalonia, with the international impact of the recognition of Franco by France and England, have destroyed the hopes of even the most deluded: the Communists. The troops on the front line feel discipline slipping and desertions increase alarmingly. Those who do not go over to the enemy leave the trenches and try to find their way home. In the cities, everyone sees the cloud of defeat and many, to avoid its consequences, seek contact with the enemy, eagerly hoping to be pardoned for their grievous fault. The air becomes putrid. Does Negrín perceive the new reality? Does anyone alert him to the seeds of decomposition? The people who surround the prime minister are, like him, committed to his resistance policy. They are Communists.[54]

Faced by the same circumstances, the CNT Regional Defence Committee set up some days earlier by Eduardo Val, Manuel Salgado, José García Pradas and Cipriano Mera had begun to make contact with other elements of the Popular Front, as well as with Casado. On the basis of a declaration drafted by García Pradas, and issued shortly after its formation, the objectives of the committee were not greatly different from those of Negrín. It proclaimed itself strong enough to make a reality of the slogan launched in mid-February by Negrín himself: 'Either we are all saved or else we all succumb to extermination and shame.' Its principal objective was 'to establish the political and military conditions that would allow us to be masters of our own fate against the enemy'. The anarchists were obsessed by fear of a preemptive coup by the Communists which would give them a monopoly of the means for evacuation and thus wanted to overthrow the Negrín government. Otherwise, their objective was to strengthen the Popular Front for a widely based resistance that would permit the negotiation of an honourable peace. It seems unlikely that they were aware of Casado's links with the Francoist Fifth Column.

Accordingly, the anarchist Defence Committee began to liaise with the leaders of other Popular Front organizations. At a meeting of the components of the Popular Front, the representatives of the CNT–FAI proposed that they take part in the creation of a 'Defence Junta or something along those lines' to replace Negrín's government. The proposal was defeated.[55] The liberal Republican parties were disgusted both with Azaña for resigning and with Martinez Barrio for prevaricating about replacing him. The Val–García Pradas–Mera committee contacted Hilario de la Cruz and Juan Gómez Egido, the president and secretary of the fiercely Caballerista Agrupación Socialista Madrileña. Through Wenceslao Carrillo and Besteiro, they were already apprised of Casado's intentions, if not his detailed plans, to overthrow Negrín. Already furious about Communist criticisms of Largo Caballero for his failure to return from France, they related scurrilous gossip about Negrín and Álvarez del Vayo and agreed unreservedly with the plans of the anarchist committee for an anti-Negrín movement.

The committee worked feverishly in a house in the calle Serrano that belonged to the Marqués de Luca de Tena, the owner of the monarchist daily *ABC*. According to García Pradas, 'Two or three times a day, Val and Salgado passed on our decisions to Casado, and during these meetings the tiniest details for the rising were ironed out. Segismundo – or Segis, as we called him – undertook liaison with those military personnel we felt were necessary. He was the most prestigious figure among them, by virtue of his professional gifts, his republican past, his subtle and far-sighted intelligence, and his opposition to any manoeuvres against the people and anti-fascist unity.' Among the reasons García Pradas gave for trusting Casado were his anti-monarchist activities before 1931, his military record and the fact that he was close to Largo Caballero.[56] It is reasonable to suppose that, both at the time and later, García Pradas was unaware of the promises made by Casado to the agents of Franco that he would prevent the escape of many leftists. There can be little doubt that he was not concerned about the fate of Communists, since his hatred for them was still palpable in a book that he published in 1974. At no point in later years did he seem to consider that his actions and those of the rest of the Consejo Nacional de Defensa were in any way responsible for the fate of the thousands of Republicans who were unable to escape.[57]

8

On the Eve of Catastrophe

Even as the British and French governments had come nearer to recognizing Franco, the situation faced by Negrín was deteriorating. The growing levels of defeatism and deafening rumours of a coup d'état being prepared by Casado fostered for those who had money a kind of eat-drink-and-be-merry, last-days-of-the-Roman-Empire atmosphere. Manuel Tagüeña and other officers recently returned from France were billeted in Madrid's Barrio de Salamanca either in the headquarters of Socorro Rojo or in those of the Quinto Regimiento on the other side of calle Lista on the corner with the elegant calle Velázquez. Líster went to the Hotel Palace to visit some of Negrín's ministers who were billeted there: 'In the bar, I was so sorry and sickened to find so many señoritos and upper-class girls and officers in flash uniforms that I had to leave.' Tagüeña recalled that:

> Madrid was awash with rumours and anxieties fomented by those who wanted to reach an agreement with the enemy in order to end the war. The most depressing thing about the situation was seeing the crowds that thronged the streets, cafés, cinemas and theatres, a strange mixture of people, among them lots of women and men in uniform. It was as if they were desperate to enjoy life before the catastrophe. There were no patrols to be seen and apart from ruined houses and the great holes in façades caused by enemy shelling, there was nothing to suggest a besieged city.

If what Líster, Tagüeña and Uribe wrote was true of the centre of Madrid, it had no equivalent in the working-class districts, where hunger and weariness jostled with fear of what would happen next.[1]

Uribe complained retrospectively that the majority of the ministers who returned from France did nothing: 'They didn't even bother to set up the service departments of their Ministries in order to pursue their basic functions. They were much more active in cabarets and suchlike places. In the hotel where they were all together, they spent hours making fun of each other regarding their real and imagined sexual conquests.' He was especially critical in this regard about the Minister of the Interior, Paulino Gómez Sáez, and the Minister of Justice, Ramón González Peña. What concerned Uribe most was that the conspirators were fully aware of the atmosphere in the Hotel Palace and the demoralization of the ministers and used their knowledge to denigrate the government and gain recruits to their cause.[2] Uribe's jaundiced account is far from presenting the entire picture. Needless to say, he did not explain how exactly he expected the ministers to create service departments. In contrast, Zugazagoitia explained the difficulties involved in being ministers without Ministries, functionaries or files: 'The existence of the Government is precarious. It lacks any administrative apparatus; it has no logistical support. The principal levers of power are not in the hands of the Ministers. They, in Madrid, send telegrams abroad, ordering the return to their responsibilities of civil servants who find it altogether more advantageous to remain in France. Accordingly, the Ministers have to adjust their activities to the limited possibilities available.'[3] Uribe forgot to mention that efforts were being made to set up Ministries in areas safer than Madrid, in the Levante.[4]

As both Tagüeña and Castro Delgado recalled, not long after their arrival in Madrid the Communist officers had been informed that a coup headed by Colonel Casado with the collusion of Besteiro was imminent. Tagüeña wrote:

The prime minister's skill inevitably ran aground on the rocks of the collapse of the will to resist provoked by a truly desperate situation. Nobody believed his promises of being able to secure the return to Spain of the equipment left in France. On the other hand, it was an illusion to think that Franco, with victory in his hands, would consider anything other than total capitulation. Negrín's efforts to negotiate an honourable peace were useless. By now, we could not even dream that resistance would enable us to gain time to wait for a favourable change in the international situation. But if the war was lost, and given that there was no hope of mercy from the enemy, we had to end it in the most dignified way with the salvation of the greatest number of at-risk people, as we had done in Catalonia.[5]

Negrín was forced to turn increasingly to committed Communist officers who had risen through the ranks of the militias because many of the career officers who had joined the party out of convenience now claimed that they could obey only the strictly military chain of command. For some time, Togliatti had been working to forestall a situation in which the Communists would find themselves in sterile isolation, the only ones committed to continued resistance.[6] A reconciliation between the PCE and Negrín saw Togliatti draft a series of proposals for stiffening the war effort and dealing with the rumoured coup by Casado. They had been presented to Negrín at some point on or around 21 February 1939. The core of these suggestions was for the fiercely loyal Modesto to replace Casado at the head of the Army of the Centre. Negrín thought that this might trigger the long-planned subversive action by Casado. Stanislav Vaupshasov, the senior Soviet guerrilla warfare adviser, later lamented that, when Negrín had been urged to remove 'the spineless, weak-willed Miaja and the highly suspect Casado', he had responded with delaying tactics and finally refused on the grounds that to do so would cause complications in the army and make it even more difficult to fight the enemy.[7]

In response to instructions from Togliatti, the PCE leadership had published a manifesto on 26 February which referred for the first time to the need to 'end the war'. It effectively reiterated the three requirements for peace made by Negrín to the Cortes in Figueras – national independence, freedom for Spaniards to decide on their political regime and, most crucially, a guarantee of no reprisals. It had actually been drafted four days previously and, according to Togliatti, had been 'personally corrected by Negrín'.[8]

Concerned about the possible consequences of making Modesto commander of the Army of the Centre, Negrín had begun to think instead in terms of replacing Casado with Lieutenant Colonel Emilio Bueno, commander of the second of Madrid's four army corps, a career officer with a PCE membership card. As the first step in the process, Casado was promoted to general on 25 February. Negrín informed him in the course of a long meeting the previous day.[9] Casado's reaction was one of slavish gratitude – which Zugazagoitia attributed to well-acted duplicity. His displeasure was confined to the plan to 'promote' him away from operational command. Bueno was ultimately loyal to Casado both as his senior officer and as a fellow freemason. Indeed, Bueno had been encouraging Casado to organize a coup and had even offered to withdraw troops from the front to support him. Now he informed Casado of Negrín's plans to kick him upstairs to be chief of staff. As Casado revealed to Domínguez, this merely increased his determination to overthrow Negrín.[10]

When ministers met Casado some days after his promotion, he was still wearing the uniform of a colonel. When asked why, he replied that his staff had not been able to get hold of the necessary gold thread to embroider his new general's stars. When he launched his coup, he told Negrín brusquely that he had refused, high-mindedly, to accept a promotion that Negrín had no right to offer. However, his previous complaints to Cordón about not being promoted and his post-war tendency to refer to himself as 'General Casado' suggest that he was rather pleased with the promotion. Indeed, two days earlier, in the presence of Hidalgo de Cisneros in Madrid, Casado had ordered his general's stars to be placed on his uniforms despite the fact that, because Azaña had resigned as President, the promotion had not been formally ratified – although it is possible that he did so in order not to alert Hidalgo de Cisneros to his disloyalty to Negrín. Manuel Tagüeña was told by a military tailor in the calle Arenal that Casado had had the general's stars embroidered on one of his uniforms.[11] Moreover, in the minutes of the Consejo Nacional de Defensa, he always referred to himself as 'General Casado'. He spoke of himself in the third person as 'General' in 1967, when writing to the Francoist historian Ricardo de la Cierva.[12]

On 27 February, Togliatti sent a message to Moscow reporting on the strong possibility of a military coup led by Casado and/or Matallana. He went on to ask: 'In such a case, do you consider that David [codename for the PCE] should seize all the levers of power and take full control of the war effort, with the consequent dangers of virtually total political isolation, with the possibilities of resistance seriously reduced and with the risk of losing both the leadership and the rank-and-file militants?' His own opinion was that the PCE should not do so. As he stated in his report of 21 May 1939, he advised the leadership against going down that road and not only to avoid the party being saddled with the responsibility of breaking up the Popular Front by force of arms. More importantly, he was convinced that defeat would be swift and inevitable because the masses, disorientated, desperate only for peace, would not have followed the PCE and even the military forces commanded by Communists would not have supported the party with the energy and determination necessary.[13]

In this depressing situation Negrín, briefly in Madrid on 27 February, called a meeting at the cabinet office (Palacio de la Presidencia) in La Castellana of the officers and commissars who had been with him in Catalonia. He thanked them warmly for returning but then, without leaving them any detailed instructions, left Madrid for Posición Yuste. He was followed by the bulk of the Communist leadership, except Pedro Checa. The two Comintern delegates Togliatti and his assistant Stoyan Minev ('Boris Stepanov') also left for the Levante, along with Modesto, Líster, Castro Delgado and other officers. As Tagüeña put it: 'Madrid was like a trap that everyone was trying to escape while the door was still ajar.' Those who remained were intensely aware of the hostility not only of the Fifth Column but also of the anarchists and erstwhile allies in the Socialist Party. Tagüeña told Domingo Girón, the organization secretary of the Madrid section of the PCE, that they should try to pre-empt the planned coup by arresting Casado. Tagüeña even drew up a rough plan for the occupation of the key buildings in Madrid and the arrest of the general staff of Casado's Army of the Centre. He had a misplaced optimism deriving from his knowledge that three of the four army corps under Casado were commanded by career officers who happened to be PCE members – the first by Luis Barceló Jover, the second by Colonel Bueno and the third by Antonio Ortega.[14] However, the views of other, more senior Communists were tempered by a sense of what a full-scale civil war within the Republican zone would mean. An internecine massacre would have done Franco's work for him and have undermined even further the chances of a mass evacuation.[15]

The depressive behaviour of Negrín, as commented on by Pedrero, Stepanov and Domínguez, and his failure to react decisively to knowledge of the machinations of Casado, Buiza and Mera lay behind a devastating judgement passed by Togliatti:

> In those months, he behaved like a man who was trying to bail out of a situation that he regarded as desperate but who did not want to be seen to betray either our party or his own past. If he let the traitors act, it was not just because of weakness or a mistaken political line but also because the coup d'état of the traitors offered him a possible way out that would leave him free of responsibility. At the same time, his disorderly life-style and fear played their part.[16]

In Madrid on 3 March, the Chilean diplomat Carlos Morla Lynch recorded in his diary rumours that Casado had rejected his promotion, had been sacked by Negrín and, with the help of Generals Matallana and Toribio Martínez Cabrera, was taking over Madrid in order to hand the city over to Franco. Such rumours could have emanated only from within Casado's own staff.[17] Martínez Cabrera, the Military Governor of Madrid, was closely involved in Casado's planning. Negrín was finally determined to respond to rumours about Casado's conspiratorial activities and was about to remove him from his active command. Casado seized the power vacuum constituted by Azaña's action to launch his coup in the late evening of Sunday 5 March, with substantial political and military support from both the CNT and sectors of the Socialist movement. Besteiro lent his immense prestige to the Consejo Nacional de Defensa formed by Casado in the hope of being able to seek an armistice. He did this despite having declared to the PSOE executive three months earlier that abandoning the Communists in order to facilitate peace talks with Franco would merely strengthen the Caudillo.[18] Casado was probably impelled to act by knowledge that the power vacuum was about to be filled by the acting President, Diego Martínez Barrio.[19]

As Negrín's friend, the American journalist Louis Fischer, wrote later, 'Negrín and del Vayo hoped, by holding out a little while longer, to extract a promise of mercy and clemency from Franco and to win time for the flight of those with a price on their heads.'[20] The idea of getting Franco to guarantee that there would be no reprisals against the defeated population was a vain one in the light of Franco's Law of Political Responsibilities, published on 13 February, under which supporters of the Republic were effectively guilty of the crime of military rebellion. In Franco's topsy turvy moral world, the 'guilty' included all those who had not supported the military coup of 1936. An earlier British diplomatic report in January had effectively endorsed Negrín's view, stating that massive reprisals could be averted only by 'a peace which was achieved without unconditional surrender or a fight to the finish.'[21]

Negrín was convinced that the struggle could have been maintained until either an adequate evacuation had taken place or the international situation changed in the Republic's favour. He wrote to Prieto on 23 June 1939: 'The measures taken – please note – even though it provoked the same incredulity as did my similar statement in April 1938, would have allowed us to go on fighting until now. To go on fighting because, even if we could not win, there was no alternative in order to save what could be saved or, at least, save our honour.'[22] Negrín had been accused by Prieto of having provoked 'the gigantic hecatomb' and 'the most disastrous end that our war could have had, an ending that those of us accused of being pessimists could never have imagined'. Prieto seems to have considered that a negotiated peace was possible and that Negrín's policy of resistance was what provoked the Francoist policy of revenge. If that was what he believed, it showed a culpable ignorance of both the chronology of and the reasons behind the Francoist repression. Negrín replied: 'We resisted and, by doing so, delayed the hecatomb by a year. Resist. Why? Well, quite simply because we knew what would happen if we capitulated. I amend your words: We knew that "the most disastrous end that our war could have had, would be an ending that those accused of being pessimists could never have imagined". How true! This is what the pessimists never wanted to see despite my insistent reiteration of the dangers.' With some bitterness, Negrín reflected on those who just wanted the war to be over: 'Without considering the millions of unfortunates who could not be saved! Without thinking of the tens of thousands for whom, even with all the wealth of Croesus, it would have been difficult to ensure a reasonable life in exile.'[23]

Prieto accused Negrín of being happy to see the coup because it exonerated him of blame. In similar vein, when asked by Castro Delgado if he had informed the party of the activities of Casado and Besteiro in Madrid, a Communist commissar in Casado's army, Daniel Ortega, replied: 'I have the impression that either they don't believe me or else they don't care if Casado and Besteiro organize a coup.' When Castro asked Miaja if it was true that he was in touch with the enemy, he just smiled.[24]

With rumours of the coup increasing, Líster was sent by Pedro Checa to Posición Yuste at the end of February. He had a revealing interview with Negrín shortly after his arrival. Negrín gave him a grim account of his meetings with the various military commanders in the Levante saying that 'they are all demoralized and the conspiracy is continuing'. Líster repeated the party line already communicated to Negrín by Togliatti that he should name trustworthy elements to various commands (by which he meant the Communist commanders who had still not been given postings after Catalonia – himself, Modesto, Tagüeña and others). Líster found Negrín noticeably demoralized:

This interview left me with a very different sensation from that produced in my previous conversations with Negrín. I departed convinced that he would make no fundamental change in the military commands, that what he wanted was to gain time and

see how events panned out. I immediately conveyed this opinion to the comrades of the politburo who had the same impression. Negrín's behaviour in those days was not what it had been
throughout the war and which had won the affection and respect
of the genuine fighters and millions of Spaniards. It was clear
that the conspiracies, the betrayals, the desertions and difficulties had ended up breaking the will to resist that Negrín had
shown throughout the war. And overcome by exhaustion and
demoralization, he lacked the necessary spirit to oppose the
conspiracies.[25]

In his later unpublished account, Uribe lamented: 'Between the
Negrín of March 1938 and after and the Negrín of the last period
there was an abyss. Previously he had demonstrated will-power and
confidence, he had sought our support and our opinions, now without actually breaking with us, he did not seek our support, he listened
to our proposals as if listening to the rain and during the whole time
that he was in the Republican zone he took no initiative that demonstrated the will to continue the struggle.'[26]

In fact, despite the impression taken away by Líster, on 3 March,
the official gazette of the Ministry of Defence published the series of
postings and promotions that Negrín had mentioned the previous
day to Casado, Miaja, Matallana and Buiza. They were largely what
the Communists had been pushing for – operational postings aimed
at securing safe evacuation. Tagüeña was made military commander
of Murcia; Etelvino Vega was made military governor of Alicante and
Francisco Galán of the naval base at Cartagena, the two ports most
crucial in Negrín's evacuation plans. Antonio Cordón and Juan
Modesto were promoted to general and Líster to full colonel. The
Group of Armies of the Centre was dissolved – which was logical
since it consisted of the entire land forces remaining to the Republic.
Negrín asserted his theoretical overall control as Minister of Defence
and Prime Minister. Miaja was removed from his position as
commander-in-chief of the armed forces of the Republic barely three
weeks after being appointed and 'promoted' away from operational
command to the empty position of inspector general of the army,

navy and air force. Matallana was promoted from the command of the army group of the centre-south zone which he had assumed on 8 February and appointed to replace Rojo as chief of the general staff. That he was given such a powerful position suggests that Negrín and Cordón remained unaware of his collusion in Casado's machinations and his links with Franco's headquarters.

The promotion of Matallana completely undermines Casado's contention that the postings were the basis of a Communist coup d'état. The two pro-Franco officers whom Matallana later claimed to have used to control Miaja, his second-in-command Lieutenant Colonel Antonio Garijo Hernández and the head of his own general staff, Lieutenant Colonel Félix Muedra Miñón, were posted to where it was believed they could not further Casado's plot. Garijo was sent to Miaja's staff and Muedra to an administrative post as head of organization in the barely functioning under-secretariat of defence recently established by Cordón in a college in Elda. Further indications that Negrín was far from trying to establish a Communist dictatorship can be deduced from his appointment of Juan Ignacio Mantecón to replace the Communist Francisco Ortega as commissar inspector of the Army of the Levante. Negrín made the appointment without consulting Jesús Hernández, whose title as commissar general of the Armies of the Centre was amended to that of inspector commissar general of the army.

Mantecón's main task was to ascertain the scale of support for Casado. He went about doing so by speaking excessively highly of Casado's military and personal qualities in order to tempt those who agreed to reveal their sympathies. His feigned enthusiasm provoked suspicion. However, he also told the Communist Lieutenant Colonel Francisco Ciutat, operations chief of the Army of the Levante, that 'Negrín had sent him to dismantle the excessive Communist apparatus that Ortega had established in the Commissariat of the Levante.' This suggests that Negrín had begun to take measures to reduce the influence of the Communists in the army that covered the area in which the planned evacuation was to take place. Certainly, although Negrín had accepted the PCE recommendation to send Galán to Cartagena, Etelvino Vega to Alicante and Tagüeña to Murcia, he rejected Communist Party recommendations to make Pedro Martínez Cartón Military Governor of Almería.[27]

These postings were later presented by Casado as part of Negrín's plan to turn the army into 'a blind instrument in his hands and those of the Communists' (the plan that had been revealed to him by divine agents). They were interpreted by the anarchists, and later by the Francoists, as proof that Negrín was the puppet of Moscow and about to stage a coup in the interests of the Communists.[28] In fact, they reflected rather the fact that the Communists were Negrín's only reliable allies in his strategy of preparing an evacuation behind a rhetoric of resistance. It made sense to put in place in the Levante energetic and determined officers capable of securing the necessary seaports and aerodromes. It was arguably too little too late. With Casado's plot nearing maturity, it was seen as a provocation. It was certainly not the Communist coup d'état denounced by García Pradas and others.[29] Moreover, the claim by Casado and the anarchists that it was the postings of 3 March that forced them to mount a coup is totally undermined by the fact that Casado had been planning his own coup over the previous months and that the anarchists had also been preparing to seize power for some weeks.

As Bolloten commented, 'coups are not generally heralded in official government journals'. Moreover, the appointments that were announced did not include ones that Casado falsely alleged had been made – Modesto as head of the Army of the Centre to replace Casado, Cordón as supreme commander of the army, navy and air force to replace Miaja, Líster as commander of the Army of the Levante to replace Leopoldo Menéndez, Tagüeña as commander of the Army of Andalusia to replace Domingo Moriones and Valentín González 'El Campesino' as commander of the Army of Extremadura to replace Antonio Escobar.[30] In any case, the publication of the postings in the Ministry gazette was not the trigger of any initiative by Casado. Earlier on 3 March, he had held a meeting with Cipriano Mera at which it appears that the final touches were put to the plan for the coup. It is worth noting that, in his brief reference to this, and in his patronizing praise of Mera's loyalty – 'a splendid officer' – Casado played down his own utter dependence on Mera's forces.[31]

On 3 March, Casado was still casting around anxiously for allies. He invited Hidalgo de Cisneros to a late lunch at Posición Jaca. His purpose was to persuade him that the only course possible was 'an honourable peace with Franco, in which there would be neither victors nor vanquished, a peace that would allow whoever wanted to leave Spain to do so'. Casado asserted that, in order to have the strong post-war army that he would need, Franco would be obliged to use Republican officers. When Hidalgo laughed at this ridiculous notion, Casado nervously exclaimed, 'Not only is what I am saying possible but I can assure you that the ranks of us career soldiers will be respected.'

When an incredulous Hidalgo asked who had given such guarantees, Casado replied solemnly that 'the British had arranged everything down to the last detail and that he had had several conversations with the British representative to whom Franco himself had given formal guarantees with only one condition: that we professional officers should remove Negrín's government and deal directly with Franco'. If Casado believed what he was saying, and was not merely lying in order to get Hidalgo aboard, it suggests a high degree of wishful thinking that casts a revealing light on his inflated perception of his relations with Franco. Hidalgo informed Negrín of this meeting but does not make it clear exactly when he did so.[32] If Casado was as sure of Franco's promises as he told Cordón and Hidalgo de Cisneros he was, it is odd that he fled Spain at the end of the war. In fact, as he had made clear to Centaño and Guitián, his intention was always to flee, albeit to do so bathed in the glory of having secured a bloodless end to the war. The implication is that he knew all along what the post-war Francoist repression would bring but clearly was not concerned about its effects on those that he regarded as Communists.

Regarding the postings announced on 3 March, Líster wrote: 'When I saw the *Diario Oficial*, I could not conceal my indignation since it was the barb that stupidly alerted the conspirators and put a weapon in their hands that was immediately exploited by Casado and company. They claimed that the promotions were proof that we Communists had returned from France in order to take over command and run the war as we pleased.' Líster's account was written when the PCE was attempting to throw blame on Negrín for permitting Casado's coup. Togliatti made a similar comment in his report of 21 May 1939 to Moscow. It is certainly the case that these appointments were interpreted by the conspirators as the Communist coup which Casado had claimed, both to his Fifth Column contacts and to the anarchists, was imminent. It goes without saying that the views of Líster and Uribe leave the Communist Party as the heroes of the hour, determined to fight on. However, as will be seen, the view of the Comintern advisers at the time was not unlike that of Negrín.[33]

After the promotions and postings had been announced, Casado spoke with Wenceslao Carrillo and they agreed that they constituted 'a real Communist coup d'état'. Writing later, Carrillo claimed hysterically that 'if the creation of the Consejo Nacional de Defensa had been delayed even by a few hours, Spain would have fallen under a Stalinist doctatorship'. The absurdity of this position rested in the fact that, even if the Communists planned to impose a dictatorship, something that was far from their intentions, the certainty of the conspirators that a Franco victory was imminent rendered it irrelevant. Neverthless, having convinced Wenceslao Carrillo that this was the case, Casado asked him to be one of the ministers of the proposed Consejo. Carrillo consulted with his fellow members of the Agrupación Socialista Madrileña who authorized him to accept and eagerly undertook to collaborate as much as possible with the Consejo Nacional de Defensa.[34] The Socialist Bruno Alonso, the commissar general of the fleet, wrote later of the postings announced by Negrín on 3 March: 'Everyone interpreted these appointments as a veritable coup d'état by which the Communist Party was taking control of all the levers of power'.[35] In retrospect, Líster suggested that 'perhaps the coup by Casado and company gave Negrín the pretext that he needed to abandon the battle-field with the dignity of a man unjustly attacked and the victim of betrayal'.

In the report by Trifón Gómez quoted by Prieto,

Negrín's government was walking over a huge store of dynamite. It just needed a spark to set off the explosion and it was provided by the unfortunate appointments of Communists to the following posts: Secretary General of the Ministry of Defence; Command of the naval base at Cartagena; the military governors of Albacete, Alicante and Murcia. If this wasn't enough, the Communist officers who had commanded the Armies of the East and of the Ebro in Catalonia were promoted, General Miaja was removed from his command and an attempt was made to remove Casado as Commander of the Army of the Centre, sending as his replacement a Communist recently promoted to general. Given the atmosphere, even if it was all done on purpose, it would have been impossible to bring together so well all the discontented elements to produce the coup.

Prieto's comment that Trifón Gómez was not part of the coup and remained in Paris as quartermaster general is disingenuous since Gómez was working in collaboration with Besteiro.[36] Moreover, neither Prieto's own views nor those of Trifón Gómez took into account the links of the Fifth Column with Casado and Besteiro.

The urgency behind Negrín's decision to make the postings of 3 March was certainly nothing to do with any desire to establish a Communist dictatorship and everything to do with securing the evacuation of those most at risk. It will be recalled that, some time after the Los Llanos meeting, Edmundo Domínguez had asked Santiago Garcés of the SIM to investigate the suspicious links between Casado and the military governors of Albacete and Murcia. Worrying as the military situation outlined on the previous day by Casado was, Negrín was about to be hit by another blow. On the morning of 4 March, he received, from the Paris Embassy, a distressing telegram from the Minister of Finance, Francisco Méndez Aspe. It made starkly clear the virtually insuperable logistical and financial obstacles in the way of supplying the centre-south zone. Moreover, Méndez Aspe asked Negrín to resolve a harsh dilemma. It was impossible, given the dwindling resources of the Republic, to pay for the necessities of both the centre-south zone and the refugee population.

New purchases having been suspended in recent weeks, existing stocks are now exhausted. I therefore request that you give me instructions. In the event of deciding on fresh acquisitions, indicate what type and what kind of goods should be bought. In addition to the cost of such purchases, money will have to be spent on shipping and insurance. It will take approximately a fortnight for delivery to Spanish ports of shipments of the new purchases. No need to tell you that to continue supplying the loyalist zone even for a short period will exhaust our economic resources and thus see the loss of the reserve funds that, in agreement with you, were set up to meet the present and future costs of the exile, which are extremely high. I wish I did not have to torment you with new problems, but I judge it to be crucial to have your decision on this which, whatever it is, will be dutifully implemented.[37]

It is more than likely that Méndez Aspe's telegram would have influenced the content of Negrín's proposed speech on resistance and peace negotiations. The cabinet was due to meet at El Poblet to discuss the text that he planned to broadcast on the morning of 6 March. Matallana, Miaja and Casado had been invited to the meeting at El Poblet but, despite Negrín's repeated efforts, only Matallana had appeared. In the evening of 3 March, Negrín had telephoned Casado and cordially invited him to the meeting. It appears that Casado accepted the invitation but immediately rang both Miaja and Matallana to check if they too had been invited. Allegedly, Miaja told him that, although he had been invited, he would not go since it 'smelled odd'. Casado decided not to go because, he claimed later, he was sure that it was a trap. Accordingly, at 10 p.m. on 3 March, Casado rang Posición Yuste to say that he would not attend because he was feeling unwell. Negrín replied that, to make the journey easier, he would send an aircraft to pick him up. Casado accepted but, when the plane arrived on the morning of 4 March, he instructed the pilot to return to Monóvar. Two hours later, Negrín rang him to ask why. Casado said that he had decided that the situation in Madrid did not permit his absence. Negrín replied that he really needed him to be present at the planned meeting and suggested that he come to Yuste with the various ministers for whom he was sending another aircraft. Casado said that that was fine and he would coordinate arrangements with them. At this point, he claimed in his memoirs, the head of his general staff came in with a copy of the issue of the Ministry of Defence gazette which contained the promotion of Modesto, and the postings of Galán, Etelvino Vega and Tagüeña. He then told the ministers that the situation in Madrid prevented his travelling with them. He put on such a convincing show of loyalty to Negrín that none of them suspected what he was planning.[38]

As well as the suspicious behaviour of Casado, one of the many other issues preoccupying Negrín was the fate of the naval base at Cartagena which was the key to his plans for an ordered evacuation. It was also crucial for the unloading of promised supplies from the Soviet Union recently negotiated by Hidalgo de Cisneros. As in many other cities in the Republican zone, there was deteriorating morale in Cartagena. Both food and raw materials for the naval arsenal and the factories were in ever shorter supply. In addition, the fleet faced constant air raids and also artillery bombardments from the Francoist fleet. Moreover, the top brass of the navy was riddled with secret supporters of Franco. General Carlos Bernal, the commander of the Cartagena naval base, hoping to be able to remain in Spain after the war, was amassing credit by appointing pro-Francoists to key positions in the base. Morale was plummeting as belief spread that the war was lost and that, since the resignation of Azaña and the recognition of Franco by the Great Powers, the government no longer had any legal existence. The government had received reports of the meeting at which Buiza had told his senior officers that the fleet had to leave in order to force the government to make peace. Locally, rumours of the imminent coup were deafening and the Fifth Column was acting ever more openly. Frenzied arrangements were being made behind the backs of the local Communists for the issuing of passports to facilitate evacuations. An office had been set up by José Samitiel, the head of civilian services, and Vicente Ramírez Togores, the head of the general staff of the naval base, where passports were issued with the signature of the French Consul.[39]

The PCE organization secretary, Pedro Checa, visited Cartagena on 3 March. He found the situation deeply alarming and reported that demoralization could be found equally among the officers, the crews and even the commissars. He discovered that three warships had already set out in the direction of Francoist-held ports, but the officers had been forced to return by the rank-and-file crews. In the case of the destroyer *Lepanto* and its captain, the Fifth Columnist Lieutenant Federico Vidal de Cubas, this was confirmed by Francoist sources. Checa tried to meet Bernal but he refused. Bruno Alonso did see him but only to repeat that the war was lost and resistance impossible.[40] Signs were mounting that something serious was afoot. On 2 March, a group of ministers, Segundo Blanco, Ramón González Peña, Tomás Bilbao, Antonio Velao and Paulino Gómez Sáez, visited Murcia with a view to establishing residences there. They were received by the Civil Governor Eustaquio Cañas, a Socialist and friend of Negrín. Not long after they had arrived, Cañas was puzzled to receive a telephone call from the Civil Governor of Madrid, José Gómez Osorio. Unknown to Cañas, Gómez Osorio was in cahoots with Casado. It quickly became apparent that Gómez Osorio had assumed that Cañas was in on the plot. To his colleague's puzzlement, Gómez Osorio asked him in a jaunty tone: 'Have that lot arrived yet? I mean the ministers. Try not to pay them too much attention and concentrate on what we are all interested in. Haven't you been told anything?' When Cañas expressed his puzzlement and asked what he was talking about, Gómez Osorio realized his mistake. He replied that it was just a joke and told him to look after the ministers.[41]

The Minister of the Interior, Paulino Gómez, had been instructed by Negrín to find out the extent of support enjoyed by Buiza for the threat made to Negrín at the meeting on 2 March with Casado, Miaja and Matallana. As will be recalled, shortly after that meeting, Buiza had returned to Cartagena and announced that, as part of the coup planned for 4 March, the fleet would put out to sea and demand that Negrín surrender his powers to a Junta Nacional which would then negotiate a 'dignified peace'. In his speech to the standing committee of the Cortes, Negrín said that, on 3 March, General Bernal had informed him that a plot was in train at the naval base in collusion with officers on board the warships. Essentially, Bernal revealed the plan hatched between Casado, Matallana, Miaja and Buiza to use the departure of the fleet to blackmail the government into resigning. Bernal, whom Negrín described as 'loyal but weak', had confessed that he lacked the will to oppose the plot.[42]

On the afternoon of 3 March, Eustaquio Cañas accompanied Paulino Gómez to Cartagena. The Minister was treated with considerable disrespect. First of all, as a joke, air-raid sirens were set off in order to give Gómez a fright. Neither Admiral Buiza nor Bruno Alonso deigned to come to the base to greet him. Both Carlos Bernal and the chief of his general staff, Vicente Ramírez, without any further niceties set about trying to convince him that all was lost and that the only possibility was surrender. In the early evening, Cañas and the Minister found Alonso in the luxuriously appointed cabin of the captain of the destroyer *Libertad*. Captain José Garcíá Barreiro spoke to the Minister in an insulting tone as he told him that the fleet could resist no more and that it was the duty of the government to make peace. Bruno Alonso's silence was taken as agreement. Shortly after the departure of Cañas and Paulino Gómez, García Barreiro joined Lieutenant Federico Vidal of the *Lepanto* and the two men tried to take their ships out to sea with the intention of going to the Francoist-held Balearics. Both were prevented by members of their crews loyal to the government.[43]

It was arranged that, the following day, the entire group of ministers would visit Cartagena. Cañas informed General Miaja who was present in Murcia. On the morning of 4 March, Miaja appeared at the offices of the Civil Governor and had a tense conversation with the ministers. When Cañas asked him in which car he would be going to Cartagena, Miaja replied that he had changed his mind and would not be going at all. Cañas said, 'Well, if I were a Minister and you refused to accompany me on an official visit, I would have you shot.' Miaja, expressing the same contempt for members of the government that he had already displayed when receiving Uribe clad only in pyjamas, retorted:'You might, but that lot wouldn't.'[44]

In fact, distrustful both of Bernal and of Buiza since the meeting at Los Llanos and in the face of ever more alarming evidence of subversion in the fleet, Negrín had already decided to send the Communist officer Lieutenant Colonel Francisco Galán to replace Bernal. Galán's brother Fermín was one of the emblematic heroes of the Republic, having been executed on 15 December 1930 for his part in the failed uprising at Jaca aimed at overthrowing the monarchy. Francisco Galán himself had been actively involved in the creation of the Quinto Regimiento which had formed the basis of the People's Army. Given his suspicions of the intentions of both Rear Admiral Buiza and Carlos Bernal, Negrín's decision to send Galán to Cartagena was perfectly understandable.[45] It would provoke some of the most decisive events of the war.

9

The Desertion of the Fleet

According to the anarchist José García Pradas, on or around 21 February 1939, Negrín ordered the Minister of the Interior Paulino Gómez to arrange for the printing of 60,000 passports. If that is true, it would have been a response to massive demand even though there could be no guarantee that those lucky enough to get their hands on a passport would be able to use it to leave Spain. On 28 February, the press carried a government statement about passports. In response to doubts arising from a profusion of passports being issued by different authorities, it stated that they would be valid for women of any age and for men not of military age – that is, not between seventeen and fifty-five. For men of military age, it was necessary also to have a safe-conduct issued by the Ministry of Defence.[1] What García Pradas cited as somehow damaging to the credibility of Negrín ignored the heaviness of the demand for passports coming from all sections of the Popular Front, Socialists, Republican parties and the CNT, who were all drawing up lists of their members for their evacuation. It was symptomatic of the degree of panic that these organizations had already started to burn their archives and that, in some cases, the more senior or wealthier elements were already heading for the port of Alicante. The Communists complained that prominent Socialists had fled to Oran with suitcases full of saffron, probably the lightest and most valuable commodity that they could take for their support in exile. There were instances of political, trade union and even military figures fleeing from Alicante, Almería and Valencia. Conflict was provoked with the Communists when they pointed out that the compilation of lists of those to be given passports for their evacuation would cause demoralization in both the military and the civilian populations.[2]

The key to any evacuation was Cartagena. Negrín had substantial concerns about the strength of pro-Francoist elements within the city. Indeed, he received a report on 15 February from the Servicio de Inteligencia Militar with details of the Fifth Column strength in the armed forces in Valencia, Orihuela, Murcia and Cartagena.[3] He had sent three ministers, Ramón González Peña, Tomás Bilbao and Segundo Blanco, to investigate the situation in Cartagena. They arrived on 17 February and appeared to be unaware of the threats made by Admiral Buiza at Los Llanos the previous day. Even after hearing the already familiar complaints of Buiza and the commissar general Bruno Alonso about the effect on morale of the Francoist bombing raids, the ministers' optimistic report about the two suggested that Buiza and Bruno Alonso were fully prepared to follow the orders of the government. However, they recommended that urgent measures be taken to strengthen the security forces in the light of the scale of defeatism and subversion there, particularly within the senior military personnel. Among other disturbing factors was the presence in Cartagena of 2,000 ex-Civil Guards whose behaviour was regarded as suspicious. The most disheartening part of their report concerned General Carlos Bernal, the commander of the naval base: 'we consider that his lack of character, of activity and of enthusiasm is a serious problem that needs urgent resolution'. The report also contained complaints about the arbitrary and authoritarian behaviour of Lieutenant-Colonel Ricardo Burillo Stohle of the Assault Guards, the elite Republican police force founded in 1932 as a counterweight to the traditionally right-wing Civil Guard. Burillo had been made head of public order for the centre-south zone by Miaja shortly before the return of the government from France. The ministers declared that it was a matter of the greatest urgency for him to be dismissed as soon as possible.[4]

The threat to remove the fleet from Cartagena made at Los Llanos by Buiza was a crucial element of Casado's planned coup. For that reason, Negrín had decided to send Lieutenant Colonel Francisco Galán to replace General Carlos Bernal as commander of the naval base. Galán received his orders from Negrín on the morning of Saturday 4 March. Not long after the appointment was announced, naval Lieutenant Antonio Ruiz, the under-secretary of the navy and previous commander of the base, went to Posición Yuste to try to persuade Negrín that the appointment would be a disaster. Given the pressure of work in El Poblet, he had to wait some hours before Negrín could see him. His arguments about the likely hostility of the senior naval staff in Cartagena were brushed aside by Negrín, who assured him that he had every faith in Galán's 'deft touch as a negotiator'. The Prime Minister told him that he should go to his house in the sierra at San Javier and not worry about the situation in Cartagena. Ruiz would be called if necessary.[5]

Ruiz's concerns reflected his awareness that the announcement of Galán's appointment in the local press in Cartagena had provoked a furore in the shore base and on board the ships.[6] Bernal himself, however, took the news of Galán's imminent arrival with great equanimity.[7] En route to Cartagena, Galán had gone to Posición Yuste to get detailed instructions from Cordón and Negrín. He was told that the coup – that is to say the plan for Buiza to take the fleet out to sea – was scheduled for 11.00 p.m. Accordingly, the 206th Brigada Mixta under Artemio Precioso, stationed at Buñol in the province of Valencia, would be sent to back him up. The idea was that they would enter Cartagena together at around 7.00 p.m. Galán stated years later that Negrín's categorical orders were 'No bloodshed! Negotiate, negotiate, and negotiate! We have virtually no rearguard left and the Republican fleet is crucial!' Galán, accompanied by the commissar general, Bibiano Osorio Tafall, set off for Cartagena. They stopped briefly in Murcia to talk to the PCE organization secretary, Pedro Checa, who reiterated to Galán that to avert the fleet's rebellion against the government planned for the night of 4 or early morning of 5 March, he should enter the town as soon as possible. Checa put Galán in contact with the commander of the tank base at Archena. Galán ordered a detachment of armoured vehicles to be outside Cartagena at 9.00 p.m. where they would find him waiting with the 206th Brigade.[8]

Having read in the local press that Galán was en route, Rear Admiral Buiza held a meeting in mid-afternoon at his headquarters on board the flagship *Miguel de Cervantes* with Bruno Alonso and a group of senior officers and commissars to decide their response. On being told that a Communist coup was imminent, the officers argued in rather hysterical fashion that, if Galán took over, 'the Communists would murder their enemies and prevent the war ending in such a way as to permit the most involved and responsible people being able to leave the central zone'. Either exhausted or just weak-willed, Bernal vacillated, saying publicly that he would not hand over to Galán, although he told Alonso that he would not oppose Negrín's orders. Buiza's officers agreed that Galán should be arrested if he took action deemed to be threatening to the fleet – which could only be interpreted by them as action aimed at preventing Buiza pursuing Casado's agenda. Throughout the day, ever more nervous delegations from the CNT and Socialist organizations visited Buiza's headquarters on the *Miguel de Cervantes* concerned by proliferating rumours that the fleet was about to put out to sea and might not return.[9]

Since the announced arrival of Galán had a considerable bearing on the plans for the fleet to depart at 11.00 p.m. as the first act of the coup, Buiza had dispatched a telegram to Matallana asking for instructions. After consulting with Casado, Matallana sent a reply to Buiza to the effect that, because of some last-minute difficulties and the need to seek more support within the army, the coup had to be delayed and therefore he was free to act as he thought best regarding the arrival of Galan. This was probably a reference to the same difficulties with politicians and officers that had led to Casado failing to send the promised peace delegation to Burgos two days earlier. Although he could rely on the anarchists, he could not count fully on the Socialists. Nonetheless, given that Casado's plans were well advanced and had widespread support among non-Communist officers, Matallana's telegram can be seen as simply giving Buiza the freedom to take the fleet out of Cartagena only in the context of an extremely short delay in the launching of the wider coup. This was confirmed by a later message from Matallana that reached Buiza at 11.40 p.m. informing him that the coup had been postponed until Monday 6 March.[10]

When Galán reached Cartagena at around 8.30 p.m., the 206th Brigade under the command of Artemio Precioso and the detachment of armoured cars from Archena had not arrived. Precioso himself had already reached the city having come on ahead to check on the logistics of his unit's proposed stay. Osorio Tafall had gone into Cartagena earlier and spoken to Buiza and Alonso. It seems to have been a bitterly heated encounter with Alonso snapping at Osorio that he and Buiza recognized neither his authority as commissar general of all the armed forces nor that of Negrín as head of the government. They told him that if Galán arrived with troops, they would take the fleet out to sea – which was, of course, their plan anyway. It was simply a ploy to deter Galán and stop him interfering with their plans. After this tense meeting, Osorio now met Galán on the outskirts of the city and urged him not to wait for Precioso and the tanks but to go the naval base without them. Osorio then went on to El Poblet to warn Negrín that the situation in Cartagena was increasingly dangerous.[11]

Accordingly, mindful of Negrín's orders to avoid bloodshed, Galán ordered Precioso to halt his unit outside the city at the village of Los Dolores. Galán went into Cartagena alone where Bernal, to the astonishment of his fellow officers, handed over command to him without objection. Before leaving the city, Bernal invited Galán and Precioso to dinner. In conversation with other officers, it was clear to Galán that they had been told that he had been sent to initiate a Communist coup. He managed to convince them that this was not the case and heard Vicente Ramírez telling other officers on the telephone, 'It is not what they told us.' At 11.40 p.m., Buiza received Matallana's message from Valencia stating that the coup had been postponed until Monday 6 March. In response, Buiza put on hold the plans to take the fleet out to sea. In the meantime, while Galán was still in conversation with officers of the base, minutes before midnight more anti-Negrín elements, too impatient to wait until Monday, took over part of the city.

They were led at the naval base by the head of the naval general staff, Captain Fernando Oliva Llamusí, and at the coastal battery by Lieutenant Colonel Gerardo Armentia of the artillery. Oliva, whose brother had been assassinated early in the war, was fiercely opposed to Negrín. Casado later claimed implausibly that Oliva's action was a coincidence, but Negrín and others were convinced that this action was part of the plans for the coup. Shortly afterwards, Galán and Ramírez were arrested by Oliva's officers who, at the very least, held views similar to those of Casado. Precioso was also detained but managed to escape. When Galán tried to telephone Posición Yuste, Oliva had him violently restrained. To his protests, Oliva replied that 'orders had been given and there was no turning back'. Galán claimed that these 'orders' emanated from the meeting held by Buiza earlier that evening at which it had been agreed that he should be arrested to stop him taking over the base. He was convinced that this had been done in collusion with Casado and was to be the first step in the coup. The fact that, in the city, Oliva's men justified their action with the slogan 'Por España y por la paz' certainly suggests that Casado had had a hand in it.[12]

If Oliva was part of the planned Casadista coup, he had jumped the gun and precipitated something altogether more pro-Francoist. To the embarrassment of both Oliva and Armentia, their action was seconded by a group of secret Nationalist sympathizers, retired rightists and local Falangists who were part of a Fifth Column operation called 'Socorro Blanco' (White Aid). They were led by a swashbuckling artillery sergeant, Calixto Molina, an eccentric figure straight out of a Viennese operetta. His men released hundreds of right-wing prisoners, among them thirty officers who had been sentenced or were awaiting trial for anti-government subversion. Ramírez said to Galán: 'This is not what we agreed. The idea was not to launch a fascist initiative; we were fighting for peace and for Spain and not for Franco.'[13] Sporadic three-way fighting broke out across the city between Galán's supporters, the pro-Casado anti-Communist Republican officers and the openly pro-Francoists. This development was clearly not part of what Buiza, Matallana, Casado and Miaja had planned. On discovering the scale of the Francoist uprising, Buiza was outraged. He telephoned Oliva and threatened to open fire on the base with his ship's heavy guns if Galán was not released. Accordingly, Oliva, in the light of the Fifth Column rebellion which had not been part of his original calculations, decided that he needed to reach an agreement with Galán.

Buiza's threat to fire on the base was his only action in favour of Galán. He refused to send any forces to help him. Had Buiza done so, he might well have been able to quash the Francoist rising before it gathered steam. Galán was left besieged by the Francoists. Concerned that, in the chaos, the crucial action of the fleet in the planned coup would be thwarted, Colonel Armentia threatened to turn his guns on the fleet if it did not leave. Buiza did not take much persuading, since he was already convinced that the local crisis in Cartagena as well as the wider situation in the centre-south zone required the implementation of what had been agreed with Casado and Matallana. The senior officers in Buiza's staff were also putting pressure on him to do this. The deal with Armentia was 'to raise anchors, go out to sea and radio the Government to hand over power to the military authorities to achieve peace and to do so if the rebel forces [in Cartagena] agreed to desist from their subversion and re-establish normality.' Armentia ordered his gunners to stand down. At 2.00 a.m. on 5 March, Buiza ordered that the fleet make preparations to sail. The lengthy process of heating the engine boilers began and family members of the crew appeared on the dockside with suitcases and bundles of possessions. However, when Armentia realized that there had been a Fifth Columnist take-over in the city, his reaction was similar to that of Oliva and he came to the base to negotiate with Galán. With his proven diplomatic skills, Galán persuaded Armentia that he had triggered something far beyond his original intentions. He confessed to Galán that he had joined the rebellion in order to see Negrín overthrown, not to instigate a Francoist uprising: 'he was overtaken by events'. At the artillery base, now in the hands of the pro-Francoists, Armentia handed over command to the retired right-wing General Rafael Barrionuevo.[14] According to Galán, in an interview published in 1971, Armentia later committed suicide. Other sources suggest that it is not known if he killed himself or died in the fighting when the forces sent by Negrín reached Cartagena.[15]

With Barrionuevo's approval, the Fifth Columnists seized control of the local radio station, Radio Flota Republicana. At around 9.00 a.m. on 5 March, the premature 'news' was broadcast that the city was in Francoist hands: 'Attention. The Nationalist fleet here. Cartagena has been liberated by the Nationalist Army which was hitherto restrained. Since last night, 4 March, Cartagena has been incorporated into liberated Spain.' This was followed thirty minutes later by another broadcast: 'Cartagena surrendered without opposition from land or sea forces. Reinforcements awaited. Franco, Franco, Franco, Arriba España.'[16]

A longer version was telegraphed to Francoist naval headquarters in Cadiz:

Cartagena has been conquered for Spain and the nationalist cause. The civilian population supports the movement with enthusiasm and no sea, land or air force offers resistance. On the contrary, they all join the movement to save Spain. The political prisoners have been freed. Reinforcements and the support of the nationalist army are urgently awaited. The ships can dock with total confidence in this port. The coastal artillery will protect the landing for greater security.[17]

As part of his efforts to resolve the situation in Cartagena, Negrín had spoken on the telephone with Matallana. He remained, of course, totally unaware of Matallana's collusion with Casado and his message to Buiza about the coup being postponed until Monday 6 March. He told him about Galán's situation and that communication with the base was difficult. Apparently, radio reception was so bad that most of the time Negrín had not been able to tell if he was actually speaking to Galán. Now, he told Matallana that he had ordered Galán or whoever it was that he had spoken to, perhaps Ramírez, to put down the revolt in Cartagena. 'I told him to inform the Admiral of the Fleet and the rebels that, at a moment when a million soldiers and civilians are carrying on the war effort and have put their trust and hopes in the fleet, their attitude is prejudicial and undermines the Government's efforts to achieve a peace without reprisals and an evacuation. They are doing so just when there are hopes of achieving this and if everyone pursues their own policy, it could provoke a catastrophe.'

Negrín told Matallana that he was sending an aircraft to bring him to El Poblet. Matallana, manifesting loyalty and concern, replied that he was prepared, if necessary, to go to Cartagena himself: 'I am ready, if you think it would be useful, to go to Cartagena because this has to be stopped peacefully, stopped peacefully if it is humanly possible.' It was left that they would talk more when Matallana reached El Poblet, but Negrín reiterated his opinion that 'It is crucial to seek at all costs a peaceful solution to this business given that it could be the spark that sets off even more serious events.' They talked about the forces to be sent and Matallana recommended that they be put under the command of 'someone energetic but very prudent'. Negrín told him that he had issued instructions for Antonio Ruiz to go to Cartagena.[18] Some hours later, Matallana telephoned Yuste and gave his excuses for not yet having left his headquarters. He said he was waiting for Casado and Miaja with whom he hoped to travel on to El Poblet. It is likely that this was merely a device to gain time while he waited to see how things developed in Cartagena. If he genuinely expected Casado, he would clearly have wanted to be able to consult with him in private before leaving for Negrín's headquarters. However, as Matallana must have known, Casado, of course, had no intention of going anywhere near Posición Yuste. Matallana arrived shortly afterwards at El Poblet ostensibly to help with efforts to resolve the situation.[19]

Galán meanwhile managed to make contact with the Civil Governor of Murcia, Eustaquio Cañas, who had been sporadically following events through his own contacts. Now able to inform Negrín about the latest developments in Cartagena, Cañas reached El Poblet shortly before 9.00 on the morning of 5 March. Negrín, visibly annoyed about what was happening in Cartagena, nevertheless calmly took control of the situation. He appointed Lieutenant Colonel Joaquín Rodríguez as overall commander of loyal units waiting outside Cartagena, Artemio Precioso's brigade, the armoured cars from Archena and a company of Assault Guards. Within half an hour, Galán had an interchange of teletypes with Negrín who asked him to give him a fuller account of the situation. He responded: 'The Artillery Regiment has rebelled, its colonel overwhelmed by a series of protests under the slogan of "peace and Spain". The fleet has made a pact with the Artillery Regiment on the following conditions: raise anchors, go out to sea, radio the government to hand over power to the military authorities to seek peace in return for the rebels laying down their arms and re-establishing normality. I beg the Minister to forgive me, I must go, but first I just need him to give orders for forces to be sent.' Negrín asked where the forces originally sent with Galán were and to whom they should now be sent. Galán explained that he had been advised by Osorio Tafall to enter the city without the 206th Brigade and had thus been unable to prevent the rebellion of the artillery. All that he knew was that the forces that had been meant to accompany him were somewhere in Murcia and thus relatively easy to locate. Meanwhile, all he could do was wait on events.

Negrín then reiterated what he had said to Galán the day before:

I consider any violence to be out of the question. It is necessary to convince the officers and others that, just at the moment when a satisfactory peace is on the horizon, their stance is undermining the efforts of the government. The fleet and the naval base are a reason for both soldiers and factory workers who long for peace without extortions or reprisals to feel confident that there can be evacuation for those who want it. This cannot be achieved if everyone pulls in a different direction. Inform the head of the fleet [Rear Admiral Buiza] and the commissar [Alonso] of this and let me know how I can speak with him [Buiza].

Galán went to telephone Buiza and read him the message. While he was away, Ramírez joined the conversation on the teletype and appealed for Negrín to agree to the request from the fleet. This provoked the suspicion in El Poblet that Galán had not actually been present during the interchange, and perhaps was under arrest, and that the entire conversation might have been fabricated. Accordingly, Osorio Tafall, pretending to be Negrín, then asked questions about his meeting the previous evening with Galán to which only Galán could know the answers. When the questions were answered correctly by Galán, who had returned to the teletype machine, Osorio revealed his identity. Galán responded by joking about the subterfuge, saying

'Gallego as always' (*siempre gallego*) – a reference to the reputation for caution of the inhabitants of Galicia.[20]

Galán had offered to renounce command of the base in the hope of taking some tension out of the situation. As the telephone conversation with Matallana had revealed, in the same spirit Negrín had decided that it would be prudent to send Antonio Ruiz to replace Galán. Ruiz was in his bed when the order to go to Cartagena arrived. It is not clear if Negrín knew that Ruiz was already party to the Casado conspiracy. At around 11.00 a.m. on 5 March, while Ruiz was en route to Cartagena, Osorio Tafall, who was with Negrín in El Poblet, managed to get through to Galán once more. Reporting that the situation was getting worse, Galán expressed his anxiety that Artemio Precioso's forces should get to Cartagena as soon as possible. Shortly afterwards, an extremely nervous Ruiz arrived.[21] Around midday, the Falangists in the radio station broadcast an instruction to all civilian Francoists in possession of weapons and who wished to join 'the victorious movement of Nationalist Spain' to go to the Plaza de San Francisco. All pro-Francoist military personnel were given orders detailing which bases they should report to for duty. To boost morale and to prepare a welcome for the expected Francoist reinforcements, an instruction was broadcast to the effect that all those in possession of a Nationalist red-and-yellow flag should fly it on their buildings while all others were to fly a white flag.

This was followed by an ultimatum to the fleet which was issued twice between 11.30 and midday: 'Attention all units of the red navy, either the fleet immediately leaves the port of Cartagena within a non-negotiable fifteen minutes or it will be subject to an artillery bombardment from the coastal batteries.' In fact, given the angles involved, the chances that the Francoists could bombard with accuracy were minimal. Shortly afterwards, the rebel elements received confirmation that their pleas for help were under consideration in Burgos. Republican land forces were meanwhile advancing on the base.[22]

In response to the earlier broadcast by the Falangists, the port was being bombed by Francoist aircraft. In the first of a series of errors provoked by the shambolic situation, the rebels who had control of the anti-aircraft batteries had opened fire on the planes believing them to be Republican. Another broadcast called on Francoist naval headquarters to send ships with reinforcements. Backed by Ramírez, Captain García Barreiro and others, Ruiz requested that Barrionuevo allow more time for the fleet to leave. Barrionuevo reluctantly agreed. Privy to Casado's plans, Ruiz presumably could see no immediate problem in the departure of the ships. He and Galán went down to the docks and were standing alongside the battle cruiser *Miguel de Cervantes*. In the light of the aircraft attacks and the threatened artillery bombardment, Ruiz said simply: 'We can't do anything here. I'm going on board.' At approximately midday, with the fleet vulnerable in the harbour, under the shore batteries, Buiza made the decision to take his ships out to sea. Left standing alone on the dockside and likely to be captured by the Francoist rebels, Galán heard Buiza shout down to him: 'Galán, come aboard.' This he did, and was received cordially by both Buiza and Bruno Alonso. In contrast, José Núñez Rodríguez, chief of the general staff of the fleet, said to him with some hostility, 'You are only a passenger here,' to which Galán replied, 'Yes, but a passenger with the rank of colonel of the Republican army.' At around 12.30 p.m., as the warships were preparing to cast off, 600 civilian refugees, men, women and children, embarked along with the most at-risk military and political personnel, except, of course, for Communists. The largely left-wing crew were not consulted about the decision to leave. Known Communist militants among the crew were arrested. At nightfall, Galán realized that the fleet had not just left port but was moving away from Spain full steam ahead. When he demanded that Buiza tell him what was going on, one of Buiza's officers threatened to have him thrown overboard.[23]

The consequences of Buiza's decision could hardly have been more dramatic. They were certainly not the objective of the Casado–Matallana–Buiza plot, but it played perfectly into the hands of the Francoists. Lieutenant Federico Vidal de Cubas, the captain of the destroyer *Lepanto*, who had tried to flee some days earlier but been restrained by pro-Negrín elements of his crew, stated later that 'We had received instructions from Franco – make the fleet leave. Once it had left, even if the onshore rising were crushed, it didn't matter to

El Poblet or 'Posición Yuste', the house just north of Elda where Negrín set up his last headquarters in February 1939.

One of the houses at 'Posición Dakar', south of Elda, where the leadership of the Communist Party established its base in February 1939.

General Vicente Rojo Lluch, Chief of Staff of the Republican Army.

Late 1938, Juan Negrín in conversation with Colonel Antonio Cordón García, the Undersecretary of the Ministry of Defence.

Negrín addresses the League of Nations in Geneva on 14 September 1937.

Negrín, Manuel Azaña and Vicente Rojo in Barcelona in the early summer of 1937.

Negrín, Azaña, General José Miaja and Valentín González 'El Campesino' inspect troops in Alcalá de Henares, November 1937.

Negrín and Colonel Enrique Líster (facing Negrín) at the Ebro front.

After the fall of Catalonia, Spanish refugees flood across the frontier into France at Le Perthus.

Segismundo Casado, his partner Norah Purcell and their daughter María Cristina in London in 1946.

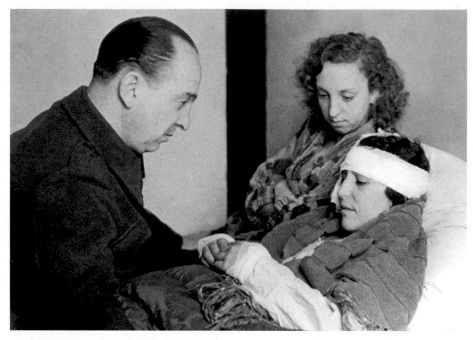

The anarchist Melchor Rodríguez, 'the Red Angel', with his daughter and his wife who was injured in a Francoist bombing raid.

Eduardo Val Bescós, organiser of the anarchist 'checas' in Madrid and a member of Casado's National Defence Junta.

General Miaja with Colonel Casado in Madrid.

The radio broadcasts announcing the creation of the Casado Junta: (*left*) Casado watches Julián Besteiro speaking and (*right*) Casado reads his own speech.

The S.S. *Stanbrook* was the last ship to leave Alicante. The captain, Archibald Dixon, managed to cram 2,638 refugees aboard.

On 25 May 1939, the S.S. *Sinaia* left Sète near Montpellier with 1,600 Spanish refugees. When it landed at the port of Veracruz in Mexico, the side of the ship carried a huge banner that read 'Negrín was right'.

us. We have achieved what we set out to do – to leave the Republic without the last bastion of resistance.'[24] Álvarez del Vayo wrote later that, when the ministers who were assembled in Negrín's headquarters at El Poblet heard that the fleet had 'set off for an unknown destination', they were uneasy: 'We little thought, however, that it had gone never to return, thus depriving the central zone of an important means of resistance, and a valuable aid if we should be faced with the unfortunate necessity of evacuating the population.'[25]

Barrionuevo was not pleased to see the departure of the Republican navy. His preference would have been to destroy it with artillery fire. He revealed this when he was arrested after Republican forces had retaken Cartagena. He told Eustaquio Cañas who interrogated him: 'I am ashamed to be a soldier and a Spaniard anything like them. They are just cowards. Ruiz, Ramírez, García Barreiro and the others begged me with tears in their eyes to let the fleet leave without firing on it from the shore batteries. They gave me their word of honour that they were going to surrender in Palma de Mallorca. Disgusted by their lack of guts, I told them to leave me in peace and I informed Franco of their intentions.'[26] He had indeed radioed Franco's headquarters twice in quick succession around 2.00 p.m. to announce that he had taken command of the city and that the fleet had left and to request that Nationalist aircraft and ships be sent. In fact, already at 11.00 that same morning, aware the Republicans were trying to retake the city, Franco had ordered troopships to Cartagena. By the time they arrived it would be too late.[27]

Meanwhile, after a night spent trying to locate them, Precioso had finally linked up with the 206th Brigade and the armoured cars from Archena and set up camp outside the city. Around mid-morning, Cañas, Lieutenant Colonel Rodríguez, Enrique Líster and Osorio Tafall had set off for Murcia and from there to Cartagena. The combined forces arrived on the outskirts just in time to see the fleet sailing out.[28] By 8.00 p.m., these forces had control of much of the city and most of the coastal batteries. Casado phoned Líster to see how things were going. Unaware of just how near Casado was to launching his coup, Líster replied, 'The rebels have been crushed and now we are concentrating on ascertaining the degree of treachery of

each of them.' Already putting the very last touches to his preparations for the coup to be launched some hours later, Casado replied
that he was delighted with the news and sent his congratulations to
Líster's men.[29]

Any excuse that the fleet could not return because of the threat
from the coastal batteries was no longer plausible. Of course, at this
stage in the evening of 5 March, for Buiza to keep the fleet at sea was
entirely compatible with Casado's plans. At some point between
midnight and 2.00 on the morning of 6 March, a teletype from
Posición Yuste was transmitted to Buiza, via the naval communications centre in Valencia, with the text: 'Minister of Defence to head of
Fleet. Official. Situation in Cartagena under control. Order the fleet
to return to base.'[30] The pro-Franco forces had barricaded themselves
in the Arsenal, the artillery depot and the military headquarters of
the base. Throughout the night of 5–6 March, unsuccessful attempts
were made to remove them. By 10.00 a.m. on 6 March, the artillery
depot was in the hands of the loyalist forces. Three hundred prisoners
were taken including General Barrionuevo. The Arsenal and the
shore batteries had been captured by 2.30 p.m.[31]

There had meanwhile been two important developments. At
around 2.30 in the morning of Monday 6 March, news of the formation of Casado's Junta reached Buiza's flagship. It could have come as
little surprise to the Admiral since it was exactly as Matallana had
telegraphed him the previous Saturday. Shortly afterwards, Casado
received the following message from Buiza: 'To President Casado.
The Fleet, in good spirits, is at Your Excellency's orders.' In the light
of the news, Galán had asked Buiza to return the fleet immediately to
Cartagena, which he declined to do. The response of the chief of the
general staff, Captain José Núñez Rodríguez, who had previously
threatened Galán, was to order the left-wing members of the crew to
be detained, claiming that it was to prevent revenge being taken for
the murder of right-wing officers on 18 July 1936. A message from
Casado to Buiza received at 7.30 on the morning of the 6th was sent
under the impression that Cartagena was still in Francoist hands: 'By
order of the President Casado, stay at sea until further orders. Trust
that this is all going well. Do not enter Cartagena until further orders.'

It is worthy of note that the ostensibly 'humble' Casado should be using the title of President.

In mid-afternoon on 6 March, with the forces under Colonel Rodríguez dispatched by Negrín now in control of Cartagena, repeated messages were sent by Rodríguez urging the fleet to return to base. On board ship, Buiza held a meeting of his general staff to debate whether to go back. A majority, either because of their long-standing pro-Francoist sympathies or in the hope of currying favour with the future regime, was fiercely determined not to return. Buiza had neither the will nor the energy to oppose them nor, very possibly, the effective authority. It was later claimed by Alonso that, unsure of the situation in Cartagena, the officers were inhibited by the presence aboard of the 600 civilian refugees and by concerns about fuel supplies. As they were midway between the Tunisian port of Bizerta and Cartagena, there was enough fuel to reach one or the other. On the grounds that, if they returned to find Cartagena in Francoist hands, it would be a disaster, they opted for Bizerta. In fact, they had already been informed that normality had been established in the port. The decision to go to Bizerta thus constituted a double treachery to both Negrín and Casado.[32] The entire Mediterranean coast was now without naval defences. On 8 March, the commander of Franco's navy, Admiral Cervera, declared a total blockade and prohibited the entry of any merchant ships into the ports of Almería, Murcia, Alicante, Valencia and Castellón.[33] Buiza felt sufficiently guilty about this, as will be seen, to try to expiate his responsibilities by joining the French Foreign Legion. He subsequently became a hero during the Second World War.[34]

The second dramatic event as far as Cartagena was concerned was provoked by the early-morning broadcast by the Falangists who had seized the local radio station. Their over-enthusiastic exaggerations triggered one of Franco's few acts of rashness in his conduct of the war effort. In response to the broadcasts of the beleaguered rebels begging for assistance, Franco had decided to send two divisions by sea, one from Castellón and the other from Málaga. On the afternoon of 5 March, approximately thirty vessels set off with 20,000 men.[35] By the morning of 6 March, the hastily assembled expedition of five unescorted transport ships was in sight of Cartagena where the forces of Rodríguez and Precioso had re-established control of the port. The plan was for a landing late in the night of 6–7 March. General Barrionuevo had revealed to Eustaquio Cañas that they were en route and the coastal batteries were ready. They fired on the improvised fleet, forcing it to withdraw to 19 kilometres outside the port, and the operation was cancelled. However, two merchant steamers which had been delayed then arrived on the morning of 7 March. Neither had radio contact with the rest of the convoy. The first, the *Castillo de Peñafiel*, withdrew when the shore guns opened fire. The other, the *Castillo Olite*, approached the entrance to the harbour. Not seeing the rest of the convoy, the captain assumed that the landing had already begun and continued forward. The coastal batteries began to fire and one of the shells hit the ship's munitions store. There were 2,112 troops on board including military lawyers sent to start the trials of what was assumed would be the defeated Republicans. When the ship was sunk more than 1,476 Nationalist troops died, 342 were wounded and 294 captured.[36]

As Rodríguez was taking control, Casadista forces led by Colonel Joaquín Pérez Salas arrived to seize control of the base. Rodríguez withdrew. Pérez Salas had orders to arrest all the Communists but made arrangements for the most endangered ones to leave on English merchant vessels. In the last days of the war, he organized more evacuations. He refused the opportunity to escape, believing that it was his duty to remain to hand the base over to the Francoists. He was arrested and shot on 4 August 1939.[37]

While the dramatic events were unfolding at Cartagena between the afternoon of Saturday 4 March and Monday 6 March, tension was rising at El Poblet. Among the various extant accounts of those days, that by one of Negrín's visitors, Dr Francisco Vega Díaz, is one of the most detailed and revealing. Vega Díaz, a one-time medical student of Negrín's, was attached to the medical services of the Army of Andalusia under Colonel Domingo Moriones Larraga. Knowing that Vega Díaz was a close friend of Rafael Méndez and also of José Puche Álvarez, the director of the Republic's military medical services, Negrín had called him to Elda in order to get his opinion of the reliability of Moriones's forces. Vega arrived on the morning of 5 March.[38] Negrín's conversations on 3 March with José Rodríguez Vega and on 5 and 6 March with Francisco Vega Díaz, as well as several other eyewitness accounts of the frenzied atmosphere at El Poblet, rather contradicted the Communist complaints about the Prime Minister's alleged inactivity. They also flatly refute the absurd accusations by Casado, García Pradas and subsequent Francoist authors about champagne-fuelled orgies.

When Vega Díaz arrived at El Poblet, after greeting him Negrín suggested that Puche take him to an orchard behind the house where they could speak candidly. Puche explained that Negrín hoped to get objective information about the Army of Andalusia from someone he could trust: 'the morale of the civilian population, the political loyal-ties of the officers [whose names Puche had written on a piece of paper], the state of both military and civilian medical services, avail-able vehicles, the role of the political commissars, food supplies, usable seaports and airports, etc'. Negrín wanted an unbiased opinion about the capacity of that sector to continue resistance. In particular, he was interested in Vega's personal opinion as to whether the obedi-ence of the military leadership could be relied upon. Vega was reluc-tant to pass an opinion on the detailed questions, but he said that in Republican Andalusia the population was weary of the war and that certain military commanders had provoked popular disgust because of the mistreatment of prisoners at a camp near Turón in Granada. At this point, Negrín rejoined Puche and asked Vega for further details. He was appalled, exclaiming: 'Yet another atrocity!'[39]

In his conversations with Negrín and Puche, Vega Díaz did not mention that on 3 March he had been ordered to dismiss all the senior surgeons who were members of the Communist Party, an order which presumably came from Casado via Moriones. Negrín then left them alone again and Puche confided in Vega that Negrín was agonizing over the possibilities of the Republic's resisting for a further three months until a European war broke out. Puche claimed that 'Negrín was terrified by the thought of Spain being involved in the inferno of another conflagration and, in his heart of hearts, felt that to continue the civil war was pointless.' In Puche's opinion,

Negrín was becoming totally disillusioned. 'He felt that he had been let down by everyone, some by their desertion, others by outright treachery. But he wanted to do his duty as a leader and an honourable man and did not want to be seen as a slippery escapee.' Puche thought that Negrín knew that these were his last hours on Spanish soil, since he was aware of events in Cartagena and expected Casado and others to mount a coup under the banners of Besteiro possibly as soon as that night. Moreover, since the resignation of Azaña, 'there was no Republic to defend and all that Negrín wanted was to find an end to the war that wasn't a dishonourable unconditional surrender'.[40]

Negrín was far from being the only one who suspected that the coup was imminent. At 3 in the morning of 5 March, Jesús Hernández went to El Poblet and had a sharp encounter with Negrín, who had just walked into the farmhouse. 'He looked unkempt, unshaven, with his trilby pulled down over his ears and his trousers tucked into his socks like a cyclist. He seemed extremely tired. I asked him rudely: "Where the hell have you been hiding so that no one can find you?" With the gesture of a disillusioned man, he responded by asking: "Do they need me?"' Hernández asked him if he was unaware of what was happening in Cartagena and with the fleet. Negrín replied sourly: 'Of course. What news is there?' Hernández related what he knew. 'There, you see,' said Negrín with bitter irony, 'I'm no longer needed for anything. What they have decided is correct. I wouldn't have done it any differently.' Cordón brought them both a glass of brandy, and Negrín took Hernández by the arm and led him to a corner of the room. 'Hernandez, my friend,' he said gently. 'When I left France for the central-southern zone, I was under the impression that there was a ninety per cent probability that I would leave my carcass here, but now that percentage has risen to ninety-nine per cent.' With tired eyes, he went on: 'There is nothing for us to do here. I do not want to preside over a new civil war among anti-Francoists.' Hernández objected that a decision to leave would lead to a total collapse and reduce everything to the most infernal chaos. Negrín replied: 'Hardly any more than now! The uprisings have already started. Now it is Cartagena and the fleet. Tomorrow it will be Madrid or Valencia. What are we supposed to do? Crush them? I don't think it's worth the trouble. The war is definitely lost. If others want to negotiate peace, I won't oppose them.' Hernández then asked what was the point of the postings and promotions announced in the *Diario Oficial*. Negrín replied: 'They were in response to the demands of your comrades. I tried to please them, knowing that it would all be useless and even prejudicial.' Hernández concluded that Negrín was a defeated man, 'already dead' as the symbol of resistance, as 'the Prime Minister and Minister of Defence who had most loyally and effectively embodied the magnificent spirit of struggle of our people in the most difficult period of our war'.[41]

Some hours after Hernández's encounter in El Poblet with Negrín, on the morning of 5 March, in Madrid, Domingo Girón, organization secretary of the PCE Madrid section, had given Manuel Tagüeña a confusing report that the Communist officers in the capital, aware of Casado's intentions, had plans to resist him. Tagüeña was not convinced. He had just received orders to go to Posición Yuste when Daniel Ortega, the Communist commissar with Casado's forces, arrived, pale and breathless. He brought the news that forces of Mera's IV Army Corps were gathering at the headquarters of the Army of the Centre, in the Alameda de Osuna in Canillejas on the north-eastern outskirts of Madrid on the road to Alcalá de Henares, code-named 'Posición Jaca'. It was clear that Casado's coup was about to begin. When Tagüeña informed Girón of this, his response made it clear that, despite what he had said earlier, the policy of the PCE was not to resist but rather to wait on events. This was because the Communist Party did not want to risk the responsibility for a final bloodstained break-up of the Popular Front, already riven by divisions. Tagüeña and his men set off for El Poblet in the evening of 5 March. Not long after their departure, Casado issued orders for their arrest.[42]

In the twenty-four hours before Casado acted, the situation in El Poblet was understandably chaotic. 'There were about twenty people distributed between the hall, the dining room and a side room from which could be heard the unmistakable voice of Álvarez del Vayo on the phone shouting to be connected to the tank base at Archena in Murcia.' Vayo was trying to ensure that a tank unit had been sent to the naval base at Cartagena as part of the effort to put down the rebellion there. A furious Negrín was trying to speak to Casado and each time he got through to his post, they told him that Casado had just left for somewhere else. Negrín turned to those with him and said: 'Casado is doing everything to avoid me!' To Vega Díaz, it seemed like a madhouse. Negrín and Vayo were trying to talk above the hubbub created by González Peña, Matallana, Uribe, Cordón, Garcés and others. They all seemed defeated and roused themselves only to accept a cup of coffee or a sandwich. Occasionally, Negrín would shout for silence and slam down the phone, but what surprised Vega Díaz most was that, in the midst of such a bear garden, the Prime Minister never lost control.[43]

In the middle of the day, there arrived the distressing news of the catastrophic decision by Rear Admiral Buiza Fernández-Palacios to take the fleet out to sea just as the forces sent by Negrín were on the verge of controlling the rebellion in Cartagena. Buiza ignored the desperate telegrams from Negrín ordering him to return. The fleet was taken to Bizerta and handed over to the French authorities, who would surrender it to Franco as soon as arrangements were made for the transfer. When Franco's emissary Rear Admiral Salvador Moreno arrived at Bizerta, many of Buiza's officers tried to ingratiate themselves by listing the ways in which they had undermined the Republic's naval war effort.[44] Buiza's decision was a devastating blow for Negrín. Without the fleet there was no way to provide the necessary security for an evacuation in mercantile vessels. The Prime Minister had hardly had time to process the news when the Casado coup took place. The consequences of that coup ensured that there would be little in the way of commercial vessels with which to organize an evacuation effort with or without naval protection.

Even with the rising in Cartagena now under control, Negrín now faced an appalling situation – the President of the Republic had resigned, Britain and France had recognized Franco and now the key to future evacuations was lost. In the course of Sunday 5 March, at El Poblet there were unmistakable signs that Casado's plot was spreading its tentacles. In the early afternoon, the commissar general of the armed forces, Jesús Hernández, rang Antonio Cordón to inform him of some suspicious and completely unjustified military activities at the headquarters of the Army of the Levante. Hernández asked Cordón to tell Negrín that if he did not use his authority as Minister of Defence to put a stop to what was going on, the Communists in Valencia would do so. The activities that concerned Hernández involved the army HQ being sealed off. A company of Assault Guards with machine guns was given orders to open fire on anyone entering or leaving Leopoldo Menéndez's headquarters. In the courtyard of the HQ building, cases of hand grenades were being unloaded. Known Communist officers had been placed under arrest. Hernández believed that these were preparations for Menéndez to support Casado.[45] When Cordón spoke to an utterly exhausted Negrín, he shrugged his shoulders and said: 'Do what you think best, Cordón. I assure you that I wish they would all just make their coup and be done with it.' This was almost identical to what Jesús Hernández claimed Negrín had said to him in the early hours of the morning. In his memoirs, Cordón claimed that Negrín repeated the remark again later on the same day.

General Manuel Matallana had just arrived at El Poblet in response to his earlier telephone conversation with Negrín about events in Cartagena. He had been promoted to chief of the general staff only the previous day. Now, he made a show of humility, saying that he was daunted by the huge responsibility and that he was embarrassed to take over a post that strictly belonged to Rojo. Cordón told him about Rojo's plans for surrender even before the final defeat in Catalonia. Despite knowing all about Rojo's views thanks to their correspondence, Matallana feigned surprise. With a virtuoso display of hypocrisy, he said: 'I didn't know that, Cordón, so we will fight on until the end. As far as I am concerned, I am old and worn out, and I have decided to stay here no matter what happens.' This was a bizarre statement for a man just forty years old. Not yet suspecting his involvement in the plot, Cordón put him on the phone to Hernández, who explained the situation. Cordón then asked Matallana, as chief of the general staff, to speak to the commander of the Army of the Levante, General Leopoldo Menéndez, and also to send him a telegram ordering him to put a stop to the suspicious movements he had ordered.

Matallana did so and Menéndez then rang to say that he had obeyed the order but that he considered that his initiatives had been no more than 'reasonable precautions'. Alarm bells went off in Cordón's head when Menéndez, who was in fact privy to Casado's conspiracy, said that he thought that his orders might not be obeyed since he was not the head of the Army Group of the Centre. This was palpably absurd given that Menéndez was supposed to be rescinding orders that he himself had issued. His remark suggested that he had been obeying orders from Casado. It was a highly suspicious indication of his collusion with Casado. Accordingly, Cordón telephoned the chief of staff of the Army Group of the Centre, Lieutenant Colonel Félix Muedra Miñón, and ordered him, in Negrín's name, to ensure that Menéndez's orders were implemented. Since Muedra was every bit as implicated in Casado's plot as were Menéndez and Matallana, it is reasonable to suppose that nothing was done.[46]

At about 5 p.m., the members of the cabinet arrived for a meeting to discuss the speech that Negrín planned to make the following day. Their lengthy debate would hinge on whether he should insist on the three conditions for peace that he had outlined to the Cortes at Figueres or whether he should make just a single demand for a guarantee that there would be no reprisals and that those at risk could be evacuated. The idea was to produce a text that would show to the world that it was Franco who stood in the way of peace because of his sadistic refusal to renounce revenge. Not long after the meeting began, Negrín came out and told Matallana to phone Miaja and tell him to join them immediately. As Matallana was speaking, it was obvious that Miaja was refusing, so Negrín went over and said in a loud voice: 'Tell General Miaja that if he is afraid to come here, I will go to him, but I cannot imagine that a general of our army would refuse to help the supreme commander and to obey an order at such a grave moment.' Matallana, who was playing a double game, then said to Miaja: 'You heard what he said, General.'

Cordón then took the receiver from him and severely reprimanded Miaja, saying: 'I cannot believe, General, that you are doing these things with the Prime Minister who needs you. Forgive me, but I think that you are behaving like an idiot. I have often told you that those who surround you are spreading banana skins in the hope that you will slip and do yourself damage. Stop being an idiot and come here, because we aren't going to eat you.' Miaja replied by questioning the recent postings; Cordón laboriously explained these to him and begged him not to throw away a distinguished reputation because he was being egged on to do so by bad advisers. Miaja then claimed that his doctors had forbidden him to travel at night and that he would come to El Poblet the next morning. The cabinet meeting continued until 11 p.m. Then the ministers, the senior officers and the administrative staff sat down to dinner.[47]

10

The Coup – the Stab in the Back

Casado had meanwhile abandoned his own base at Posición Jaca on the road to Barajas and, in preparation for launching his coup, had set up camp in the Ministry of Finance in the calle de Alcalá, from where Miaja had led the defence of Madrid during the siege of 1936. Now, Val, Salgado, González Marín and García Pradas entered the building at 8.45 p.m. on the night of 5 March 1939 to be followed shortly afterwards by Besteiro and Wenceslao Carrillo. García Pradas had sent anarchist squads to take over the offices of the two principal Republican radio stations, Unión Radio and Radio España. The anarchists who supported Casado had been led to believe that the creation of the Consejo Nacional de Defensa constituted a counter-coup against what he had alleged was an imminent coup by Negrín. The chaos at El Poblet underlines just how absurd was this view. The assembled conspirators put the final touch to the announcement that would be made shortly. Besteiro declined the presidency on the grounds that it should be held by a senior general. Casado also refused and the name of General Miaja was proposed. The offer was made to him only when he reached Madrid in the early hours of 6 March and was happily accepted. Besteiro accepted the dual post of Vice-President and Minister of Foreign Affairs. Only after the building had been surrounded by forces led by Lieutenant Colonel Cipriano Mera was the formal public announcement of the Consejo made at midnight in a radio broadcast by Besteiro.[1]

Not long after the arrival of the anarchists Besteiro and Carrillo, the commissar inspector of the Army of the Centre, Edmundo Domínguez, reached the Ministry of Finance. Because Casado was suffering from his ulcers, he was lying fully clothed on a bed. Despite his stomach pains, he was intoxicated with delight that his plans were about to reach fruition. A visibly worried and taciturn Wenceslao Carrillo was sitting on Casado's bed. The anarchists Val, García Pradas and Manuel González Marín could barely conceal their pleasure at what was happening. Inevitably, since Domínguez was regarded as a friend of Negrín's, the atmosphere was tense and hostile. Val and García Pradas pressed him threateningly to declare himself for or against the Consejo Nacional de Defensa. To have declared against would have guaranteed his arrest and possible execution. To avoid declaring in favour, he claimed that, as vice-president of the UGT, he could not make any statement until there was a meeting of the union executive.

Obviously annoyed, Casado snapped: 'It's up to you whether to make statements or not; we can do without you and the UGT.' His arrogance had got the better of him because, in order to give the impression that the proposed Consejo represented all forces, the agreement of the UGT was crucial. When Domínguez remained silent, Casado tried to pressure him with the lie that the UGT secretary general José Rodríguez Vega was in agreement. When Domínguez questioned this, Casado had to admit that Rodríguez Vega had done no more than express a desire to see the end of the war. Domínguez, virtually a hostage, then sat in a corner observing the passage of events. In the hours before the formal announcement, much of the time was spent by the conspirators in exchanging ludicrously scurrilous gossip about Negrín, claiming that he ate as much as four men, consuming tortillas of twelve eggs and sleeping with three different women each night. Besteiro seemed to be influenced by this and, convinced that Negrín mistreated his ministers, pompously expressed his distress that Negrín did not maintain the dignity of his post.

So hurriedly put together was the final scene that the conspirators had still not assigned their various posts and the political attributions to go with them. When Casado claimed that the Consejo Nacional de Defensa (CND) would represent the PSOE, the CNT, the Republican parties and the UGT, Domínguez objected. Exchanging glances with Besteiro, Casado proclaimed that the PSOE was represented by Besteiro – which was anything but true, but not something to which

Domínguez could object. However, when Casado said that Wenceslao Carrillo represented the UGT, Domínguez insisted that this was not the case. Eventually, Carrillo claimed that, as president of the Casa del Pueblo de Madrid (the Socialists' meeting place and effective headquarters), he could appear as representing the Agrupación Socialista Madrileña. Casado then declared that Rodríguez Vega would represent the UGT, to which Domínguez objected that he had not been consulted. Casado agreed to delay the announcement of his councillors and their party affiliation until it was possible to consult Rodríguez Vega. When it was nearly time to make the radio broadcasts announcing the formation of the CND, Casado said, with childish glee, 'Just imagine their faces when they hear!'[2]

Besteiro spoke from the cellars of the Ministry. Hunched over the radio microphones, his voice trembling with emotion, he defended the motives of those involved: 'That the time has arrived to declare the truth and rip down the net of lies that surrounds us is an unavoidable necessity, a humanitarian duty, and is demanded by the supreme law that the innocent masses be saved.' He was either deliberately lying or else bizarrely mistaken when he asserted that the Negrín government had been wandering around France ever since the collapse of Catalonia. He alleged that the government,

> with its concealment of the truth, its half-truths and deceitful propositions, can have no other aim than to gain time; time that has been lost for the interests of the bulk of citizens, soldiers or civilians. And this policy of delay can have no other point that to feed the sick hope that the complications of the international situation will unleash a catastrophe on a universal scale in which, along with us, the proletarian masses of many nations will perish. Public opinion in the Republic is tired of this policy of catastrophic fanaticism, of complete submission to foreign orders, with its total indifference to the sorrow of the Nation …
> I speak to you from this Madrid which has known suffering and knows how to suffer its martyrdom with moving dignity … I speak to you to say that it is in defeat that it is necessary for individuals and nations to show their moral courage. It is

possible to lose but with honour and dignity, without denying one's faith, without being crushed by misfortune. I tell you that a moral victory of this type is worth a thousand times more than a material victory achieved by dint of deceit and vilification.

When he finished, he wept.[3]

The formal declaration of the Consejo was read out by Miguel San Andrés, a minor figure of Izquierda Republicana. José García Pradas claimed later that he had drafted the text. It certainly echoed the declaration made by the CNT's Comité Regional de Defensa ten days earlier. Indeed, as in that statement, its declared aims were similar to those proclaimed by Negrín and suggested that the reasons behind the coup were to do with his failure to provide strong leadership. It gave no inkling of the collusion of Besteiro and Casado with the Fifth Column.

> As revolutionaries, as proletarians, as anti-fascists and as Spaniards, we could no longer go on passively accepting the lack of foresight, the lack of policies, the lack of organization and the irresponsibility demonstrated by the Government of Dr Negrín ... Many weeks have passed since the war in Catalonia came to an end with a general desertion. All the promises that were made to the people in the most solemn moments were forgotten; every duty ignored; every undertaking criminally trampled underfoot. While the people sacrificed many thousands of its best sons on the bloody altar of battle, many of those who had set themselves up as leaders of the resistance abandoned their posts and sought in shaming and shameful flight to save their lives even at the cost of their dignity ... To avoid this, to wipe out so much shame and prevent further desertion at the most serious moments, the Consejo Nacional de Defensa has been constituted and in the name of this entity, which found its powers in the gutter where they had been thrown by the so-called government of Dr Negrín, we speak to every worker, to every anti-fascist and to every Spaniard to guarantee that no one will flee from the fulfilment of their duties nor elude the responsibilities

implicit in their promises … Not one of the men whose duty is here will leave Spain until everyone who wants to has left, not just those who can. We advocate resistance so that our cause should not be buried in derision and shame; and to achieve this we call for the help of all Spaniards and we guarantee that no one will fail in their obligations. 'Either we are all saved or else we all succumb to extermination and shame.' So said Dr Negrín and the Consejo Nacional de Defensa assumes as its first, last and only task to convert those words into reality.[4]

Then Mera spoke, his speech degenerating into a series of cheap insults directed at Negrín whom he called a traitor, a criminal and a thief. He accused him of causing the defeat in Catalonia and of selling out the Republic 'for gold and orgies'. Mera was followed finally by Casado. The last words of his speech (written for him by García Pradas) were addressed to Franco. 'In your hands, not in ours, is peace or war.' They effectively put an end to any possibility of peace conditions from Franco. As Rodríguez Vega put it later: 'This literary masterpiece was a brilliant example of how to express in bellicose language an unbreakable commitment to surrender.'[5]

Initially, since Besteiro refused to assume the presidency, Casado did so for several hours until the arrival of Miaja, who was given the formal title. Nevertheless, for the three weeks of his Junta's existence, it was widely, and correctly, assumed that Casado was in complete charge. General Miaja later claimed that he had accepted the presidency of the CND only after Negrín had left Spain. This is simply untrue. It is certainly the case that he was not consulted about the finer details before Casado and Besteiro went on air. Nevertheless, he had been party to the machinations of Casado and Matallana at least since that first lunch on 2 February at which anti-Negrín sentiments had been aired.[6] The actual timing of Casado's proposal to Miaja remains difficult to determine, although the formal announcement of his appointment as President of the Consejo Nacional de Defensa is dated 5 March.

When the initial broadcasts were being made, Miaja was asleep in his headquarters in Torrente on the outskirts of Valencia, codenamed

'Posicion Pekín'. After hearing the speeches, one of the officers of his escort woke him. Miaja immediately phoned Casado who, plagued by the pain provoked by his ulcers, was again lying on his bed. He got up to talk to Miaja and, knowing how important it was to get him aboard, immediately invited him to come to Madrid and join them. While still connected to Miaja, Casado turned to those present and said: 'He says we are a bunch of scoundrels for going ahead without him.' As he held the phone up, others shouted for Miaja's benefit, 'Tell him to come!' and Casado resumed the conversation, saying: 'Now you hear it, General, we all want you to come and be with us.' After further brief exchanges, Casado repeated: 'Come, please come, you will be our leader and we will obey you.' Whispering to the others that Miaja had agreed, he ended the conversation with the words: 'We are waiting for you, General. At your orders!'

Casado then turned again to the others and said: 'He is arriving in the nick of time. His prestige will silence those who aren't happy. It really helps the Consejo.' According to Ángel Pedrero who was present, Miaja wanted to know what his role in the Junta would be. Besteiro said: 'This is a real issue. What should his role in the Consejo be?' Casado hesitated and then barked: 'I've no idea! I couldn't care less.' Several of those present suggested that he be made President. It is likely that Pedrero was conflating this conversation with the one that had taken place some hours earlier when the idea of offering Miaja the presidency had first been mooted. Pedrero claimed later that Casado, 'to prevent him provoking a difficult situation, decided to offer him the presidency of the junta' on the grounds that he was the appropriate person as commander-in-chief of the army. This differed slightly from Domínguez's recollection in that he has Casado saying: 'That's fine. Let him be President. I'm not proud. I am only interested in Spain and the people. I am satisfied just to command the Army.' He then said: 'This will please the general and, when he arrives, we can decide on the ministerial positions for one another.'[7]

Since Casado had urged him to come to Madrid as soon as possible, ignoring the alleged doctor's orders that he had cited to Cordón as an excuse for not travelling, Miaja quickly set off for the capital. He was accompanied by his two adjutants, Lieutenant Colonel José Pérez

Martínez and Comandante Mario Páramo, his secretaries and his guards. They arrived in the early morning of 6 March and stayed for about twenty-four hours while Casado supervised the battle that now raged as Communist forces in Madrid resisted his coup.[8] The arrival of Miaja and his entourage caused great delight in the cellars of the Ministry of Finance. Casado greeted him with the words: 'We have won! Everything is settled.' Miaja replied jovially: 'Bandits! You jumped the gun!' Those not in the secret of all of Casado's machinations were surprised by this and asked Miaja if he had been part of the plot all along. He replied: 'Naturally, and I had my speech already written to broadcast it to the nation.' One of his secretaries took some sheets of paper from his briefcase and showed them around before Casado seized hold of them and took the opportunity to play on Miaja's vanity. 'Not to worry, General,' he said, 'these notes will be read out today and they will have a big impact!'[9]

Domínguez meanwhile managed to persuade Casado to let him telephone Rodríguez Vega. In front of so many hostile witnesses, Domínguez was unable to say much about what was going on. However, Rodríguez Vega, detecting the nervous tone of Domínguez's voice, realized what was happening. Casado spoke to him and sent a car for the short journey from UGT headquarters to the Ministry. On the way, the driver told Rodríguez Vega about the coup. When he reached the Ministry cellars, Casado announced bluntly: 'It's all done. We have defeated Negrín's government.' Rodríguez Vega responded by saying that he and Domínguez had to leave to call a meeting of the UGT executive to resolve its official position regarding the CND. Casado, who clearly wanted to hold on to Domínguez as a hostage, was forced to agree. The two UGT leaders then walked to the union's headquarters in nearby calle Fuencarral. They and the other two members of the executive committee, Claudina García and Antonio Pérez Ariño, were opposed to Casado. The UGT president, Ramón González Peña, was with Negrín in El Poblet. It was impossible to contact El Poblet, and many representatives of various federations were in favour of supporting the Junta. In a heated meeting, it was decided that, to avoid divisions in the movement, the UGT should agree to be represented in the CND. A reluctant Antonio Pérez, who had a long-standing friendship with Besteiro, was nominated to take that role.[10]

Casado was anxious to proceed to the announcement of a cabinet. It was a meaningless gesture aimed at giving the impression that a government existed with representation of all anti-Negrín and anti-Communist forces. Casado, Besteiro and Miaja acted entirely on their own initiative. The 'cabinet' was a fiction which obscured the truth that this was a military junta pure and simple. None of the participants had the unanimous support of the organizations they claimed to represent. For example, the list published on the evening of 6 March did not include Pérez since the full agreement of the UGT was not secured until thirty hours later and only then as a gesture to avoid dividing the movement. Participation in Casado's junta was never authorized by the executive committee of the PSOE.[11] The final cabinet announced was: President, General Miaja; Foreign Minister and Vice-President, Besteiro; Minister of the Interior, Wenceslao Carrillo (PSOE); Minister of Defence, Casado; Minister of Finance, Manuel González Marín (CNT); Minister of Justice, Miguel San Andrés (Izquierda Republicana); Minister of Education, José del Rio (Unión Republicana); Minister of Public Works, Eduardo Val (CNT); Minister of of Labour, Antonio Pérez (UGT). It was described by the correspondent of the London *Times* as 'a pitiful mummery – a cabinet of the doomed, born out of despair'.[12] The two Republicans were virtually unknown and the same was true of the CNT and UGT representatives. As a government, it was meaningless in that the only 'ministries' with anything like real functions were those of Defence under Casado and Interior under Wenceslao Carrillo, both of whom would play key roles in crushing opposition to the coup.

Popular desire for an end to the war was intensified by anarchist and Socialist hostility to the Communists who had advocated resistance to the end. Having presented itself as the 'party of victory', Francoist triumphs meant that the PCE was now widely seen as the 'party of defeat'.[13] The coup's success was also owed to several other factors. The CNT which had suffered at the hands of the PCE was thirsting for revenge.[14] Moreover, most professional army officers, even those with Communist membership cards, failed to oppose

Casado. They had joined the PCE because it offered discipline and efficacy but they were not in any real sense Communists.[15] However, despite the fact that the Casado coup struck a real chord with both civilians and soldiers, the importance of Besteiro's contribution should not be underestimated. Having stood aside from Republican politics and so carefully nurtured his reputation for rectitude, his participation bestowed a moral legitimacy on the Casado Junta which it would not otherwise have had. It is difficult to know just how aware Besteiro was of the implications of what he was doing – which was to render pointless the bloodshed and the sacrifices of the previous three years by emulating the military coup of 18 July 1936 against an alleged Communist danger. His physical privations may have had some impact on his mental health. The exiled ex-Prime Minister Manuel Portela Valladares was told by a doctor who had treated Besteiro at the end of the war that the professor was *gagá*.[16] For years, Besteiro had fought off tuberculosis, and the war years in Madrid, without decent food or warmth in the winter, had taken their toll.[17] On the other hand, his own privations do not explain his wilful ignorance of the Francoist repression.

Besteiro seems to have thought that he could achieve great things in the way of reconciliation. The moderate Socialist Enrique Tierno Galván, who met him in the last months of the war, believed that Besteiro thought himself 'destined to be the moral barrier that could be placed between the victors and the vanquished to avoid reprisals'. He was persuaded that his historic role was to stand between both sides and 'be the father of the helpless once weapons had been laid down'. Besteiro considered that his own superior moral rectitude and his marginalization during the war would carry weight with the Francoists. It was a view compounded of arrogance and ignorance.[18] The revenge wreaked by the Nationalists in captured Republican cities was well known. Yet Besteiro managed not to know, perhaps because he was eager to believe the false information about Francoist clemency given him by his Falangist contacts.[19] Antonio Luna García certainly told him that Franco offered to guarantee the life and liberty of all of those who were guiltless of common crimes and contributed to the bloodless surrender of the Republic. Like many less sophisticated and less well educated than himself in towns all over Spain, he accepted this claim.[20]

The ministers and the senior officers who were with Negrín at El Poblet had just finished dinner when Besteiro's speech was broadcast at midnight, followed by those by San Andrés, Mera and Casado himself. Up to that point, the conspirators had managed to carry out their activities in relative secrecy, most crucially in terms of the involvement of Generals Matallana and Menéndez. As has been seen, formally at least Negrín had dismissed the rumours reported to him by Cordón, Domínguez and the air force chief Hidalgo de Cisneros and had given the impression that he was convinced by Casado's pretence of total hierarchical obedience. It is not clear whether this was the consequence of his total exhaustion, a misplaced confidence that Casado would not manage to bring off his planned coup or an unconscious desire to see someone else take on the job of ending the war.[21]

In the immediate aftermath of the broadcast, a flurry of three-way telephone conversations took place between the headquarters of Negrín, Casado and Leopoldo Menéndez. Those involved were, in El Poblet, Negrín, his ministers, Manuel Matallana, Antonio Cordón and Ignacio Hidalgo de Cisneros; in the Finance Ministry in Madrid, Casado and members of his Junta; and, in Valencia, General Menéndez. There exist numerous versions of what was said in the course of these contacts. From the Madrid end, there are four broadly similar accounts by Casado himself, plus one by José García Pradas, one by the commissar inspector of the Army of the Centre and vice-president of the UGT, Edmundo Domínguez, and one by José Rodríguez Vega, secretary general of the UGT, all of whom were present in the Finance Ministry. From the Yuste end, there are accounts by Negrín, Vicente Uribe, Antonio Cordón, Julio Álvarez del Vayo, Santiago Garcés and Francisco Vega Díaz, all of whom were in El Poblet, and by Julián Zugazagoitia, who was able to talk shortly afterwards to all those who were present. From the Valencia end, there exists an account by Lieutenant Colonel Francisco Ciutat, operations chief of the Army of the Levante. The recollections of all of these protagonists broadly coincide in terms of the general drift of conversations but there are differences in terms of timings and sequencing, usually as a consequence of the passage of time before the protagonists recorded their memories. The most detailed and convincing source in terms of timings is the contemporary diary of Antonio Cordón, and this is the one that is followed here in establishing the basic sequence of events throughout the night.

According to Casado, on hearing the various speeches, Negrín telephoned him to demand explanations. In contrast, Cordón claimed that Casado had phoned Matallana at El Poblet to give him the news that the coup had taken place. Certainly at some point after the broadcasts, Matallana spoke to Casado. According to Zugazagoitia, 'His reproaches to the rebel could hardly have been more conventional and formulaic. His voice expressionless, his pulse racing, he stammered out his rebukes and short answers … His nervousness gave the game away.' Matallana had then passed the telephone to Negrín and, according to Cordón, Casado, using language reminiscent of the military conspirators of 1936, said to Negrín: 'We have risen in arms.' 'Against whom?' asked Negrín. 'Against some rebels, against you,' replied Casado. When Negrín addressed him as 'general', he claimed that he refused his promotion because it came from an illegal government and that this was why he had established his Junta. Negrín told him that what he was doing was madness and dismissed him from all his posts. Casado, speaking loudly for the benefit of his fellow rebels, who were listening avidly, used a tone that, according to Edmundo Domínguez, was 'rough and boastful'. When Negrín told him that he was dismissed, he replied rudely: 'Look, Negrín, all that means nothing to me now. You and your ministers are no longer the government; you don't have the power or the prestige to keep going, let alone to arrest us.'

Casado claimed later that, in the course of their conversation, Negrín had offered to hand over power to him. The alleged interchange went as follows:

Negrín: 'I understand that there is still time for us to make some arrangement.'

Casado: 'I do not understand what you mean. I believe that everything is arranged.'

Negrín: 'At least I must ask you to send a representative so that I may hand over the powers of government, or I will send one to Madrid with this mission.'

Casado: 'Don't worry about that. You can't hand over what you haven't got. Actually, I am taking up the powers which you and your government have abandoned.'

In fact, the offer to hand over power came not from Negrín personally but later in the interchange. Casado was conflating here his subsequent conversations with the ministers Giner de los Ríos and Paulino Gómez and with Hidalgo de Cisneros and Cordón.

After putting down the phone, Negrín returned to the dinner table and, without a word, sat down. With a look of utter dejection, he put his head in his hands. Cordón was struck by the way the ministers, whom he had seen trembling and upset at far less serious moments, took the news calmly, as if they were in on the secret. When he later commented on this, Negrín simply said, 'Naturally, Cordón.'[22] Uribe and José Moix Regas, the Minister of Labour, bitterly criticized their colleagues for 'the despicable treachery' committed by the parties to which they belonged and insinuated that they bore some responsibility for not foreseeing what was going to happen.[23]

Paulino Gómez then stood up and took the telephone. He urged Casado to think carefully about what he was doing. He said that a reasonable solution could be found and that he would leave for Madrid immediately. Casado replied that he had nothing against him personally but that, given that the coup was directed at Negrín's government, it would not be prudent for Gómez to come to Madrid since his safety could not be guaranteed. Gómez then passed the receiver to Cordón. Cordón addressed Casado in friendly terms, not as under-secretary of the Ministry of Defence but as a comrade-in-arms, and told him that he could not have fully thought through what he was doing. Casado replied harshly: 'Cordón, in my opinión the government has not acted as it should have done. There's nothing to be done with these politicians; they are all idiots and we are fed up with their foolishness and time-wasting.' Cordón responded tactfully: 'Now is not the time to argue about the government's actions. Now it is crucial to think about the people and, thinking about their best interests, it is crucial to proceed calmly and avoid anything that might lead to more people being killed or hurt. I think you should send here a representative of that Junta you have formed to explain why you have rebelled.' Irascible as ever, Casado replied: 'No! I will send nobody nor do I wish any contact with that government!' Cordón repeated that he should do so, arguing that the government was still recognized by the United States, Mexico and other nations that were ready to help mediate. 'If this is about getting a peace settlement with honourable conditions and guarantees for our people … and if it is necessary to replace the government then it must be done legally so that the negotiations with these nations can continue. To do anything else is madness and a crime.' To this, Casado just stated: 'That government is not legal.'

Cordón pointed out that, even if Negrín's government were illegal, without a formal transfer of powers Casado's Junta would be even more illegal and would not have the advantage of the international recognition still enjoyed by Negrín. He ended with an appeal to Casado's good sense: 'I ask you to think calmly about all of this and that you explain it to the Junta or whatever it is you have formed. At least that way we can ensure between all of us that the war does not end in a sad and dirty manner, with us killing each other, handing ourselves over to the enemy and leading the people to yet another sacrifice.' After a lengthy pause, Casado said hesitantly: 'What's done is done!' Cordón finished the conversation, saying, 'I hope that tonight at least you will not do anything irrevocable,' to which Casado replied simply: 'All right, I promise. Salud.'[24]

Negrín and the ministers then reconvened to continue the cabinet meeting in the light of the bombshell from Casado. Cordón began to telephone the principal military commanders and soon became aware of the full extent of the treachery. When he asked General Leopoldo Menéndez, the commander of the Army of the Levante, what he knew about Casado's coup, Menéndez prevaricated, reluctantly saying that 'he had heard something about it on the radio'. When Cordón pressed him further about his reaction, Menéndez replied evasively that he awaited the orders of General Matallana. Cordón pointed out that this was not an appropriate response given that the person demanding an answer was the under-secretary of defence on behalf of the Prime Minister and Minister of Defence. He then stated that standing there next to him was Matallana himself who would certainly condemn Casado's action. He passed the receiver to Matallana, who replied to whatever Menéndez said only with monosyllables. He thereby confirmed to Cordón that they were both in on the conspiracy.

Feeling that nothing was to be gained by revealing his outrage, and concerned only to gain time for the government to act, Cordón simply took the phone back from Matallana and told Menéndez about the conversation he had had earlier with Casado. Menéndez replied: 'I agree that we must do everything possible to prevent armed conflict between us. We must all make sure that the first shot is not fired and you can contribute greatly in that regard.' This accords closely with the account of Lieutenant Colonel Ciutat, according to which Menéndez replied 'that there should not be a war within the war, that we should not take up arms against those we have fought alongside, something that could only benefit the enemy'.

At this point, Cordón, obviously with the agreement of Negrín and the cabinet, asked Menéndez to telephone Casado and stress the need to avoid internecine bloodshed. He also asked Menéndez to transmit an offer to maintain the legal status of the Republic by means of a hand-over of powers from the government to the Junta. To facilitate this, the government would send its resignation by telegram to Martínez Barrio. He then asked Menéndez not to take any military initiative that 'could unleash a catastrophe'. Menéndez agreed to phone Casado and to get back to Cordón with his response. He ended with the rather alarming words: 'I promise that tonight we won't do anything that could be seen as an attack on El Poblet.'[25]

The only encouraging responses that Cordón was able to elicit came from Colonel Antonio Escobar in Extremadura and Colonel

Domingo Moriones Larraga in Andalusia, who both replied that they supported Negrín.[26] In the meantime, Menéndez spoke to Casado. He passed on the message from Cordón about a transfer of powers and they discussed the significance of the cryptic answers given by Matallana to both of them. They concluded erroneously that Matallana was being held as a hostage. Regarding the offer, Casado claimed later to have said: 'You are the fifth person commissioned to pass on this message. Dr Negrín has given the same authority to the ministers Giner de los Rios and Gómez, to the under-secretary of the army and to the chief of the air force and I have told all of them, as I am telling you, that I do not wish to have these powers handed over to me. On the other hand, I authorize you to tell Dr Negrín that if within three hours General Matallana is not at his headquarters, I shall shoot every member of the government.' Lieutenant Colonel Ciutat reported later that 'then, Menéndez had spoken on the telephone to Casado who told him that, after consulting with the Junta, they refused to receive any authority from those who did not have it to give because the government was not constitutionally legitimate'.[27]

Casado's version, while broadly in tune with other accounts, telescopes the sequence of events and, typically, attributes to himself a virtually exclusive role in the Ministry of Finance. According to Edmundo Domínguez, Besteiro played an important part in encouraging Casado to reject the offers of a transfer of powers, advising him: 'Better not to have anything to do with them. We don't even know what is hidden behind the offer.' Domínguez also recounts a conversation in which Del Val berated the anarchist minister Segundo Blanco for suggesting a hand-over of powers. Santiago Garcés claimed later that there had been a suggestion that Trifón Gómez, the quartermaster general and a close friend of Besteiro, could be the intermediary in any hand-over. Domínguez was astonished by the rejection of the offer since it meant renouncing access both to government funds held outside Spain and to existing diplomatic links with other countries. It reflected the frivolity of the anarchists and the arrogance of Casado and Besteiro in that they were blinded by their desire to humiliate Negrín.[28]

More and more bad news was reaching El Poblet. There were reports of Communists and other supporters of Negrín being captured and held hostage. In his capacity as head of the Servicio de Inteligencia Militar, Santiago Garcés spoke to the commander of the SIM for the Army of the Centre, Ángel Pedrero, and ordered him to arrest Casado, which he refused to do.[29] Cordón received distressing news about the activities of the erstwhile Communist Lieutenant Colonel Ricardo Burillo Stohle of the Assault Guards. Earlier in the war, Burillo had been a highly effective police chief in Barcelona and helped put a stop to anarchist atrocities. However, he had turned against the Communist Party after being expelled in mid-1938 for failures on the Extremadura front. He was described by Cordón as 'on the verge of lunacy'. Togliatti claimed that Burillo was a key figure in Casado's coup, having made the bulk of the organizational preparations. He had allegedly purged the Assault Guards of Communists and was now in a position to use them against the party. In the series of postings published on 3 March, Burillo had been dismissed as head of public order and put under the orders of Cordón. He claimed that the postings were illegal and so he had prevented Etelvino Vega from taking over as Military Governor of Alicante.[30]

Even before the broadcasts by the members of Casado's junta, Wenceslao Carrillo had telephoned Eustaquio Cañas, the Civil Governor of Murcia, and asked him if he was aware of developments in Madrid. Before Cañas could reply, Carrillo brusquely told him that he would shortly be receiving a telegram from him and hung up. Having just returned briefly from Cartagena, and knowing nothing of the imminent announcement of the creation of the Junta, Cañas was nonplussed by Carrillo's message. Shortly afterwards, a telegram arrived, albeit not from Carrillo but from Colonel Burillo and General José Aranguren Roldán: 'With the forces at your disposal, under the orders of Colonel Aizpuru, leave for Yuste (Alicante) and proceed to arrest the Government of Negrín, especially Negrín himself, Álvarez del Vayo and Uribe. Take the rest of the government into your custody.' Colonel Gabriel Aizpuru Maristany, the commander of the Assault Guards in Murcia, had received a similarly worded telegram. Having discussed it, they decided to ignore the order. A few minutes after midnight, the telegram announced by Carrillo arrived in Cañas's office: 'State quickly if you accept the authority of the recently constituted Junta. If not, think about the consequences.' Cañas tried desperately to make contact with Posición Yuste but could not get a telephone link. His principal concern was still the revolt in Cartagena. Having ensured the loyalty to himself of the Assault Guards, and in ignorance of the situation at Yuste, he decided to play for time and finally, at around 3 a.m., he replied ambiguously to Carrillo: 'In reply to your telegram, I await further orders.' At some point, he must have been able to contact Cordón, who noted in his diary that Burillo had issued orders for the arrest of everyone at Posición Yuste.[31]

Meanwhile, Matallana's facial expression and body language revealed ever more signs of agitation in the wake of his compromising pantomimes on the telephone with both Casado and Menéndez. Cordón thought that he was both afraid and ashamed of the way in which his fellow conspirators had acted. Nevertheless, at the same time, he felt himself committed to joining them. Lamenting what had happened, Matallana offered himself as an intermediary with Casado. Cordón, convinced that the 'organizers of the betrayal would not unleash violence as long as Matallana, our only "hostage", remained with us', insisted that he should not leave until the cabinet had finished deliberating.

In the course of the night, Cordón tried to contact Ménendez in Valencia but connections were difficult. At about 5.30 a.m., Menéndez telephoned back. Previously polite, his tone now was brutally aggressive. Cordón recalled: 'He no longer spoke as a subordinate and a comrade but as an enemy who, sensing victory, had thrown himself unreservedly into the conspiracy.' Menéndez related his conversation with Casado about Matallana being held as a hostage (which was not the case). Cordón told him that Matallana was free to leave whenever he wished, although he should wait until the cabinet meeting was over, given that he was chief of the general staff and its conclusions might affect him. Menéndez demanded to speak to Matallana. When Cordón gave him the receiver, he was amazed to hear Matallana respond to something said by Menéndez by exclaiming: 'But I am detained' (*Pero hombre, ¡si estoy detenido!* – in Spanish, *detenido* can mean either 'detained', as in 'delayed', or 'under arrest'). Seeing Cordón's astonished expression, Matallana corrected himself, saying 'I mean I am delayed [*retenido*]. I wish I could be there and every-where else at the same time! You need to be patient.'[32]

When Matallana handed the telephone back to Cordón, Menéndez barked: 'Listen, Cordón, it can't go on like this for another minute. What has the cabinet decided?' Cordón replied that the meeting was about to finish and so he did not know what its conclusions were. Menéndez said: 'All right. Whether it's finished or not, Matallana has to come here, safe and sound, immediately and you have to come with him.' Cordón tried to calm him down: 'I think you're losing your head, Menéndez. I've already told you that Matallana can leave when-ever he wants and, if you're worried about his safety, you can take whatever precautions you think necessary on the road, although I think it's a bit over the top. As for me going with him, why should I? I am not obliged to do so either as his friend or as under-secretary of the Ministry of Defence.'

Menéndez then snapped, 'Very well, but the government has to make a decision,' to which Cordón simply said: 'I'll pass on the message but I'm not the cabinet.' Menéndez now issued a threat: 'Well, take note of this. If Matallana isn't here soon, we will shoot all those we have arrested in Madrid. I have already agreed on this with Casado. And not just that. We will also shoot all of you.' Cordón replied calmly: 'Understood. For my part, I can only tell you that nothing has happened to Matallana and he will leave for Valencia in a few minutes if it is authorized by the Minister [that is, Negrín] from whom he has to seek permission. You ought to stay calm. Salud.'

While Cordón was talking to Menéndez, the cabinet meeting had come to an end. The decision had clearly been taken to abandon Spain since Negrín was packing suitcases. Matallana asked Negrín for permission to leave, which was immediately granted. With tears in his eyes, Matallana embraced each of the ministers and senior officers in turn. The last was Negrín, who said: 'Tell your comrades that their behaviour has been unworthy of them.'

Saying that he was going in order to do everything he could to ensure that 'things turn out as well as possible', Matallana set off by car shortly afterwards. As he left the room, bitter smiles were provoked when someone said: 'You won't be coming back.'[33] Menéndez's threats meant that, against the clearly hostile intentions of the Consejo Nacional de Defensa, the only forces at Negrín's disposal in the area were the eighty *guerrilleros* who guarded Posición Yuste.

Tagüeña reached El Poblet at dawn on 6 March. There he received contradictory news. He was informed on the one hand of Casado's success in Madrid, and on the other that the previous day's uprising by the Fifth Column in Cartagena had been crushed. Nevertheless, at 4.00 a.m., Rear Admiral Buiza had sent a message to the effect that the fleet would not return to Cartagena. The quashing of the last hopes for evacuation was devastating.[34] Negrín had no inclination to see internecine strife within the Republic. With a tone of resignation, he told Hidalgo de Cisneros: 'Our job now is to try to gain time. On no account quarrel with Casado.'[35] This is consistent with the offer made to Casado by Paulino Gómez for Negrín to transfer his powers to the Junta. Clearly, such a transfer could hardly be legal since Casado had no legal basis for his military coup.

In fact, despite these efforts, after Menéndez's last phone call it was obvious to Negrín that to stay at El Poblet was tantamount to handing himself over to Casado. Francisco Vega Díaz described how Negrín, 'with a look of great sadness and disgust that he didn't have before, called for silence and said to his ministers and the rest of his staff in a hoarse voice choked with emotion: "We are all ready, aren't we? So, no more doubts. Let's go!"' Shortly before, he had telephoned Colonel Antonio Camacho Benítez, head of the air force in the centre-south zone, at his headquarters in Los Llanos and ordered him to send two Douglas DC-2 passenger aircraft to the airfield at Monóvar to be ready for departure. According to Camacho's secretary, José Manuel Vidal Zapater, his commander was deeply reluctant to send the aircraft because once they got to France they would be sequestrated. Vidal claimed that Camacho, unable to disobey out of hand, quickly invented the excuse that he could send only one because the other was in need of repairs. In this version, Negrín therefore had to make do with only one aircraft and, in consequence, it would be so overloaded with the ministers and their luggage that it was able to take off only with the greatest difficulty. It almost certainly the case that Camacho was reluctant to release the aircraft. However, Vidal Zapater's version is contradicted by several eyewitness accounts which concur in asserting that Negrín and his cabinet departed in two Douglas DC-2s.

Having made the decision for everyone to leave, Negrín announced that he would meet his ministers and the rest of the staff at the airfield. According to Stepanov, he regarded it as a debt of honour to say goodbye to Togliatti and Stepanov and the senior Communist Party members, Dolores Ibárruri, Uribe, Hidalgo de Cisneros, Cordón, Líster and Modesto. At approximately 10.00 a.m., accompanied by Uribe and Moix, Santiago Garcés, Álvarez del Vayo, Negrín and his aides Benigno Rodríguez and Manuel Sánchez Arcas went to the cluster of houses, 3 kilometres to the south of Elda, known as Posición Dakar, where the senior Communists were staying. The other ministers and their staff left El Poblet in a line of cars followed by a van loaded with suitcases, briefcases, files, two or three cases of brandy and champagne and the machine guns of the guards. They went ahead to the airfield known as El Fondó at Monóvar to await the arrival of Negrín and Vayo.[36]

When Negrín took his leave of Vega Díaz, after thirty hours without sleep, the stress that he had suffered was palpable – he appeared 'pale, haggard, his eyelids swollen, unshaven and soaked in sweat. In comparison with the man I used to know and I had seen in the last few hours, he looked like an invalid without hope.' Nevertheless, Vega regarded the dignity and humanity with which Negrín had behaved as 'superhuman'. When he arrived at Posición Dakar, according to Pasionaria's secretary, Irene Falcón, 'Negrín's face was grey and tense.'[37]

Once Negrín had reached Posición Dakar, the senior Communist figures tried to get him to change his mind about leaving. Togliatti proposed that a last effort should be made to secure an agreement between the government and Casado's Junta to avoid a fratricidal bloodbath. It was a device to gain time in order to ascertain the scale of support enjoyed by Casado and the possibilities of opposing him.

To this end, Pedro Checa sent emissaries out across the central zone. Tagüeña, for instance, went to Alicante to make sure that the port was still in government hands.[38] Determined to prevent the unnecessary sacrifice of Republican blood, Negrín immediately sat down to write a conciliatory declaration which he handed to Benigno Rodríguez so that he could take it to be broadcast. Rodríguez returned shortly afterwards to report that the radio transmitter had been dismantled. Accordingly, the message was sent to Menéndez for retransmission to Casado. It called for any eventual transfer of powers to be carried out without violence. Negrín's text pointed out that there was no fundamental discrepancy between the Casado Junta's proclaimed objectives and the government's commitment to a peace settlement without reprisals.

The full text read as follows:

The Government over which I preside has been painfully surprised by a movement in whose aims of a swift and honourable peace free from persecutions and reprisals, and guaranteeing the country's independence (as announced by the Junta in its manifesto to the country), there appear to be certain discrepancies. My Government also considers that the reasons given by the Junta in explanation of its actions are unjustifiable. It has consistently laboured to retain that spirit of unity which has always animated its policy, and any mistaken interpretation of its actions can only be due to the impatience of those who are unaware of the real situation. If they had waited for the explanation of the present position, which was to have been given tonight in the Government's name, it is certain that this unfortunate episode would never have taken place. If contact between the Government and those sectors who appear to be in disagreement could have been established in time, there is no doubt whatever that all differences would have been removed. It is impossible to undo what has been done, but it is nevertheless possible to prevent serious consequences to those who have fought as brothers for a common denominator of ideals, and – most particularly – to Spain. If the roots of mischief are pruned in time they may yet grow a good and useful plant. On the altar of the sacred interests of Spain we must all offer up our weapons, and if we wish for a settlement with our adversaries, we must first avoid all bloody conflict between those who have been brothers in arms. The Government therefore calls upon the Junta which has been constituted in Madrid and proposes that it should appoint one or more persons to settle all differences in a friendly and patriotic manner. Inasmuch as it is of interest to Spain, it is of interest to the Government that, whatever may happen, any transfer of authority should take place in a normal and constitutional manner. Only in this way can the cause for which we have fought remain unsullied. And only thus can we preserve those advantages in the international sphere which still remain to us through our limited connections. In the certainty that as Spaniards the Junta will give heed to our request. Juan Negrín[39]

When the message reached the Ministry of Finance in Madrid, Casado read it out loud to his assembled collaborators. There were mutters of protest from the anarchists and others. Commenting that Negrín's offer reflected concern for the interests of the Republic and of Spain, José Rodríguez Vega offered to go to Elda and accept the transfer of powers on behalf of the Consejo Nacional de Defensa. He pointed out that this would ensure that there would be no violence between the Consejo and supporters of the government. Given that Casado was anxious to secure the approval of the UGT for his Junta, he gave the impression that he was inclined to accept, saying: 'It seems like a good idea.' He then turned to Julián Besteiro and said: 'Do you hear what Rodríguez Vega is saying? There's a lot to be said in favour of a transfer of power. I certainly think it's a good idea.' Apparently, Besteiro replied that there should be no negotiations with the government and he was supported in this by General Miaja, who shouted: 'No way, no way! Pay them no attention. It's a trap to gain time!'[40] In consequence, no reply was sent to Negrín.

In fact, despite the cynical, or perhaps fearful, speculations of those who surrounded Casado, Negrín had made the offer as a way of avoiding violence. The arrogant dismissal of it by Besteiro, Miaja and the anarchists opened the way to precisely the mini-civil war that Negrín had hoped to prevent. Rodríguez Vega and Edmundo Domínguez, both of whom disapproved of the Consejo's action, had left the Finance Ministry to hold a meeting of the UGT executive. En route, they went to see Rafael Henche, the Alcalde of Madrid. In his office, they found the quartermaster general, Trifón Gómez. Both expressed their disapproval of the way in which Casado had acted.[41] According to Irene Falcón, Casado had responded to the peace initiative with a broadcast ordering the arrest of Negrín, Álvarez del Vayo, Uribe, Líster, Modesto and all the members of the PCE politburo. She was unaware that Wenceslao Carrillo had already sent instructions to this effect to Ricardo Burillo. Rodríguez Vega remarked on the fervour with which Wenceslao Carrillo set about arresting Communists and his readiness simply to have them shot.[42] Lieutenant Colonel Francisco Romero Marín recorded later, 'We had to leave Madrid with pistols in our hands because there were controls everywhere, but we managed to reach Elda.'[43]

After the text had been sent, Negrín is alleged to have said to Álvarez del Vayo in German: 'Ich, auf alle Fälle, werde gehen' (I, in any case, am going). At about 2.30 p.m., Tagüeña arrived back from Alicante with the news that the recently appointed Military Governor of the province, Etelvino Vega, had been arrested and the city taken by supporters of Casado. Warned that Casadista forces were approaching Elda, and thus faced with the prospect of being captured and used by Casado as a bargaining chip with Franco, Negrín declared: 'Señores, we cannot stay here a moment more because they will arrest us. I think we should all leave.' He and Álvarez del Vayo set off for the airfield at Monóvar where they arrived shortly after 3 p.m. The remainder of the cabinet was waiting impatiently. Álvarez del Vayo wrote later: 'We were greeted by the justified, if restrained, indignation of our colleagues, who like ourselves had had nothing to eat, and who had, besides, been waiting for six hours in the blazing sun.' The last refreshment taken by Vayo and Negrín on Spanish soil was a cup of coffee before they left Posición Dakar, made for them by Irene Falcón on the instructions of Pasionaria.[44]

As they were leaving Posición Dakar, they encountered the chief Soviet military adviser, Mikhail Stepanovich Shumilov (alias 'Shilov'), Stanislav Vaupshasov and his interpreter, who were also waiting to be evacuated. They asked Negrín to provide two Douglas aircraft for the evacuation of themselves and the other Russians who were part of the security forces guarding the house. Negrín could do nothing to help them, not least in the light of Camacho's reluctance to send the aircraft that he had requested for the evacuation of the government. Vaupshasov wrote bitterly that 'Negrín sheepishly replied that he no longer had any power and all that he could do for us was to thank us for our services. Well, as they say, thanks for nothing! Nevertheless, the ex-prime minister wrote a letter of introduction to the commander of the Los Llanos air base near Albacete Colonel Cascón. We took this kind note but it was useless since there were no aircraft at the base.' Colonel Manuel Cascón Briega Cascón was Camacho's second-in-command.

While they were talking, Negrín's adjutant arrived to report that the rebels had captured Albacete and that he must hasten to Monóvar where the planes were waiting for him. 'Negrín hastily shook hands and virtually ran to his car.' Santiago Garcés, who accompanied Negrín, recalled that the cabinet left for France in two Douglas transport aircraft. Antonio Cordón, who was with Negrín until shortly before his departure, also recalled there being two Douglas DC-2s, not one, as alleged by Vidal Zapater. Enrique Líster, who was guarding the airfield at Monóvar, also wrote of protecting the departure of two Douglas aircraft. Given the number of ministers and other senior staff, it is difficult to see how they, together with trunks of official documents and the large quantities of luggage described by Francisco Vega Díaz, could all have been accommodated in one fourteen-seater aircraft. It would be a long and dangerous flight over Francoist-held territory. After crossing the French border en route to Toulouse, Negrín would never again set foot in Spain.[45]

While Negrín had been drafting the message to Casado, it was decided that Dolores Ibárruri must be safeguarded at all costs. Accordingly, accompanied by Cordón, Jesús Monzón, Romero Marín and some others, she had left for Oran in Algeria. They arrived around 1.00 p.m. They travelled in a De Havilland DH-89 Dragon Rapide from the Escuela de Polimotores (multi-engined aircraft flying school) at Totana where the commander was a Communist called Ramos.[46] After Negrín and Vayo had left Posición Dakar, the rest of the PCE politburo held a meeting at the El Fondó aerodrome, the last to be celebrated during the war. It was really a question of ratifying a decision already imposed on the politburo and the Comintern delegates by Casado's failure to respond to the peace initiative. Given that Casado's Consejo Nacional de Defensa was now the only effective authority in the country, to fight against it signified another civil war. As the partisans of Republican unity, the PCE could not undertake the responsibility of fighting against the rest of the Popular Front. Moreover, Togliatti believed that, even if a decision to fight had been taken, the Communists would have been defeated given the scale of the forces ranged against them and the scale of defeatism within their own ranks. After all, with Franco recognized by the Great Powers, and the Soviet Union looking at alliance with Nazi Germany, it would have been a hopeless fight. Because the radio was out of action, Togliatti had lost contact with Moscow and dispatched Irene Falcón to Albacete with coded messages to be sent from there. When she arrived, the local Communists had disappeared, either arrested, fled or gone underground. She was able to return to Elda only with enormous difficulty. Líster and the *guerrilleros* held off Casado forces that were approaching the airfield. Hidalgo de Cisneros recalled seeing the headlights of the trucks bringing anarchist troops loyal to Casado to capture the remaining Communists. The last to leave flew to France at dawn on 7 March. Tagüeña reached Toulouse on 7 March and took a train to Paris, where he was astonished to read in the press of the following day that the Communists in Madrid were resisting the Casado forces. Togliatti, Checa and Claudín had remained in the hope of organizing the evacuation of militants. They were arrested by Casado's forces, but Claudín used his long-standing friendship with Prudencio Sayagués, the head of the local SIM, to secure their release.[47]

Eustaquio Cañas spent all of 6 March involved in the operations to put down the rebellion in Cartagena. When he returned to Murcia, shortly after reaching his office he received a telephone call from the Socialist Pascual Tomás who was working with Wenceslao Carrillo. Despite having been elected as PSOE deputy for Murcia with Communist votes, Tomás now urged Cañas 'to put all his energy behind the Junta until the Communist scum are smashed once and for all'. On the morning of 7 March, Cañas was informed that a large troopship was approaching Cartagena. It was, of course, the *Castillo Olite*. He hastened to the naval base and arrived in time to see the horrific scenes when the ship exploded. On his return to Murcia, he found several individuals who had come to seek refuge from the terror being unleashed by Burillo throughout Valencia and Alicante. Among them was the Socialist Ricardo Mella, who had just been removed as Civil Governor of Alicante. Burillo himself arrived in Murcia at midday on 8 March where he peremptorily ordered Cañas to arrest all Communists in Murcia, which he declined to do. After a violent confrontation, Cañas threw him out of his office and Burillo left muttering threats.[48]

11

Casado's Civil War

Through arrogance or ignorance, Casado, Besteiro and their fellow rebels harboured utterly naive expectations of what an early end to the war would bring. In contrast, Negrín was fully aware of the consequences of a catastrophic defeat. He had seen with his own eyes the horrors experienced by the defeated Republicans in France where they had encountered humiliation and hardship, though at least they had not experienced the hatred that could be expected from the Francoists in terms of trials, torture, imprisonment and executions. When he heard the news of the coup, Vicente Rojo, who had never forgiven Casado for his treachery during the battle of the Ebro, wrote: 'What will they do when Franco tells them that he doesn't recognize their authority to negotiate with him?'[1] In the basement of the Ministry of Finance during the first hours of Casado's Consejo de Defensa, Besteiro asked naive questions about Negrín which suggested prejudice rather than hard information about the government against which he was rebelling. Witnesses described him as nervous and fidgeting with his hands, chain-smoking, his eyes shining, emanating an air of otherworldliness. According to Eduardo Domínguez, everything about Besteiro's behaviour in the Ministry cellars suggested that he was 'infantile, weak and washed-out'.[2]

With Negrín and his ministers on their way to France and the Communist leadership flying to Algeria, the opposition faced by the Casado Junta was perhaps unexpected. At what was to be the last meeting of the PCE on Spanish soil until after the death of Franco, armed resistance against Casado seemed to have been ruled out. It was later alleged that, as organization secretary, Pedro Checa failed to communicate decisions adequately to his comrades.[3] That was clearly a factor in the events of the week following the coup when a group consisting of the secretary of the Madrid Communist organization, Domingo Girón, Isidoro Díeguez, Vicente Pertegás and Francisco-Félix Montiel orchestrated the resistance from Villa Eloísa, a house in Ciudad Lineal on the eastern outskirts of the city.[4] The Communist leaders and rank and file in Madrid, who had always enjoyed a degree of autonomy from the rest of the party, were simply not ready to throw away two and a half years of struggle against Franco. An even more powerful motivation lay in the fact that the Communists in Madrid suspected with very good reason that it was Casado's intention to use them as his payment to Franco for the concessions that he thought he would receive. The view of the Madrid Communists that to capitulate to Casado was to capitulate to Franco was shared by the Trotskyist Manuel Casanova. Writing at the time, he denounced the cowardice of the PCE leadership and urged all workers to forget their hatred of Stalinism and join in the battle against Casado: 'We are faced with a conspiracy whose objective is to open the doors to Franco by smashing the revolutionary base of the Communist Party. Today, in Madrid, what is happening is a stab in the back by treacherous generals who want, by the destruction of the Communists, to prepare the way for capitulation to Franco.' Even though the POUM and the anarchists had often made common cause, Casanova wrote with disgust of the role of the CNT–FAI: 'Val and Mera are going down a criminal road: they are handing over the proletariat of Madrid to the gang of capitulators and, indirectly, to Franco.'[5]

General Miaja's secretary, Fernando Rodríguez Miaja, wrote later: 'In my opinion, Negrín's government which found itself buffeted by that whirlwind of confusions found an unexpected way out thanks to the ambition of the recently promoted General Segismundo Casado in his determination to act as the principal protagonist on the basis of his belief that he could find the solution that would end the war and thereby become the saviour of Spain.'[6]

Negrín's activities after he reached France did not suggest that he had found a way out that was easy. He had already started to make arrangements for the Republic to have funds in exile before returning to Spain from Toulouse on 10 February 1939.[7] Now, in Paris, Negrín continued to use government resources to keep the centre zone supplied with food and equipment. He had also made arrangements for ships to evacuate the tens of thousands who were fleeing from the Francoist advances.[8] He wrote later to Prieto:

> From Paris, we continued to work to avoid the collapse of the zone by ensuring that the needs in terms of food, raw materials and fuel were met. Efforts were made to overcome the difficulties of supplying war matériel despite the blockade. Before the outrageous desertion of the fleet, the most urgent items for Cartagena – detonator fuses for anti-aircraft shells and fighter aircraft – were on their way. Sufficient tonnage had been contracted for the evacuation of forty to fifty thousand people per fortnight and, through friendly intermediaries, arrangements were made for them to be admitted into Algeria and Tunisia. The bulk of the few refugees who did escape from the centre did so in our ships. The reasons why others were not saved were 1) until the last moment, Casadista functionaries would not permit them to leave; 2) the precipitate nature of the final collapse saw the French authorities restrict facilities for admission, something that would not have happened if the capitulation had not been so rapid; 3) the rebel blockade prevented our poor compatriots from leaving.[9]

Negrín was right on all counts. The loss of the fleet's capacity to prevent the Francoist blockade of the Levante coast ensured that the French ships that he had chartered would not risk going into Alicante and Valencia to pick up the desperate refugees milling on the docksides. The Junta did everything possible to prevent people leaving until, according to its egalitarian rhetoric, everyone who wanted to do so could leave. In its manifesto, the Consejo Nacional de Defensa accused the members of Negrín's cabinet and the Communist leadership of shamefully abandoning their posts without mentioning that they had left El Poblet to avoid being arrested and handed over to Franco. In the end, as will be seen, with the exception of Besteiro, Miguel San Andrés Castro and Antonio Pérez García, the behaviour of the members of Casado's 'cabinet' was significantly more shameful. That was not just because, despite their 'heroic' rhetoric, they ensured their own escape but because they had given little thought to the time-consuming complexities of evacuation. It was not just a question of merchant ships to carry the evacuees and a fleet to escort them through the Francoist blockade. Passports and other documentation had to be prepared, arrangements made for political asylum and money provided for the sustenance of the refugees. Another huge failure of the Casado Junta was that, even if all of the above preparations had been made, no thought was given to the transport of those most at risk from Madrid and other inland towns to the coast.[10]

From Paris too, Negrín reprimanded the Republic's Ambassador in the United States, Fernando de los Ríos, for a public declaration, made on the advice of Prieto, that the Negrín government had no constitutional basis and that he therefore recognized the Consejo Nacional de Defensa. In the opinion of Negrín, if De los Ríos believed that the CND was the only legitimate authority, he should have resigned. Instead, De los Ríos's action thus contributed to Franco being recognized by the United States. A directive was issued to the Republic's ambassadors in countries that had not yet recognized Franco ordering them not to comment on the changed situation other than to point out that the Casado coup had undermined the efforts of Negrín's government to protect the population against reprisals and ensure safe evacuation.[11]

Casado's action was rewarded by Franco in the form of a de facto ceasefire. As the Caudillo's notes to his staff on 25 February had made clear, his army had more than ample means to occupy Madrid 'by force, when and how it pleases, [so] the surrender must be without conditions'. Nevertheless, it was worth waiting for Casado's coup since it would save the cost of a final offensive against the centre-south zone.[12] Only in Madrid did Casado's coup meet serious armed resistance, in the first days at least. In part, this was a response to Wenceslao Carrillo's order that the police should arrest Communists whenever possible.[13] Elsewhere there was little fighting. The commanders of the three other armies, General Leopoldo Menéndez in Valencia, Colonel Domingo Moriones Larraga in Andalusia and

Colonel Antonio Escobar Huertas in Extremadura, were principally concerned to avoid senseless slaughter among the troops under their command. Without considering the consequences for the mass of the Republican population after defeat, they merely saw the Casado coup as a way to end the war. In Madrid, in theory, the PCE had the advantage because three of Madrid's four army corps were commanded by career officers who were PCE members. However, they were all tempted by Casado's promises that Franco would permit their incorporation into his post-war army. The commander of the II Army Corps of the centre, Colonel Bueno, although a member of the Communist Party, was a friend of Casado, a fellow freemason, and had refused to replace him on 25 February. Now, he feigned illness and was replaced by his second-in-command, Major Guillermo Ascanio. Ascanio managed to persuade one of the others, Colonel Luis Barceló Jover, pro-Communist commander of the I Corps of the Army of the Centre, that there was no chance of Franco forgiving their 'military rebellion'.[14]

Pressed by the officers on his own staff, Barceló had reluctantly disobeyed Casado's orders to move against Communist units. He decided to join Díeguez and Montiel in Ciudad Lineal and assume command of the Communists' military action. In fact, doubts have been expressed as to who really commanded the Communist forces, Barceló, Ascanio or Pertegás. Certainly, Communist units surrounded Madrid, and for several days there was fierce fighting in the capital. To the delight of Franco, Cipriano Mera's troops were withdrawn from the Guadalajara front to fight the Communists. According to Wenceslao Carrillo, this was done in cooperation with the Francoists, who undertook not to advance and even to look after the abandoned Republican trenches. It is clear that Franco was desperate for Casado to defeat the Communists. Carrillo boasted later that anarchist units were permitted to cross the key Arganda bridge across the River Jarama south-east of the capital, transit across which was usually dangerous given that it was within range of Francoist artillery. There were suspicions that the movement of Casado's forces was coordinated with Francoist attacks.[15] According to the senior Falangist Antonio Bouthelier, General Manuel Matallana who was in charge of the CND's forces held desperate interviews with representatives of the

SIPM and went so far as to beg tearfully for Franco to occupy Madrid and so rescue the beleaguered Consejo Nacional de Defensa. Needless to say, his pleas were ignored since the Francoist high command preferred to wait a few days, let Casado defeat the Communists and then enter Madrid unopposed.[16]

On 7 March, to avoid being trapped in the Ministry of Finance, Miaja and his entourage set off for Tarancón, 82 kilometres to the south-east of the capital, where they established headquarters, known as 'Posición Chamberí'. Over the next few days, Miaja organized the dispatch of troops to Madrid to assist in quelling the Communist resistance and to block the arrival of Communist forces intending to join their comrades. At one point, in conversation with José González Montoliú of the PCE, he claimed that he had no influence over Casado, insisting 'I am just a figurehead who counts for nothing.' When the Communist opposition to Casado had been crushed, Miaja returned to Madrid on 12 March and established himself in the Presidencia building in the Castellana. He took advantage of his position to arrange the exchange of his son, who was a prisoner of the Francoists, for the Falangist Miguel Primo de Rivera.[17]

Ever since Cipriano Mera had been given command of the IV Army Corps, he had put every possible obstacle in the way of the Communists, and particularly of the Civil Governor of Guadalajara, José Cazorla. Edmundo Domínguez believed that this had undermined morale among the Republican forces in the area.[18] The support of the IV Army Corps, with its four divisions (the 12th, 14th, 17th and 23rd), was crucial to Casado's success. When the Consejo Nacional de Defensa was announced, the 300th Guerrilla Brigade and 1st Armoured Brigade, based in Alcalá de Henares, had remained faithful to Negrín. With the Communists on the verge of defeating Casado's coalition after the first confrontations on 5, 6 and 7 March, Mera mobilized the 14th Division, under his anarchist comrade Liberino González, to surround Alcalá de Henares. There was fierce fighting with the Guerrilla unit which held the city and which had also occupied nearby Torrejón de Ardoz. Only after Casado had sent more troops from Madrid did Alcalá de Henares and Torrejón de Ardoz fall on 9 March. The local town council declared its recognition of the CND, expelled the PCE representatives and closed down the Communist Party headquarters. Mera's forces then pushed eastwards to Barajas, entering the capital through Ciudad Lineal.[19] When Mera reached the Finance Ministry, he found Besteiro seriously ill on a camp bed in the cellars. Mera offered to have him escorted to his home, but he refused: 'I have undertaken to carry out a job with the Conseja and will carry it out until the last moment.'[20]

The commander of the Army of Extremadura, Colonel Antonio Escobar Huertas, had, after initial dithering, declared for Casado. Having told Negrín in the early hours of the morning of 6 March that he supported the legitimate government unreservedly, it is to be presumed that he now regarded the Consejo Nacional de Defensa as the legitimate government. After all, in Barcelona in July 1936, Escobar had loyally declared in favour of the Republic despite his deeply Catholic convictions. When he finally went into action after declaring for Casado it was to crush the Communist resistance in Ciudad Real led by the parliamentary deputy Pedro Martínez Cartón. Once the Communists had been defeated, he used all his energies to put pressure on Casado and Besteiro to hasten peace negotiations with Franco. Nevertheless, Escobar was executed in Barcelona on 8 February 1940, largely for his role in 1936 in preventing the military uprising in the Catalan capital.[21]

Escobar played a key role in securing victory for Casado in Ciudad Real and doing so with minimum bloodshed. In fact, the anarchist Civil Governor, David Antona, had pursued a fiercely anti-Communist policy for some time. Casado's coup was opposed by the tank base in the town of Daimiel, north-east of the provincial capital, and by some Guerrilla units. Together they occupied the Ayuntamiento and other major public buildings and cut communications with Madrid. Casado was concerned that they would advance on the capital. Meanwhile, troops loyal to Negrín, under Martínez Cartón, threatened the town of Puertollano in the south-west of the province. In the provincial capital, on 7 March, numerous members of the PCE and the JSU, together with some *guerrilleros*, retreated into the PCE headquarters. Wenceslao Carrillo ordered their rebellion crushed and anarchist units armed with machine guns, with tank support, assaulted the building. Faced with such superior forces, the Communists surrendered. Colonel Escobar ordered the arrest of the commanders of tank and guerrilla brigades. His intervention ensured a negotiated settlement. By the afternoon of 11 March, all opposition to the Consejo Nacional de Defensa in Ciudad Real had been crushed.[22]

An offer by José Rodríguez Vega, secretary general of the UGT, to act as peacemaker was accepted eagerly by Ángel Pedrero but rejected out of hand by Wenceslao Carrillo.[23] In the event, the PCE leadership seems to have decided that to fight on could achieve no more than a Pyrrhic victory. With the bulk of the Communist leadership forced into exile to avoid capture by Casadista forces, Jesús Hernández had taken over effective direction of the PCE. Togliatti, Checa and Claudín were briefly under Casadista arrest and, after escaping, went into hiding. Hernández created a new politburo made up of Jesús Larrañaga, José Palau, Sebastián Zapiráin and Pedro Martínez Cartón and assumed direct control of the resistance against the Consejo Nacional de Defensa. On 9 March, Hernández issued a belligerent manifesto calling on Communist commissars and army officers not to relinquish their commands or surrender their arms until the Popular Front had been restored and the persecution of the PCE had come to an end, with prisoners released and its press allowed to function normally. If this was not done, tank units would be used against the CND. Hernández's manifesto was contradicted by another much more conciliatory one written by Togliatti that was published on 12 March.

In the event, it was Togliatti's view that prevailed. This was helped by the fact that the commander of the Army of the Levante, General Leopoldo Menéndez, was altogether less intransigent than Casado and Wenceslao Carrillo. At the suggestion of Francisco Ciutat, it was agreed that the organization of the evacuation of militants was the principal issue. Accordingly, the priority was to maintain the legal status of the party and its capacity to function openly. Menéndez had been shocked by the unrestrained hatred of the Communists shown by Carrillo and Casado and was open to some kind of agreement with the party. The obstacle would be Burillo. Nevertheless, Menéndez agreed to meet José Palau to discuss liberty of action for the party and its press and a commitment to carry out no reprisals in return for Communist military units remaining inactive. This would lead to subsequent complaints from Casado and Carrillo that those in the Levante had not sent forces to support them in the fight against the Communists in Madrid.

However, in many places outside Madrid, there was a feeling even in Communist units that the war was lost and, even if it were possible to defeat the Junta, that it would still not be possible to defeat Franco. For example, the commanders of the XX and XXI Army Corps, Colonels Gustavo Durán and Ernesto Güemes, both regarded as members of the PCE, had refused to oppose the CND on the grounds that, with Negrín in exile, it constituted the only legal power. Similarly, in the Army of Andalusia, the Communist officers were divided, with many siding with the CND. Some key commanders had decided that there was no point in continuing the fight. These included Domingo Ungría, head of the XIV Guerrilla Army Corps that had protected the Negrín cabinet and the PCE leadership in their last days in Spain, Valentín González 'El Campesino' and Lucio Santiago. While negotiations were proceeding with General Menéndez, Hernández ordered fifty tanks and armoured cars, a machine-gun battalion and other forces to cut off the roads to Valencia. Although Menéndez regarded the Communist demands as reasonable, he did not appreciate Hernández's threats and responded by arresting some Communist officers. In this stalemate, neither side had an appetite for conflict. In the event, a relatively peaceful end was in sight when at dawn on 11 March General Matallana communicated the decision of the CND to recognize the legal status of the PCE, to free prisoners, to authorize the Communist press and to reopen the party's offices. Although rightly unsure of the sincerity of the offer, conscious of the reluctance of their units to take part in a mini-civil war, aware too that resistance was fizzling out in Madrid, Hernández and the rest of the politburo agreed to accept the terms offered.[24] In the event, the anti-Communist zeal of Wenceslao Carrillo would ensure that Matallana's promises were not fulfilled.

Another key factor that persuaded the politburo to contemplate terms was the knowledge that the Casadistas had managed to capture

Domingo Girón on the first day of fighting. As a result the Communist effort would lack an overall leader.[25] Moreover, there was no appetite on the part of the Communists to overthrow the Junta and take power. Since the Casado coup had put paid to any possibility of serious resistance, such a strategy would merely saddle the PCE with responsibility for a defeat that was inevitable.[26] Accordingly, first Pedro Checa and then Palmiro Togliatti sent instructions to the PCE to stop the fighting and negotiate with Casado in the hope that this might give party cadres the opportunity to prepare for evacuation for many members and clandestinity for those who had to remain. Checa's emissaries arrived in the early hours of 9 March and pointed out that, beyond Madrid, pro-Casado forces were in the ascendant. After heated debate among the Communists, an offer was submitted that day to make peace in return for the release of hostages and a place on the Consejo Nacional de Defensa. The intransigent reply from the CND was as follows:

1) All units to lay down their weapons and return to the posts occupied on the day the Consejo Nacional de Defensa was created;

2) All civilian and military personnel arrested by the rebel side to be handed over to the Consejo Nacional de Defensa;

3) The Consejo Nacional de Defensa undertakes to judge the events of the last days without partisan passion;

4) Substitution of all commanders and commissars according to procedures to be decided on by the Consejo Nacional de Defensa;

5) The Consejo Nacional de Defensa will free all prisoners belonging to the Communist Party who have not committed criminal acts;

6) The Consejo, once this conflict is resolved, is prepared to listen to the representatives of the Communist Party (Headquarters. 12 March 1939).[27]

A conciliatory reply was drafted by Togliatti. Obviously, while it is an absurd exaggeration to suggest that Stalin connived at the final defeat of the Republic, it was not in the interests of the Soviet Union to drag out a lost cause.[28] The Communist reply, as drafted by Togliatti, was:

We have lived through six days of fighting in Madrid and the Communist Party believes that to prolong it further will do terrible harm to the fatherland. For this reason, it has decided to use its influence in favour of a ceasefire because of the supreme duty to unite all our forces in the war against the invaders, with an enemy offensive imminent on one or other of our battle-fronts, and bearing in mind the circumstances in which the Negrín government felt it necessary to leave Spain. The Communist Party, which has at no time carried out acts nor had aims contrary to its well-known political line, declares today that without the unity of our people, all resistance is impossible. And it calls upon all sectors to reach a positive and fruitful agreement in the interests of our independence and our freedom. We have seen that the agreements of the Consejo Nacional de Defensa regarding an internal peace settlement exclude any kind of reprisals. In those circumstances, we not only abandon all resistance against the constituted power but we the Communists, at the front, in the rearguard, in the workplace and in battle, will also continue to give the fatherland, with our blood and our lives, an example of sacrifice, heroism and discipline.[29]

The instructions for Communist surrender were taken to the PCE in Madrid on 12 March by Togliatti's wife Rita Montagnana. Togliatti was in hiding in Valencia with Ettore Vanni, the editor of the newspaper *La Verdad*.

Almost immediately, there were many trials of the Communists who had fought against the CND. Those who were found guilty of military rebellion were still in prison when Madrid fell to the Francoists at the end of March. The majority were shot.[30] According to Wenceslao Carrillo, only two were shot by the Casado Junta, Lieutenant Colonel Luis Barceló Jover and José Conesa Arteaga, a Communist political commissar accused of ordering the execution of Socialists captured when the headquarters of the Agrupación Socialista Madrileña was attacked. Casado appeared as a witness for the prosecution. In the view of Edmundo Domínguez, Casado was motivated by an intense personal resentment of Barceló. When the sentence was discussed in the Consejo Nacional de Defensa, Antonio Pérez of the UGT and Besteiro spoke in favour of clemency, but they met an implacable determination to see Barceló and Conesa shot on the part of both Casado and Carrillo. When Eustaquio Cañas pleaded with Casado to be benevolent, he reacted violently, screaming that Barceló would be shot.

Lieutenant Colonel Bueno received a death sentence that was commuted to imprisonment on the grounds that, although he had been head of the II Army Corps which had resisted the CND, he had played no part in events because he had claimed to be ill and bedridden and had merely lacked the courage to oppose the Communists in his general staff. The execution of Barceló and Conesa marked the end of the dominance of the Communist Party in the central zone.[31]

With the Communists prepared to surrender and their senior leadership in exile, the anarchists and anti-Communist elements of the PSOE seized the opportunity for revenge. Expelling Communists from various political organizations and committees seemed a singularly futile exercise with the final disaster imminent.[32] When the JSU headquarters in Alicante were taken over by supporters of Largo Caballero, the local Socialist Youth Federation (Federación de Juventudes Socialistas, or FJS) was reconstituted. Busts of Lenin and large portraits of JSU leader Santiago Carrillo were destroyed in an iconoclastic rage.[33] If they had taken Casado's anti-Communist pronouncements to be sufficient to satisfy Franco's objectives, they were sadly in error. As the Caudillo's public statements about his post-victory objectives had made unmistakably clear, all those who opposed him were Communists. Franco had clarified further his plans for the defeated in a widely publicized interview given to Manuel Aznar on 31 December 1938. He divided them into hardened criminals beyond redemption and those who had been deceived by their leaders and were capable of repentance. Even for those who repented, there would be no amnesty or reconciliation, only punishment to guide them to their 'redemption'. Prisons and labour camps would provide the necessary purgatory for those with minor 'crimes' – that is to say, without blood on their hands. Others could expect no better fate than death or exile.[34] In the light of these declarations, it is astonishing that Casado took Franco's 'promises' about what awaited those without blood on their hands to mean no punishment at all.

It is difficult to believe that the anarchists and Socialists who engaged in acts of revenge against the PCE could have imagined that they would thereby improve their own lot in a post-war Francoist Spain. It is utterly impossible to believe that, even if he was seduced by dreams of special treatment for army officers, Colonel Casado did not know what Franco had in mind for civilians. Nevertheless, on two occasions before his coup, on 18 and 27 February 1939, he deliberately undermined attempts by Negrín to negotiate with Franco.[35] Moreover, both directly and indirectly, he scuppered Negrín's plans for an orderly evacuation. Not only did he leave prisoners neatly detained for Franco's forces, but his coup also opened the way to Admiral Buiza effectively relinquishing the port of Cartagena in Murcia as a possible base for evacuation.[36]

Other alternatives were few. On 10 March 1939 the Foreign Office had instructed British officials in Valencia that the Royal Navy would not evacuate refugees without Franco's permission. Moreover, Chamberlain showed that he was prepared to do no more for prisoners than accept Franco's word at face value. Speaking in the House of Commons on 28 February the British Prime Minister assured MPs that he had asked the Spaniard not to carry out reprisals and added that 'Franco has committed himself to the law as established before the outbreak of the Civil War.' This attitude perhaps explains why the British government proved reluctant to act on the last-minute plea from Denys Cowan that it help facilitate the evacuation of thousands of leading Republicans in exchange for the final prisoners remaining in the hands of the Republic. If this did not happen, Cowan felt thousands whose only desire was for peace would be slaughtered.[37]

There is considerable debate over the numbers of those killed, wounded and taken prisoner in the mini-civil war against the Communists and the savage battle for control of Madrid. Recent researchers have differed wildly in their calculations. Ángel Bahamonde has referred to 'around two thousand casualties', which includes both dead and wounded. In his earlier book with Javier Cervera, he gave the figure of 20,000 based, it seems on a report by the Communist Jacinto Barrios.[38] The debate began with Casado himself. In an attempt to inflate his merit as an anti-Communist and denigrate the Communists who had opposed him, Casado claimed in his 1939 memoirs that 30,000 prisoners had been taken in the fighting, although by 1968 he had reduced this figure to 15,000.[39] Dr Manuel Aguilera Povedano, on the basis of the figures in the Registro Civil de Madrid, reached the figure of 243 dead and 2,000 taken prisoner.[40] On the basis of documentation from the Army of the Centre, General Ramón Salas Larrazábal gave the figure of 233 deaths and 564 wounded. He commented that the correlation of dead to wounded was 'terrifyingly high' in relation to normal battlefield averages. He concluded that this might have been because those who were slightly wounded may have just gone to their homes rather than to hospital, but concluded that it was much more likely that the bitter hatred between Communists and anarchists simply ensured that prisoners were murdered.[41]

In fact, some prisoners were shot on both sides, although there were exceptions. Melchor Rodríguez, heeding warnings from Casado that he was on a Communist black-list, set up a machine gun in his house. At one point during the conflict in Madrid, he was indeed arrested by Communist forces. Despite talk of shooting him, he was quickly released. Similarly, Trifón Gómez and the Civil Governor of Madrid, José Gómez Osorio, had been captured by the Communist forces but released unharmed. After the fighting was over, Carrillo's secretary Sócrates Gómez told Eustaquio Cañas how he had disposed of Communist prisoners in a deep sewer in an old convent. Vicente Girauta, the Director General de Seguridad, told Cañas that hundreds of Communist prisoners had been murdered.[42] Another senior member of the CND who fell into Communist hands was José García Pradas who, consumed by panic, sent a message to Casado, Val, Salgado and González Marín begging them to declare a ceasefire in exchange for his freedom. They ignored his plea but he survived.[43]

Once it became clear that the Communists in Madrid faced defeat, the Consejo Nacional de Defensa met on 12 March to discuss the future. It was agreed to seek direct negotiations with Franco's head-quarters despite the fact that the Consejo held no cards. With characteristic myopia or megalomania, in his memoirs Casado wrote that 'the Communist uprising did not weaken the position of the Consejo Nacional de Defensa in the peace negotiations because it was eloquently demonstrated that the Consejo had more than enough authority to inspire confidence in the other side in the war'.[44] Casado seems to have thought that he could negotiate with Franco as an equal yet, as a result of the fighting, the Republic was even weaker than before. The coup and the elimination of the Communists had thrown away the most powerful card left to the Republic in any negotiation – the threat of a last-ditch, Numantine resistance. Negrín had perceived the value of that threat; Casado did not. Indeed, by defeating the Communists, Casado had given Franco another reason not to need any negotiations. It also meant that the anti-Communism that tied Casado and the anarchists together was no longer operating to prevent divisions within the Consejo Nacional de Defensa. Morale was lower than ever, especially among Communists, and many soldiers had simply left their units and gone home. As Méndez Aspe had warned Trifón Gómez in February, the food supply situation was disastrous. Malnourished soldiers and civilians had little will to resist further. There were widespread and vague hopes of evacuation, which also disinclined people to think in terms of resistance.

The peace conditions proposed were indicative both of the demands of the anarchists on the Consejo and of Casado's inflated sense that he was dealing with a roughly equal interlocutor. Along with a formal document setting out the conditions, Casado sent a letter to Franco whose terms revealed his own megalomania. In it, he stated benevolently that he recognized that the Republic had lost the war and declared, 'We are not trying to impose conditions.' However, he did ask for facilities so that those who wished to leave Spain could do so: 'If this petition is agreed to, surrender will take place under conditions that have never been seen before in history and that will astound the world.'[45] The version of the conditions that were published later in both his memoirs and the account by Wenceslao Carrillo were as follows:

FIRST: Categorical and definitive declaration of national integrity and sovereignty.

SECOND: An assurance that both civilian and military elements who took part honestly and cleanly in this long and hard war will be treated with the greatest respect as to their persons and their interests.

THIRD: Guarantees that there will be no reprisals nor sanctions other than those imposed as sentences laid down by the competent courts, which will acept all kinds of proof including the testimony of witnesses. *For the avoidance of misunderstandings, political and common crimes should be defined and delimited clearly.* [The sentence in italics is included in the original manuscript and in the memoirs published by Casado in London. However, it is omitted from the version published by Casado in Madrid in 1968, presumably in order to avoid underlining the gratuitous brutality of the victorious Francoists.]

FOURTH: Respect for the life, liberty and rank of the professional officers who have not committed any common crime. [The demand for the rank (*empleo*) of army officers to be respected was an astonishing example of Casado's lack of realism.]

FIFTH: Respect for the life and liberty of the commissars and soldiers who rose through the militias that have not committed any common crime.

SIXTH: Respect for the life, liberty and interests of public servants under the same conditions.

SEVENTH: The granting of a minimum period of 25 days to permit the evacuation of those people who wish to leave Spanish territory.

EIGHTH: That in the zone under discussion neither Italian nor Moorish troops will be used.[46]

At the same time as these 'conditions' were being drafted, Casado contacted Abbington Gooden, the British Consul in Valencia, with a request for the participation of the Royal Navy in a scheme for the evacuation of 'about 10,000 people'. Since this was something that the Foreign Office had been reluctant to do for Negrín before the Anglo-French recognition of Franco, the chances of British help were remote. Gooden told Casado that 'His Majesty's Government considered the consent of the Spanish Government as an essential prerequisite to any assistance on their part in organised, large-scale evacuations.' Gooden wrote to Lord Halifax that it was to be assumed that, on taking power, the Consejo Nacional de Defensa should have been 'sure of having the means for such evacuations at their disposal'. He went on to comment: 'However, it subsequently came to light that the Council's preparations in this direction were a shining example of vagueness, muddle, vacillation and inability to say nay to all and sundry petitioners for assistance in fleeing the country.'[47]

Whether Casado knew it or not, the fact was that decisions on evacuation were more in Franco's hands than in those of the Consejo Nacional de Defensa. On 14 March, Franco's representative in London, the Duque de Alba, reported to the Minister of Foreign Affairs, the Conde de Jordana, that Lord Halifax had assured him that no action would be taken without the consent of Burgos but that British naval assistance for an evacuation would be available, if Franco requested it. On 15 March, the Foreign Office received a brusque response to the effect that 'General Franco would not be prepared to agree to the evacuation of a single red in ships of the

Royal Navy.' In response to Casado's proposal, Franco rejected it out of hand, demanding immediate and total unconditional surrender.[48]

The relative ease with which the Casado Junta triumphed in the struggle against the Communists within the centre-south zone demonstrates just how misplaced are the accusations that the Republic was in the grip of a Soviet stranglehold. That success was owed largely to Mera's troops, and that signified a problem for Casado.[49] The anarchists had been motivated to join him in his treachery by their visceral anti-Communism and their hostility to Negrín. That was the consequence of Negrín's cooperation with the Communists in imposing a centralized war effort. While Casado opposed Negrín's policy of resistance, the anarchists blamed the Prime Minister for the defeat at the Ebro and the loss of Catalonia and, by implication, for not resisting effectively. However, according to the anarchist chronicler José Peirats, there were two lines within the Movimiento Libertario with regard to the inevitable defeat of the Republic – the CNT was fatalistic and the FAI was determined to react. This was illustrated by the fact that a plenum of regional committees (Pleno de Regionales) of the FAI held in Valencia on 19 January 1939 had condemned the action of the government as inadequate, but the CNT regional committees decided on 6 February that it was not appropriate to try to overthrow Negrín.[50] In the event, it was a hard core of FAI militants, Val, Salgado and García Pradas, that bypassed the myriad committees and failed to inform either Mariano Vázquez (secretary general of CNT – now in France) or Segundo Blanco (the CNT minister in Negrín's cabinet) about their links with Casado. Their desire for a free hand was understandable, given that on 16 February, it will be recalled, Mera had been reprimanded by the liaison committee of the CNT-dominated Movimiento Libertario Español for his participation in Casado's conspiracy. In the weeks before the creation of the CND and in the mini-civil war from 6 to 12 March, the determination of the Mera–Val–Salgado–García Pradas group to destroy the Communists was more important to them than the wider issues of the war. It may also explain why they did not investigate Casado's links with the Fifth Column, although the links of Salgado and Val with Antonio Bouthelier and Julio Palacios suggest culpable naivety if not actual complicity.[51]

The anarchists' burning hatred of the Communists and Negrín was shared by Wenceslao Carrillo and other Socialist supporters of Largo Caballero, bent on revenge for the fall of their hero in May 1937. Negrín and Álvarez del Vayo were formally expelled from the Agrupación Socialista Madrileña on 16 March. The anti-Negrín tone of the Socialist media matched that of the anarchists. In the press and on the radio, Negrín and the Communists were blamed for every setback during the war. Russian aid was portrayed as deeply sinister, while criticism of Franco, of Fascist Italy and of Nazi Germany virtually disappeared from the pages of the Republican press. The increasingly pacifist tone of the media saw the population reassured, in the same terms used by Casado to recruit support for his coup, that those with no blood on their hands need fear nothing from Franco. There were accusations that the Communists had stockpiled confiscated valuables – as, of course, had the anarchists and the Socialists.[52]

The attacks on Negrín and the Russians and the diminution of criticism of Franco, Hitler and Mussolini reflected the desire, conscious or otherwise, of Casado's allies in Madrid to ingratiate themselves with Franco. Resistance as advocated by Negrín was portrayed on both sides of the lines as a Russian plot. Franco had told the journalist-cum-propagandist Manuel Aznar on 31 December 1938, 'it remains Russia's intention to destroy us, to corrupt us, to bring us ever lower. It must be smashed.'[53] Already in February 1939, in order to strengthen the position of Casado, Franco himself had issued orders for the intensification of a propaganda initiative by radio, with thousands of leaflets dropped on Republican territory. He ordered that the campaign stress the cowardice of Azaña in fleeing to France and the vileness of the resistance policy of Negrín, Uribe and Álvarez del Vayo. Republican resistance was to be portrayed as operating in the interests of Russia and its proponents as agents of the Comintern uprooted from their fatherland and paid by murky elements.[54] In Madrid, among the numerous articles criticizing Negrín and the Communists, the most virulent came from the pen of Javier Bueno, the Caballerista director of the Socialist evening newspaper *Claridad*. 'And now? The Republic has broken its ties with Moscow. Now what has Franco got to say?' Along similar lines was an article in *El Socialista* on 13 March that dismissed the role of the Communists in the war effort as an anti-Spanish strategy on the part of the puppets of the Kremlin.[55]

The Socialist press was clearly influenced by a document of guidance to the press drawn up by Besteiro in the early days of the Consejo Nacional de Defensa. Its references to Dostoevsky's *The Brothers Karamazov* recalled his long-standing resentment of Negrín. His analysis of the war and the impending defeat was blindly anti-Communist and implicitly pro-Francoist. Indeed, the most startling feature of the document was its praise of the Francoist collaboration with the Anti-Comintern Pact established in 1937 between Nazi Germany, Fascist Italy and imperial Japan:

> It's our own fault that we have been defeated, although to include myself in the blame is pure rhetoric. We have been defeated as a nation because we let ourselves be dragged along by the Bolshevik line which is perhaps the greatest political aberration known down the centuries. Russia's foreign policy, in the hands of Stalin and perhaps in reaction to domestic failures, has been turned into a monstrous crime that goes way beyond the macabre imaginings of Dostoevsky and Tolstoy (*The Brothers Karamzov*, *The Power of Darkness*). The reaction against this error of the Republic is genuinely represented by the Nationalists who, whatever their defects, have fought in the great anti-Comintern crusade. But those of us, few or many, who have suffered the Bolshevik contagion of the Republic not only have rights but also have a pool of experience, sad and tragic if you like, but valuable precisely because of that. And that experience cannot be ignored without gravely damaging the construction of the Spain of the future.[56]

When Besteiro wrote that the fault for defeat lay within the Socialist Party, but not with himself, he was actually revealing his own resentment about the way in which he had been sidelined from the PSOE leadership, as well as indicating something about his motivation in joining the Casado Junta. He spoke to Rodríguez Vega about Largo Caballero in the most contemptuous terms and also exposed the extent to which he was motivated by a desire for revenge against those to the left of him within the PSOE. He likewise revealed just how faulty his memory was when he said, 'The responsibility for everything that has happened in the Party and, as a result, in the country as a whole, falls on Prieto for joining with Caballero simply in order to destroy me.'[57] In 1935, when Besteiro was eliminated from the PSOE leadership stakes, Prieto and Largo Caballero were locked in a fierce mutual enmity.[58]

Edmundo Domínguez was aware how much a desire for revenge motivated Besteiro and believed that 'resentment and spite had unhinged him. He did not fight to defend his own life. In fact, deep down he seemed not to be bothered about losing it. He was putting an end to a political situation which had seen him sidelined for years. Once again his name was briefly in lights and it would be enriched for posterity. His passions and his hatred of Negrín were more powerful than any consideration of the loss of his freedom or indeed the loss of the freedom of many Spaniards.'[59]

The Valencian Socialist Eduardo Buil Navarro was shocked that Besteiro and Carrillo and other Socialists had decided to take part in the Casado Junta without formal authorization from either the PSOE or the UGT. He was even more perplexed by the discovery that their anti-Communism could wipe out the memory of nearly three years of comradeship in the fight against Franco. He wrote shortly after the end of the war:

> We received a slogan from Madrid: 'More than anti-fascist, it is necessary to be anti-Bolshevik.' We Valencian Socialists who were forced to yield to the fait accompli of the Consejo Nacional de Defensa rejected that slogan as incompatible with our ideological principles. The active element of the CND was made up of anarchist forces with whom we had fought side by side and coexisted throughout the war even though we had different doctrinal views, of those Socialists who were always out of touch

with Party discipline, of the spiteful, the malcontents, the waver-
ers of every stripe, the defeatists, those who supported the
Munich pact, the resentful, the men of good faith who longed
for any end to their agony and those who had no choice but to
accept it.[60]

In the course of the conflict, civil governors and military authorities
received orders from the CND to arrest the principal Communist
militants in their area. Eustaquio Cañas, for example, the Civil
Governor of Murcia, received on 17 March 1939 a telegram from
Madrid signed by Wenceslao Carrillo: 'Proceed to arrest all prominent Communists in the province under your command.' Carrillo was
also determined to see Communists expelled from their positions in
trade unions. As the prisons were being filled by these new prisoners,
right-wingers and Fifth Columnists were being released. Among
them in Madrid was Manuel Valdés Larrañaga, the head of the clandestine Falangist organization. Valdés had managed to persuade the
director of the prison in which he was held to release all the detainees
in case they became victims of the Communist resistance against
Casado – a decision upheld by Wenceslao Carrillo. In Valencia,
Colonel Ricardo Burillo started to free members of the Falange and,
in Cartagena, the new commander of the naval base, Colonel Joaquín
Pérez Salas, was doing the same.[61]

Despite claims by Wenceslao Carrillo and others to the contrary,
many Communists were left in prison, where they were found, and
executed, by the Francoists. This was especially true of the areas in the
centre such as Madrid, Guadalajara and Alcalá de Henares. Within
Guadalajara itself, Mera arrested the principal local officials who
supported Negrín. José Cazorla, the Civil Governor, was tricked into
going to Mera's headquarters in the Palacio Tardó del Monte Ibarra.
He had been told that it was a meeting to evaluate the advances being
made by the Francoists around Madrid.[62] In fact, throughout the
provinces of the Republican zone, Casado attempted to establish
absolute control as quickly as possible by suspending all party political activity and banning the activities of the PCE. All mayors and
town councillors belonging to the PCE were removed. In Cuenca, the

predominance of an anarchist administration and the presence of the 17th Division ensured that José Laín Entralgo, the head of the local PCE, after contacting Uribe, would decide to submit to the Casado Junta. However, some Communists resisted but were quickly defeated. Those unable to flee to Valencia were arrested when PCE headquarters were closed down.[63]

After the Negrinista forces in Ciudad Real had surrendered, over sixty of the principal leaders of the provincial PCE and JSU were imprisoned. Emulating their comrades in Alicante, the young Socialists dissolved the local JSU and recreated the provincial Juventud Socialista. David Antona had implemented Wenceslao Carrillo's orders with greater zeal than most civil governors. He kept the Communist prisoners under lock and key and they were handed over to the Francoists at the end of the war. Because Antona had promised to release them before the Francoists arrived, they had refrained from organizing a break-out. In Puertollano, large numbers of Communists were left to be arrested by the Francoists. Several were shot, along with their Casadista jailers who had assumed that they would be spared as a reward for handing over the prisoners.[64]

In Almería, when it became clear that the local UGT, PSOE and CNT had declared their support for Casado, there was confusion and disillusionment within the PCE. To avoid arrest, large numbers of militants in the smaller towns of the province either went into hiding or else ostensibly accepted the Casado Junta. In Almería itself and smaller towns, the headquarters of the PCE, the JSU and the Communist-dominated women's organization, Mujeres Antifascistas, were closed down after they had been ransacked. On 13 March, the provincial committee of the PCE went to see the Civil Governor, Cayetano Martínez, to request that the persecution of Communists be stopped. He had just received instructions from Wenceslao Carrillo to arrest them, which he reluctantly did. They were released on 27 March. Some militants were still in jail when the Francoists arrived, although more than fifty managed to seize a fishing boat and reach Algeria.[65]

In Granada, the entire provincial committee of the PCE was arrested and was still behind bars when the Francoists arrived. In the provincial capital itself and in smaller towns like Guadix and Benalúa, JSU offices were smashed up. In Cordoba, in response to the order of Wenceslao Carrillo, men and women of the PCE were imprisoned. Although none were left in prison for the Francoists, their detention until 28 March meant that they were unable to flee and therefore were faced with the dilemma of arrest by the Francoists or fleeing to the sierra to join the guerrillas. In Jaén, seventy Communist officers were arrested. At the end of the war, on 27 March, the Casadistas locked all seventy in a church in Villacarrillo, having told them that they were being taken to Alicante. They were captured by the Francoists and several shot, along with the Casadistas who had brought them to Villacarrillo. Prisoners in Madrid were left behind. Indeed, as soon as the Dirección General de Seguridad, the national police headquarters, was in Francoist hands, orders were issued to police stations instructing them to hand over prisoners to the Army of Occupation.[66] Others were moved to Valencia. Some managed to take advantage of the general confusion, but many were handed over to the Falange, including Guillermo Ascanio, Daniel Ortega, Eugenio Mesón Gómez and Domingo Girón.[67]

A member of Mera's forces, the anarchist Joaquín Piñol, who was a senior officer in the IV Army Corps, wrote later: 'I recall the bitter moment when I had to disarm and arrest Communist officers because another war had started within the Republican ranks in an accursed fashion. In Spain, the Communists wanted to continue the war. Today, I think that they were right. The rest of us wanted to end the war but first to defeat the Communists. And in that we were mistaken.'[68]

In Guadalajara, those who were arrested were taken to a hunting lodge near the village of Mohernando in the north of the province. Among them were the Civil Governor José Cazorla, Ramón Torrecilla Guijarro (his police chief) and Juan Raposo (the secretary of Socorro Rojo Internacional). They were forced to dig graves and told that, if they did not sign a document of support for the CND, they would be buried in them. Around thirty women were imprisoned in the convent of San Ginés, among them Cazorla's wife, Aurora Arnáiz, and Clotilde Ballesteros, the head of the local PCE and wife of Juan

Raposo. The baby son of Cazorla and Aurora Arnáiz had died during their detention. Aurora and Cazorla managed to escape along with Ramón Torrecilla.[69] Shortly before the arrival of the Francoist forces at the end of March, a few prisoners had the good fortune to be released by their guards. Many more were handed over to the Francoists by Mera's troops of the IV Army Corps to be imprisoned, many to be tortured and others to be shot.[70]

When Alcalá de Henares was captured by Casado's forces, many prisoners were taken and others from Madrid were brought there. According to Casado himself, 'the Communist uprising ended with 15,000 prisoners being detained around Alcalá de Henares. The problem of feeding them was extremely difficult.'[71] Although Casado's figure seems excessively high, it is certainly the case that a substantial number of Communist militants and army officers loyal to Negrín were taken prisoner and squeezed into a concentration camp known as 'Caño Gordo'. Those prisoners were still there when a Francoist column headed by Colonel Antonio Sagardia Ramos occupied Alcalá de Henares. They were quickly joined by large numbers of left-wingers and trade unionists.[72]

Casado Reaps the Whirlwind

Victory over the Communists now exposed the contradictions between the aims of the FAI and those of Casado. Mera assumed that he could now take his troops back to Guadalajara in order to resume their defensive duties. He was taken aback when, at a meeting on 13 March 1939, in Matallana's presence, Casado proposed that he leave the IV Army Corps and take command of the Army of Extremadura. A shocked Mera recalled a meeting in Casado's house with Val, García Pradas, Salgado and his chief of staff, Antonio Verardini Díez de Ferreti. He reminded Casado that he had proposed that, once the Junta was in power, Mera should take charge of the Army of the Centre to ensure that negotiations with Franco could take place from the strongest position possible. At that time, Casado had made two incendiary suggestions that appealed greatly to Mera and the other anarchists present but were unlikely to have been sincere. These were that, before any approach was put to Burgos, thirty or forty thousand Francoist hostages should be herded together in one place and that dynamite should be placed in the mercury mines of Almadén with the threat that, if reasonable peace conditions were not reached, the hostages would be killed and the mines blown up and rendered useless for many years. Mera was to be the person who would brandish these two threats in negotiations with the Francoists. Now, Mera told Casado that, if his proposed transfer to the Army of Extremadura meant that plans had been changed and that the threats were no longer part of any negotiation, he must offer his resignation. Casado refused to accept Mera's resignation and simply did not respond to his accusation that he was reneging on his early belligerency. In subsequent conversation with Val, García Pradas and Salgado, Mera was left with the impression that his suspicions of Casado were well founded.[1] With Casado occupied running the Consejo Nacional de Defensa, command of the Army of the Centre was given to Colonel Manuel Prada.

Casado's suggestions to Mera about pro-Francoist hostages echoed remarks that he had made to his Fifth Column contacts alleging that the Communists had similar plans. To the Francoists, he had claimed that the Communists had enormous black-lists of people to be executed ranging from right-wing prisoners and foreign diplomats to non-Communist leftists. He alleged that large quantities of dynamite had been buried ready to blow up important buildings. He added that his men had managed to recover 700 tonnes but that there were still 900 unaccounted for. He also claimed that the Communists had plans for plunder on a massive scale before they headed for the coast. In both cases, it appears that he was lying – in the case of the anarchists, to prove his seriousness as an ally against Franco and, in the case of the Fifth Column, to underline his anti-Communist credentials.[2]

It would not be long before Eduardo Val, José García Pradas, Manuel Salgado and Manuel González Marín began to share Mera's discomfort at the readiness of Casado to bow before ever more imperious Francoist demands. There were frequent confrontations with the police as *Castilla Libre*, the main anarchist daily in Madrid, attempted to bypass Casado's censorship machinery. As late as 25 March, anarchists and others were arrested for sticking up posters saying 'We must resist'.[3] According to the fanciful account of García Pradas, the anarchists elaborated a dual strategy. On the one hand, there were broadcasts to the Francoist zone calling for peace, the naive hope being that they would stimulate 'a clamour for peace' that would put pressure on Franco to agree to a negotiated peace settlement. On the other, this would be backed up by the creation of eight or ten suicide columns, each of a thousand well-armed volunteers, to be sent into the enemy zone to try to stimulate an anti-Franco uprising or die trying. Needless to say, nothing was actually done to create these guerrilla columns.[4]

Nevertheless, in broadly similar terms, on 15 March, Juan López, secretary general of the Movimiento Libertario Español since 7

March, made a broadcast on Unión Radio de Madrid. While agreeing with the need for an honourable peace, he insisted that this did not mean peace at any price. Indeed, his words about the need for resistance were hardly different from those of Negrín and could not have been in starker contradiction to the aims of Casado:

> As long as there are any Spanish anti-fascist forces still standing, and I mean us in particular, all resources will be exhausted in order to impose the conditions that we are prepared to accept … If we are ready for peace we are also ready for war. The supreme effort to achieve peace will be successful only if resistance is organized and does not cease until our conditions are met. The enemy, despite sealing our frontiers and aiming to blockade the entire coastline of the loyalist zone, needs to realize once and for all that it is not facing a docile and defeated people, whatever the adversity that it faces. If we are ready for peace we are also ready for war. A war of extermination! That is to say a supreme heroic effort as a worthy flourish with which to crown so much heroism and so much blood spilled. If we have the nobility to proclaim our intention to make peace, it is because we do not lack the steely courage to mount a final resistance if our enemies want to make the lunatic and foolish error of entering the territory still held by the Spanish Republic waving the sword of conquest. If that is the price, there will be neither peace nor any kind of agreement.[5]

López's broadcast has to be seen in the context of the growing number of desertions from the front and of incidents of fraternization between Republican and Francoist troops. Such disintegration of Republican strength threatened any project of staged withdrawal and ordered evacuation, although the shipping situation made that highly unlikely anyway. Accordingly, in a similar tone to that adopted by López, the National Committee of the Movimiento Libertario Español made a feeble attempt to remedy the situation. It issued its last manifesto on 22 March with a message with which Negrín would not have disagreed. Alarmed by the extent to which the creation of the Consejo

Nacional de Defensa was being presented by the Fifth Column as the end of the war and the humiliating surrender of the Republic, the manifesto declared that the setting up of the CND was 'an initiative to safeguard the independence of Spain and the dignity of all. The conflict continues on the same basis as before.' This declaration of war aims was far from what Casado had in mind: 'No matter what more or less concealed fascists may say, the Consejo Nacional de Defensa will countenance no settlement that might imply dishonour for the workers, the surrender of anti-fascists or humiliation for any who today adhere proudly to the same ideological positions they held on 19 July [1936].'

Despite a spurious effort to suggest that Negrín had planned to evacuate only a few leaders and sacrifice the bulk of the Republican masses, the declaration went on in terms that replicated the Prime Minister's aspirations:

> there are conditions attached to our peace. It will not be a craven 'every man for himself' affair in which those with the means of escape take to their heels, betraying their comrades and leaving them to the mercy of the enemy, but rather a decorous arrangement permitting all who so desire to leave Spain, and guaranteeing those who stay behind against all threat of reprisals, criminal treatment and extermination. In the absence of these conditions and whatever others may ensure the complete independence of our country, there will be no peace.

Despite these efforts to distinguish the CND's plans from those of Negrín, López's earlier declaration demonstrated that hatred of the Communists had blinded the anarchists to the reality that their war aims were indistinguishable from those of Negrín, that is to say sufficient resistance to permit a staged evacuation. It had also blinded them to the real ambitions of Casado. The manifesto ended with the seemingly rousing but ultimately empty words, 'All Spanish anti-fascists must stand together, ready to continue the war until the peace is won.'6

An interesting light on Casado's alleged belief in Franco's promises is cast by the declarations Ángel Pedrero made to his interrogators.

Questioned about valuables confiscated from right-wing prisoners, Pedrero stated that, by February 1939, the SIM held jewels, watches and other items worth about 35,000 pesetas. When Casado formed his Junta, Pedrero informed him of this. Casado told him to distribute the valuables among the agents of the SIM 'so that when they went into exile they could meet their first expenses'. The Consejo de Defensa had arranged to borrow ten million French francs through a contact in the British Chamber of Commerce. Similar arrangements were being made with contacts in the Papal Nunciature. Pedrero's interrogators were surprised when he told them that Casado was confident of having access to four billion francs made up of moneys owed the Republic for exports and moneys that would be withheld from payments to foreign suppliers. The end of the war came before Casado was able to implement these plans. Casado was also trying to freeze the bank accounts held by Negrín outside Spain.[7]

Besteiro was ludicrously sanguine about the future. On 11 March 1939, he spoke to the Civil Governor of Murcia, Eustaquio Cañas, who found him in the Ministry of Finance 'lying on a hospital bed in the basement, his blue pallor, his emaciated features, his extreme thinness giving him the appearance of a corpse'. To Cañas's utter astonishment, Besteiro confidently assured him that 'those of us who have responsibilities, especially in the union organization, cannot just walk away. I am sure that virtually nothing is going to happen. Let us wait on events, and perhaps we can reconstitute a UGT of more moderate character, something along the lines of the British trades unions. Stay at your post as Governor, everything will be fine, I assure you.' Cañas could not credit that a man of Besteiro's intelligence could be so oblivious of the nature of the Civil War. He asked himself, 'Who can have deceived him, and with what promises, so that he can be ignorant of what is going to happen here?'[8]

A similar testimony to Besteiro's almost infantile incomprehension of the situation facing the Republic came from the head of the clandestine Falangist organization, Manuel Valdés Larrañaga. While awaiting his own transfer to the Francoist zone, Valdés, accompanied by Antonio Luna, had a long meeting with Besteiro in the cellars of the Finance Ministry. In the early evening, its electricity out of action, the Ministry's corridors were in almost total darkness apart from the faint light of oil lanterns. They found their way to the basement where they came upon Besteiro, in pyjamas, lying on an iron bedstead in a room that appeared more like a monk's cell than the office of the Vice-President of the government. The room stank of stale tobacco smoke. Smoking without pause, the emaciated Besteiro spoke to them with remarkable frankness about his contacts with the Francoist authorities. He recognized that he and Casado had nothing to bargain with but outlined his personal objectives for the inevitable surrender. His hope was that there would be a great theatrical scene on the esplanade in front of the Nuevos Ministerios in Madrid which would emulate the Abrazo de Vergara, the ceremonial embrace between Generals Espartero and Maroto which on 31 August 1839 had brought to an end the First Carlist War. Besteiro's idea was that Franco would be presented with a sword of victory and that the victory parade that followed would not include German and Italian troops. Besteiro went on to tell Valdés that he had lost his faith in trade unions: 'Look at the state of me. I am a sick and exhausted man who does not have long to live, but my dejection is more moral and physical. At the end of my life, I have ended up crushed by everything that I have always defended.'[9] Inspired by promises made to him by the Fifth Column or to Casado by his military friends within the Francoist high command, Besteiro's naivety may have been the consequence of the illusory optimism which is said to be a symptom of tuberculosis. In later years, when he was Spanish Ambassador in Austria, Luna García privately expressed his chagrin that Franco, after promising 'life and liberty' to those who helped avoid a massacre, 'went and shot them all'.[10]

Bizarrely, Besteiro seems to have assumed that life for the Socialist movement under Franco would be similar to the privileged existence it had experienced under the dictatorship of Primo de Rivera. His own writings during these days show the remarkable extent to which his fierce anti-communism had fed a bizarre complacency about the Francoists. In the document of guidance that he drafted for the press, he revealed his naive hopes for the future:

To believe that one half of Spain could destroy the other half would be a new lunacy that would put an end to any possibility of affirming our national character. It was a danger that we risked and from which we have escaped miraculously. To construct the Spanish character of tomorrow, the victorious Nationalist Spain will have to take into account the experience of those who suffered the errors of the bolshevized Republic or else risk losing itself in by-ways that lead only to failure. The useful Republican masses cannot demand – without losing their dignity – any share of the booty of the war but they can and should demand their post at the constructive labour front.[11]

If anything bordered on lunacy, it was his idea that any Republicans might expect to share in the victor's spoils of war. He fondly believed that the experience of those who had displayed anti-Communist attitudes within the Republican zone was something upon which the Francoists would want to draw for the reconstruction of the Spain of the future. He suggested that the contribution of the Casado Junta to shortening the war should be recognized by the victors.

Franco's firing squads and concentration camps, however, would not limit their work to Communists. It is astonishing that Besteiro could have remained ignorant of Franco's refusal to give any undertakings to the British and American governments concerning reprisals, declaring his patriotism, high-mindedness and generosity to be an adequate guarantee. William Bullitt, the US Ambassador in France, had been sufficiently disturbed by the terms of Franco's Law of Political Responsibilities to challenge the Nationalists' representative in Paris, José María Quiñones de León. He told him, he reported to Washington, that:

I had been shocked to read in the London *Times* of Tuesday March 7 the summary of a law on 'political responsibilities' signed by General Franco last month designed according to the preamble to punish all persons who contributed by act or omission 'to forge Red subversion, maintain it incandescent for more than 2 years and place obstacles in the path of the providential and inevitable triumph of the National movement' ... I said to Quinones de Leon that I was certain that it would shock American public opinion to learn that 'grave passivity' had been made a crime and pointed out that although there was to be no death penalty for 'political responsibilities' all other penalties were to be inflicted and everyone in the Republican area except active Franco sympathizers was to be placed in the position of a criminal. I asked Quinones de Leon how this law could be reconciled with the statement that the courts of justice would apply only the laws existing on July 16, 1936.

Quiñones was unable to answer.[12]

If Bullitt could have been aware of the implications of Franco's measures, it is barely credible that Besteiro, whose concern for the fate of ordinary Spanish Republicans was ostensibly more urgent than that of an American diplomat in another country, was not. Despite Besteiro's naive hopes, active anti-Communists, liberal republicans, Socialists and anarchists, as well as many who were simply non-political, would be victims of the savage repression, including Besteiro himself.

Among the miscalculations of both Besteiro and Casado must be included a failure to take into account the international situation. Indeed, the international context was a subject regarding which they seemed to have neither knowledge nor interest.[13] In mid-March, José Rodríguez Vega went to see Besteiro to urge him to follow up the initiatives taken by Negrín and Álvarez del Vayo with the British and French governments. To his surprise, Besteiro responded flatly 'that it did not seem to him to be appropriate for him to take initiatives of this kind since he did not regard himself as belonging to a regular government: "I have come here only to make peace and, if in a few days, that has not happened, I am leaving."'[14]

Negrín had hoped to hold on until an international war altered the attitudes of London and Paris towards the Spanish Republic. He had been severely undermined by the Munich Agreement which had rendered useless, not to say fatal, the titanic sacrifices of the battle of the Ebro. However, another opportunity occurred within ten days of

Casado's coup. On 15 March, German troops entered Prague and completed the take-over of Czechoslovakia begun six months earlier. There is a possibility that things might have changed in the Republic's favour had Casado not been so totally committed to surrender. However, the reactions of the British and French governments were supine. As the French Ambassador to London said to Sir Alexander Cadogan, 'it is embarrassing for our two governments to have to watch events of this kind and to confess that we are powerless to influence them'. Lord Halifax told the German Ambassador that 'what had taken place was in flat contradiction with the spirit of the Munich Agreement, which had surely contemplated that, if such questions affecting the whole structure of European confidence were to arise, they would be found capable of settlement by consultation and not by the method of naked application of force'. He warned the Ambassador that he understood 'Herr Hitler's taste for bloodless victories, but one of these days he would find himself up against something that would not be bloodless.' This was followed up on 17 March when Halifax instructed the British Ambassador in Berlin, Sir Nevile Henderson, to inform the German government that His Majesty's Government regarded the invasion of Czechoslovakia as a repudiation of the Munich Agreement and devoid of any basis of legality. Two weeks later, Neville Chamberlain would announce his guarantee to Poland.[15]

Besteiro would be one of the few of the Junta's twenty-eight members to stay in Madrid. On 18 March 1939, he told Regina García, editor of the Socialist daily *La Voz*, 'I will stay with those who cannot save themselves. Of course, we will arrange the departure from Spain of many comrades who have to go, and who will leave by sea, by land or by air; but the great majority, the masses, they can't leave, and I, who have always lived with the workers, will continue with them and with them I will stay. Whatever is their fate will be mine.'[16] He was seemingly unaware that the Casado coup had in itself severely sabotaged any chance of a properly organized evacuation of those in danger. Moreover, the Anglo-French recognition of Franco meant that Republican currency now had no value outside the centre-south zone.

In any case, the manifesto of the Consejo Nacional de Defensa read out in the early hours of 6 March by the representative of Izquierda Republicana, Miguel San Andrés, suggested that evacuation was not an immediate priority: 'Not one of the men whose duty is here will leave Spain until everyone who wants to has left, not just those who can.'[17] According to Evaristo Jorge Moreno, secretary general of the Agrupación Socialista de Valencia, one of Wenceslao Carrillo's first measures was to prohibit all preparations for evacuation, and it was not until it was too late that a decision was taken to create evacuation committees.[18]

When it was finally decided to do something, responsibility was given to Antonio Pérez. According to a report by Abbington Gooden on 26 March, Pérez was utterly overwhelmed since he had no idea of the numbers requiring evacuation and had no reliable information as to whether ships had been chartered.[19] In fact, many individuals who could afford to do so were simply making their own arrangements. The Izquierda Republicana deputy for Alicante, Eliseo Gómez Serrano, noted in his diary on 12 March that hundreds of people were lining up on the docks to go aboard the shabby British tramp steamer *Ronwyn*. For 200 francs or 50 silver pesetas, they could buy a passage to Oran – although, as he noted two days later, when they reached Algeria they were not allowed to disembark. Gómez Serrano was surprised that people were so anxious to leave as he was quietly confident that the repression would be relatively mild, short-lived and applied only to extremists: 'I still don't believe there is any need to go into exile. One would need to be very sure to do so ... For the first few weeks there will be an "extra-legal justice" aimed at eliminating those who are in the way, a purging of the "reds" of this zone, with the authorities pretending to be shocked, proclaiming themselves innocent of such crimes and, once they are over, declaring that they will "pursue" them until they have "put an end to them". By 22 March, having just read the spine-chilling account of the repression in Andalusia in 1936 written by the head of Queipo de Llano's propaganda apparatus, Antonio Bahamonde, Gómez Serrano was horrified. And when negotiations between Casado and Franco did not produce 'an honourable peace', he wrote on 26 March: 'The CND has been despicably cheated and so have the rest of us. Nothing else could have been expected from the enemy that we face. After all, they are fascists.' Nevertheless, like many, he was confident enough to remain in Spain. On 2 April, he would be arrested, subjected to a military trial three weeks later, found guilty of 'support for military rebellion' and shot.[20]

Besteiro made some effort to facilitate the escape of others through his lifelong friend and comrade Trifón Gómez. Gómez, quartermaster general of the Republican army, was in Paris negotiating refuge in Mexico for the Republicans who had to flee.[21] However, Besteiro negated his efforts by refusing to allow any national resources, the income from the export of agricultural products or minerals, or the accumulated jewellery and other confiscated valuables, to be used for those who needed to flee. José Rodríguez Vega suggested to him that, to finance the evacuation and to help the exiles in French concentration camps, the proceeds from exports be used and that an agreement be made with Negrín to gain access to government funds held abroad. Besteiro refused point-blank and gave vent to a series of insulting remarks about Negrín and his ministers. His logic was that the national wealth was needed in Spain for post-war reconstruction and that Franco would treat those who stayed behind in Spain all the better for having thus safeguarded resources. As for those forced into exile, 'they would find in foreign solidarity whatever they needed'.[22]

The hunched figure of Besteiro sat on a sofa chain-smoking to the end. He was described by García Pradas as 'dried-out, cadaverous, a virtual skeleton, looking like a mummy'.[23] His faith in Franco's good-will sustained him to the end of the war. On 27 March, he urged Cipriano Mera to escape along with Casado, saying: 'I have had no function whatsoever in the war, apart from these last moments when I have tried with you to avoid greater sufferings for our people. The victors can do with me what they please. They will arrest me but perhaps they will not dare to kill me.'[24] Besteiro would be the most senior Republican political figure to choose to stay with his constituents rather than escape. It was suicidal to stay, yet he did so, with a sense of pride. Just before the end, asked by José del Río, secretary of the Consejo de Defensa Nacional, if he thought that Franco would have him shot, he replied, 'Yes; I accept that possibility and I even desire it. I am not afraid to die, because with my sixty-nine years and my physical ailments, what better service could I lend to the cause of the workers who have been left without a flag and without leaders? If my name could be a flag for them then I would prefer to be shot!'[25] In the appeal against his sentence, however, he claimed proudly, and with a hint of malice, that by staying he had also underlined the contrast between himself and those of his colleagues who had escaped. He had made the same point earlier to one of the future escapees, José García Pradas: 'I am not leaving. Our rivals have called me a traitor and I am staying in Madrid so that my sentence will answer them.'[26]

In the meantime, no reply had been received from Franco to the conditions drafted by Casado on 11 March, discussed by the CND the next day and then sent to Burgos. An anxious Casado arranged through the Fifth Column for a message to be dispatched to Franco's headquarters requesting that he and Matallana go to Burgos for negotiations, but Franco was not prepared to accept such a senior delegation lest it appear that these were discussions between equals. Accordingly, Casado had to agree that those to be sent would be Lieutenant Colonel Antonio Garijo Hernández and Major Leopoldo Ortega Nieto.[27] They went to Burgos on 23 March where they were received at Gamonal aerodrome by Colonels Luis Gonzalo Victoria and José Ungría Jiménez and Majors Eduardo Rodríguez Madariaga and Carmelo Medrano Ezquerra. Casado's proposals for a staged surrender and evacuation were dismissed out of hand. Colonel Victoria told them that they merely 'represented a defeated army'. A shocked Garijo admitted that the Republic was defeated but placed on the table a copy of the concessions offered to Casado by Lieutenant Colonel José Centaño de la Paz and Manuel Guitián on 20 February at Posición Jaca. In return, Casado's emissaries were presented with Franco's demands for unconditional surrender, starting with the symbolic handing over of the Republican air force two days later and the laying down of arms by the entire Republican army four days later. Garijo and Ortega pointed out that this was simply not enough time and that it would be difficult to persuade all units of the army to surrender. While Casado's emissaries were being given something to eat, Victoria and Ungría consulted with Franco about the concessions cited by Garijo. They returned with a vague undertaking that everything would be 'favourable as far as clemency was concerned'. It was made clear that Franco refused to sign any document that might give the impression that the war had ended as a result of any pact or compromise between the two sides. It was unconditional surrender or nothing.[28]

Garijo and Ortega returned to Madrid and, between 11.00 p.m. on 23 March and 2 a.m. the following morning, gave the Consejo Nacional de Defensa a report of their meeting. In the accounts of the session left by Casado and Wenceslao Carrillo, what the two emissaries said differed in tone from the one written by Colonel Victoria. It is possible that the encounter itself was cordial and then the two sides chose to report to their superiors in the terms that they expected to hear. However, the sugar-coated account given by Casado and Carrillo is utterly implausible. Allegedly, Garijo and Ortega claimed that Victoria and Ungría had said that the Nationalist government had no interest in interpreting the word 'criminal' in such a way as to justify putting many Republicans on trial and would simply apply the code of justice effective before 18 July 1936. Accordingly, all those who had been obliged to carry out military duties in the Republican army would have nothing to fear from the Nationalist government. They had been assured that Franco had no intention of persecuting the workers for their membership of trade unions or political parties that had opposed the Nationalist movement. Moreover, while the possessions of Republicans would be confiscated according to the Law of Political Responsibilities, they would be left enough to live with dignity.

In the Casado–Carrillo version, the Francoist officers in Burgos claimed that no obstacles would be put in the way of those who wished to leave and asked for an estimate of the likely numbers. When Garijo and Ortega gave the figure of 10,000, they were told that it seemed too few. Then Victoria and Ungría allegedly requested that the Nationalist authorities be advised of the departure of any boat with exiles on board in order to ensure that it would not be attacked by Francoist warships. Finally, they said that Franco would lift the siege on the ports indicated by the CND to allow the evacuation but would not provide any means of transport for that purpose. Needless to say, if these promises were made, it is certainly the case that Franco had no intention of keeping them. Interestingly, according to Casado's version but not mentioned in Wenceslao Carrillo's account, Garijo reported that Victoria and Ungría had said that the Francoists 'wanted the members of the Consejo Nacional de Defensa to go into exile and, if they did not have an aeroplane big enough, a three-engine aircraft would be supplied'. If Victoria and Ortega had indeed said that Franco was happy to facilitate the evacuation of more than 10,000 Republicans, it is odd that special mention should have needed to be made regarding the members of the CND. In the event, the Fifth Column was given instructions not to impede the departure from Madrid of Casado and his entourage, who were thus given free passage out of Spain.[29]

Contrary to the apparent benevolence regarding thousands of evacuees, Victoria and Ortega transmitted Franco's implacable demand that the hand-over of the air force take place between 3.00 and 6.00 p.m. on 25 March and that of the remainder of the armed forces of the Republic on 27 March. The difficulty for the Consejo in complying was immense in both cases. There was a strong possibility that the pilots, instead of taking the aircraft to the designated landing field, at Los Llanos, would simply fly abroad for fear of reprisals. As for the armed forces, to meet the detailed demands from the Francoists, which included inventories and location of all weaponry and munitions, neutralization of minefields and barbed-wire traps, and lists of personnel, would have required several weeks. At the same time, the Nationalist refusal to sign any agreement put the Consejo in a difficult position in terms of explaining its humiliation to the Republican population. If, as was more than likely, the Nationalists did not keep to their oral undertakings, Casado feared that he would be regarded as a traitor who had deceived those who had followed him. Nevertheless, the meeting ended with both Besteiro and Casado expressing their confidence in the earlier concessions sent by Franco in February.[30]

It was obvious that those promised concessions had been replaced by the brutal diktat of 23 March. The CND therefore decided on 24 March that another meeting in Burgos was required in an attempt to get a written clarification of Franco's terms. Lieutenant Colonel Antonio Garijo Hernández and Major Leopoldo Ortega Nieto returned to Gamonal on 25 March and had to explain why the surrender of the air force had not taken place as demanded two days earlier. Their claim that technical difficulties had made it impossible was dismissed by Victoria and Ungría as a subterfuge to hide the CND's lack of control over the Republic's armed forces. In fact, the original demand for this to happen within forty-eight hours was impossible for the CND, as Franco well knew. It was a way of ensuring the most humiliating collapse of the Republic by claiming that the CND's failure required a major military offensive which would end up as an unopposed victory parade. On being informed by Victoria that the air force had not been handed over and that Casado's emissaries wanted written terms, Franco ordered the conversations terminated. When Garijo returned to Madrid and reported to the CND, the main preoccupation of Casado was, once again, that the population of Madrid might think that he had betrayed them. The next morning, Franco ordered the final offensive, which had been in preparation for several days.[31]

The surrender of the Republican air force eventually took place on 29 March when the remaining aircraft were flown to the aerodrome of Cuatro Vientos outside Madrid. Despite promises to the contrary, the pilots were immediately arrested and shortly afterwards subjected to summary trials. Colonel Antonio Camacho Benitez, the head of the Republican air force in the centre-south zone, had left Spain, but the commander of the base at Los Llanos, Colonel Manuel Cascón Briega, refused to flee on the grounds that he could not abandon his men. He had ensured that all matériel was handed over in the best condition possible with full inventories, disarmed his men and placed all weapons in the base armoury. He had taken his decision some months before. His dignified and courageous behaviour was linked to a belief that such a gesture of goodwill would influence the Francoists and redound in creating an atmosphere of benevolence which might benefit those about to be taken prisoner. He naively believed that his track record as a career officer who had belonged to no political party and simply obeyed orders, with strict obedience to military discipline, would work in his favour. The first enemy forces to reach Los Llanos were Italians, who treated Cascón with great courtesy while also plundering everything that they could from the base. The arrival of Spanish units saw things get worse. The officers were arrested and subjected to trial, many given death sentences and others prison sentences of up to thirty years. Cascón was subjected to humiliation, being stripped of his uniform and forced to clean latrines. He was shot on 3 August 1939.[32]

In the course of the last week of March, the futility of Casado's and Besteiro's plans was brutally exposed. Troops all along the line were surrendering or just going home, although some took to the hills from where they kept up a guerrilla resistance until 1951. Jesús Hernández was given the task of organizing the departure of the last remaining elements of the PCE leadership – Isidoro Diéguez, Pedro Checa, Vicente Uribe and others, with their wives and children. He had located, in the hills behind Cartagena, two airfields. One was the Escuela de Polimotores at Totana from which Pasionaria had flown three weeks before and where there remained three De Havilland Dragon passenger planes, and the other a small military airfield where there remained some Russian aircraft not handed over with the rest of the air force. Protected by a group of the *guerrilleros* from the XIV Army Corps, they occupied the two airfields and seized the planes. The passengers were distributed among them – the senior party leadership in the Dragons and the more junior ones in the Russian planes. Togliatti's plane was the last to leave. In the early-morning cold, the engine at first would not start. The security guards escaped from the warehouse where they had been tied up. As they began shooting, the engine fired up and the plane began to taxi down the runway. The planned destination was Oran in Algeria but strong winds blew the plane in the direction of Mostaganem. They were given a heroes' welcome before being arrested by the French authorities and stripped of their belongings. Having a Soviet passport, Togliatti was allowed to leave the following day; Hernández was let go two months later.[33]

In Extremadura, the forces of General Juan Yagüe advanced and found virtually no opposition. They captured 30,000 men and seized 2,000 square kilometres of territory. The Consejo Nacional de Defensa met on the evening of 26 March and decided to order no resistance against the Francoists, effectively authorizing a completely disorganized demobilization of the Republican armies. On 27 March, a gigantic and virtually unopposed advance was launched against Madrid from Toledo in the south and from Guadalajara in the north. Franco's forces simply occupied deserted positions. Soldiers from both sides were seen embracing in the Casa de Campo park. Colonel Adolfo Prada Vaquero made contact with Franco's headquarters to arrange the time and place for the formal surrender of the capital.[34] Within Madrid and other Republican cities, the Fifth Column was out, careering through the streets in cars and trucks waving Falangist and monarchist flags. In the capital, in the course of 27 March, the main utilities, water, gas, electricity and telephone networks, had been taken over by the Fifth Column. By the next day, fascist salutes and slogans were being flaunted. The last foreign correspondent to leave Madrid, O'Dowd Gallagher of the *Daily Express*, wrote 'They were bawling their heads off in triumphal hysteria in broad daylight.'[35]

At dawn on 28 March, Casado ordered Colonel Prada to effect the hand-over. In the Ciudad Universitaria, Prada formally surrendered to Colonel Eduardo Losas. He was immediately arrested. The red and yellow Francoist flag was raised over the Ministry of Finance. The Nationalists entered an eerily silent Madrid. Melchor Rodríguez similarly handed over the Ayuntamiento. At roughly the same time, General Menéndez in Valencia and Colonels Escobar and Moriones in Extremadura and Andalusia gave orders for the troops under their command to lay down their arms. City after city, Alicante, Jaén, Cartagena, Cuenca, Guadalajara, Ciudad Real, fell bloodlessly. By 31 March, all of Spain was in Nationalist hands. Negrín's peace offer to Franco had been that, in return for an undertaking not to carry out reprisals and to permit the evacuation of the civilian and military personal at risk of persecution, he could have a bloodless final victory. With the collusion of Casado, Franco was able to pursue his basic aim of inflicting reprisals on the greatest possible number of Republicans.[36]

Much of the suffering undergone in the recently conquered areas was the direct consequence of the Casado coup. The bravado of the anarchists and their talk of scorched earth, suicide squads and Numantine resistance came to nothing. Cipriano Mera had made a worthless promise that if the Consejo Nacional de Defensa did not secure an honourable peace his men would fight on, yet he was one of the escapees. While the Communist prisoners were being handed over to the Francoists, many anarchists and Socialists fled to the eastern coast. Casado told the members of the Junta to go to Valencia. Miaja, accompanied by his aides de camp and his nephew Fernando Rodríguez Miaja, who acted as his private secretary, had already left Madrid for Valencia by car on 26 March. Earlier that morning, he had given an interview to O'Dowd Gallagher and invited him to have a glass of sherry. When Gallagher murmured his appreciation, Miaja leaned forward and said, 'It's special, even for me.' The journalist added:

> He poked me in the stomach and laughed comfortably, his shoulders shaking. He would talk about anything but peace. 'I have news, of course, but you will understand it is impossible for me to tell you. The situation changes fast and what I might say now might be quite wrong in a few hours' time. I don't want anyone to say that Miaja put about fake stories.' One thing he said, however, referred to the question of possible reprisals if Franco came in. 'My hands are clean of blood.' He went on: 'All the same, I'd rather be shot than sent to jail. I could not live in jail. I would rot.'

On the morning of 28 March, Miaja went to see the British Consul, Abbington Gooden, and pleaded for himself and his staff to be evacuated on a British ship. Gooden told him that he would have to seek instructions from London. When Gooden got permission to comply, Miaja had already made the decision to move on to Alicante. He and his companions left their uniforms behind and travelled in civilian clothes. Not long after reaching San Juan in the early hours of the morning of 29 March, they heard on the radio that Murcia was in

Francoist hands. After a brief encounter with Ángel Pedrero, who would be captured the following day in the port of Alicante and, after imprisonment and lengthy interrogation, would be shot, they reached the airport of Rabasa. At 10.30 a.m., they flew to Oran in an aircraft that had been a personal gift from Haile Selassie, the Negus of Ethiopia, who was a supporter of the Spanish Republic. They remained in Algeria until 13 April when they sailed to Marseilles. They reached Paris on the 15th and remained for a week in the Cuban Embassy before travelling on to Havana, where Miaja was the guest of Fulgencio Batista for two weeks. He then established his definitive exile in Mexico.[37]

Remarkably, Negrín had cordial relations with Miaja in Paris. Prieto wrote to the exiled Prime Minister:

How can you forget General Miaja, President of the Consejo Nacional de Defensa, who gave the protest movement against you all the force of his popularity which is enormous both inside and outside Spain? I don't believe that you exonerate Miaja. I know that in a cabinet meeting held in France you spoke of him harshly. But now that the insults are directed against Casado, Miaja is greeted with kindness. In Paris, you feverishly sought contact with him not to reprimand him but to show him effusive friendship. And, at your initiative, you dined with him. The lady who gave lodging to Miaja in Paris requested his permission to invite you to sit down with him and Miaja, knowing it was the wish both of yourself and the illustrious lady, agreed. In Mexico, you have had affectionate meetings with Miaja and, here in Mexico, Álvarez del Vayo sat next to him at a public banquet. How can one explain this treatment to which, according to rumours, has to be added financial help of an exceptional kind?

It is certainly true that there was a cordial meeting between the two at a dinner in the Cuban Embassy where Miaja was staying. It is also true that Negrín offered to help him out financially.[38]

On 26 March, Burgos had demanded that white flags be raised as Franco's troops made their final advance. That same night, the CND broadcast a call for the flying of white flags of surrender which guaranteed that the Republican lines would soon be deserted.[39] Until the last minute, the anarchists had talked of using dynamite to blow up the uninhabited buildings in the centre of Madrid and of sending suicide units behind the Francoist lines to be the basis of a guerrilla war. At a meeting of the Consejo Nacional de Defensa on 26 March, Manuel Amil declared, 'We have to make sure that the dynamite in Madrid will have the desired effects and that we take full advantage of the situation.' This was a reaction to the realization that Casado had deceived them.[40]

On the night of 27 March, Casado and several other members of the CND made speeches on Madrid Radio that were published in the next morning's papers. Although they might be considered partly an effort to prevent panic in the population, González Marín's broadcast was largely an attempt to dissociate the anarchists from Casado's call for white flags. The speech contained enough downright mendacity to raise the question whether González Marín was motivated more by cynicism or by self-delusion. His theme was 'every man should remain at his post'. He started by claiming that the motivation behind the coup d'état of 5 March had been to remove Negrín's government in order to organize a more effective war effort involving the entire population: 'Time was pressing and we could not allow chaos and disorder to be the undignified end of a war in which so much blood and heroism had been squandered.' To achieve victory in the war may well have been one of the anarchists' aims, albeit not one shared by Casado. This laudable aim had not been achieved, González Marín claimed, because of the chaos left behind by Negrín. In consequence, it became necessary to limit the Junta's objectives to the quest for an honourable peace that would guarantee national independence, safety from reprisals for anti-fascists and a guarantee that those who wanted to leave the country could do so.

In equally mendacious terms, Casado made a speech congratulating himself for the fact that 'I can state that in the entire loyalist zone there has not been one single incident contrary to the plan conceived by us.' He went on to make the astonishing claim that there was complete normality both inside Madrid and within the armed forces.

Of a city in the grip of cold fear, he declared: 'In Madrid, there is complete tranquillity. The streets are as bustling as ever, full of citizens commenting on the latest news, with no sign of nervousness or of anyone acting on their own initiative.'[41]

By 28 March, the streets of Madrid were thronged with soldiers who had abandoned their weapons and were just walking home. At a gathering of senior anarchists at the offices of *Castilla Libre*, Eduardo Val declared in Churchillian terms: 'We will defend ourselves however and wherever we can. We will fight like cornered wildcats and we will make them pay dearly for our heads.' Manuel González Marín chipped in: 'The more than one hundred thousand men that the fascists will sacrifice when they win should not go to the slaughterhouse with bovine resignation but rather fight like men and die killing.' When Salgado said that they should fight until an evacuation had been organized, González Marín said: 'If necessary, we will turn the ten provinces that we still control in the centre-south zone into gigantic Numantias.' Val remarked sententiously, 'The entire Consejo Nacional supports our unshakeable decision to resist whatever the cost. The only doubt is Besteiro. The others, all the others ...' They managed to keep up their morale by deceiving themselves that a revolutionary guerrilla war was possible. In terms earlier attributed by Julio Palacios to the Communists, they talked of organizing a massacre of known fascists within the Republican zone. Eduardo de Guzmán was commissioned to write manifestos in favour of continued resistance to be distributed as pamphlets and to be published in the anarchist press. González Marín declared confidently that they could rely on Miaja. He was evidently unaware that Miaja had already fled two days earlier. They were all nonplussed when they heard on the radio the CND calling for white flags.[42]

On 27 March, Captain Rafael Sánchez Guerra, secretary of the Junta, had advised Casado to remain in Madrid on the mistaken grounds that nothing would happen to him. Sánchez Guerra's misplaced confidence may well have derived from the fact that he himself had protected many right-wingers in the course of the war. Moreover, he was the son of a distinguished conservative prime minister, José Sánchez Guerra, and had served as secretary to the first

President of the Republic, Niceto Alcalá Zamora. Apparently convinced, Casado said he would stay. He then went to a meeting with Salgado. In early hours of the morning of the next day, however, Casado told Sánchez Guerra that he had changed his mind and was about to fly to Valencia. He claimed that this was to make sure that there would be no atrocities committed by the defeated when the news reached Valencia that Madrid had fallen. This apparently altruistic motive was later contradicted in Casado's memoirs when he admitted that he had left on advice from Franco's headquarters.

Nevertheless, Casado told Sánchez Guerra that there were two spare seats on his plane if he and his wife wanted to go to Valencia with the other members of the CND. Sánchez Guerra refused despite Casado insisting that, with the imminent arrival of Franco's forces, he was in great danger. Sánchez Guerra had decided to stay with Besteiro. He went into the Ministry cellar to see how Besteiro had passed the night and asked him if he was going to wait for the Francoists in the Ministry or at his home. Besteiro replied: 'I think it is better to wait to be arrested here to avoid unpleasant scenes for my family.' Referring to his Madrid constituents, he spoke again with a hint of arrogance: 'One cannot abandon those who have put their faith in one. My presence here can prevent much bloodshed; I can prevent many injustices being committed. I will be the wall that holds back the avalanche that is coming.' Meanwhile, in the early-morning frost, the official cars to take Casado's party to the aerodrome at Barajas were warming up in the courtyard behind the Finance Ministry. Casado, now in civilian clothes, bade an emotional farewell to the other two. Shortly afterwards, Sánchez Guerra had some contradictory thoughts. Praising Casado to the skies, he noticed some officers also out of uniform, and indignantly called them cowards. He went home to change into uniform and, while he was having his breakfast, he saw from his window girls in blue Falangist shirts singing the Falange anthem 'Cara al Sol'. He reflected that they were the same girls that he had often seen in the red shirts of the JSU singing the 'Internationale'.[43]

It is obvious from Guzmán's account that Val, García Pradas and Salgado, on the basis of what they had been told by Casado, were either convinced that there would be adequate shipping for a complete evacuation or else were lying in an effort to maintain morale or worse to cover their own retreat. Equally, it could have been that Casado was lying to them or was sufficiently megalomaniac to assume that all was well. Nevertheless the next morning, when Guzmán arrived at the Madrid offices of the Comité Regional de Defensa for a planned meeting with Val and García Pradas, he found the building deserted and was told that the pair had been called away urgently by Casado.[44]

Meanwhile, a Delegation for Spanish Evacuation and Relief of the French Comité Internationale de Coordination et d'Information pour l'Aide à l'Espagne Republicaine had arrived in Valencia in the early hours of 27 March. They came on the small French freighter *Lézardrieux*, bringing food supplies and aiming to help organize the evacuation of those whose lives were in peril. The delegation consisted of three French parliamentary deputies (Albert Forcinal, Albert Rigal and Charles Tillon), three other Frenchmen (Dr Jacob Maurice Kalmanovitch, the anthropologist Bernard Maupoil and the journalist André Ulmann), three English members (Sir George Young, Lord Faringdon and the Quaker Barbara Wood), an American, Major Thompson, and an Anglo–Finn, Laurin 'Konni' Zilliacus. The final report of the Committee stated that:

> The total number that required and might have received evacuation if the British and French Governments had put the resources within reach at the disposal of the Delegation, would have been in the order of sixty thousand. The total number that the Delegation could have dealt with but for instructions issued by those Governments would have been about 6,500. The total number that were evacuated within the two days was no more than 650.

The blame for this was laid on the British and French governments and on Casado.[45]

In the course of 27 March, the delegation met Leopoldo Menéndez, the commander of the Army of the Levante, who presided over the evacuation committee set up only a few days earlier. The first order of business was the selection of those to be evacuated on the *Lézardrieux*.

With relatively equitable distribution of Republican groups, including Communists, 'A list of 350 approved by the delegation assembled at the port with numbered tickets that night (11 p.m.) and about 30 more were added later. The *Lezardrieux* left with them about dawn (28th March) and was boarded by a Nationalist cruiser but allowed to proceed.' Unfortunately, the same spirit of cooperation did not apply in Alicante.[46]

The flimsiness of Casado's claims about regarding evacuation as a priority was revealed in his dealings with the international delegation. They met a wildly over-optimistic and complacent Casado at 5 p.m. on 28 March not long after he had reached Valencia. Laurin Zilliacus wrote later: 'At our first meeting with him that afternoon, he did not, as he writes in his book, tell us that we might have three days. He was self-confident, and told us we probably had twenty-five or thirty days, since, he explained, while Franco had rejected his plan of surrender, he was actually moving according to it (or even more slowly).' Zilliacus' account tallies with the official report of the Comité Internationale in which it is stated that Casado had told the delegation that both sides had presented plans for the transfer of power. He claimed that the Francoist plan was not practical and that, although the CND's plan had been rejected as a matter of form, it was being followed. The transfer, he said, was to be completed in thirty days and the Nationalists were three days behind on the schedule. He told the delegation that he had had assurances from Franco that there would be no obstacles to evacuation and 'gave an optimistic account of Spanish ships available'. According to Zilliacus,

Casado also told us at this meeting that he had ships for some 10,000 refugees. There is no doubt of this because I remember agreeing with one of my colleagues as we left the room that this was good news indeed, although it made our efforts seem almost redundant. Later the same evening Casado called us in again and this time he said he thought we should have a week, but it might be only three days or – with a shrug – even only twenty-four hours. When pressed about the ships he made it plain that he had none. Apparently he had earlier referred to an optimistic

view of the capacity of *our* ships. Next morning at 7.30 he sent
for us, and said he was surrendering the town in a few minutes
… Reading Casado's self-justification confirms me in the view I
formed of him and his role at the time. I do not believe he was
the Machiavellian instrument of pseudo-democratic governments. I do believe he was a wishful thinker with grandiose
sentiments and exalted ideas about himself.[47]

André Ulmann also wrote about the interview with Casado in
Valencia. He claimed that Casado had suggested that all available
ships should go to Alicante, because it was the port furthest from the
battlefront. Moreover, Casado guaranteed that it would be the last
port to be occupied by Franco's forces. He based this on the claim that
Franco had promised him not to oppose the evacuation. Using words
that he would repeat on the radio later in the day, he said that,
although there was nothing on paper, since the victor could not be
asked to humiliate himself, he had assured the delegation that Franco's
word could be trusted because he had kept every promise that he had
made. Accordingly, that night, the most at-risk Republican militants
and army officers went to Alicante. The next morning, Wednesday 29
March, on the basis of Casado's assurances, Ulmann and Charles
Tillon went to Alicante to help with the evacuation. They were furious when they learned that Casado himself had chosen to go to
Gandía, halfway between Valencia and Alicante. They were even
more outraged to discover that the same British and French warships
that had been ordered not to protect merchant shipping hoping to
collect refugees in Alicante had been given instructions to go to
Gandía. Ulmann learned from those of the delegation who went to
Gandía that the town had been taken over by Falangists who, far from
impeding Casado's departure, had sent him refreshments while he
was waiting to embark.[48]

For those who ended up in Alicante, it was a very different story.
After a hair-raising journey, Guzmán had reached Valencia where
Val, Salgado and García Pradas had already arrived, having come by
plane with Casado on 28 March. Guzmán learned that Casado had
told them and the other members of the Consejo Nacional de Defensa

that Franco had given assurances that anyone who wished to be evacuated would be allowed to do so. This was absurd in the light of the
Law of Political Responsibilities and the experience of the repression
elsewhere. Guzmán attended a press conference given by Casado on
29 March at which he told his audience that there were sufficient
ships on the way to secure the evacuation of everyone who desired it.
García Pradas and Salgado confirmed to Guzmán that there would
adequate shipping at Alicante and that was where they were telling
the would-be refugees to go. They assured him that they would not
leave until everyone else had got away. When Guzmán took his leave
of them, García Pradas's last words were: 'We will embark only once
everyone is safe. Or else we will be killed trying to prevent a single
anti-fascist being left on land.' This was a lie. Rodríguez Vega, who
had managed to reach Valencia, went in search of Casado. He bumped
into Mera, who was also looking for Casado. Mera was furious about
the flight of the CND from Madrid and feared that he would be left
behind. When Casado appeared, it quickly became apparent that he
had virtually nothing organized for the evacuation other than for
himself and the staff of the CND.[49]

Nothing had been done until 23 March when Wenceslao Carrillo
had issued vague orders to the civil governors to form evacuation
committees but gave no details of how any evacuation was to take
place. Inevitably, nothing was done, but civil governors, such as
Cañas, were left with the impression that the Junta in Madrid believed
that their order had magically resolved the issues surrounded the
evacuation. In the words of the Valencian Socialist leader Evaristo
Jorge Moreno, the plans of the Consejo Nacional de Defensa 'consisted
simply in entrusting the salvation of our comrades to a chaotic and
terrifying "every man for himself"'. Casado advised Rodríguez Vega
and Mera, as Val and García Pradas had told Guzmán, that they
should go to Alicante, where he claimed evacuation would be possible. José Rodríguez Olazábal, president of the Audiencia Provincial
(high court) of Valencia, was also told by Casado that the only chance
of evacuation was from Alicante. Once in Alicante, Guzmán learned
that a caravan of cars with Casado, the members of the Consejo
Nacional de Defensa and the anarchist high command had left

Valencia on 29 March. Rodríguez Olazábal and his family never reached Alicante because Falangists and other Fifth Columnists were blocking the road. They did, however, reach Gandía.[50]

Despite telling Guzmán that they would be the very last to leave, García Pradas, Val, Salgado and González Marín were driven to Gandía the following day with Casado. Before they left, Casado accepted an offer from the Legation of Panama to offer asylum to his (second) wife, Carmen Santodomingo, and a number of senior Republicans who did not want to leave Spain. Shortly afterwards, the Francoists attacked the Panamanian Legation and arrested them all, remarkable payment for the fact that Panama had saved many hundreds of right-wingers during the war. Casado's wife was imprisoned with prostitutes.[51] García Pradas later described the flight to Gandía of Casado and the rest of the Consejo Nacional de Defensa:

> The drivers, with pistols in their hands, guarded the cars with the engines running. They pulled away at high speed. In the lead, there was a Chrysler with Casado, Val and I don't know who else, then, in a Packard, Salgado, two others and myself and behind, in a Rolls-Royce, González Marín and other comrades. The brakes were squealing, the gears grinding. The drivers seemed ready to run over anyone who got in the way. We went towards the port in Valencia so as not to go through the city centre and, once we were on the outskirts, we got on to a road going south towards Alicante.

García Pradas wrote that they were really heading for Alicante, but that Fifth Column uprisings along the way made it impossible to go any further than Gandía. The claim that he and the rest of Casado's party had been forced to go to Gandía was an absurd attempt to obscure the special treatment arranged for their departure by Franco. Casado himself wrote: 'since there was nothing left for us to do in Valencia, the Consejeros met and, after a brief discussion, we decided to set out for the port of Gandía.'[52] The choice of Gandía as their destination would have been strange if it had not been where their prearranged rescue awaited them. Casado was telling only part of the truth.

The decision to head for Gandía was almost certainly not taken on the morning of 29 March. The previous evening, Abbington Gooden had informed Casado that a British warship would be waiting in Gandía for his party. The commander of British naval forces in the western Mediterranean, Rear Admiral John Tovey, wrote to the Admiralty that 'care will be taken to exclude undesirables', unaware presumably of the blood-stained antecedents of Val, Salgado, González Marín and García Pradas. While Franco was not prepared to give written permission for Casado's party to be evacuated, the Foreign Office was informed by the Spanish Embassy in London that he would turn a blind eye.[53]

Shortly before leaving Valencia, Casado had made a broadcast at the request of the local Falange from the studios of Radio Valencia. He called for calm and made a feeble attempt to justify Franco's refusal to negotiate. 'It is not possible to doubt the good faith of the victors ... We have secured a decent and honourable peace with the best possible conditions and without bloodshed.' He repeated what he had been saying for days:

I can guarantee that in the entire loyalist zone, nothing has happened that was not part of the plans made by us when we assumed constitutional power in Republican Spain on 5 March. According to Franco's promises, all those who have not committed crimes of blood will retain their freedom. Generalísimo Franco has promised me that there will be no opposition to the evacuation. He has not signed any document to this effect since that would have been a humiliation that cannot be required of a victor but you can trust his word. He has fulfilled all the promises that he has made me. ¡Viva España![54]

The broadcast was yet another example of Casado's duplicity. Franco's entire war effort had been aimed at the annihilation of as many Republicans as possible. That he never intended to fulfil any of the promises made on his behalf to Casado would be demonstrated, if it needed demonstrating, by the naval blockade which prevented the evacuation of tens of thousands of would-be evacuees. Shortly after making his broadcast in praise of Franco's good faith, Casado claimed to Abbington Gooden that he was perfectly aware of Franco's bad faith. However, the terms in which he did so were testimony to his megalomania. He told Gooden that the Caudillo's determination to put Republican army officers on trial was because 'General Franco bore a personal grudge against him for having robbed him of the kudos of crushing Communism in Madrid.'[55]

As García Pradas well knew, when the caravan with 163 members of Casado's staff and their families left for Gandía, with the top personalities in the luxury limousines leading the way, it had already been arranged with the British Consul Abbington Gooden that they would leave from the port. García Pradas goes on to recount that Leopoldo Menéndez and two members of his staff, Colonels Francisco Ciutat and Gustavo Durán and Juan Ignacio Mantecón of Izquierda Republicana, the commissar of the Army of the Levante, were already in Gandía. Durán had been wandering around Valencia about to hand himself over to the Francoists when he bumped into a friend who put him in touch with a British official who got him to Gandía. The novelist Max Aub describes a row between García Pradas and Menéndez, probably about who did or did not have the right to escape. In the light of Menéndez's efforts in Valencia, it might reasonably be supposed that the row concerned the duplicitous instructions issued by Casado and the rest of the CND, García Pradas included, that refugees should head for Alicante.[56]

In fact, Abbington Gooden had received permission from London to allow those on the dockside in Gandía to embark on the British destroyer HMS *Galatea*. However, the members of the Consejo Nacional de Defensa seemed anxious to keep the prearranged British evacuation to themselves. When Rodríguez Olazábal unexpectedly arrived in Gandía and was told by Albert Forcinal and Sir George Young that this was the only place from which evacuation was now possible, he was furious. He confronted Casado, more or less accusing him of being a liar.[57] Even more dramatic was the experience of two members of the executive committee of the Agrupación Socialista de Valencia, Serafín Sánchez and Gerardo Jiménez Hernández, and two other prominent Socialists. They were heading for Alicante when, on the outskirts of Gandía, they ran into a unit of frontier guards who were covering the flight of the CND's caravan of cars from Valencia. The commander of the unit, also a Valencian Socialist named Nieto, advised them to go to the port of Gandía as their best chance of escape. However, when they reached the dockside, Wenceslao Carrillo tried to stop them embarking on *Galatea*, something he had no right to do. There was some pushing and shoving, until Gerardo Jiménez drew his pistol and threatened Carrillo, who was finally obliged to stand aside so that they could go aboard.[58] When groups of armed Republicans arrived, demanding to be permitted to embark on *Galatea*, Rear Admiral John Tovey, and Casado agreed that they be told, mendaciously, that if they went to Alicante there would be ships to evacuate them.[59]

Of the enthusiastic Numantine revolutionaries, Val, Salgado and González Marín, along with García Pradas, managed to escape to England. García Pradas claims that they were evacuated on HMS *Sussex* but in fact they left on *Galatea* since *Sussex* was bound for Palma de Mallorca to repatriate Italian prisoners taken by the CND. While *Galatea* was being loaded, an armed Francoist merchant ship, the *Mar Negro*, arrived, but it stood off the port and its contingent of troops waited for the refugees to be taken aboard *Galatea* before landing. This was clearly done on Francoist orders. After all the members of Casado's Junta who wished to escape had been brought on board *Galatea* in the early hours of the morning of 30 March, the Francoist troops landed and occupied the town. The following morning, Casado, who was prostrate from a combination of exhaustion and his abdominal problems, was transferred to the hospital ship HMS *Maine* accompanied by the other members of the CND. There is little doubt about London's role in Casado's evacuation. Casado was praised by the Captain of *Galatea* for staying on in Valencia 'to keep order' despite having been offered the chance to leave on a French warship. There was a delay in the final authorization for him to be taken aboard a British vessel, but that had been given the previous evening. It was thus no coincidence that when *Galatea* put into Gandía at 4.30 in the afternoon of 29 March, Casado happened to be there awaiting evacuation.[60]

In a passage in the 1968 Spanish edition of his memoirs, not included in the English edition of 1939, Casado claimed that he had planned to stay in Spain. It was certainly plausible that he should have aimed to do so, given his contacts with the Fifth Column and his repeated claims that Franco would respect the ranks of officers who had helped bring the war to an end. In 1968, in tune with his usual self-aggrandizement, he attributed his desire to stay to 'my duty as an officer'. He made no mention of his hopes of remaining in Spain as the honoured officer who had, as he announced to the Fifth Column, astounded the world. However, there followed a passage that, alongside a respectful deference towards Franco, contained a glimmer of truth. Casado wrote that he had refrained from staying because 'our representatives who negotiated peace in Burgos, brought a suggestion from the Generalísimo that the members of the Consejo Nacional de Defensa should leave Spain. Given the Generalísimo's position as the victor and mine as the vanquished, I took the suggestion as an order although I could not understand its meaning. I found the explanation when they informed me that the illustrious Señor Besteiro had been sentenced to thirty years in prison.'[61] It was more than a suggestion. Garijo and Ortega had informed the CND on 23 March that Franco would facilitate the departure of its members. He reneged on all but this one of his insinuated promises about facilitating evacuation and refraining from reprisals. Accordingly, as Casado inadvertently revealed, saving him and the other members of his Junta from facing the same fate as awaited Besteiro was the crumb that Franco considered to be an appropriate reward for their services.

Betrayed by Casado's coup, tens of thousands of desperate Republican men, women and children fled from Madrid on 28 March 1939 pursued by Falangists. They headed for Valencia and Alicante. They had been promised by Casado's Junta that there would be ships to take them into exile. In fact, there was no chance of that. In his memoirs, Casado asserted that the overriding concern of the Consejo Nacional de Defensa was the evacuation of all those who wanted to leave Spain. He cited the report allegedly given by Colonel Garijo on his return from Burgos to the effect that Franco's negotiators, Colonels Victoria and Ungría, had implied that the Generalísimo would tolerate the evacuation of at least 10,000 Republicans. He pointed out that Trifón Gómez had been sent to Paris to ascertain whether the ships chartered by Negrín from the Mid-Atlantic Shipping Company could be used. He then went on to blame Negrín for scuppering this aim. Casado conveniently forgot that Besteiro had objected to any government resources being used to charter ships. He also claimed that the CND had 'made every effort humanly possible to evacuate those who wanted to leave Spain'.

This was just another of Casado's lies. On 26 March Abbington Gooden and a British officer, Colonel Hay, had met Antonio Pérez Garcia, of the UGT, 'minister of labour' (*consejero de trabajo*) in the National Defence Council. His department had been given the task of arranging the evacuation of leading Republicans. Gooden's report on the meeting could hardly have been more devastating:

We both gained the impression that this gentleman is completely dazzled and incapable of coming to any decision. He told us vaguely that lists of persons to be evacuated were being prepared, but he had no idea of how many persons would be included in them and could give us no figures between a minimum of 10,000 and a maximum of 40,000. He has made no arrangements for chartering of ships and talks vaguely of persons evacuated proceeding to Mexico. No arrangements appear to have been made with French Government for receiving them in transit. The Council appears to be incapable of formulating any plan but in this connexion it must be remembered that they have little money abroad, no ships for evacuation, no diplomatic mission to plead their cause and inadequate means of communication with foreign countries.[62]

The mitigating factors listed by Gooden were, of course, the consequence of the refusal of Besteiro, Miaja and Casado on 6 March to accept Negrín's offers of a formal hand-over of power.

The last boats to leave, organized by the Federación Provincial Socialista of Alicante, were the British steamers *Stanbrook*, *Maritime*, *Ronwyn* and *African Trader*. They carried 5,146 passengers. In fact, according to the head of the SIM, the *Stanbrook* was one of the ships that belonged to the Mid-Atlantic line that Negrín had bought for the Republic. Another was the *Winnipeg* which might have been able to take as many as 6,000 refugees, but it was prevented by a Francoist warship from entering the port. The greatest number to escape were on the *Stanbrook*, whose captain, Archibald Dixon, on his own initiative, permitted every possible space inside and out to be crammed with evacuees. In contrast, the captain of the *Maritime* refused to let more than thirty-two important politicians embark.[63] Many smaller vessels, fishing boats and pleasure craft, made the hazardous journey to Algeria. The very last of the ships to leave Alicante, the *Stanbrook*, precariously carried 2,638 refugees. There were passengers crammed on the deck and in the holds, and its plimsoll line was well below the surface of the water. The ship was attacked by Francoist aircraft but miraculously, without lights, Captain Dickson managed to manoeuvre through the rebel gauntlet. The *Stanbrook* reached Oran in Algeria. For nearly a month, the French authorities refused to let Captain Dickson disembark his passengers, even though they were short of food and water, in conditions of extreme overcrowding. The French relented only when there was a danger of contagious illnesses spreading. Finally, the refugees were taken to internment camps.[64]

Over the next few days, those who had arrived too late were joined by thousands more refugees from all over the remaining Republican territory. In despair, many committed suicide, some throwing themselves into the water, others shooting themselves, others still slitting their throats. One eyewitness, Laurin Zilliacus, a member of the delegation sent by the Comité Internationale de Coordination to help with the refugees, recalled that 'When, finally, a Franco warship appeared, and after it, like a mockery, our helpless ships, over a hundred of the refugees committed suicide by drowning or cutting their veins on the jagged edges of opened tins.' Edmundo Domínguez put the number of suicides at forty-five and the Italian commander, General Gastone Gambara at sixty-eight.[65] In the vain hope that ships would arrive, an evacuation junta was set up in the port by Colonel Ricardo Burillo, who had received instructions from Carrillo to take charge. In the Comandancia Militar of the port, a group of senior

Republican figures tried to keep order while drawing up lists of those to be allotted places on the ships. As well as Burillo, there was José Rodríguez Vega of the UGT, José Gómez Osorio, the Civil Governor of Madrid, Rafael Henche, the Alcalde of Madrid, and Pascual Tomás and Carlos Rubiera of the PSOE. Pascual Tomás was allowed to leave on an Air France aircraft in order to negotiate the speedier arrival of ships for the evacuation. Some vessels came into view but, with their captains fearful of interception by the Francoist navy, they either left empty or turned back before even reaching the docksides at Valencia and Alicante. Having already recognized Franco, neither London nor Paris were prepared to let their navies intervene against the rebel fleet. In Alicante, the refugees waited in vain for three and a half days without food or water. Children died of inanition. The Mexican government offered to take all the refugees but Franco refused, declaring that they were all prisoners of war and must face the conse-quences. On Friday 31 March, the city was occupied by Italian forces. A deal was brokered by the Consul of Argentina, with the support of the French and Cuban consuls, whereby the Italians undertook to provide safe-conducts to those who wanted to leave Spain if the approximately 12,000 Republicans gave up their weapons. The Republicans agreed but the Italians were then overruled once more by Franco. When two ships carrying Francoist troops arrived, the majority of the refugees were herded away and the remainder followed the next morning.[66] Families were violently separated and those who protested beaten or shot. The women and children were taken into the city centre where they were kept for a month packed into a cinema with little food and without facilities for washing or changing their babies. The men – including boys from the age of twelve – were marched either to the bull-ring in Alicante or to a large open field outside the town known as the Campo de los Almendros.[67]

As the last hopes of evacuation on a British or French ship vanished, the numbers of suicides increased. As the prisoners were forced to file past their corpses, one remarked, 'Soon, we'll envy the dead.' They were stripped of money, watches, valuables and decent jackets and coats by the troops sent to watch them. As they were marched to the improvised concentration camp, they passed further piles of corpses of men who had been shot 'while trying to escape'.[68] The camp was known as the Campo de los Almendros simply because it was an orchard of almond trees. For six days, 45,000 prisoners were kept virtually without food or water, sleeping in mud in the open, exposed to the wind and the rain. On two occasions in six days, they were fed – the first time with a small tin of sardines between four and a small loaf of bread between five, and the second with a small tin of lentils between four and a *chusco* (a small bread roll) between five. The prisoners stripped the trees of the young unripe nuts and then resorted to eating the leaves and the bark. Only the fact that they were surrounded by machine-gun emplacements prevented mass break-outs.[69]

Repent at Leisure?

Besteiro, Sánchez Guerra and others remained in the basement of the Ministry of Finance throughout 28 March 1939. Antonio Luna García, Besteiro's friend and Fifth Column contact, had come to be present and 'protect' them in case of unpleasantness when the Francoists arrived. While there, he had inappropriately treated them to a pompous recital of the programme of Falange Española. In the evening, a group of Falangists appeared led by a very short man called Ángel Luque who greeted them with a fascist salute and the words 'Arriba España!' Besteiro responded with a nod, at which point the diminutive Falangist asked him angrily: 'Have you not learned the greeting of the New Spain?' Besteiro replied drily, 'No. And the worst thing is that, at my age, I'm afraid that it is going to be hard work learning it.' To the astonishment of Luque, the guards and staff of the Ministry continued to treat Besteiro and Sánchez Guerra with respect. When dinner was served, they invited Luque to join them and, in the droll recollection of Sánchez Guerra, 'despite his meagre volume, he ate with the appetite of a much bigger person'. The next day, the Ministry was occupied by Francoist troops. Besteiro and Sánchez Guerra and others were arrested and taken later that evening to the prison of Porlier.[1]

Besteiro's confident prediction that he would be a barrier against mass reprisals was greatly mistaken, yet his naive optimism about the new situation continued for some time. On 30 April, he wrote to his wife from prison: 'We will all leave here rather battered, or maybe (who knows?) perhaps we will leave toughened up. I am not pessimistic about our situation. We will have to give up some things but they are things which, given our lifelong habits and our moral standards, we are ready to give up. I still hope that we can find a dignified way of making a living, on top of the reparations that are owed us, or certainly to you.'[2] That Besteiro believed there would be 'reparations' for his trial and the suffering undergone by himself and his wife is testimony to his delusions about Franco.

Sánchez Guerra was tried for the 'crime' of 'aiding the military rebellion' (*auxilio a la rebelión militar*). Numerous Francoists spoke up for him and referred to his efforts to save conservatives during the war. He was able to point out that he had had nothing to do with Casado's exigent peace conditions and that he had advised him simply to sue for peace. He was able to point out that while he was a lieutenant in Morocco, serving with the local mercenaries of the Regulares Indígenas in 1920, he had been wounded. His bravery had been noted by Franco himself, who had written in his diary 'What a soldier!' Sánchez Guerra was awarded the Medalla Militar for gallantry. He appealed for Queipo de Llano to be a witness on his behalf. Queipo sent a telegram declaring that there was nothing against Sánchez Guerra. But he was tried in mid-May 1940, found guilty and sentenced to life imprisonment. When he was released in 1946 afer a partial amnesty, he went to Argentina. He returned to Spain and spent his last years in a Dominican monastery in Villalva, Navarra, where he died in 1964.[3]

Nearly sixty-nine years old, on 8 July 1939 Besteiro faced a court martial of insurrectionary generals for the alleged crime of 'support for the military rebellion' (*el delito de adhesión a la rebelión militar*). The absurd charges were brought against him despite his efforts to secure peace and despite the anti-communism which inspired his participation in the Casado Junta, an act of military rebellion against the government of Juan Negrín.[4] Indeed, his peace mission to London and his links with Casado were among the central accusations against him at his court martial. The prosecutor, Lieutenant Colonel Felipe Acedo Colunga, recognized that Besteiro was an honest man, innocent of any crime of blood, yet demanded the death sentence. Acedo's long speech made it clear that Besteiro's crime was to have rendered Socialism more acceptable by making it moderate. It is difficult also to avoid the conclusion that the Francoists, unable to try Azaña, Negrín, Largo Caballero and the other major figures of the Republic, poured all their hatred into the trial of Besteiro.[5]

When the time came to appeal against the sentence of life imprisonment, Besteiro composed a plea of mitigation in which it was usual both to confess and to excuse oneself. He wrote:

Without committing the indignity, which I would never have committed, of going over to the side which, according to my view of things, had to be, at the end of the day, the victor, I could easily have adopted a more cautious position which would have permitted me, either inside or outside Spain, to save my life, my reputation, my interests and those of my family. I did not do so because I understood my duty to be unequivocally to remain in the breach, facing all dangers, not to fudge my position nor reduce my influence so as to seek salvation in a kind of political anonymity, but rather to proclaim it clearly and affirm it as much as possible, to make use of the moral force that the adoption of such an attitude might provide me on behalf of my fellow citizens who had been fully put to the test by misfortune, and on behalf of the country in which I was born and to which I wish to belong. I have remained faithful to this rule down to the last moment, a moment when I risked everything in order to put an end to an impossible situation and to save the Spanish people greater misfortunes than those which they had already suffered. It is well known that I have had opportunities to leave Spain, not only with ease but with positive advantages both at the time and for the future. But there were two moments which illustrated the tenacity with which I have maintained my position. These two moments were 7 November 1936 and 28 March 1939. On the first of those dates, the violence with which the Nationalist troops could have entered Madrid made me fear that I might be one of victims of the struggle. On the second of those dates, even though it was clear that there would be no attack on Madrid, the news that I had been removed from my Professorial chair and the unjust attacks to which I had been subjected by the Nationalist radio allowed me to have no illusion about the fate which awaited me in the first days. Nevertheless, on both occasions, ignoring advice from all quarters to leave the country, or at least to go into hiding for some time, I decided, without hesitation, to remain at my post. The reasons for my decision are complex: the desire not to re-establish a long-dead solidarity with others who were fleeing; a repugnance both for the very idea of flight, especially since I did not have to flee, and for making a show in foreign parts of the tragedies of my own fatherland; the conviction that I could appear before the most severe judges with my head held high and my conscience clear.[6]

The initial sentence of life imprisonment was commuted to thirty years of hard labour. He was confined first in the Monasterio de Dueñas in the province of Palencia until the end of August 1939 and then in the prison of Carmona in the province of Seville. In his seventieth year, with his health broken by lack of adequate food and medical attention, he was forced to undertake hard physical work, scrubbing floors, cleaning latrines. When his final illness, a fatal blood-poisoning contracted during this latter activity, struck in mid-September 1940, his beloved wife, Dolores Cebrián, travelled immediately to Carmona but was refused permission to see him and was kept waiting eight days until the eve of his death on 27 September.[7]

The dignity and courage shown by Besteiro during the last days of the Spanish Civil War and the injustice of his fate at the hands of the Francoists have to be weighed against the lives lost as a result of the Casado fiasco. Besteiro's comportment throughout the war, first standing aside from the Republican cause then participating in the Casado Junta, was born of a curious mixture of innocence and arrogance. Always thin-skinned behind his dignified exterior, he was deeply wounded by his treatment at the hands of the left during the internal party feuds of 1934–6. His understandable outrage was compounded by his conviction that the left Socialists were simply wrong in rejecting his definition of the historical moment. His inter-pretations of practical political issues were often theoretical abstrac-tions elaborated with an Olympian detachment from day-to-day realities. This was particularly the case with regard to fascism. His personal sensitivities and his conviction of his theoretical correctness seem to have combined to produce a sense of overwhelming moral superiority. Out of that sense was born his optimistic belief that his unblemished past would earn him Francoist clemency. His well-meaning but somewhat self-regarding views in 1939 stood in stark contrast to the reality of the Caudillo's determination to annihilate all the values of the Republic. Besteiro's case was considered personally by Franco. The fact that he was refused medical treatment and any commutation of his sentence reflected the determination of the Caudillo to destroy him.[8] Franco was essentially making an example even of a man who had done nothing to oppose the military rising and had done more than most to put an end to Republican resistance. Besteiro's tragedy was that, having lost what little faith he had in the Republic and his Socialist comrades, he chose instead to place his trust in his executioner.

Another example of the vindictiveness of the Francoist 'justice' facilitated by Casado's coup even with those who had worked hard to stop the repression in the Republican zone was the fate of the anar-chist Melchor Rodríguez. As Director of Prisons in November 1936, he had saved many lives. Indeed, his successful efforts to save rightists in Madrid had led some of his anarchist comrades to suspect him of being a traitor. Even his wife became convinced that, at best, he had naively let himself be used by the Fifth Column. His refusal to acknowledge her suspicions led to her leaving him in early 1939. When, at dawn on 28 March, the Alcalde of Madrid, Rafael Henche, left for Valencia, Melchor accepted Besteiro's suggestion that he replace Henche as mayor.[9] He awaited the arrival of the Francoist troops and formally surrendered the capital to them and then simply went home. Confident that his services to the Francoists would ensure that nothing would happen to him, Melchor did not hide. A journal-ist from the Catholic newspaper *Ya* interviewed him after he had attended an event in honour of two dramatists, the Alvarez Quintero brothers. In the interview, he insinuated that he had some sympathy for the new regime. The following day, 13 April 1939, he was arrested and taken to prison where he enjoyed a degree of privilege, although he was shunned by his fellow prisoners. He was tried by a Francoist military tribunal in December. After an energetic defence by Ignacio Arenillas de Chaves, the extremely competent military lawyer who had defended Besteiro, he was found not guilty. However, the chief prosecutor of the Madrid military region (Auditor de la Primera Región Militar) rejected the verdict and insisted on a retrial.[10]

Melchor Rodríguez was tried again on 11 May 1940 accused of a crime that took place in Madrid at a time when he was in Valencia. A young and inexperienced defender was appointed two days before the trial. He was not permitted to meet his client or given any of the trial documents until the trial had actually started. The trial was rigged with false testimonies. The prosecutor, Leopoldo Huidobro Pardo, was a Carlist who was bitterly hostile towards the left in general and the anarchists in particular having undergone some frightening experiences in Madrid during the war. He accused Melchor of being a bloodthirsty gunman and demanded the death penalty. However, the pantomime was ruined by the unscheduled appearance of General Agustín Muñoz Grandes, who spoke on Melchor's behalf and presented a list of over 2,000 rightists whose lives he had saved. Among them were many aristocrats and one of the founders of the Falange, Raimundo Fernández Cuesta. Muñoz Grandes, as the main witness on Melchor's behalf, outranked everyone else in the room. The planned death sentence was commuted to twenty years and one day, and he was sent on 1 March 1941 to the prison of El Puerto de Santa María in the province of Cádiz. Then, Muñoz Grandes, as Capitán General, or commander, of the Madrid military region, commuted his sentence to twelve years and a day, which gave him the possibility of provisional liberty.[11]

Melchor Rodríguez was one of the few senior members of the Casado Junta who had remained in Madrid, naively believing that, since he had no blood on his hands, he had nothing to fear. Another still in Spain was Ángel Pedrero. In late March, Pedrero had been provided by Casado with the considerable sum of 2,500 pesetas in Francoist currency and also carried a large quantity of confiscated jewellery and other valuables. Having delayed his departure to take his loved ones with him, he reached the port of Alicante too late to catch the last boat out. Imprisoned in the Campo de los Almendros with 200 of his men, he remarked prophetically that they were all doomed because of what they knew about the Fifth Column and its betrayals. Pedrero meant that the empty boasts of those who now claimed falsely to have been Fifth Columnists would be exposed if he lived. He was sentenced to death on 20 February 1940 and executed by garrote vil.[12] There is also the case of the Socialist Ricardo Zabalza, who had supported the CND in his capacity as a member of the executive committee of the PSOE. He was also trapped in Alicante and shot in Madrid on 24 February 1940.[13]

After Besteiro, the most senior member of the Casada Junta to fall into the hands of the Franco regime was the anarchist Cipriano Mera. He had escaped Spain on 29 March 1939 and got to Oran in Algeria. By trade a bricklayer, during the Civil War he had joined the CNT militia and risen to the rank of lieutenant colonel, and had commanded the IV Army Corps. In Algeria, he was interned in a concentration camp along with other Spanish refugees. They were then incorporated into work battalions. Mera escaped and after various adventures reached Casablanca. He was frequently arrested, sent to camps, released, arrested again and interrogated, yet he was given permission to go to Mexico. Arrested again before he could do so, a Francoist request for his extradition was heard on 13 January 1942. It was successful and he was handed over to the Francoist authorities in Spanish Morocco on 20 February and eventually taken to Spain in April. He was court-martialled in Madrid on 26 April, accused of military rebellion as well as of murders and looting. He was condemned to death but, after some months, his sentence was reduced to life imprisonment. In the aftermath of the Second World War, as Franco reacted to the defeat of the Axis, Mera was among many prisoners released provisionally in 1946.[14]

The other principal anarchist members of the Junta were more fortunate than Mera and managed to escape with Casado to England.

Given the British government's reluctance to accept Republican refugees, it was remarkable that men notorious for their roles in the anarchist *checas* of Madrid should have been given asylum. José García Pradas and Manuel Salgado remained in London until their deaths many years later. García Pradas worked as a waiter, then as a broadcaster on the Spanish service of the BBC, and was a prolific writer and translator. Salgado also worked in the catering business and became manager of a restaurant. Manuel González Marín and Eduardo Val Bescós never settled in England and eventually moved to France.[15] Juan López Sánchez and his wife lived in various parts of England and Scotland, for a time at first in the Oxford home of Salvador de Madariaga. He was one of Casado's most assiduous correspondents.

There were many army officers who had supported Casado's Junta and, before that, had worked on behalf of the Francoists. They made no attempt to go into exile at the end of the war, confident that their services would either be rewarded or at least protect them. Despite Casado's optimistic promises that they could keep their rank and Franco's assurances that nothing would happen, his collaborators were put on trial and given long prison sentences. Although they spent less time in jail than many loyal Republicans, they were expelled from the army and stripped of their pensions. Since, like so many, they faced punitive fines under the terms of the Law of Political Responsibilities, their families were often left destitute. After their release, they had to look for whatever work was available no matter how inappropriate. Matallana, for instance, despite testimonials from prominent members of the Fifth Column and Franco's intelligence service, the SIPM, was put on trial in August 1939 and sentenced to thirty years. However, he was rewarded for his efforts in that, within a year, his sentence had been commuted to twelve years, and eleven months later he was released. Nevertheless, he faced considerable financial difficulties until he found a job with a construction company. Despite determined efforts, he was never able to secure his return to the army.[16]

In a case that revealed the absurdity of the Francoist judicial system, Diego Medina Garijo, Casado's personal physician, was arrested shortly after the end of the war. He was accused by a Captain

Antenor Betancourt González of having been involved in the assault by a Republican crowd on the Cuartel de la Montaña in Madrid in July 1936 where in fact he had gone in his capacity as a doctor to treat wounded soldiers. He was interrogated, and evidence collected, throughout the summer while under house arrest. The court received numerous testimonials from other army officers to the effect that he had saved many lives, including priests, monks and other pro-Francoists. Manuel Valdés Larrañaga, the head of the clandestine Falange, provided an enthusiastic account of Medina's services to the Fifth Column in terms of medical assistance, the provision of false documents and certificates to permit rightists to avoid military service and hiding individuals being sought by the SIM. There was an equally warm testimonial from Antonio Bouthelier, who described him as a 'fervent patriot' and praised his role in converting Casado to the Francoist cause. Julio Palacios spoke in similar terms. At his court martial on 14 August, the case was dismissed. However, four days later, that verdict was set aside and he was taken to a higher court where the prosecution called for him to be sentenced to four years in prison. On 29 August, another court martial found him not guilty. However, on 9 September, the chief prosecutor of the Madrid military region insisted on a further retrial at which he was accused of 'aiding the military rebellion' for his service in the Republican army. The fact that he could not have done all the things that he did for the Francoist cause had he not been an officer was not considered and he was sentenced to three years and one day. However, he was released because his case fell under the terms of a general pardon for those sentenced to less than six years and a day.[17] Not long after Medina had been pardoned, Casado wrote a will in which he named him as guardian of his children, Segismundo and María del Carmen Casado Santodomingo. In the same document, he instructed his children, who were still toddlers, to reject any offer of financial help from his brother César or his own ex-wife María de las Mercedes Condado y Condado, 'letting them know that I make this request because of their abominable conduct towards me during my time in exile'.[18]

Matallana's second-in-command, Lieutenant Colonel Antonio Garijo Hernández, had collaborated closely with him in sabotaging the diversionary operations planned by Vicente Rojo during the battle of the Ebro. He had flown to Burgos to negotiate a peace settlement on Casado's behalf. When he was tried in June 1940, he was given glowing testimonials by prominent members of the Fifth Column, by the SIPM, by Antonio Bouthelier of the clandestine Falange, by Diego Medina Garijo, himself undergoing trial, and by Franco's lifelong friend, General Camilo Alonso Vega. He was sentenced to six years and pardoned by Franco two days later. He was allowed to keep his pension as a retired officer.[19] The head of Matallana's general staff, Lieutenant Colonel Félix Muedra Miñón, was tried in August 1939. He was sentenced to thirty years in prison. Within a year, this had been reduced to six years, and ten months later he was granted provisional liberty. However, like Matallana, he had been expelled from the army and lost his pension. A friend wrote to Vicente Rojo in 1956 to describe how he had met Muedra and found him selling soap and bleach in a little shop.[20]

Of the Casadistas who managed to escape, it was Admiral Buiza whose later career gave the clearest signs of remorse for the consequences of his actions. After the arrival of the fleet in Bizerta in Tunisia, he was confined in a French concentration camp. After his release, he joined the French Foreign Legion. In recognition of his rank in the Spanish Republican navy, he was admitted with the rank of captain, only the second person in the history of the Legion to be given this honour, the other being a member of the Danish royal family. He fought against the Germans in French North Africa and was promoted to the rank of lieutenant colonel. After the armistice following the French defeat, Buiza was obliged to leave the Legion and went to Oran, where he lived selling toys door to door until he got a job as the accountant in a soap factory. When the Allied invasion of French North Africa took place in November 1942, he joined the Corps Franc d'Afrique, a Gaullist anti-Vichy unit. He was decorated for his exploits as his unit fought in the Tunisian campaign of early 1943 against Rommel's Afrika Korps. When the company transferred en masse to the Free French army in the summer of 1943, he was asked to continue but declined, saying he had had enough. There seem to have been health reasons for this decision, as well as his impending marriage to an elementary school principal from the port of Mostaganem in Algeria. Nevertheless, his name would adorn one of the half-track armoured cars of the Division Leclerc that liberated Paris. Among the Spaniards in General Philippe Leclerc's 2nd Armoured Division, Buiza was something of a legend. Most of the Spanish contingent in the division had previously fought in the Corps Franc d'Afrique. The half-track of the 3rd Platoon, 9th Company, baptized as 'Amiral Buiza', was the only vehicle in the unit to carry the name of a real person. The others bore the names of Republican victories such as Guadalajara, Teruel and Ebro and there were none called 'Pasionaria', 'Negrín' or 'Durruti' and certainly no others with any link to Casado. After the war, Buiza took part in clandestine operations to smuggle Jewish settlers into Palestine.[21]

Despite fulfilling none of his promises or predictions, and precipitating the collapse of the Republic in the worst imaginable circumstances, Casado, unlike Buiza, never showed any indication that he felt regret or remorse for his actions. Yet, he cannot have failed to realize that, far from saving lives, he had facilitated the Francoist repression and left tens of thousands of Republicans vulnerable to imprisonment, torture and execution. Franco himself had made it clear that his war effort was undertaken with deliberate slowness in order to facilitate the purging of Republican territory. As each area fell into his hands, a savage repression followed. That reality together with numerous declarations by Franco as well as the Law of Responsibilities made it unavoidably clear that the aim was to eradicate for ever the ideals and hopes stimulated by the Republic. The actions of Casado and the Consejo Nacional de Defensa helped Franco fulfil that ambition. As the Valencian Socialist Eduardo Buil wrote:

The Republic was surrendered to Franco. Ninety-five per cent of our best men were left in Spain, men impossible to replace, men that we needed for the future. Many have been shot accused of monstrous crimes that they did not commit. Others languish in prisons or concentration camps, subjected to the most inhuman treatment. The judgement of history will be severe with those culpable of the final disaster, a disaster that could have been avoided. Their historical duty was to avoid it at all costs.[22]

In exile, Casado wrote many letters that give the impression that he was unaware of any negative consequences of his coup. He was never given to self-criticism, but his complacency may have been intensified by the privileged treatment he was given in London. He received a stipend from the British Committee for Refugees from Spain but, as a result of an intervention by the Foreign Office, his allowances were set at a higher rate than that received by other beneficiaries. After the Second World War broke out in September 1939, he was given a job in the Spanish section of the BBC. He commentated on military issues using the pseudonym 'Coronel Juan de Padilla'. According to Ángel Viñas, the BBC World Service was 'one of the places which British Intelligence used to camouflage contacts that might be useful in the future'. In the course of 1939 when he was writing the first version of his memoirs, *The Last Days of Madrid*, it appears that he was being given guidance on its tone by contacts in MI6. The published version of late 1939, for which he had been given an advance of £100, was written and translated in record time. It sold well, was reviewed favourably and set the tone for future interpretation of the last days of the war. In January 1940, efforts were made through the press section of the British Embassy in Madrid by Casado's one-time contact in Madrid, Denys Cowan, to help his wife Carmen Santodomingo de Vega obtain a passport. Despite the support of two of Casado's military friends (Generals Juan Yagüe Blanco and Fernando Barrón y Ortiz) and the one-time head of the SIPM (Colonel José Ungría Jiménez), the application was blocked by the Falangist Director General de Seguridad, José Finat Escrivá de Romaní, Conde de Mayalde.[23]

In consequence, Casado would not be reunited with his wife until more than twelve years after they had parted in Valencia in March 1939. In the meantime, in 1941, he had begun a relationship with a thirty-five-year-old Englishwoman, Mrs Norah Purcell. She was something of an intellectual. She spoke Spanish and also French and was later to be the translator of the letters of Antoine de Saint-Exupéry. In February 1939, she was divorced from her husband, the British colonial administrator and sinologist Victor Purcell, from whom she had been estranged since 1935.[24] Casado lived with Norah for six years. It appears that he never fully mastered English. They had a daughter, María Cristina, who died in 1947. In that year, he went to work first in Colombia for Cicolac and, from 1949, in Venezuela for Indulac, both subsidiary companies of the Swiss multi-national Nestlé. The British Consulate in Bogotá was instructed by the Foreign Office to give him every facility and his UK entrance visa was extended so that he could return to London whenever he wished. In the event, he did not return. Despite a long separation, he remained in love with Norah. He frequently wrote love-sick letters, begging for news of her. He suspected that she had started another relationship, writing in June 1950 that 'the doubt is consuming my blood'. In December 1952, he was asking for news of 'Norah and the Jackal', presumably a reference to her new partner. In late 1951, he had brought his wife and his son and daughter to Venezuela only because he feared that a new war might break out in Europe. It was a decision that he would regret bitterly. In the letter of December 1952, he confessed to his friend and one-time aide de camp Rafael Fernández de la Calzada that his renewed family life was 'unenviable', that he and Carmen Santodomingo were incompatible and that their marriage was doomed. A year later, he wrote: 'My family problem gets worse with every passing day and I have reached the conclusion that unfortunately Carmen and I are totally incompatible. This is going to end badly. I have suggested that it would be better if she went back to Spain but she just digs her heels in.'[25]

His emotional turmoil regarding the women in his life was intermittent. The one constant in his life in exile was his total confidence that he was right and that he occupied a position of importance almost on a par with that of Franco. He wrote to Cipriano Mera in late August or early September 1939, when many of his own collaborators such as Colonel Manuel Cascón Briega, as well as many other Republican officers, had already been executed.[26] A bemused Mera commented: 'With overwhelming optimism, he claimed that we would all soon be back in Spain and we Republican army officers would return with the same rank that we had at the end of the war.' Mera replied that, while he accepted the possibility that Casado might have better sources of information, he could not share his hopes. He ended by saying that, if indeed things were as Casado asserted, then they should meet and that, if a visa could be arranged, he was ready to go to London. Casado never replied.[27]

Casado's letters to Rafael Fernández de la Calzada are immensely revealing in many ways. One in particular is the fact that he always addressed him rather patronizingly in the familiar *tú* form while, for the thirty years of their voluminous correspondence, Rafael addressed him respectfully as *usted*. Other letters emanated megalomania and self-pity in equal measure. In March 1940, Casado wrote to Franco, as if to an equal, expressing sadness at the execution of Colonel Antonio Escobar and commenting mildly, 'Your Excellency broke the word you gave in the peace concessions.'[28] In November 1945, he wrote to the anarchist ex-minister Juan López, claiming that he had successfully asked Franco to spare the lives of Rafael Henche and the brother of Manuel Irujo, the Basque politician and one-time Minister of Justice under Negrín. He sent López a copy of a telegram to Franco asking for a pardon for the Valencian anarchist Sigfrido Catalá 'Lohengrin', who was secretary general of the CNT and head of the Madrid committee of the Alianza Nacional de Fuerzas Democráticas (National Alliance of Democratic Forces, the non-Communist anti-Franco front). He had been arrested in Madrid in December 1945 and the following July sentenced to death. Casado's telegram read: 'Segismundo Casado to Generalísimo Franco: I beg Your Excellency pardon Sigfrido Catalá. His honesty and upright character justify the request that I am making.' The sentence was later commuted to thirty years' imprisonment. It is not known if Casado's telegram influenced Franco's decision.[29]

In a letter to Juan López, on 9 April 1941, Casado expressed, as he had done with Mera, wild optimism about the imminent removal of Franco. He revealed both his satisfaction in his own achievements and his readiness to return to Spain as part of an authoritarian government. His constant assumption was that he would be playing a prominent, if not indeed the central, role in whatever regime replaced Franco's dictatorship.

> If the idea is to return to the old politics with all its vices and bad habits, I will oppose it. If, on the other hand, the country decides that it wants to be governed energetically, honourably and honestly, then I will be a modest but determined warrior in that undertaking. I am incapable of joining the ranks of unscrupulous politicians. When I left Spain, I was a remarkably dynamic and temperamentally violent man. What I have seen in exile, the climate of England and possibly the passing of time are factors that have dramatically altered my way of being. It is possible that the sun in Spain might return me to how I used to be. When I examine my life, I do not regret any of the many things for which I worked and suffered, in my modest field of action, despite the meagre results. But I can assure you that I will not wear myself out to no purpose. Throughout my life, I have squandered energy without concern for myself; I have been far too generous with my labour in contrast with the selfishness of others. For every single person who has expressed their thanks, I have found one hundred ungrateful wretches. For every selfless person, I have found thousands interested in feeding their bastard appetites.[30]

A regular feature of Casado's correspondence was his narcissism. On 1 January 1947, he sent Juan López a letter that underlined the perspicacity of the judgement made by Konni Zilliacus in 1939 ('I do believe he was a wishful thinker with grandiose sentiments and exalted ideas about himself'). Eight years after the disaster of the end of the war, Casado wrote to López: 'I believe that if we Spaniards are incapable of making peace for ourselves, no one else will do it for us. I, with men of goodwill, wanted to make peace in 1939 and I failed. For trying to be the redeemer of Spain, they damn near wanted to crucify me.'[31] His sense of his own indispensability for a post-Franco Spain was revealed in a letter in the late spring or early summer of 1949 to

Rafael Fernández de la Calzada. He instructed him to inform the Republican government-in-exile in Paris that:

> The problem of Spain is not in the hands of Franco and the Falange. The key is in the hands of the Army. They will not accept any solution that does provide an absolute guarantee of their lives and their salaries. I have reliable reports that, without my intervention, they are not ready to negotiate in order to find a solution. Our politicians did not inspire confidence in the officer corps because they don't think that they are capable of implementing their commitment to a change of regime, not for lack of desire but for lack of the strength of purpose to do so.[32]

In March 1949, he wrote to Fernández de la Calzada from Venezuela in terms which revealed his inflated self-image but also something about what he believed to be the nature of his relationship with the British government. 'I have heard from Paris that the English have finally realized that the only solution left to them for making a deal with Franco is me. I have been told that almost certainly within a couple of months they will propose my return to London. If this is true, I will give it serious thought. For ten years I have maintained my dignity and I am not ready for them to squander my prestige.'[33]

Three months later, although the call from Whitehall had not come, he wrote to Fernández de la Calzada with undented confidence: 'These days I am very sought after by my friends over there. They insist that I return to London because – according to them – that is where my place is now. If I were to decide to go, they would provide me with every facility to travel to London and to live there without any financial worries. *I have refused them categorically*. They could have thought of this in 1947, when they let me leave.'[34] Two weeks later, he wrote in similarly arrogant terms about what he insinuated was an approach from British diplomatic representatives:

> They have spoken to me here about the same business. I have no interest in speaking to groups or groupuscules no matter how respectable they might seem. I learned many things over there.

One of the things I learned best is how to make myself respected and how to insist that I be treated with the proper consideration. I am not prepared to negotiate with some clique or other. If they regard me as indispensable to finding a solution [to the problem of Franco] – something of which I have been convinced for a long time now – then let them say so; but not with hints but face to face and frankly. They have a representative here whom I know and with whom I would be happy to discuss the question and reach an agreement but I'm not up for any other game.[35]

In the first years of his exile, Casado was in touch with Indalecio Prieto, Salvador de Madariaga, Juan López and other exiled Republican figures, and even with the heir to the throne Don Juan de Borbón. As his hopes dwindled, his references to Franco became more insulting, a common symptom of Republican impotence. In 1954, he had started to refer to the dictator as 'Paco'. By March 1956, in response to student riots in Spain, he called him 'Frank the Short' (Paco el Corto). In August that year, his optimism was rekindled. He announced with delight that the Venezuelan press was reporting that he was about to return to Spain as president of a military directory, along with the captains general of Catalonia, Burgos and Granada, to replace Franco. It is more than likely that the Venezuelan reports reflected some input from Casado himself or from one of his cronies. Nevertheless, by October, he was claiming never to have expected any political change in Spain. As his frustration with the continued survival of Franco intensified, he referred to him in a letter of July 1959 as the 'Jewish dwarf' (*el JUDÍO ENANO* – in capitals).[36]

Neither his early optimism about the imminent fall of Franco nor his hopes that he would play a key role in a post-Franco Spain came to anything. By the late 1950s, he was no longer talking in terms of returning to Spain in triumph to replace Franco. His health was deteriorating with lung and prostate issues added to his intermittent gastric problems. He was increasingly unable to travel all over Venezuela as he had done before. When he considered talking to his employers about possible changes in his work patterns, he revealed his underlying anti-Semitism in speaking of their 'Jewish mentality'.

In equally cantankerous terms, he complained: 'I can't get used to the inconvenience and impertinences of my family.' By 1957, aware that General Rojo had returned to Spain, he was beginning to think about making his own arrangements to go back.[37] There were various problems. In May 1944, the Franco regime had condemned him in his absence to a sentence of twelve years and one day in prison for the 'crime' of being a freemason. Even if this sentence were not enforced, he still needed enough money on which to live, which his pension from Nestlé would not cover. This eliminated London as another possible destination. He also considered establishing residence in Portugal or Tangier. By January 1960, he had decided to return to Spain. In September, he wrote that he had been given guarantees that the regime would not molest him. He added that he didn't care what the Republican opposition thought of him. However, on 4 May 1961, he wrote that friends in Spain had advised him not to return because he would be arrested as soon as he set foot in the airport of Barajas. Two months later, he had been told that it was the intention of the War Ministry to put him on trial. Nevertheless, despite additional fears that in the event of the left ever returning to Spain, he would be vulnerable to the Communists, he and his wife set off for Barcelona in September 1961.[38]

All went well in Spain until June 1962 when he made the mistake of applying for a military pension in respect of his army service from 1911 to 1939. This triggered an investigation into his past as a Republican and a freemason. The proceedings lasted until 1965. He was treated relatively gently because of his services during the Civil War and, in his own defence, made much of his anti-communism and his triumph over Negrín. Eventually, the charges of military rebellion were dropped but the sentence of twelve years and one day for having been a freemason was upheld. He was not imprisoned, although he was briefly placed under house arrest and lost any chance of the desired military pension. Throughout this time, both his health and his bank balance were deteriorating. He had chronic asthma as well as prostate and cardiac problems. Indeed, in 1966, he suffered a minor heart attack. To resolve his financial predicament, he came up with the idea of reviving the memoirs that he had published in London in

1939, first in the form of a series of articles in the newspaper *Pueblo* and then in book form.[39]

He wrote to Fernández de la Calzada on 1 April 1967: 'To make up for that pig's ear of a book that I wrote in London which, as well as lacking documentation, was disorganized rubbish, I have now decided to write a truly historical book. I have sufficient index cards to make it a book that I am sure will sell like hot cakes because, apart from its historical and dramatic interest, it will be the first book of the many that have been written that will be impartial.' Astonishingly, two months later, Casado wrote again to say that the book was finished. Fernández de la Calzada was less amazed by the speed of completion than he was to be told by Casado's friend and one-time member of the CND José del Rio that 'it is going to be sponsored by an organization or department of the Spanish Government'. He wrote to Casado warning him against becoming a cat's-paw of the propaganda apparatus of the Franco regime. Casado replied sadly that his financial situation gave him no choice. If he wrote it as he wished, he would be forced to leave Spain. Thus, it had to be published in Spain 'with all the problems that that entails, but for it to be a success, given my situation, I need to be given facilities and I can't get them without compromising. What else can I do?' The bulk of the text was serialized from 28 October to 14 November 1967 in *Pueblo*, the evening newspaper of the Falangist 'vertical syndicates', the regime's official corporative trade unions. It was published in book form in mid-1968 some months before his death on 18 December. No mention was made in the text of Casado's dealings with the Fifth Column and the Francoist intelligence services in the months before his coup. Even more than the earlier English version, with which it had much in common, the book set out to prove that Negrín was a puppet of Moscow. For all his boasts in exile about triumphantly returning to Spain to replace Franco, Casado's activities when he came back, as before he had left, were in the service of Franco.[40]

On the day after the would-be redeemer had left Spain, Negrín addressed the standing committee of the Republican Cortes in Paris with a coherent defence of his policy that was in stark contrast to what Casado had tried to do.

Resist? For what? To enter Burgos in triumph? We never thought or spoke in such terms. Gentlemen, to proclaim a policy of resistance implies a confession that one lacks the means to destroy the enemy but that higher reasons oblige one to fight on to the last. To do so means stimulating and encouraging the warlike spirit in the fighting troops. We defended essential things for our country because we believed that Spain in Franco's hands was headed for perdition and ruin … My deepest convictions told me that it was necessary to resist to save our country and it was also necessary to resist so as not to perish because only a blind man could not see that the triumph of our enemies signified the annihilation of all those who were fighting at our side. It was necessary to save them, both for them and also in the interests of Spain, since if we had won, we would not have pursued a policy of persecutions and reprisals. That was the line that the Government followed with the full approval of public opinion. But now, if the policy of persecution followed since the first months of the war is continued, the country will be destroyed because the seeds of rancour and hatreds that it will leave behind will be such that its stain will never be washed away … That was the basis of the resistance policy. Six or eight months more of resistance, which were possible, would have forced our enemies to modify their policy and the end of the war would have been different.

Negrín went on to discuss the Casado coup in detail. In the event, he demonstrated that his hopes of resistance as the only way to save more Republicans had been dashed as much by the coup of Colonel Casado as by Franco himself. More in sadness than in anger, he declared that 'Unfortunately, what has actually happened is lamentable proof that the policy of the Government was the only one that could be followed. Whoever surrenders to the mercy of a pitiless and merciless enemy is already lost and we were not obliged to surrender. We could still have resisted and that was our obligation. It was an obligation and a necessity to stay there and save those who are now being forced into concentration camps or going to be murdered.' As things had turned out, thanks to Casado, the Republic ended 'in catastrophe and shame'.[41]

Negrín was not alone in believing that resistance had been possible. Even after the fall of Catalonia, the US Ambassador, Claude Bowers, wrote to the journalist Louis Fischer, a friend of Negrín, relating his own 'emphatic' efforts to get President Roosevelt to lift the embargo on arms sales to the Republic. He had bombarded the President with letters and dispatches pointing out that, by maintaining the embargo, 'we are placing a premium on illegality and contributing to the success of the aggressor or fascist powers'. He wrote, 'I believe the embargo would have been lifted but for the fall of Barcelona. That created a new situation and raised the question whether it is worthwhile now. Personally, if they carry on the fight in the central zone, I think it is worthwhile.' When Negrín addressed the standing committee of the Cortes in Paris on 31 March 1939 to denounce Casado's action and justify his own resistance policy, he lamented the failure of arms deliveries without which it had been impossible to defend Barcelona. In this regard, Bowers wrote to Fischer about the massive superiority of Axis deliveries to Franco and commented, 'It is noteworthy that during that two and a half months Chamberlain and Bonnet were exerting themselves as never before to prevent arms from reaching the legal Government.'[42]

In a rather different spirit from Casado's self-obsession and bitter resentment about his fate, Negrín in exile was first and foremost concerned with the welfare of his fellow exiles. That is why he had arranged for funds to be taken to France to permit the establishment of the Servicio de Evacuación de los Refugiados Españoles (SERE). The bulk of those funds were hijacked by Prieto, but the SERE still managed to help around 10,000 Republican refugees in terms of paying their transport to Mexico, their rent and maintenance when they arrived and initial finance for small business enterprises.[43] During the Second World War, he worked against insurmountable odds to rebuild Republican unity in the hope of being able to present the Allies with a viable alternative to Franco. While still in France, although he maintained the legitimacy of his government, its remaining authority had been undermined by the standing committee of the Cortes which had declared itself to be the only legitimate Republican institution. When he was reluctantly allowed into England by the British government in June 1940, he was forbidden to engage in political activities. Indeed, desperate not to upset the Franco regime whose neutrality was being sought, the government constantly and unsuccessfully pressured him to leave.[44] This is not the place to discuss the complex and bitter relations among the exiled political leaders and especially within the PSOE. Suffice it to say that his efforts were thwarted and, in August 1945, his political career came to an end when he was not invited to participate in the first government-in-exile.[45]

Thereafter, Negrín devoted himself to cultural and scientific pursuits and to his family. Like Casado, he suffered frequent abdominal and heart problems, but that was the end of any resemblance. Unlike the hyper-sensitive Casado, Negrín made a constant effort to remain on speaking terms with all those with whom he was called upon to deal. This included those who had betrayed him, as in the case of General Miaja, those who had let him down, as in the case of General Rojo, and even those who had turned on him, as in the case of Indalecio Prieto. For the last seventeen years of his life, he lived happily with his partner Feliciana López. With his estranged wife Marie Fiedelmann from whom he had separated in the mid-1920s, he sustained a cordial relationship regarding their common concern for their children.[46]

On 5 September 1952, four years before his death, Negrín wrote from Mexico to his friend the American journalist Herbert Matthews who had asked him about his conversations in London with George Orwell, who had died in 1950. He commented openly about what he perceived to have been his own errors and those of others:

Spain was often a matter of conversation, generally in connection with the daily developments of the World War, and occasionally recollecting bygone episodes of our Civil strife. I remember now that, when this point was touched, he [Orwell] was very eager to enquire about the policy, internal and external, of the government I headed; the changes in the line of

conduct of the war which I introduced; our problems and difficulties; the many mistakes I later realized to have committed,
which I frankly confessed to him though some of them were
unavoidable and would have had to be repeated once more,
even after the foregone experience; our way of handling the
motley conglomeration of incompatible parties, labour unions
and dissident groups and, also, the frequently self-appointed,
largely unconstitutional local and regional 'governments' with
which we had to trade; our foreign policy, especially our relations with Russia, having to take into account that the U.S.S.R.
was the only great power supporting us internationally, and
prepared to provide us, on the basis of cash payment (we never
demanded it gratuitously from anyone) with the necessary
weapons; the causes of our defeat which I held, and still hold, as
due more than to the shortage of armaments, to our incom-
mensurable incompetence, to our lack of morale, to the
intrigues, jealousies and divisions that corrupted the rear, and
last, but definitely not least, to our immense cowardice. (When
I say 'our' I point, of course, not to the brave who fought to
death or survived after all sorts of ordeals, nor to the poor
hungering and starving civilians. I mean 'we,' the irresponsible
leaders who, having been unable to prevent a war that was not
inevitable, contemptibly surrendered when it could be still
fought and won. And I make no discrimination among the 'we.'
As with original sin, there is a solidarity in the responsibility,
and the only baptism that can whitewash us is the acknowledg-
ment of our common faults and wrongdoings.)[47]

It is difficult to imagine Casado making such a self-critical analysis.

Juan Simeón Vidarte wrote of the end of the war: 'the tragic story
of the surrender of Madrid showed the world that Negrín and the
PSOE executive were right. Unfortunately, there was no other policy
other than that of resistance.'[48] When the exiles reached the port of
Veracruz in Mexico in the Sinaia, the side of the ship carried a huge
banner that read 'Negrín tenía razón' (Negrín was right).

ABBREVIATIONS

ASM: Agrupación Socialista Madrileña (Madrid Socialist Group)

CND: Consejo Nacional de Defensa (National Defence Junta)

CNT: Confederación Nacional del Trabajo (National Confederation of Labour – anarcho-syndicalist trade union)

CRD: Comité Regional de Defensa (Regional Defence Committee of CNT–FAI (qq.v))

FAI: Federación Anarquista Ibérica (Iberian Anarchist Federation – direct action group created in 1926)

FJS: Federación de Juventudes Socialistas (Socialist Youth Federation – merged in 1936 with the Communist Youth to form the JSU (q.v.))

GRU: Glavnoe Razvedupravlenie (Soviet Military Intelligence)

JSU: Juventudes Socialistas Unificadas (United Socialist Youth – created in 1936 from the fusion of Socialist and Communist youth movements)

MLE: Movimiento Libertario Español (Spanish Libertarian Movement – uniting the CNT (q.v.), the FAI (q.v.) and the Juventudes Libertarias)

PCE: Partido Comunista de España (Spanish Communist Party)

PCF: Parti Communiste Français (French Communist Party)

POUM: Partido Obrero de Unificación Marxista (Workers' Marxist Unification Party – anti-Stalinist Marxist group persecuted during the Civil War as Trotskyist)

PSOE: Partido Socialista Obrero Español (Spanish Socialist Party)

SERE: Servicio de Evacuación de los Refugiados Españoles (Service for Evacuation of Spanish Refugees)

SIM: Servicio de Inteligencia Militar (Military Intelligence Service
– Republican)
SIPM: Servicio de Información y Policía Militar (Military
Intelligence and Police Service – Francoist)
UGT: Unión General de Trabajadores (General Union of Workers –
Socialist trades union federation)

NOTES

Abbreviations Used in Notes
AFPI: Archivo Fundación Pablo Iglesias; AGMAV: Archivo General Militar de Ávila; AGR: Archivo General Rojo; AGRM: Archivo General Regional de Murcia; AHN: Archivo Histórico Nacional; AHPCE: Archivo Histórico del Partido Comunista de España; AJLS: Archivo Juan López Sánchez; AMP: Archivo Marcelino Pascua; FJN: Fundación Juan Negrín; *FRUS: Foreign Relations of the United States 1939*, vol. II (Washington, DC: Government Printing Office, 1956–7); TMM: Sección 'Tesis, Manuscritos y Memorias' (of AHPCE); TNA: The National Archives, London

Chapter 1: An Avoidable Tragedy

1. José García Pradas, *Cómo terminó la guerra de España* (Buenos Aires: Ediciones Imán, 1940) p. 50.
2. Herbert L. Matthews, *A World in Revolution. A Newspaperman's Memoir* (New York: Charles Scribner's Sons, 1971) p. 45.
3. Marcelino Pascua, 'Semblanza de Juan Negrín', Archivo Histórico Nacional, Archivo Marcelino Pascua (henceforth AHN, AMP), Caja 1, carpeta 12, p. 3.
4. Ángel Bahamonde Magro, *Madrid 1939. La conjura del coronel Casado* (Madrid: Ediciones Cátedra, 2014) pp. 15–16.
5. Juan-Simeón Vidarte, *Todos fuimos culpables* (Mexico City: Fondo de Cultura Económica, 1973) p. 857.
6. Ernest Hemingway, 'Preface', in Gustav Regler, *The Great Crusade* (New York: Longmans Green, 1940) p. vii.
7. On the Casado coup, the fullest account is by Ángel Viñas and Fernando Hernández Sánchez, *El desplome de la República* (Barcelona: Editorial Crítica, 2009). For the Communist reaction, Santiago Carrillo, *Memorias*, 2nd edn (Barcelona: Editorial Planeta, 2006) p. 319. On Casado's reputation at the time, see Julián Zugazagoitia, *Guerra y vicisitudes de los Españoles*, 2nd edn, 2 vols (Paris: Librería Española, 1968) II, pp. 194–5.
8. Carrillo, *Memorias*, p. 299; Francisco-Félix Montiel, *Un coronel llamado Segismundo. Mentiras y misterios de la guerra de Stalin en España* (Madrid: Editorial Criterio-Libros, 1998) pp. 82–3. On British relations with Casado, see Angel Viñas, 'Playing with History and Hiding Treason: Colonel Casado's Untrustworthy Memoirs and the End of the Spanish Civil War', *Bulletin of Spanish Studies: Hispanic Studies and Researches on Spain, Portugal and Latin America*, vol. 91, nos 1–2, 2014, pp. 295–323. For a

refutation of the charge that Casado was a British agent, see Michael Alpert, *The Republican Army in the Spanish Civil War 1936-1939* (Cambridge: Cambridge University Press, 2013) pp. 283-4.

9. Manuel Tagüeña Lacorte, *Testimonio de dos guerras* (Mexico City: Ediciones Oasis, 1973) p. 308.

10. Allen to Fischer, 30 July 1962, Jay Allen Papers.

11. Coronel Segismundo Casado, *Así cayó Madrid. Último episodio de la guerra civil española* (Madrid: Guadiana de Publicaciones, 1968) pp. 65-7, 78-80; Ángel Viñas, 'Segismundo Casado López. Colonel', in Javier García Fernández, ed., *25 militares de la República* (Madrid: Ministerio de la Defensa, 2011) pp. 213-18; Bahamonde, *Madrid 1939*, pp. 38-46.

12. Montiel, *Un coronel llamado Segismundo*, pp. 88-93; Carlos Blanco Escolá, *Vicente Rojo, el general que humilló a Franco* (Barcelona: Editorial Planeta, 2003) pp. 236-7.

13. Edmundo Domínguez Aragonés, *Los vencedores de Negrín*, 2nd edn (Mexico City: Ediciones Roca, 1976) pp. 28-30.

14. Fernando Rodríguez Miaja, *Testimonios y remembranzas. Mis recuerdos de los últimos meses de la guerra de España* (Mexico City: Imprenta de Juan Pablos, 1997) p. 168.

15. Colonel Segismundo Casado, *The Last Days of Madrid. The End of the Spanish Republic* (London: Peter Davies, 1939) pp. v-vi.

16. Ricardo de la Cierva, *1939. Agonía y victoria (El protocolo 277)* (Barcelona: Editorial Planeta, 1989) p. 75.

17. Jesús I. Martínez Paricio, ed., *Los papeles del general Vicente Rojo. Un militar de la generación rota*

(Madrid: Espasa Calpe, 1989) p. 112.

18. Dolores Ibárruri, *El único camino* (Madrid: Editorial Castalia, 1992) p. 582.

19. Ángel L. Encinas Moral, ed., *Las causas de la derrota de la República española. Informe elaborado por Stoyán Mínev (Stepanov), Delegado en España de la Komintern (1937-1939)* (Madrid: Miraguano Ediciones, 2003) p. 214.

20. Antonio Bouthelier and José López Mora, *Ocho días de revuelta comunista. Madrid 5-13 marzo 1939* (Madrid: Editora Nacional, 1940) pp. 5-6.

21. Fernando Vázquez Ocaña, *Pasión y muerte de la Segunda República española*, 2nd edn (Madrid: Biblioteca de la Cátedra del Exilio/ Fondo de Cultura Económica de España, 2007) pp. 89-93.

22. Helen Graham, *Socialism and War. The Spanish Socialist Party in Power and Crisis, 1936-1939* (Cambridge: Cambridge University Press, 1991) p. 158; Vázquez Ocaña, *Pasión y muerte*, pp. 104-7.

23. Indalecio Prieto, *Cómo y por qué salí del Ministerio de Defensa Nacional. Intrigas de los rusos en España (Texto taquigráfico del informe pronunciado el 9 de agosto de 1938 ante el Comité Nacional del Partido Socialista Obrero Español)* (Mexico City: Impresos y Papeles, S. de R.L., 1940) pp. 94-6; Zugazagoitia, *Guerra y vicisitudes*, pp. 84-5; Vidarte, *Todos fuimos culpables*, pp. 845-66

24. Gerald Howson, *Arms for Spain. The Untold Story of the Spanish Civil War*, 2nd edn (New York: St Martin's Press, 1999) pp. 130-5, 234-5; Helen Graham, *The Spanish Republic at War 1936-1939* (Cambridge: Cambridge University Press, 2002) pp. 317-18; Dominique Grisoni and Gilles Herzog, *Les*

Brigades de la mer (Paris: Grasset, 1979) p. 121; José Luis Alcofar Nassaes, *Los asesores soviéticos en la guerra civil española: Los mejicanos* (Barcelona: Dopesa, 1971) pp. 92–4.

25. In Prague in the autumn of 1959, Vicente Uribe wrote a series of reports for the official histories of the PCE and of the Civil War then being compiled. They contain important reminiscences regarding the latter stages of the war and can be found in the Archivo Histórico del Partido Comunista de España (henceforth AHPCE), Dirigentes/Vicente Uribe/Escritos/Artículos/27/3.4, Extenso Informe (cited henceforth as Uribe, 'Informe'). Here, Uribe, 'Informe', p. 62.

26. Enrique Moradiellos, *Don Juan Negrín López* (Barcelona: Ediciones Península, 2006) p. 412; Manuel Azaña, *Obras completas*, 4 vols (Mexico City: Ediciones Oasis, 1966–8) III, pp. 477, 537.

27. Antonio Elorza and Marta Bizcarrondo, *Queridos Camaradas. La Internacional Comunista y España, 1919–1939* (Barcelona: Editorial Planeta, 1999) pp. 422–3.

28. Tagüeña, *Testimonio*, p. 205.

29. Zugazagoitia, *Guerra y vicisitudes*, II, p. 214; General Vicente Rojo, *¡Alerta los pueblos! Estudio político-militar del período final de la guerra española*, 2nd edn (Barcelona: Ariel, 1974) p. 66.

30. Vicente Rojo, Informe, 20 de septiembre de 1938, Barcelona, AHN, Archivo General Rojo (henceforth AGR), Caja 2/4, pp. 1–5.

31. Ibid., pp. 6–9.

32. Ángel Viñas, 'Mitos que se derrumban, controversias que se aclaran', in Sergio Millares Cantero, ed., *Juan Negrín el estadista. La tranquila energía de un hombre de Estad›* (Las Palmas: Fundación Juan

Negrín, 2005) pp. 88–9; Howson, *Arms for Spain*, pp. 242–3; Ángel Viñas, *El honor de la República. Entre el acoso fascista, la hostilidad británica y la política de Stalin* (Barcelona: Editorial Crítica, 2009) pp. 436–51.

33. Rojo, Informe, 20 de septiembre de 1938, AHN, AGR, Caja 2/4, pp. 10–15.

34. José Manuel Martínez Bande, *La batalla del Ebro*, 2nd edn (Madrid: Editorial San Martín, 1988) pp. 252–68.

35. Helen Graham, 'Casado's Ghosts: Demythologizing the End of the Spanish Republic', *Bulletin of Spanish Studies: Hispanic Studies and Researches on Spain, Portugal and Latin America*, vol. 89, nos 7–8, 2012, pp. 263–4.

36. Pedro Corral, *Desertores. La guerra civil que nadie quiere contar* (Barcelona: Debate, 2006) pp. 285–340; Graham, *The Spanish Republic at War*, pp. 373–9.

37. Vidarte, *Todos fuimos culpables*, p. 885.

38. Moradiellos, *Negrín*, pp. 406–7

39. Rafael Méndez, *Caminos inversos. Vivencias de ciencia y guerra* (Mexico City: Fondo de Cultura Económica, 1987) pp. 170–1.

40. *Documents on German Foreign Policy*, Series D, vol. III (London: HMSO, 1951), pp. 760–1, 767–8, 775–9, 782–8, 802.

41. Rojo, *¡Alerta los pueblos!*, pp. 102–5, 123–4, 212–14; José Manuel Martínez Bande, *La campaña de Cataluña* (Madrid: Editorial San Martín, 1979) pp. 41–60.

42. Herbert L. Matthews, *The Education of a Correspondent* (New York: Harcourt Brace, 1946) pp. 147–9.

43. Matthews, *A World in Revolution*, p. 47.

Chapter 2: Resist to Survive

1. Manuel Aguilera Povedano, *Compañeros y camaradas. Las luchas entre antifascistas en la Guerra Civil española* (Madrid: Actas Editorial, 2012) pp. 249–50.

2. Zugazagoitia, *Guerra y vicisitudes*, II, p. 131; Indalecio Prieto, *Convulsiones de España. Pequeños detalles de grandes sucesos*, 3 vols (Mexico City: Oasis, 1967–9) III, pp. 223–5; Vidarte, *Todos fuimos culpables*, pp. 764–5, 786.

3. Casado, *The Last Days*, pp. 51–2; Ramón Salas Larrazábal, *Historia del Ejército popular de la República*, 4 vols (Madrid: Editora Nacional, 1973) II, pp. 2286–7; Alpert, *The Republican Army in the Spanish Civil War*; Antonio Cordón, *Trayectoria (Recuerdos de un artillero)*, ed. Ángel Viñas (Seville: Espuela de Plata, 2008) pp. 559–60.

4. Montiel, *Un coronel llamado Segismundo*, pp. 26, 108–9

5. *El Socialista*, 22, 24 February 1931; Partido Socialista Obrero Español, *Convocatoria y orden del día para el XIII Congreso ordinario* (Madrid: Gráfica Socialista, 1932) pp. 77–83; Andrés Saborit, *Julián Besteiro* (Buenos Aires: Losada, 1967) pp. 200–3.

6. *El Socialista*, 25, 26, 28, 30 January 1934; *Boletín de la Unión General de Trabajadores*, February 1934; Gabriel Mario de Coca, *Anti-Caballero. Una crítica marxista de la bolchevización del Partido Socialista Obrero Español* (Madrid: Ediciones Engels, 1936) pp. 137–42; Paul Preston, *The Coming of the Spanish Civil War. Reform, Reaction and Revolution in the Second Spanish Republic 1931–1936*, 2nd edn (London: Routledge, 1994) pp. 137–8.

7. Saborit, *Besteiro*, p. 251; Prieto, *Convulsiones*, III, pp. 331–2.

8. Preston, *The Coming of the Spanish Civil War*, pp. 113–15.

9. Zugazagoitia, *Guerra y vicisitudes*, I, p. 182.

10. Gabriel Jackson, *The Spanish Republic and the Civil War 1931–1939* (Princeton, NJ: Princeton University Press, 1965) pp. 441–2.

11. Vidarte, *Todos fuimos culpables*, pp. 758–60. See also Jackson, *The Spanish Republic*, pp. 470–1.

12. Enrique Tierno Galván, *Cabos sueltos* (Barcelona: Bruguera, 1981) pp. 26–7.

13. Uribe, 'Informe', pp. 52–8; Viñas and Hernández Sánchez, *El desplome*, p. 67; Viñas, *El honor de la República*, pp. 381–6.

14. Rojo (Perpignan) to Negrín, 18 de febrero de 1939, AHN, AGR, Caja 5, pp. 29–34.

15. Fernando Hernández Sánchez, *Guerra o revolución. El Partido Comunista de España en la guerra civil* (Barcelona: Editorial Crítica, 2010) pp. 347–51; Viñas and Hernández Sánchez, *El desplome*, pp. 147–8.

16. José Peirats, *La CNT en la revolución española*, 2nd edn, 3 vols (Paris: Ediciones Ruedo Ibérico, 1971) III, pp. 169–93, 195–216; Viñas and Hernández Sánchez, *El desplome*, pp. 156–67.

17. Mariano Ansó, *Yo fui ministro de Negrín* (Barcelona: Editorial Planeta, 1976) pp. 220–2; Zugazagoitia, *Guerra y vicisitudes*, II, pp. 145, 176; Uribe, 'Informe', p. 57.

18. Uribe, 'Informe', p. 60.

19. Bahamonde, *Madrid 1939*, pp. 79–81.

20. 'Declaración del testigo don Luis de Sosa y Pérez' and 'Declaración de don Antonio Luna García', in Ignacio Arenillas de Chaves, *El proceso de Besteiro* (Madrid: Revista de Occidente, 1976) pp. 188–96. See also *ibid.*, pp. 240, 323–8; Julián Besteiro, *Cartas desde la prisión* (Madrid: Alianza Editorial, 1988) pp. 128, 138; Emilio Lamo de

Espinosa and Manuel Contreras, *Filosofía y política en Julián Besteiro*, 2nd edn (Madrid: Editorial Sistema, 1990) pp. 113–16; La Cierva, *1939*, pp. 49–52.

21. Bouthelier and López Mora, *Ocho días de revuelta comunista*, pp. 9–10; Javier Cervera, *Madrid en guerra. La ciudad clandestina 1936–1939*, 2nd edn (Madrid: Alianza Editorial, 2006) pp. 260, 265–6, 340–1, 386–9; Ángel Bahamonde Magro and Javier Cervera Gil, *Así terminó la Guerra de España* (Madrid: Marcial Pons, 1999) pp. 259–60; Bahamonde, *Madrid 1939*, pp. 49–50.

22. On Bertoloty, see Hoja Matriz de Servicios de D. Ricardo Bertoloty Ramírez, comandante, Cuerpo de Sanidad, Archivo General Militar, Segovia; Cuerpo de Sanidad, Médicos Segundos, in *Anuario Militar de España* (Madrid: Ministerio de la Guerra, 1936) p. 580. On the later relationship with Franco, see Jaime Peñafiel, *El General y su tropa. Mis recuerdos de la familia Franco* (Madrid: Temas de Hoy, 1992) pp. 154–6.

23. Bahamonde and Cervera Gil, *Así terminó la Guerra*, pp. 249–50, 256–8, 265; Cervera, *Madrid en guerra*, p. 387; La Cierva, *1939*, pp. 21, 51–4, 57–8; Declaración prestada por Ángel Pedrero García, AHN, FC-Causa General, Caja 1532, Exp. 30, p. 51.

24. R. G. Skrine Stevenson, 'Report on a Visit to the Southern Zone of Republican Spain', December 4 to December 15, 1938, TNA, FO 371, W114/114/41.

25. Bahamonde, *Madrid 1939*, pp. 47–8, 55–6; Peirats, *La CNT*, III, pp. 180, 183. On the political function of the commissariat, see Alpert, *The Republican Army in the Spanish Civil War*, pp. 174–201; James Matthews, *Reluctant Warriors. Republican Popular Army and Nationalist Army Conscripts in the Spanish Civil War, 1936–1939* (Oxford: Oxford University Press, 2012) p. 70; Santiago Álvarez, *Los Comisarios Políticos en el Ejército Popular de la república. Aportaciones a la historia de la Guerra Civil española (1936–1939). Testimonio y reflexión* (Sada-A Coruña: Ediciós do Castro, 1989) pp. 168–73.

26. Matthews, *The Education*, pp. 148–9.

27. Bahamonde, *Madrid 1939*, pp. 107–9.

28. Rojo, *¡Alerta los pueblos!*, pp. 68–85; Juan Perea Capulino, *Los culpables. Recuerdos de la guerra civil 1936–1939* (Barcelona: Ediciones Flor del Viento, 2007) pp. 451, 455–6; Enrique Castro Delgado, *Hombres made in Moscú* (Barcelona: Luis de Caralt, 1965) pp. 629–31; Juan Modesto, *Soy del Quinto Regimiento (Notas de la guerra española)* (Paris: Colección Ebro, 1969) pp. 259–64; Jesús Hernández, *Yo fui un ministro de Stalin* (Madrid: G. del Toro, 1974) pp. 261–2; Salas Larrazábal, *Historia del Ejército popular de la República*, II, pp. 2043–7, 2056–7; José Manuel Martínez Bande, *El final de la guerra civil* (Madrid: Editorial San Martín, 1985) pp. 45–76, 81–4; Bahamonde, *Madrid 1939*, pp. 57–9, 82; Domínguez Aragonés, *Los vencedores*, pp. 59–66.

29. Palmiro Togliatti, *Opere IV: 1935–1944* (Rome: Editori Riuniti, 1979) p. 380.

30. Bahamonde, *Madrid 1939*, pp. 80–91.

31. Juan Miguel Campanario, Carlos Díez Hernando and Javier Cervera Gil, 'El enigma del general republicano Manuel Matallana Gómez, Jefe del Estado Mayor de Miaja: ¿Fue un miembro activo de la Quinta Columna?', paper delivered at the Conference 'La Guerra Civil

Española, 1936–1939', Madrid, 28 November 2006, pp. 2–6; Bahamonde, *Madrid 1939*, pp. 90–104.

32. Togliatti, *Opere IV*, p. 383; Bouthelier and López Mora, *Ocho días*, pp. 7–8.

33. Matthews, *The Education*, pp. 143–4.

34. Viñas and Hernández Sánchez, *El desplome*, pp. 101–2; Diego Martínez Barrio, *Memorias* (Barcelona: Editorial Planeta, 1983) pp. 402–5; Cipriano de Rivas Cherif, *Retrato de un desconocido. Vida de Manuel Azaña* (Barcelona: Ediciones Grijalbo, 1980) pp. 390–1.

35. Juan Negrín, *Textos y discursos políticos*, ed. Enrique Moradiellos (Madrid: Centro de Estudios Políticos y Constitucionales & Fundación Juan Negrín, 2010) p. 347.

36. Miaja to Negrín, 30 January 1939, Miaja Papers, Hoover Institution, Bolloten Collection, Box 9, folder 38; a more readable text is reproduced in Rodríguez Miaja, *Testimonios y remembranzas*, pp. 92–3; Bullitt to Hull, 8 February 1939, *Foreign Relations of the United States* [henceforth *FRUS*] *1939*, vol. II (Washington, DC: Government Printing Office, 1956) pp. 740–2.

37. Joan Villarroya i Font, *Els bombardeigs de Barcelona durant la guerra civil (1936–1939)*, 2nd edn (Barcelona: Publicacions de L'Abadia de Montserrat, 1999) pp. 278–9; Josep Pernau, *Diario de la caída de Cataluña* (Barcelona: Ediciones B, 1989) pp. 200–1; Perea Capulino, *Los culpables*, p. 483.

38. Ramón Lamoneda, 'Manifiesto de la CE del PSOE', Mexico, 15 November 1945, *El Socialista*, no. 10, January 1946, reproduced in Ramón Lamoneda, *Escritos políticos* (Madrid: Fundación Pablo

Inglesas, 2012) pp. 238–9. See also Graham, *The Spanish Republic at War*, p. 381.

Chapter 3: The Power of Exhaustion

1. Montiel, *Un coronel llamado Segismundo*, p. 88; Ignacio Iglesias, *La fase final de la guerra civil (De la caída de Barcelona al derrumbamiento de Madrid* (Barcelona: Editorial Planeta, 1977) pp. 77–80; García Pradas, *Cómo terminó la guerra*, pp. 57–8.

2. Ivo Banac, ed., *The Diary of Georgi Dimitrov* (New Haven: Yale University Press, 2003) pp. 93–5.

3. Paul Preston, *The Spanish Holocaust. Inquisition and Extermination in Twentieth Century Spain* (London: HarperCollins; New York: W. W. Norton, 2012) pp. 383–423; Luis Araquistain, *Sobre la guerra civil y en la emigración* (Madrid: Espasa Calpe, 1983) pp. 178–87; Cervera, *Madrid en guerra*, pp. 241–67, 289–95, 381–412.

4. Carrillo, *Memorias*, pp. 300–3.

5. R. G. Skrine Stevenson, 'Report on a Visit to the Southern Zone of Republican Spain', December 4 to December 15, 1938, TNA, FO 371, W114/114/41; Graham, 'Casado's Ghosts', pp. 258–9; Hugh Thomas, *The Spanish Civil War*, 3rd edn (London: Hamish Hamilton, 1977) p. 863; Iglesias, *La fase final*, pp. 20–2. On the situation in Barcelona, see Francisco Lacruz, *El alzamiento, la revolución y el terror en Barcelona* (Barcelona: Librería Arysel, 1943) p. 264 n. 1.

6. Carrillo, *Memorias*, pp. 298–300; Ronald Fraser, *Blood of Spain. The Experience of Civil War 1936–1939* (London: Allen Lane, 1979) p. 488; Casado, *Así cayó Madrid*, p. 85.

7. Fraser, *Blood of Spain*, pp. 487–8.

8. Cipriano Mera, *Guerra, exilio y cárcel de un anarcosindicalista* (Paris: Ruedo Ibérico, 1976)

pp. 174–5; Viñas and Hernández Sánchez, *El desplome*, pp. 177–80; Graham, 'Casado's Ghosts', p. 266.

9. Graham, *Socialism and War*, pp. 226–31.

10. Actas de la Comisión Ejecutiva, 15 November 1938, Archivo de la Fundación Pablo Iglesias (henceforth AFPI), AH-20-5; Dolores Ibárruri et al., *Guerra y revolución en España 1936–39*, 4 vols (Moscow: Editorial Progreso, 1966–77) IV, p. 166; Lamoneda, *Posiciones políticas*, p. 96.

11. Azaña, *Obras*, IV, p. 895; Rivas Cherif, *Retrato de un desconocido*, p. 394; Ansó, *Yo fui ministro de Negrín*, p. 222; Saborit, *Besteiro*, pp. 285; Zugazagoitia, *Guerra y vicisitudes*, II, pp. 190–1; R. G. Skrine Stevenson, 'Report on a Visit to the Southern Zone of Republican Spain', December 4 to December 15, 1938, TNA, FO 371, W114/114/41.

12. Zugazagoitia, *Guerra y vicisitudes*, II, pp. 173, 178.

13. Azaña, *Obras*, IV, pp. 895–6; Togliatti, *Opere IV*, pp. 352, 356.

14. Declaración prestada por Ángel Pedrero García, AHN, FC-Causa General, Caja 1532, Exp. 30, pp. 51–2; Bahamonde and Cervera, *Así terminó la guerra*, p. 373.

15. Francisco Franco Bahamonde, *Palabras del Caudillo 19 abril 1937–7 diciembre 1942* (Madrid: Ediciones de la Vicesecretaría de Educación Popular, 1943) p. 476.

16. Josep Cruanyes, *El papers de Salamanca. L'espoliació del patrimoni documental de Catalunya* (Barcelona: Edicions 62, 2003) pp. 15–51; Paul Preston, *Botxins i repressors. Els crims de Franco i dels franquistes* (Barcelona: Editorial Base, 2006) pp. 101–13.

17. Zugazagoitia, *Guerra y vicisitudes*, II, pp. 172, 244.

18. *Ibid.*, pp. 194–6, 270; Ansó, *Yo fui ministro de Negrín*, p. 230.

19. 'Declaración de don Antonio Luna García', in Arenillas, *El proceso*, pp. 192–3; *ibid.*, p. 241; Cervera, *Madrid en guerra*, pp. 391–5; Bahamonde and Cervera, *Así terminó la guerra*, pp. 264–6; Viñas and Hernández Sánchez, *El desplome*, pp. 91–3; La Cierva, *1939*, pp. 74–6; José Manuel Martínez Bande, *Los cien últimos días de la República* (Barcelona: Luis de Caralt, 1973) pp. 119–21, Casado, *Así cayó Madrid*, pp. 208–9.

20. La Cierva, *1939*, pp. 79–80, 91, 110, 118, 120–1; Casado, *Así cayó Madrid*, p. 200. Cf. Casado, *The Last Days*, p. 276.

21. Telegram from General Staff to Miaja, 23 January 1939, Miaja Papers, Hoover Institution, Bolloten Collection, Box 9, folder 38; Rodríguez Miaja, *Testimonios y remembranzas*, p. 91.

22. Uribe, 'Informe', p. 65; Antonio López Fernández, *El general Miaja, defensor de Madrid* (Madrid: G. del Toro, 1975) pp. 259–61.

23. Uribe, 'Informe', p. 63.

24. Casado, *Así cayó Madrid*, pp. 199–200; Rodríguez Miaja, *Testimonios y remembranzas*, pp. 47–8.

25. Julio Álvarez del Vayo, *Freedom's Battle* (London: Heinemann, 1940) p. 277.

26. José Manuel Vidal Zapater, 'Los Llanos (Albacete) 1939', unpublished manuscript (Madrid, 1994) pp. 2–5. I am grateful to Ricardo Miralles and Ángeles Gómez Egido for making it possible for me to use this document. See also Ricardo Miralles, *Juan Negrín. La República en guerra* (Madrid: Ediciones Temas de Hoy, 2003) p. 409, and Viñas and Hernández Sánchez, *El desplome*, pp. 190–2.

27. Estado Español, Ministerio de la Gobernación, *Dictamen de la comisión sobre ilegitimidad de poderes actuantes en 18 de julio de*

1936 (Barcelona: Editora Nacional, 1939) pp. 9–13; Manuel Álvaro Dueñas, *'Por ministerio de la ley y voluntad del Caudillo'. La Juridicción Especial de Responsabilidades Políticas (1939–1945)* (Madrid: Centro de Estudios Políticos y Constitucionales, 2006) pp. 84–121.

28. Vázquez Ocaña, *Pasión y muerte*, pp. 61–2.

29. Vidarte, *Todos fuimos culpables*, pp. 855–7.

30. Vayo to Pascua, 6 February 1939, AHN, AMP, Caja 1 (bis), carpeta 22.

31. Negrín to Pascua, 18 February 1939, AHN, AMP, Caja 1, carpeta 19; Zugazagoitia, *Guerra y vicisitudes*, II, p. 227; Martínez Barrio, *Memorias*, pp. 402–4; Cordón, *Trayectoria*, 2nd edn, pp. 698–9; Álvarez del Vayo, *Freedom's Battle*, pp. 281–2.

32. Azaña to Ossorio, 28 June 1939, Azaña, *Obras*, III, pp. 551–2; Pascua, 'Azaña en la Embajada de París', undated report, AHN, AMP, Caja 1, carpeta 9, p. 4a.

33. Pascua, 'Azaña en la Embajada de París', undated report, AHN, AMP, Caja 1, carpeta 9, pp. 1–4; Zugazagoitia, *Guerra y vicisitudes*, II, pp. 234–5.

34. Rivas Cherif, *Retrato de un desconocido*, pp. 416–19.

35. Viñas and Hernández Sánchez, *El desplome*, p. 111.

36. Cristina Elia Rodríguez Gutiérrez, 'Julio Álvarez Del Vayo y Olloqui. Biografía Política de un Socialista Heterodoxo', unpublished doctoral thesis (Universidad Nacional de Educación a Distancia, Madrid, 2013) pp. 426–8.

37. Negrín, *Textos y discursos políticos*, p. 350.

38. Azaña to Ossorio, 28 June 1939, Azaña, *Obras*, III, pp. 549–54; Martínez Barrio, *Memorias*, pp. 402–5; Rivas Cherif, *Retrato de un desconocido*, p. 415.

39. Carles Pi Sunyer, *La República y la guerra. Memorias de un político catalán* (Mexico City: Ediciones Oasis, 1975) p. 630.

40. Rivas Cherif, *Retrato de un desconocido*, p. 416; Zugazagoitia, *Guerra y vicisitudes*, II, p. 228; Ansó, *Yo fui ministro de Negrín*, p. 238.

41. Stevenson to Halifax, 8 February 1939, TNA, FO 371/24127, W2559/8/41.

42. Herbert Matthews, 'Figueras Capital of Loyalist Spain', 'Conflict to Go On', 'Toll of 500 feared in Figueras Raids', *New York Times*, 28 January, 6, 4 February 1939; Matthews, *The Education*, pp. 170–1.

43. Zugazagoitia, *Guerra y vicisitudes*, II, p. 214.

44. Frank C. Hanighen, ed., *Nothing but Danger* (New York: National Travel Club, 1939) pp. 267–8; Matthews, *The Education*, pp. 174–8.

45. For the full text of the speech, see Negrín, *Textos y discursos políticos*, pp. 312–26.

46. Zugazagoitia, *Guerra y vicisitudes*, II, pp. 217–19; Juan López, *Una misión sin importancia (memorias de un sindicalista)* (Madrid: Editora Nacional, 1972) pp. 145–51. In López's account of several days spent in France with a CNT mission, the most outspoken critic of Negrín was Largo Caballero's acolyte Rodolfo Llopis.

47. Matthews, *The Education*, p. 178.

48. Stevenson to Halifax, 8 February 1939, TNA, FO 371/24127, W2559/8/41.

49. Richard Alan Gordon, 'France and the Spanish Civil War', unpublished doctoral thesis (Columbia University, New York, 1971) p. 360; Claude G. Bowers, *My Mission to Spain* (London: Gollancz, 1954) p. 407.

50. Ambassador in France (Bullitt) to the Secretary of State Cordell Hull, 3

February 1939, *FRUS 1939*, II, pp. 735–6.

51. Enrique Moradiellos, *El reñidero de Europa. Las dimensiones internacionales de la guerra civil española* (Barcelona: Ediciones Península, 2001) p. 244.

52. Stevenson to Halifax, 8 February 1939, TNA, FO 371/24127, W2559/8/41; Rivas Cherif, *Retrato de un desconocido*, p. 417

53. Viñas and Hernández Sánchez, *El desplome*, p. 111.

54. Stevenson to Halifax, 8 February 1939, TNA, FO 371/24127, W2559/8/41; Thurston to Hull, 6 February, Bowers to Hull, 6 February, Bullitt to Hull, 8 February 1939, *FRUS 1939*, II, pp. 737, 740–2.

55. Juan Negrín et al., 'Discurso en el Palacio de Bellas Artes, México D.F., 1 de agosto de 1945', *Documentos políticos para la historia de la Republica Española* (Mexico City: Coleccion Málaga, 1945) pp. 25–6; Zugazagoitia, *Guerra y vicisitudes*, II, pp. 218, 241–2.

56. Vidarte, *Todos fuimos culpables*, p. 912.

57. Lawrence Fernsworth, *Spain's Struggle for Freedom* (Boston: Beacon Press, 1957) p. 234. On Fernsworth, see Paul Preston, *We Saw Spain Die. Foreign Correspondents in the Spanish Civil War* (London: Constable, 2008) pp. 9–12, 43, 122–3.

58. Graham, 'Casado's Ghosts', pp. 23–4.

59. Méndez, *Caminos inversos*, pp. l04–6.

60. Indalecio Prieto and Juan Negrín, *Epistolario Prieto y Negrín. Puntos de vista sobre el desarrollo y consecuencias de la guerra civil española* (Paris: Imprimerie Nouvelle, 1939) p. 37.

61. Negrín, *Documentos políticos*, pp. 26–7.

62. López Fernández, *El general Miaja*, pp. 262–8.

63. *Ibid.*, pp. 269–77.

64. Uribe, 'Informe', p. 64; Zugazagoitia, *Guerra y vicisitudes*, II, p. 230; Viñas and Hernández Sánchez, *El desplome*, p. 184.

65. Iglesias, *La fase final*, pp. 74–5; Rojo, *¡Alerta los pueblos!*, p. 166.

66. Zugazagoitia, *Guerra y vicisitudes*, II, pp. 229, 241; Viñas and Hernández Sánchez, *El desplome*, pp. 83–4.

Chapter 4: The Quest for an Honourable Peace

1. López, *Una misión sin importancia*, pp. 187–93.

2. Azaña to Ossorio, 28 June 1939, Azaña, *Obras*, III, p. 540; Marcelino Pascua, 'Semblanza de Juan Negrín', AHN, AMP, Caja 1, carpeta 12, pp. 10–12.

3. Bahamonde, *Madrid 1939*, p.14.

4. Togliatti, *Opere IV*, pp. 380–1, 388.

5. *Mundo Obrero*, 23, 24, 25 December; *La Voz*, 24 December; *El Socialista*, 24 December; *Claridad*, 25 December; *Heraldo de Madrid*, 25 December 1936; *Mundo Obrero*, 28, 30 April, 14, 15 May 1937.

6. Procedimiento Militar contra José Cazorla Maure, AHN, FC-Causa General, Caja 1525-1, pp. 4–5, 11–14, 25, 31–2; AHN, FC-Causa General, Caja 1526-3, Exp. 5, p. 201. Conesa was executed by the Casado Junta: *ABC* (Madrid), 15, 24 March 1939; Luis Español Bouché, *Madrid 1939. Del golpe de Casado al final de la guerra civil* (Madrid: Almena Ediciones, 2004) pp. 55, 57, 141.

7. *Mundo Obrero*, 13 March 1937.

8. *Mundo Obrero*, 14 April 1937; intervention of Cazorla at Junta dc Defensa, Julio Aróstegui and Jesús Martínez, *La Junta de Defensa de Madrid* (Madrid: Comunidad de Madrid, 1984), pp. 445–7. On López de Letona, see Cervera, *Madrid en guerra*, pp. 324, 371–3, 451

9. Vidarte, *Todos fuimos culpables*, p. 392; Cervera, *Madrid en guerra*, pp. 250, 412.
10. Manuel Tarín-Iglesias, *Los años rojos* (Barcelona: Editorial Planeta, 1985) pp. 92–3.
11. Peirats, *La CNT*, III, pp. 278–81; Amaro del Rosal, *Historia de la UGT de España 1901–1939*, 2 vols (Barcelona: Grijalbo, 1977) II, pp. 900–1.
12. López, *Una misión sin importancia*, pp. 96–104.
13. *Ibid.*, pp. 169–93,
14. Negrín, Discurso en Londres, 14 de abril de 1942, Santiago Álvarez, *Negrín, personalidad histórica. Biografía*, 2 vols (Madrid: Ediciones de la Torre, 1994) II, pp. 158–9; Azaña to Ossorio, 28 June 1939, Azaña, *Obras*, III, pp. 543–54; Rojo, *¡Alerta los pueblos!*, pp. 165–7; Martínez Paricio, ed., *Los papeles del general Vicente Rojo*, pp. 128–32.
15. Martha Gellhorn to Eleanor Roosevelt, 5 February 1939, in Caroline Moorehead, ed., *Selected Letters of Martha Gellhorn* (London: Chatto & Windus, 2006) pp. 72–3.
16. Rojo, *¡Alerta los pueblos!*, pp. 167–8.
17. Negrín to Prieto, 23 June 1939, *Epistolario Prieto y Negrín*, pp. 46–7; Moradiellos, *Negrín*, pp. 414, 429, 448.
18. Vayo to Pascua, 13 February; Vayo to Negrín, 15 February; Azaña to Negrín 16 February; Negrín to Pascua, 18 February 1939, in Marcelino Pascua, 'Azaña en la Embajada de París', AHN, AMP, Caja 1, carpeta 9, pp. 4–5.
19. *Ibid.*, pp. 4–6. See also Negrín to Pascua, 18 February 1939, AHN, AMP, Caja 1, carpeta 19.
20. Castro Delgado, *Hombres made in Moscú*, p. 643; Tagüeña, *Testimonio*, pp. 301–2; Méndez, *Caminos inversos*, pp. 106–7.
21. Burnett Bolloten, *The Spanish Civil War. Revolution and Counterrevolution* (Hemel Hempstead: Harvester Wheatsheaf, 1991) p. 688. On Díaz Tendero, see Cordón, *Trayectoria*, 2nd edn, pp. 410–11.
22. Salas Larrazábal, *Historia del Ejército popular*, II, p. 2285.
23. Pedro María Egea Bruno, 'Miguel Buiza Fernández-Palacios, Almirante habilitado', in García Fernández, ed., *25 militares de la República*, pp. 157–60; Victoria Fernández Díaz, *El exilio de los marinos republicanos* (Valencia: Universitat de València, 2009) pp. 152–4; Viñas and Hernández Sánchez, *El desplome*, pp. 190, 200–1; Viñas, *El honor de la República*, p. 498; Michael Alpert, *La guerra civil española en el mar* (Madrid: Siglo XX, 1987) pp. 144–5; Fernando Moreno de Alborán y de Reyna and Salvador Moreno de Alborán y de Reyna, *La guerra silenciosa y silenciada. Historia de la campaña naval durante la guerra de 1936–39*, 4 vols (Madrid: Gráficas Lormo, 1998) IV, p. 2723.
24. Martínez Bande, *El final*, pp. 88–102; report by Fernando Sartorius, *ibid.*, pp. 353–9; Salas Larrazábal, *Historia del Ejército popular*, II, pp. 2237–9; Alpert, *La guerra civil española en el mar*, pp. 349–51; Bruno Alonso, *La flota republicana y la guerra civil de España (Memorias de su comisario general)* (Seville: Espuela de Plata, 2006) pp. 150–1.
25. Rojo to Negrín, 12, 13 February 1939, AHN, AGR, Caja 5, carpeta 8; Ansó, *Yo fui ministro de Negrín*, pp. 238–9; Zugazagoitia, *Guerra y vicisitudes*, II, pp. 228–32; Togliatti, *Opere IV*, p. 388; Tagüeña, *Testimonio*, p. 303; José Andrés Rojo, *Vicente Rojo. Retrato de un general republicano* (Barcelona: Tusquets Editores, 2006) pp. 287–8; Moradiellos, *Negrín*, pp. 439–40;

Graham, *The Spanish Republic at War*, pp. 396–9.

26. Uribe, 'Informe', pp. 63–4.
27. Negrín to Pascua, 16 February 1939, AHN, AGR, Caja 5, carpeta 8.
28. López, *Una misión sin importancia*, p. 250.
29. Pascua to Negrín, 14, 19 February 1939, AHN, AMP, Caja 2, carpeta 19; Zugazagoitia to Pascua, 12 February, 3 April 1940, Pascua to Zugazagoitia, 27 March 1940, AHN, AMP, Caja 2 (bis), carpeta 16 (exilio); Graham, *The Spanish Republic at War*, p. 398 n. 26; Rojo, *¡Alerta los pueblos!*, pp. 168–9.
30. Tagüeña, *Testimonio*, pp. 300–1; Cordón, *Trayectoria*, 2nd edn, p. 683; Méndez, *Caminos inversos*, pp. 106–7. I have mainly referred to this version of Cordón's memoirs, edited by Ángel Viñas, because it contains more detail than the first edition, produced in Romania and published in Paris in 1971. However, very occasionally the text of the 1971 edition contains snippets of information not in the later and much fuller original edited by Professor Viñas.
31. Rojo to Negrín, 12 February; Rojo to Pascua, 13 February; Pascua to Negrín, 14 February 1939, AHN, AGR, Caja 5, carpeta 8; Rojo, *¡Alerta los pueblos!*, pp. 165–70; Rojo, *Vicente Rojo*, pp. 276–8; Santos Juliá, *Vida y tiempo de Manuel Azaña 1880–1940* (Madrid: Taurus, 2008) pp. 450–1.
32. Rojo, *¡Alerta los pueblos!*, pp. 153–4; Pi Sunyer, *La República y la guerra*, p. 626. For a fiercely contrary view, see Perea Capulino, *Los culpables*, pp. 470–1.
33. Zugazagoitia, *Guerra y vicisitudes*, II, pp. 241–3.
34. *Epistolario Prieto y Negrín*, pp. 46–7; Amaro del Rosal, 'El Tesoro del Vita', *Historia 16*, no. 95, 1984, p. 13; Amaro del Rosal, *El oro del Banco de España y la historia del Vita* (Barcelona: Grijalbo, 1977) pp. 81–93; Viñas and Hernández Sánchez, *El desplome*, pp. 136–9; Gabriel Jackson, *Juan Negrín. Spanish Republican War Leader* (Brighton: Sussex Academic Press, 2010) pp. 294–5.

35. Moradiellos, *Negrín*, pp. 425–6; Del Rosal, 'El Tesoro del Vita', pp. 11–14; Del Rosal, *El oro del Banco de España y la historia del Vita*, pp. 81–93; Jackson, *Juan Negrín*, pp. 294–5. For a breakdown of what was sent, see Del Rosal, 'El Tesoro del Vita', p. 16; Ángel Herrerín López, *El dinero del exilio. Indalecio Prieto y las pugnas de posguerra (1939–1947)* (Madrid: Siglo XXI de España Editores, 2007) p. 9.
36. Castro Delgado, *Hombres made in Moscú*, pp. 643–4.
37. Rojo, *¡Alerta los pueblos!*, p. 167.
38. Bahamonde, *Madrid 1939*, pp. 65–70, 82–4; Luis F. Villamea, *Gutiérrez Mellado. Así se entrega una victoria* (Madrid: Fuerza Nueva Editorial, 1996) pp. 24–38; Fernando Puell de la Villa, *Gutiérrez Mellado. Un militar del siglo XX (1912–1995)* (Madrid: Biblioteca Nueva, 1997) pp. 100–17.
39. Tagüeña, *Testimonio*, pp. 303–4; Enrique Líster, *Nuestra guerra* (Paris: Colección Ebro, 1966) p. 249; Enrique Líster, *¡Basta! Una aportación a la lucha por la recuperación del Partido*, 2nd edn (Madrid: G. del Toro, 1978) pp. 169–71; Bolloten, *The Spanish Civil War*, pp. 500, 689.
40. Romero Marín, Interview, *Cuadernos para el Diálogo*, 2ª época, 172, 14 August 1976, p. 22.
41. Cordón, *Trayectoria*, 2nd edn, pp. 684–8; Rojo, *¡Alerta los pueblos!*, p.169.
42. Uribe, 'Informe', p. 64.
43. Ignacio Hidalgo de Cisneros, *Cambio de rumbo (Memorias)*, 2

vols (Bucharest: Colección Ebro, 1964) II, pp. 248–51; Cordón, *Trayectoria*, 2nd edn, p. 685; Zugazagoitia, *Guerra y vicisitudes*, II, p. 234; Azaña to Ossorio, 28 June 1939, Azaña, *Obras*, III, p. 239; Rivas Cherif, *Retrato de un desconocido*, p. 425.

44. Negrín to Pascua (for General Rojo), 18 February 1939, Rojo to Negrín, 18 and 19 February 1939, 'Las posibilidades de resistencia en la región central', AHN, AGR, Caja 5, carpeta 8.

45. Graham, *The Spanish Republic at War*, pp. 396–9; García Fernández, ed., *25 militares de la República*, p. 837; Tagüeña, *Testimonio*, p. 301; Cordón, *Trayectoria*, 2nd edn, p. 682; Modesto, *Soy del Quinto Regimiento*, p. 275.

46. Rojo, *¡Alerta los pueblos!*, p. 168.

47. Azaña to Negrín, 25 February 1939, AHN, AMP, Caja 1, carpeta 13, and in Pascua, 'Azaña en la Embajada de París', AHN, AMP, Caja 1, carpeta 9, pp. 7–8; Martínez Barrio, *Memorias*, pp. 405–7.

48. Viñas and Hernández Sánchez, *El desplome*, pp. 132–3.

Chapter 5: Casado Sows the Wind

1. Francisco Largo Caballero, *Mis recuerdos. Cartas a un amigo* (Mexico City: Editores Unidos, 1954) pp. 250–5; Constancia de la Mora, *In Place of Splendor* (New York: Harcourt, Brace, 1939) pp. 397–8; David Wingeate Pike, *Vae Victis! Los republicanos españoles refugiados en Francia 1939–1944* (Paris: Ruedo Ibérico, 1969) p. 25.

2. Julio Aróstegui, *Largo Caballero. El tesón y la quimera* (Barcelona: Debate, 2013) pp. 670–2; Domínguez Aragonés, *Los vencedores*, pp. 40–3; Hernández Sánchez, *Guerra o revolución*, p. 421.

3. Togliatti, *Opere IV*, pp. 384–6; Graham, *The Spanish Republic at War*, pp. 403–5; *Mundo Obrero*, 10–12, 14 February 1939; Hernández Sánchez, *Guerra o revolución*, pp. 421–2; Elorza and Bizcarrondo, *Queridos Camaradas*, pp. 429–31.

4. Domínguez Aragonés, *Los vencedores*, pp. 103–4.

5. Louis Fischer, *Men and Politics. An Autobiography* (London: Jonathan Cape, 1941) pp. 425–6, 213, 246.

6. Líster, *Nuestra guerra*, pp. 249–50.

7. Encinas Moral, ed., *Las causas de la derrota*, p. 176; Elorza and Bizcarrondo, *Queridos Camaradas*, p. 431.

8. Tagüeña, *Testimonio*, p. 309.

9. Cordón, *Trayectoria*, 2nd edn, p. 689. The first edition, Antonio Cordón, *Trayectoria (Recuerdos de un artillero)* (Paris: Colección Ebro, 1971) pp. 470–1, has the following version of Cordón's comment on Negrín: 'not in the sense of a leader determined to take the reins to direct events but rather as a decent man who wishes to ease his conscience and accept the sacrifice even if he is aware of its possible futility'. That is followed by the comments about further resistance being possible.

10. Bolloten, *The Spanish Civil War*, p. 925 n. 21. In a letter dated 14 January 1940 (Papers of Jay Allen), Constancia de la Mora wrote: 'These last three days we have [*sic*] Bolloten here with us. He has brought me seven chapters of his book, which will be really THE historical documentary study of the war. I wish you could see some of it! It is simply marvellous … ALL from our side; but it is a most fascinating political as well as historical and military study of the war, with details and data that no one – I am sure – has or can ever get … the thing now is to find some kind of a foundation or society … or

university to give him a sum or an advance that will enable him to live at the rate of $20 a week! Have you any suggestions as to whom he could write? Obviously we have thought of Negrín or other sources, but all these he very justly rejects, for immediately the book would be branded as propaganda etc. and would lose all its value.'

11. *Epistolario Prieto y Negrín*, p. 37.
12. Vayo to Pascua, 25 February 1939, AHN, AMP, Caja 1 (bis), carpeta 22.
13. Negrín to De los Ríos, 10 March 1939, AHN, AMP, Caja 2, carpeta 11.
14. On Besteiro, Domínguez Aragonés, *Los vencedores*, p. 213; Trifón Gómez's report, *Epistolario Prieto y Negrín*, pp. 116–20.
15. Hernández, *Yo fui un ministro de Stalin*, p. 268.
16. *ABC* (Madrid), 10 February 1939.
17. FJN, Carpeta 97 'Final Guerra', 30A–B. See also Viñas and Hernández Sánchez, *El desplome*, pp. 223–4.
18. Ibárruri, *El único camino*, pp. 591–2.
19. AHN, FC-Causa General, Caja 1532, Exp. 30, pp. 52–3.
20. On the earlier meeting with the three generals and others, Casado, *Así cayó Madrid*, pp. 199–200. On the 7–8 February meeting at Los Llanos, see José Manuel Vidal Zapater, 'Los Llanos (Albacete) 1939' (Madrid: unpublished manuscript, 1994) pp. 2–5. Casado makes no mention of the meeting on 7 or 8 February.
21. On the links between Mera and Casado, see Mera, *Guerra, exilio y cárcel*, pp. 193–4; Domínguez Aragonés, *Los vencedores*, pp. 109–11.
22. *El Socialista*, 11 February 1939; Negrín, *Textos y discursos políticos*, p. 351.
23. Zugazagoitia, *Guerra y vicisitudes*, II, p. 246.

24. Negrín, *Textos y discursos políticos*, p. 358; Zugazagoitia, *Guerra y vicisitudes*, II, pp. 246–7; Alonso, *La flota republicana*, pp. 152–4.
25. Álvarez del Vayo, *Freedom's Battle*, pp. 275–6; Miralles, *Juan Negrín*, p. 313.
26. Encinas Moral, ed., *Las causas de la derrota*, pp. 183–4; Viñas and Hernández Sánchez, *El desplome*, pp. 95–7.
27. Uribe, 'Informe', pp. 64–5.
28. Casado to Negrín, 15 February 1939, Archivo Fundación Juan Negrín, Carpeta 66, 97–9; Casado, *Así cayó Madrid*, pp. 113–16. In Casado, *The Last Days*, pp. 106–13, he gave a similar account but dated this interview as taking place on 25 February. For a slightly different interpretation of the episode, see Moradiellos, *Negrín*, pp. 431–2.
29. Domínguez Aragonés, *Los vencedores*, pp. 107–8.
30. 'Declaración de don Antonio Luna García', in Arenillas, *El proceso*, pp. 192–3; *ibid.*, p. 241; Cervera, *Madrid en guerra*, pp. 391–5; Bahamonde and Cervera, *Así terminó la guerra*, pp. 264–6; Viñas and Hernández Sánchez, *El desplome*, pp. 91–3; La Cierva, *1939*, pp. 74–6; Martínez Bande, *Los cien últimos días*, pp. 119–21, Casado, *Así cayó Madrid*, pp. 208–9.
31. On Franco's supervision of the links between the SIPM and Casado, see Bahamonde, *Madrid 1939*, pp. 140–3; Bahamonde and Cervera, *Así terminó la guerra*, p. 315.
32. Martínez Bande, *Los cien últimos días*, pp. 121–2. Casado's intention to escape, *ibid.*, p. 125.
33. Ibárruri et al., *Guerra y revolución*, IV, p. 240.
34. Togliatti, *Opere IV*, p. 388; José Ramón Valero Escandell, *El territorio de la derrota. Los últimos días del Gobierno de la II República en el Vinalopó* (Petrer: Centre

d´Estudis Locals del Vinalopó, 2004) pp. 48–50.

35. *El Socialista*, 14 February 1939.

36. Graham, *The Spanish Republic at War*, pp. 396–401.

37. Pablo de Azcárate, *Mi embajada en Londres durante la guerra civil española* (Barcelona: Ariel, 1976) p. 121.

38. Cabinet minutes, 8 February 1939, TNA, CAB 23/97.

39. Johnson to Hull, 14 February 1939, *FRUS 1939*, II, pp. 744–5; Peter Anderson, 'The Chetwode Commission and British Diplomatic Responses to Violence behind the Lines in the Spanish Civil War', *European History Quarterly*, vol. 42, no. 2, 2012, pp. 251–2; Bahamonde and Cervera, *Así terminó la guerra*, pp. 222–3; Enrique Moradiellos, *La perfidia de Albión. El Gobierno británico y la guerra civil española* (Madrid: Siglo XXI, 1996) p. 350.

40. Cabinet minutes, 15 February 1939, TNA, CAB 23/97.

41. Halifax to Hodgson, 15 February 1939, TNA, FO 371/24152, W2729/1443/41; Cabinet minutes, 22 February, 1939, TNA, CAB 23/97; Azcárate, *Mi embajada*, pp. 124–6; Luis Romero, *El final de la guerra* (Barcelona: Ariel, 1976) p. 132.

42. Halifax to Stevenson, 14 February 1939, TNA, FO 371/24148, W2734/374/41; British Embassy to Department of State, 18, 22 February 1939, *FRUS 1939*, II, pp. 748–51; Cabinet minutes, 22 February 1939, TNA, CAB 23/97; Azcárate, *Mi embajada*, p. 127.

43. Negrín, Discurso en Londres, 14 de abril de 1942, Álvarez, *Negrín*, II, pp. 160–2; Graham, 'Casado's Ghosts', pp. 269–70; 'Cuadro de abastecimientos al 1 de marzo de 1939', documentary appendix to Viñas and Hernández Sánchez, *El desplome*, CD-ROM, pp. 187–8;

Domínguez Aragonés, *Los vencedores*, pp. 122–3.

44. Morel report, 3 February 1939, quoted by Miralles, *Juan Negrín*, p. 408.

45. Casado, *Así cayó Madrid*, pp. 122–7; Miralles, *Juan Negrín*, pp. 312–14, 409; Togliatti, *Opere IV*, pp. 388–9; Romero, *El final*, pp. 149–56; Bahamonde and Cervera, *Así terminó la guerra*, pp. 321–3; Moradiellos, *Negrín*, pp. 436–7; *Actas de la Diputación Permanente. Congreso de los Diputados*, 31 de marzo de 1939, p. 9 (printed version p. 352).

46. Casado, *Así cayó Madrid*, pp. 199–200; Romero, *El final*, p. 119.

47. Ansó, *Yo fui ministro de Negrín*, pp. 244–5; Romero, *El final*, pp. 153, 172; Álvarez del Vayo, *Freedom's Battle*, p. 283.

48. Hernández, *Yo fui un ministro de Stalin*, pp. 269–70; Alpert, *La guerra civil española en el mar*, p. 353. On the bombardment of Cartagena, see TNA, FO 371/24109, W698/4/41; FO 371/24127, W2988/8/41, FO 371/24128, W4294/8/41, W4535/8/41.

49. Álvarez del Vayo, *Freedom's Battle*, p. 278; Hernández, *Yo fui un ministro de Stalin*, pp. 269–70; Uribe, 'Informe', p. 67.

50. Rojo to Negrín, 19 February 1939, AHN, AGR, Caja 5, carpeta 8; Rojo, *Vicente Rojo*, pp. 282–90; Moradiellos, *Negrín*, p. 440.

51. Rojo to Miaja, 19 February 1939, AHN, AGR, Caja 5, carpeta 8.

52. Bahamonde, *Madrid 1939*, p. 147.

53. Campanario, Díez Hernando and Cervera Gil, 'El enigma del general republicano Manuel Matallana Gómez, Jefe del Estado Mayor de Miaja: ¿Fue un miembro activo de la Quinta Columna?', pp. 2, 6–14.

54. Negrín to Pascua, 27 February 1939, AHN, AMP, Caja 2, legajo 19.

55. Rojo, *Vicente Rojo*, p. 278; Manuel

Azaña, *Obras completas*, ed. Santos
Juliá, 7 vols (Madrid: Centro de
Estudios Políticos y
Constitucionales/Taurus, 2008)
p. 747.
56. Negrín, Discurso, 14 de abril de
1942, Álvarez, *Negrín*, II, pp.
159–60.
57. Bolloten, *The Spanish Civil War*,
p. 689.

Chapter 6: Negrín Abandoned
1. Declaración prestada por Ángel
Pedrero García, AHN, FC-Causa
General, Caja 1532, Exp. 30, p. 53.
2. Casado, *Así cayó Madrid*, p. 136.
3. Uribe, 'Informe', p. 66; Irene Falcón,
*Asalto a los cielos. Mi vida junto a
Pasionaria* (Madrid: Temas de Hoy,
1996) pp. 171–2. Irene had worked
as a secretary with Ramón y Cajal,
ibid., pp. 30–1.
4. Álvarez del Vayo, *Freedom's Battle*,
pp. 283–5.
5. *Epistolario Prieto y Negrín*, pp.
120–1.
6. Encinas Moral, ed., *Las causas de la
derrota*, pp. 174–6; Graham,
Socialism and War, pp. 158–9, 236;
Miralles, *Juan Negrín*, pp. 315–17;
Moradiellos, *Negrín*, pp. 438–9.
7. Zugazagoitia, *Guerra y vicisitudes*,
II, p. 244.
8. Manuel Azaña, *Obras completas*, 4
vols (Mexico City: Ediciones Oasis,
1966–8) IV, pp. 875–9; Joan Llarch,
Negrín ¡Resistir es vencer!
(Barcelona: Editorial Planeta, 1985)
p. 26
9. Encinas Moral, ed., *Las causas de la
derrota*, p. 176; Santiago Garcés,
interview with Heleno Saña, 'Habla
un ayudante de Negrín', *Índice*, 15
June 1974, p. 8; Llarch, *Negrín*,
p. 27.
10. Rojo, *Vicente Rojo*, pp. 280–1.
11. Togliatti, *Opere IV*, pp. 387–9;
Cordón, *Trayectoria*, 2nd edn,
pp. 690–6; Moradiellos, *La perfidia
de Albión*, p. 355.

12. Cabinet minutes, 8 March 1939,
TNA, CAB 23/97.
13. Cowan to Consul-General at
Marseilles for onward transmission
to FO, 22 February 1939, TNA, FO
371/24127, W3150/8/41. Cowan
was on board HMS *Devonshire* off
the coast near Valencia.
14. Casado, *The Last Days*, p. 273;
Álvarez del Vayo, *Freedom's Battle*,
pp. 289–90.
15. Martínez Bande, *Los cien últimos
días*, p. 130.
16. *Ibid.*, pp. 122–3.
17. Bahamonde and Cervera, *Así
terminó la guerra*, pp. 314, 326–7;
Martínez Bande, *Los cien últimos
días*, pp. 123–5.
18. *Documentos inéditos para la historia
del Generalísimo Franco* (Madrid:
Fundación Nacional Francisco
Franco, 1992) I, pp. 292–3.
19. Martínez Bande, *El final*, pp. 150–1;
Casado, *Así cayó Madrid*, pp. 208–9.
20. On the realities of what Franco's
triumph would mean for the
defeated in the last areas to be
captured, see Preston, *The Spanish
Holocaust*, pp. 471–517.
21. Martínez Bande, *Los cien últimos
días*, p. 126.
22. Domínguez Aragonés, *Los
vencedores*, pp. 98–9; Cordón,
Trayectoria, 2nd edn, p. 692.
23. Declaración prestada por Ángel
Pedrero García, AHN, FC-Causa
General, Caja 1532, Exp. 30, p. 52.
24. Testimonio del procedimiento
sumarísimo de urgencia seguido
contra el Jefe del SIM, Ángel
Pedrero García, AHN, FC-Causa
General, Caja 1520–1, Exp. 1,
pp. 106–8.
25. Domínguez Aragonés, *Los
vencedores*, pp. 90, 100.
26. *Ibid.*, pp. 103–4; Graham, 'Casado's
Ghosts', pp. 270–1.
27. Mera, *Guerra, exilio y cárcel*; Joan
Llarch, *Cipriano Mera. Un
anarquista en la guerra civil española*

(Barcelona: Producciones Editoriales, 1977); Romero, *El final*, pp. 122–3, 181.

28. César M. Lorenzo, *Los anarquistas españoles y el poder* (Paris: Ruedo Ibérico, 1972) p. 264.

29. Eduardo de Guzmán, *La muerte de la esperanza* (Madrid: G. del Toro, 1973) p. 27.

30. Gregorio Gallego, *Madrid, corazón que se desangra* (Madrid: G. del Toro, 1976) pp. 151–3.

31. Ricardo Sanz, *Los que fuimos a Madrid. Columna Durruti 26 División* (Toulouse: Imprimerie Dulaurier, 1969) pp. 107–8.

32. Juan García Oliver, *El eco de los pasos* (Barcelona: Ruedo Ibérico, 1978) pp. 306, 323, 526.

33. On Eduardo Val, see Preston, *The Spanish Holocaust*, pp. 262–3, 280, 297, 377, 384–7, 390; Felipe Sandoval, 'Informe de mi actuación', AHN, FC-Causa General, Caja 1530–1, Exp. 1, pp. 201–6, 216, 222. There is a short and anodyne biographical sketch in Miguel Íñiguez, *Enciclopedia histórica del anarquismo español*, 3 vols (Vitoria: Asociación Isaac Puente, 2008) I, p. 1740.

34. Lorenzo, *Los anarquistas*, p. 173.

35. This is apparent in the virulently anti-Communist tone of his book, *Cómo terminó la guerra* and in his many articles in *CNT*. Íñiguez, *Enciclopedia histórica del anarquismo español*, I, pp. 707–8 (García Pradas), II, p. 1546 (Salgado); Gallego, *Madrid*, p. 353.

36. Gallego, *Madrid*, p. 353; Procedimiento militar sumarísimo contra José Cazorla Maure, AHN, FC-Causa General, Caja 1525-1, pp. 6, 14–16.

37. Arenillas de Chaves, *El proceso de Besteiro*, pp. 448–9; Julio Palacios, 'Diario de un testigo de la liberación de Madrid', *ABC* (Madrid), 2 April 1961.

38. Peirats, *La CNT*, II, pp. 215–25, III, pp. 83–99.

39. *Ibid.*, III, pp. 177–82.

40. *ABC* (Madrid), 24 January 1939, p. 4.

41. *ABC* (Madrid), 8 February 1939, p. 1.

42. Mera, *Guerra*, pp. 193–7; Peirats, *La CNT*, III, pp. 288–9.

43. García Pradas, *Cómo terminó la guerra*, pp. 51–4.

44. On Mancebo, see Preston, *The Spanish Holocaust*, pp. 273–4, 375; AHN, FC-Causa General, Caja 1525-1, pp. 3–4; Causa General, *La dominación roja en España* (Madrid: Ministerio de Justicia, 1945) p. 159; Gallego, *Madrid*, pp. 126–7.

45. The fullest account of the meeting in the calle Miguel Ángel is by Gregorio Gallego, 'La CNT acuerda sublevarse contra el doctor Negrín', *Historia y Vida*, special issue, 4, 1974; Isaac Martín Nieto, 'Anarcosindicalismo, resistencia y grupos de afinidad. La comisión de propaganda confederal y anarquista (1937–1939)', *El Futuro del Pasado*, no. 1, 2010, pp. 597–611; Viñas and Hernández Sánchez, *El desplome*, pp. 180–1.

46. Peirats, *La CNT*, p. 291.

47. On Pedrero, see Preston, *The Spanish Holocaust*, pp. 277–8; Declaración de Pedrero, AHN, FC-Causa General, Caja 1532, Exp. 30, pp. 8, 39.

48. Alfonso Domingo, *El ángel rojo. La historia de Melchor Rodríguez, el anarquista que detuvo la represión en el Madrid republicano* (Cordoba: Editorial Almuzara, 2009) pp. 256–9, 267–8. Information about the meetings between Sánchez Guerra and Melchor Rodríguez derives from interviews given to Alfonso Domingo by Melchor's daughter Amapola (Alfonso Domingo to Paul Preston, 30 August 2014).

49. José Rodríguez Vega, 'Notas autobiográficas', in *Estudios de Historia Social* (Madrid), no. 30, July–September 1984, pp. 278–9; Viñas and Hernández Sánchez, *El desplome*, p. 286.

50. Gooden to FO, 28 February 1939, TNA, FO 371/24128, W3576/8/41.

Chapter 7: In the Kingdom of the Blind

1. Orencio Labrador recounted his role in the coup and the consequent divisions within the PSOE at the time in a long letter to Largo Caballero, 26 November 1945, Francisco Largo Caballero, *Obras completas*, 16 vols (Madrid and Barcelona: Fundación Largo Caballero/Instituto Monsa, 2003–9) XIV, pp. 5599–607.

2. Wenceslao Carrillo, *El último episodio de la guerra civil española. Marzo de 1939* (Toulouse: Juventudes Socialistas Españolas, 1945) pp. 9–10; Graham, *Socialism and War*, p. 239, 299; Domínguez Aragonés, *Los vencedores*, p. 105.

3. Rodríguez Vega, 'Notas autobiográficas', pp. 279–80.

4. Arenillas de Chaves, *El proceso de Besteiro*, p. 435.

5. Juan Negrín, Intervención ante la Diputación Permanente de las Cortes, Paris, 31 March 1939, in Negrín, *Textos y discursos políticos*, p. 353; Zugazagoitia, *Guerra y vicisitudes*, II, p. 251; Domínguez Aragonés, *Los vencedores*, pp. 103, 107–8; García Pradas, *Cómo terminó la guerra*, p. 51; Hernández, *Yo fui un ministro de Stalin*, p. 276.

6. Líster, *Nuestra guerra*, pp. 251–2; Uribe, 'Informe', pp. 67–8.

7. Mera, *Guerra, exilio y cárcel*, pp. 198–200.

8. Hodgson to Halifax, 21 February 1939, TNA, FO 371/24148, W3417/374/41; British Embassy to Department of State, 22 February 1939, *FRUS 1939*, II, pp. 751–2.

9. Hansard, HC Deb 14 February 1939, vol. 343, cols 1558–9, 23 February 1939, vol. 344, col. 573.

10. Sir Alexander Cadogan, *The Diaries of Sir Alexander Cadogan 1938–1945*, ed. David Dilkes (London: Cassell, 1971) p. 149.

11. Halifax to Hodgson, 27 February 1939, TNA, FO 371/24148, W3238/374/41.

12. Hansard, HC Deb 27 February 1939, vol. 344, cols 871–6.

13. FO Note, 'The Position in Spain', annex to cabinet minutes, 2 March 1939, TNA, CAB 23/97.

14. Hansard, HC Deb 28 February 1939, vol. 344, cols 1099–1119.

15. Cadogan, *The Diaries*, p. 154.

16. Azcárate, *Mi embajada*, pp. 128–9.

17. TNA, FO 371/24129, W6704/8/41; Anderson, 'The Chetwode Commission', pp. 251–2; Moradiellos, *El reñidero de Europa*, p. 245

18. Cabinet minutes, 2 March 1939, TNA, CAB 23/97.

19. Cordón, *Trayectoria*, 2nd edn, pp. 692–6

20. Cowan to FO, 22 February 1939, TNA, FO 371/24127, W3150/8/41; Gooden to FO, 23 February 1939, FO 371/24128, W3571/8/41, Gooden to Tovey, 5 March 1939, FO 371/24128, W3851/8/41; Moradiellos, *La perfidia de Albión*, p. 356.

21. Martínez Bande, *El final*, pp. 160–1.

22. Martínez Bande, *Los cien últimos días*, pp. 127–8.

23. *Ibid.*, p. 129.

24. Castro Delgado, *Hombres made in Moscú*, p. 648; Tagüeña, *Testimonio*, p. 311; Llarch, *Negrín ¡Resistir es vencer!*, p. 245; Glicerio Sánchez Recio et al., *Guerra civil y franquismo en Alicante* (Alicante: Instituto de Cultura Juan Gil-Albert, 1991) pp. 49–51; Valero Escandell, *El territorio de la derrota*, pp. 51, 74, 80–1, 106. Both of the

latter sources provide excellent maps.

25. Líster, *Nuestra guerra*, pp. 253–4.
26. Uribe, 'Informe', p. 68.
27. Valero Escandell, *El territorio de la derrota*, pp. 71–6.
28. Stanislav Vaupshasov, *Na trevozhnykh perelrestkakh: zapiski chekista* (Moskva: Voenizdat, 1988). I have used the digital edition at http://militera.lib.ru/memo/russian/vaupshasov/18.html which is unpaginated. The references are from the chapter entitled 'On the Eve of Disaster' (Накануне катастрофы). I am grateful to Dr Boris Volodarsky both for locating this and for help with the translation.
29. Francisco Ciutat, 'Informe al Comité Central sobre los acontecimientos durante el golpe de Casado', 3 May 1939, reproduced on CD-ROM appendix to Viñas and Sánchez Hernández, *El desplome*, pp. 219–23.
30. FJN, Carpeta 97, 'Final Guerra', 7.
31. On Dakar, see Valero Escandell, *El territorio de la derrota*, pp. 100–2.
32. García Pradas, *Cómo terminó la guerra*, pp. 17, 33–4; Diego Sevilla Andrés, *Historia política de la zona roja* (Madrid: Editora Nacional, 1954) p. 508.
33. Líster, *Nuestra guerra*, p. 278; Boris Volodarsky, 'Soviet Intelligence Services in the Spanish Civil War, 1936–1939', unpublished doctoral thesis (London School of Economics, 2010), pp. 119–22, 167, 238; A. K. Starinov, *Behind Fascist Lines. A First-hand Account of Guerrilla Warfare during the Spanish Revolution* (New York: Ballantine Books, 2001) p. 282.
34. Rodríguez Vega, 'Notas autobiográficas', p. 280.
35. Zugazagoitia, *Guerra y vicisitudes*, II, pp. 252–3; Cordón, *Trayectoria*, 2nd edn, pp. 706–8; Casado, *Así cayó Madrid*, pp. 132–3.

36. Casado, *Así cayó Madrid*, p. 187; Alpert, *La guerra civil española en el mar*, pp. 354–5; Alonso, *La flota republicana*, p. 161.
37. Zugazagoitia, *Guerra y vicisitudes*, II, p. 253; Modesto, *Soy del Quinto Regimiento*, p. 281.
38. Casado, *The Last Days*, pp. 125–9; Casado, *Así cayó Madrid*, pp. 131, 141–2; *Pueblo*, 31 October, 1 November 1967; Viñas and Hernández Sánchez, *El desplome*, pp. 225–9.
39. See the text of the telegrams sent via Ambassador Pascua urging Azaña to return, Marcelino Pascua, 'Azaña en la Embajada de París – Documentación', pp. 6–11, AHN, AMP, Caja 1, carpeta 9; Negrín to Azaña, 18, 27 February 1939, draft text of telegrams, FJN, Carpeta 97, 'Final Guerra', 53A–D, 54; Moradiellos, *Negrín*, pp. 440–1.
40. Pascua to Negrín, 27 February 1939, FJN, Carpeta 97, 'Final Guerra', 39A–B.
41. Marcelino Pascua, 'Azaña en la Embajada de París', AHN, AMP, Caja 1, carpeta 9, pp. 9–10; Pascua to Álvarez del Vayo, 27 February 1939, FJN, Carpeta 97, 'Final Guerra', 44A–C; Manuel Azaña, *Obras completas*, 4 vols (Mexico: Ediciones Oasis, 1966–8) III, p. 567; Rivas Cherif, *Retrato de un desconocido*, pp. 427–35; Zugazagoitia, *Guerra y vicisitudes*, II, pp. 235–6.
42. Pascua to Negrín, undated telegram, FJN, Carpeta 97, 'Final Guerra', 41A–B.
43. Rojo, *Vicente Rojo*, pp. 291–3; Rojo, *¡Alerta los pueblos!*, pp. 169–70.
44. Pascua to Zugazagoitia, 27 March 1940, AHN, AMP, Caja 2 (bis), carpeta 16 (exilio).
45. Viñas and Hernández Sánchez, *El desplome*, pp. 245–7.
46. Martínez Barrio to Negrín, 3 March 1939, FJN, Carpeta 97, 'Final

Guerra', 3A–C; Martínez Barrio, *Memorias*, pp. 408–15; Zugazagoitia, *Guerra y vicisitudes*, II, pp. 236–9; Viñas and Sánchez Hernández, *El desplome*, p. 252.

47. Ibárruri, *El único camino*, p. 608; Negrín, Intervención ante la Diputación Permanente de las Cortes, Paris, 31 March 1939, in Negrín, *Textos y discursos políticos*, pp. 360–1; Ibárruri et al., *Guerra y revolución en España*, IV, pp. 279–80.

48. Encinas Moral, ed., *Las causas de la derrota*, pp. 176, 201, 213; 'Informe a Stalin', Viñas and Hernández Sánchez, *El desplome*, p. 549.

49. Viñas, *El honor de la República*, p. 516.

50. La Cierva, *1939*, p. 75; Casado to Juan López, 1 January 1947, Archivo General Regional de Murcia, Archivo Juan López Sánchez (henceforth AGRM, AJLS), JLS,998/1,192.

51. Negrín, Intervención ante la Diputación Permanente de las Cortes, Paris, 31 March 1939, in Negrín, *Textos y discursos políticos*, p. 360.

52. Benigno Rodríguez to Negrín, 26 February and undated but 5 March 1939, Blas Cabrera to Negrín, FJN, Carpeta 97 'Final guerra', 77, 78, 79; *ABC* (Madrid), 2 March 1939.

53. Pascua telegraphed Negrín on 3 and 4 March to say that he had given Martínez Barrio all those telegrams that had actually reached him, FJN, Carpeta 97, 'Final Guerra', 42A–B, 43A–B; Martínez Barrio, *Memorias*, pp. 415–20; Zugazagoitia, *Guerra y vicisitudes*, II, pp. 239–40.

54. Zugazagoitia, *Guerra y vicisitudes*, II, pp. 241–3.

55. Rodríguez Vega, 'Notas autobiográficas', p. 280.

56. García Pradas, *Cómo terminó la guerra*, pp. 53, 58–61; Peirats, *La CNT*, III, pp. 297–8.

57. José García Pradas, *¡Teníamos que perder!* (Madrid: G. del Toro, 1974) p. 13.

Chapter 8: On the Eve of Catastrophe

1. Líster, *Nuestra guerra*, p. 251; Tagüeña, p. 305.

2. Uribe, 'Informe', pp. 65–6.

3. Zugazagoitia, *Guerra y vicisitudes*, II, pp. 244–6.

4. Valero Escandell, *El territorio de la derrota*, pp. 48–50.

5. Tagüeña, *Testimonio*, p. 305; Castro Delgado, *Hombres made in Moscú*, pp. 646–7.

6. Aldo Agosti, *Palmiro Togliatti* (Torino: UTET, 1996) pp. 240–1.

7. Vaupshasov, *Na trevozhnykh perelrestkakh: zapiski chekista*.

8. Togliatti *Opere IV*, p. 389; Elorza and Bizcarrondo, *Queridos camaradas*, pp. 432–3; Bolloten, *The Spanish Civil War*, p. 711.

9. *ABC* (Madrid), 26 February 1939; Casado, *The Last Days*, p. 106.

10. Togliatti *Opere IV*, pp. 388–92; Vaupshasov, *Na trevozhnykh perelrestkakh: zapiski chekista*; Cordón, *Trayectoria*, 2nd edn, pp. 702–3; Ibárruri et al., *Guerra y revolución*, IV, pp. 258–9; Zugazagoitia, *Guerra y vicisitudes*, II, pp. 251–4; Casado, *The Last Days*, p. 127; Domínguez Aragonés, *Los vencedores*, p. 108; Arenillas de Chaves, *El Proceso de Besteiro*, p. 432.

11. Tagüeña, *Testimonio*, p. 307.

12. On Casado's duplicity regarding his promotion, see Cordón, *Trayectoria*, 2nd edn, p. 692; Modesto, *Soy del Quinto Regimiento*, p. 280; Álvarez del Vayo, *Freedom's Battle*, pp. 290–1; Zugazagoitia, *Guerra y vicisitudes*, II, p. 254; La Cierva, *1939*, p. 75.

13. Agosti, *Palmiro Togliatti*, p. 241; Togliatti, *Opere IV*, p. 390

14. Tagüeña, *Testimonio*, pp. 306–7.

15. Falcón, *Asalto*, p. 109.

16. Togliatti, *Opere IV*, p. 389.
17. Carlos Morla Lynch, *España sufre. Diarios de guerra en el Madrid republicano* (Seville: Editorial Renacimiento, 2008) p. 727.
18. Ramón Lamoneda, *Posiciones políticas-documentos-correspondencia* (Mexico City: Roca, 1976) p. 96.
19. Viñas and Sánchez Hernández, *El desplome*, pp. 116, 134, 252–4.
20. Fischer, *Men and Politics*, p. 559.
21. Michael Richards, *A Time of Silence: Civil War and the Culture of Repression in Franco's Spain, 1936–1945* (Cambridge: Cambridge University Press, 1998) p. 44; TNA, FO 371/24126, W1215/8/41.
22. *Epistolario Prieto y Negrín*, p. 37.
23. *Ibid.*, pp. 17, 44–5.
24. Castro Delgado, *Hombres made in Moscú*, pp. 647–8.
25. Líster, *Nuestra guerra*, pp. 252–4. Líster, admitting that he did not have exact recollection of dates, implies that this meeting took place on 2 or 3 March. However, since he then refers to the promotions that were announced on 2 March as taking place on the day after or the day after that, it is reasonable to assume that his interview with Negrín probably took place on 1 March.
26. Uribe, 'Informe', pp. 71–2.
27. Salas Larrázabal, *Historia del Ejército popular*, IV, pp. 3400–8; Bahamonde and Cervera, *Así terminó la guerra*, pp. 342–4; Viñas and Hernández Sánchez, *El desplome*, pp. 228–37; on Mantecón, see Francisco Ciutat, 'Informe al comité central', pp. 227–8, and on Martínez Cartón, see 'Informe a Stalin', p. 55; Pedro Checa, 'Informe sobre los acontecimientos del 1 al 24 de marzo de 1939', p. 252 (reproduced in documentary appendix, on CD-ROM, to *El desplome*).
28. Manuel Aznar, *Historia militar de la guerra de España (1936–1939)* (Madrid: Ediciones Idea, 1940) pp. 841–2; Sevilla Andrés, *Historia política de la zona roja*, pp. 510–12; Ricardo de la Cierva, *1939*, pp. 160–1; La Cierva, *La victoria y el caos. A los sesenta años del 1 de abril de 1939* (Madrid: Editorial Fénix, 1999) pp. 424–6.
29. Ibárruri, *El único camino*, pp. 608–9; Salas Larrazábal, *Historia del Ejército popular*, II, p. 2333.
30. Bolloten, *The Spanish Civil War*, pp. 713–17; Casado, *Así cayó Madrid*, pp. 131, 142.
31. Casado, *Así cayó Madrid*, pp. 143, 166.
32. Hidalgo de Cisneros, *Cambio de rumbo*, II, pp. 253–4; Álvarez del Vayo, *Freedom's Battle*, pp. 289–90. In fact, Hidalgo de Cisneros does not specify the day but Bahamonde and Cervera, *Así terminó la guerra*, give the date of the meeting as 3 March.
33. Líster, *Nuestra guerra*, p. 254; Togliatti, *Opere IV*, pp. 392–3.
34. Carrillo, *El último episodio*, p. 10
35. Alonso, *La flota republicana*, p. 174.
36. Prieto to Negrín, 3 July 1939, *Epistolario Prieto y Negrín*, pp. 119–20.
37. Méndez to Negrín, 3 February 1939, AHN, AMP, Caja 2, carpetas 17 and 19. See the commentary on this of Moradiellos, *Negrín*, pp. 448–9.
38. Casado, *Así cayó Madrid*, pp. 144–7; Zugazagoitia, *Guerra y vicisitudes*, II, pp. 253–5. See Juan Miguel Campanario, 'Los ascensos y nombramientos de militares comunistas en marzo de 1939, la sublevación del coronel Segismundo Casado y el hallazgo del Diario Oficial del Ministerio de Defensa Nacional del día 5 de marzo cuya existencia se desconocía', Ponencia presentada en el X Congreso de la Asociación de Historia

Contemporánea, que se celebró en Santander el 16–17 de septiembre de 2010, pp. 18–21.

39. Alonso, *La flota republicana*, pp. 160–1, 171–2; Zugazagoitia, *Guerra y vicisitudes*, II, pp. 247–50, 255–6; Juan Martínez Leal, *República y guerra civil en Cartagena (1931–1939)* (Murcia: Universidad de Murcia/Ayuntamiento de Cartagena, 1993) pp. 326–8.

40. Checa, 'Informe', pp. 249–53; Ibárruri et al., *Guerra y revolución*, IV, pp. 282–3; Fernández Díaz, *El exilio de los marinos republicanos*, pp. 57, 92; Martínez Bande, *El final*, p. 192.

41. Report by Eustaquio Cañas, 'Marzo de 1939. El último mes', in AFPI, ARLF-172-30, pp. 12–13. Cañas erroneously refers to him as Pérez Barreiro.

42. Negrín, Intervención ante la Diputación Permanente de las Cortes, Paris, 31 March 1939, in Negrín, *Textos y discursos políticos*, p. 358. Both Modesto, *Soy del Quinto Regimiento*, p. 282, and Ibárruri et al, *Guerra y revolución*, IV, p. 282, state that the withdrawal of the fleet was to take place on 2 March but 4 March is a more likely date.

43. Cañas, 'Marzo de 1939', pp. 13–14.

44. Ibid., p. 14.

45. 'Memorias del coronel Galán', *Pueblo*, 26 October 1971, p. 40; Alonso, *La flota republicana*, pp. 174–203; Alpert, *La guerra civil española en el mar*, pp. 353–5.

Chapter 9: The Desertion of the Fleet

1. *ABC* (Madrid), 28 February 1939; García Pradas, *Cómo terminó la guerra*, p. 36.

2. 'Informe a Stalin', pp. 62, 80 (reproduced in documentary appendix, on CD-ROM, to Viñas and Sánchez Hernández, *El desplome*).

3. FJN, Carpeta 28, 17A–C.

4. Informe de González Peña, Bilbao & Blanco, 20 February 1939, FJN, Carpeta 28, 16A–C.

5. Coronel Jesús Pérez Salas, *Guerra en España (1936 a 1939)* (Mexico City: Imprenta Grafos, 1947) pp. 240–1; Manuel D. Benavides, *La escuadra la mandan los cabos*, 2nd edn (Mexico City: Ediciones Roca, 1976) p. 523.

6. Negrín, Intervención ante la Diputación Permanente de las Cortes, Paris, 31 March 1939, in Negrín, *Textos y discursos políticos*, pp. 358–9; Martínez Bande, *El final*, p. 194.

7. Bernal to Miaja, 4 March 1939, FJN, Carpeta 28, 6.

8. 'Informe de Francisco Galán sobre su actuación como jefe de la base naval de Cartagena', AHPCE, Sección 'Tesis, Manuscritos y Memorias', Carpeta 35, Exp. 9 (henceforth AHPCE, TMM, 35/9) p. 1 (reproduced on CD-ROM appendix to Viñas and Sánchez Hernández, *El desplome*, p. 201); 'Memorias del Coronel Francisco Galán', *Pueblo*, 28 October 1971, p. 14; Martínez Bande, *El final*, pp. 197–9.

9. Viñas and Hernández Sánchez, *El desplome*, pp. 271–2; Alonso, *La flota republicana*, pp. 174–5; Martínez Leal, *República y guerra civil en Cartagena*, p. 336

10. Zugazagoitia, *Guerra y vicisitudes*, II, p. 256; Benavides, *La escuadra*, p. 519; Iglesias, *La fase final*, pp. 134–5. Alonso, *La flota republicana*, p. 173, refers to Matallana's telegram as emanating from the army chiefs, which clearly meant Matallana and Casado, but gives no text. On the message regarding the postponement, see Ibárruri et al., *Guerra y revolución*, IV, p. 284; 'Informe de Galan', p. 204.

11. Alonso, *La flota republicana*, pp. 176–7; Benavides, *La escuadra*, pp. 519–20.

12. 'Informe de Galán', AHPCE, TMM, 35/9, pp. 2–4; 'Memorias del Coronel Francisco Galán', *Pueblo*, 28 October 1971, p. 14; Martínez Bande, *El final*, pp. 192–6, Martínez Leal, *República y guerra civil en Cartagena*, pp. 338–9.

13. 'Informe de Galán', AHPCE, TMM, 35/9, pp. 3–5; Alonso, *La flota republicana*, pp. 179–80; Romero, *El final de la guerra*, pp. 207–8.

14. 'Informe de Galán', AHPCE, TMM, 35/9, pp. 5–6; Ibárruri et al., *Guerra y revolución*, IV, pp. 285–6; Fernández Díaz, *El exilio de los marinos republicanos*, pp. 27–8; Martínez Leal, *República y guerra civil en Cartagena*, pp. 340–4; Martínez Bande, *El final*, pp. 200–2; Alpert, *La guerra civil española en el mar*, pp. 354–60.

15. 'Memorias del Coronel Francisco Galán', *Pueblo*, 28 October 1971, p. 14; Benavides, *La escuadra*, p. 540; Pérez Salas, *Guerra en España*, p. 243.

16. Handwritten drafts of the texts of the various messages were captured when the Republicans retook Cartagena. See FJN, Carpeta 28, 1A–H. Transcripts of the actual broadcasts, *ibid.*, 18A–B; 'Informe de Galán', AHPCE, TMM, 35/9, pp. 12–13.

17. FJN, Carpeta 28, 1B–C.

18. Transcript of telephone conversation between Negrín and Matallana in the early hours of 5 March, FJN, Carpeta 28, 10A–B; also in Carpeta 28, 1999-03-22 11.03.46 and 1999-03-22 11.04.24. The telegraphic style of the document makes interpretation difficult. Moradiellos, *Negrín*, p. 449, takes it that Negrín was giving orders to Matallana rather than informing him of the orders he had given to those at the base.

19. Transcript of second telephone conversation between Negrín and Matallana on 5 March, FJN, Carpeta 28, 13A–B.

20. Interchange of teletypes between Negrín and Galán and Vicente Ramírez, FJN, Carpeta 28, 14A–B, 11A–B; 'Informe de Galán', AHPCE, TMM, 35/9, pp. 8–10; Report by Eustaquio Cañas, 'Marzo de 1939. El último mes', in AFPI, ARLF-172-30, pp. 15–17; Benavides, *La escuadra*, pp. 532–4; Alonso, *La flota republicana*, pp. 181–2.

21. Transcript of telephone conversation between Osorio Tafall and Galán, FJN, Carpeta 28, 9; 'Informe de Galán', AHPCE, TMM, 35/9, pp. 10–12.

22. Texts of radio broadcasts and messages, FJN, Carpeta 28, 1A–H; 18A–B; 'Informe de Galán', AHPCE, TMM, 35/9, pp. 12–13; Pérez Salas, *Guerra en España*, pp. 241–3; Benavides, *La escuadra*, pp. 526–7.

23. 'Informe de Galán', AHPCE, TMM, 35/9, pp. 13–15; 'Memorias del Coronel Francisco Galán', *Pueblo*, 28 October 1971, p. 14; Benavides, *La escuadra*, pp. 526–7; Viñas and Hernández Sánchez, *El desplome*, pp. 276–7; Martínez Leal, *República y guerra civil en Cartagena*, pp. 333–43.

24. Benavides, *La escuadra*, p. 534; Martínez Bande, *El final*, p. 192.

25. Álvarez del Vayo, *Freedom's Battle*, pp. 292–3.

26. Cañas, 'Marzo de 1939', pp. 22–3.

27. Martínez Bande, *El final*, pp. 212–14.

28. Cañas, 'Marzo de 1939', pp. 17–18.

29. Líster, *Nuestra guerra*, pp. 255–6.

30. 'Informe de Galán', AHPCE, TMM, 35/9, pp. 16–17.

31. Martínez Bande, *El final*, pp. 215–17.

32. Viñas and Hernández Sánchez, *El desplome*, pp. 279–83; Galán, 'Informe', pp. 214–16; Pedro María Egea Bruno, 'Miguel Buiza Fernández-Palacios, Almirante

habilitado' in García Fernández, ed., *25 militares de la República*, pp. 177–8; Benavides, *La escuadra*, pp. 544–5; Alonso, *La flota republicana*, pp. 187–90.

33. Martínez Bande, *El final*, p. 233.
34. Pérez Salas, *Guerra en España*, p. 244; Egea Bruno, 'Miguel Buiza Fernández-Palacios', pp. 184–6.
35. Alonso, *La flota republicana*, pp. 181–4; Martínez Bande, *El final*, pp. 219–26; Martínez Leal, *República y guerra civil en Cartagena*, pp. 346–8; Zugazagoitia, *Guerra y vicisitudes*, II, pp. 260–7; Bahamonde and Cervera, *Así terminó la guerra*, pp. 421–38.
36. Martínez Leal, *República y guerra civil en Cartagena*, pp. 355–9; Almirante Juan Cervera Valderrama, *Memorias de Guerra (1936–1939)* (Madrid: Editora Nacional, 1968) pp. 375–9; Martínez Bande, *El final*, pp. 226–32; Eladi Mainar, José Miguel Santacreu and Robert Llopis, *La agonia de la II República* (Valencia: La Xara, 2014) pp. 31–3; Luis Miguel Pérez Adán, 'El hundimiento del Castillo de Olite', *Revista Cartagena histórica*, no. 2, January 2003, *passim*; for an eyewitness account, see Cañas, 'Marzo de 1939', pp. 24–5.
37. Benavides, *La escuadra*, pp. 542–3; Pérez Salas, *Guerra en España*, pp. 247–9.
38. Francisco Vega Díaz, 'El último día de Negrín en España', *Claves de la Razón Práctica*, no. 22, May 1992, pp. 60–3. This fascinating account is entirely credible, although the title of the article is somewhat confusing regarding timings. Vega Díaz writes as if everything he describes occurred in the course of 5 March, but also refers to events that took place on 6 March such as the departure of Negrín and his ministers. No facts are distorted and the confusion probably arises from

the fact that he was writing sixty years later.
39. *Ibid.*, pp. 60–1.
40. *Ibid.*, p. 61.
41. Hernández, *Yo fui un ministro de Stalin*, pp. 280–1.
42. Tagueña, *Testimonio*, pp. 310–11; Falcón, *Asalto*, pp. 169–70
43. Vega, 'El último día', pp. 61–2.
44. 'Informe de Galán', AHPCE, TMM, 35/9, pp. 19–20; Alpert, *La guerra civil española en el mar*, pp. 360–2.
45. Viñas and Hernández Sánchez, *El desplome*, pp. 328–32.
46. Cordón, *Trayectoria*, 2nd edn, pp. 712–13.
47. *Ibid.*, pp. 713–14.

Chapter 10: The Coup – the Stab in the Back

1. García Pradas, *Cómo terminó la guerra*, pp. 65–71.
2. Domínguez Aragonés, *Los vencedores*, pp. 150–6.
3. For the text of his speech, *El Socialista*, 7 March 1939; the description of Besteiro, García Pradas, *Cómo terminó la guerra*, pp. 71–2; Romero, *El final*, pp. 261–3.
4. Romero, *El final*, pp. 263–4.
5. Domínguez Aragonés, *Los vencedores*, p. 160; Rodríguez Vega, 'Notas autobiográficas', p. 282; Romero, *El final*, pp. 267–8.
6. Casado, *Así cayó Madrid*, pp. 199–200; Romero, *El final*, pp. 119.
7. Declaración prestada por Ángel Pedrero García, AHN, FC-Causa General, Caja 1532, Exp. 30, p. 54; Domínguez Aragonés, *Los vencedores*, p. 168.
8. Rodríguez Miaja, *Testimonios y remembranzas*, pp. 53–5. The decree appointing Miaja, dated 5 March 1939, is reproduced in *ibid.*, p. 95.
9. Domínguez Aragonés, *Los vencedores*, p. 176.
10. *Ibid.*, pp. 178–85; Rodríguez Vega, 'Notas autobiográficas', pp. 281–3; Pere Gabriel, *Historia de la UGT. Un*

sindicalismo de guerra (Madrid: Siglo XXI, 2011) pp. 496–7.

11. Gabriel, *Historia de la UGT*, pp. 498–9.

12. Fernsworth, *Spain's Struggle for Freedom*, p. 235.

13. Palmiro Togliatti, 'Relazione del 21 maggio 1939', *Opere IV*, pp. 343–410; Graham, *Socialism and War*, pp. 234–5.

14. Preston, *The Spanish Holocaust*, ch. 11.

15. Togliatti, 'Relazione del 21 maggio 1939', *Opere IV*, pp. 343–410; Viñas and Hernández Sánchez, *El desplome*, p. 48; Tagüeña, *Testimonio*, p. 321; Bahamonde and Cervera, *Así terminó la guerra*, pp. 377–8, 386–9, 416–18.

16. Manuel Portela Valladares, *Dietario de dos guerras (1936–1950). Notas, polémicas y correspondencia de un centrista español* (Sada-A Coruña: Ediciós do Castro, 1988) p. 152.

17. Jackson, *The Spanish Republic*, p. 471.

18. Tierno Galván, *Cabos sueltos*, pp. 26–7, 34; cf. Gabriel Morón, *Política de ayer y política de mañana. Los socialistas ante el problema español* (Mexico City: Talleres Numancia, 1942) pp.142–3.

19. Lamo de Espinoa and Contreras, *Besteiro*, p.116.

20. 'Declaración de don Antonio Luna García', in Arenillas, *El proceso*, p. 193.

21. Zugazagoitia, *Guerra y vicisitudes*, II, p. 252; Cordón, *Trayectoria*, 1st edn, pp. 486–7.

22. Casado, *The Last Days*, pp. 149–50; Casado, *Así cayó Madrid*, pp. 157–8; 'Las memorias inéditas del Coronel Casado', *Pueblo*, 2 November 1967, p. 17; Cordón, *Trayectoria*, 2nd edn, pp. 714–15; Zugazagoitia, *Guerra y vicisitudes*, II, pp. 257–8; Domínguez Aragonés, *Los vencedores*, pp. 170–1; García Pradas, *Cómo*

terminó la guerra, pp. 75–6; Álvarez del Vayo, *Freedom's Battle*, pp. 293–4.

23. Viñas and Hernández Sánchez, *El desplome*, p. 322.

24. Cordón, *Trayectoria*, 2nd edn, pp. 715–17; Álvarez del Vayo, *Freedom's Battle*, pp. 294–5.

25. Cordón, *Trayectoria*, 2nd edn, p. 718; Francisco Ciutat, 'Informe al Comité Central sobre los acontecimientos durante el golpe de Casado', 3 May 1939, reproduced on CD-ROM appendix to Viñas and Sánchez Hernández, *El desplome*, p. 229.

26. Negrín, Intervención ante la Diputación Permanente de las Cortes, Paris, 31 March 1939, 'Discurso pronunciado en Londres el 14 de abril de 1945', in Negrín, *Textos y discursos políticos*, pp. 479–80; Cordón, *Trayectoria*, 2nd edn, p. 719.

27. Casado, *The Last Days*, pp. 153–5; Casado, *Así cayó Madrid*, pp. 158–9; Ciutat, 'Informe', p. 229; Miralles, *Juan Negrín*, p. 323.

28. Domínguez Aragonés, *Los vencedores*, pp. 171–2; Santiago Garcés, interview with Heleno Saña, 'Habla un ayudante de Negrín', *Índice*, 15 June 1974, p. 9.

29. Declaración prestada por Ángel Pedrero García, AHN, FC-Causa General, Caja 1532, Exp. 30, p. 54; Cordón, *Trayectoria*, 2nd edn, p. 720.

30. On Burillo, see Viñas and Hernández Sánchez, *El desplome*, pp. 232, 338, 540, 558; Español Bouché, *Madrid 1939*, pp. 67, 121; Encinas Moral, ed., *Las causas de la derrota*, p. 175; Togliatti, *Opere IV*, p. 383 and the remarks on the eve of his execution to Rafael Sánchez Guerra, *Mis prisiones. Memorias de un condenado por Franco* (Buenos Aires: Editorial Claridad, 1946) pp. 115–17.

31. Cañas, 'Marzo de 1939', pp. 19–20; Cordón, *Trayectoria*, 2nd edn, p. 721.

32. Cordón, *Trayectoria*, 2nd edn, p. 720; Uribe, 'Informe', pp. 68–70.

33. Cordón, *Trayectoria*, 2nd edn, pp. 721–2; Vega, 'El último día', p. 62.

34. Tagüeña, *Testimonio*, pp. 311–12.

35. Bolloten interviewed Hidalgo de Cisneros in Mexico shortly after the war, Bolloten, *The Spanish Civil War*, p. 730.

36. Vega, 'El último día', p. 62; Falcón, *Asalto*, pp. 172–3; Vidal Zapater, 'Los Llanos (Albacete) 1939' p. 7; Zugazagoitia, *Guerra y vicisitudes*, II, pp. 258–9; Líster, *Nuestra guerra*, pp. 256–7.

37. Vega, 'El último día', p. 62; Falcón, *Asalto*, p. 173.

38. Togliatti, *Opere IV*, p. 396; Ansó, *Yo fui ministro de Negrín*, p. 252; Encinas Moral, ed., *Las causas de la derrota*, p. 192.

39. The text is reproduced in Martínez Bande, *El final*, pp. 252–3 and, in English, in Álvarez del Vayo, *Freedom's Battle*, pp. 298–9. See also Uribe, 'Informe', pp. 70–1; Togliatti, *Opere IV*, pp. 397–8; Tagüeña, *Testimonio*, pp. 312–14; Falcón, *Asalto*, pp. 171–4; Ibárruri et al., *Guerra y revolución*, IV, p. 297.

40. Rodríguez Vega, 'Notas autobiográficas', pp. 282–3.

41. *Ibid.*, p. 283.

42. Falcón, *Asalto*, p. 174; Rodríguez Vega, 'Notas autobiográficas', p. 283.

43. Romero Marín, Interview, *Cuadernos para el Diálogo*, 2ª época, 172, 14 August 1976, p. 22.

44. The remark apparently made by Negrín in German is quoted by Manuel Tuñón de Lara, *La España del siglo XX*, 2nd edn (Paris: Librería Española, 1973) p. 670, and Miralles, *Juan Negrín*, pp. 323–4. Tuñón de Lara was a friend of Tagüeña (see *Testimonio*, p. 309). Álvarez del Vayo and Tuñón de Lara became friends in exile. Accordingly, the remark was almost certainly reported by him to Tuñón. The final remark and the coffee were recalled by Irene Falcón, *Asalto*, p. 175.

45. Vaupshasov, *Na trevozhnykh perelrestkakh: zapiski chekista*; Álvarez del Vayo, *Freedom's Battle*, p. 301; Santiago Garcés, interview with Heleno Saña, 'Habla un ayudante de Negrín', *Índice*, 15 June 1974, pp. 9–10; Cordón, *Trayectoria*, 2nd edn, p. 726; Líster, *Nuestra guerra*, p. 256. On the five DC-2s in Republican Spain, see Gerald Howson, *Aircraft of the Spanish Civil War 1936–1939* (London: Putnam, 1990) pp. 121–6.

46. Falcón, *Asalto*, p. 176; Valero Escandell, *El territorio de la derrota*, pp. 163–6; Encinas Moral, ed., *Las causas de la derrota*, p. 205; Howson, *Aircraft of the Spanish Civil War*, pp. 23–4, 107; Hernández, *Yo fui un ministro de Stalin*, p. 335.

47. Togliatti, *Opere IV*, pp. 324–5, 390–1, 397–9; Falcón, *Asalto*, pp. 174–5; Tagüeña, *Testimonio*, pp. 314–19; Líster, *Nuestra guerra*, pp. 256–7; Romero, *El final*, pp. 274–5; Hidalgo de Cisneros, *Cambio de rumbo*, II, pp. 257–9; Ibárruri et al., *Guerra y revolución*, IV, pp. 303–4; Hernández, *Yo fui un ministro de Stalin*, p. 307.

48. Cañas, 'Marzo de 1939', pp. 23–5.

Chapter 11: Casado's Civil War

1. Martínez Paricio, ed., *Los papeles del general Vicente Rojo*, p. 112.

2. F. Ferrandiz Alborz, *La bestia contra España. Reportaje de los últimos días de la guerra española y los primeros de la bestia triunfante* (Montevideo: CISA, 1951) p. 73.

3. Hernández Sánchez, *Guerra o revolución*, p. 455; Ibárruri et al., *Guerra y revolución*, IV, p. 304.

4. Ibárruri et al., *Guerra y revolución*, IV, pp. 304–17; Elorza and Bizcarrondo, *Queridos Camaradas*, p. 436; Viñas and Hernández Sánchez, *El desplome*, pp. 347–50.

5. Manuel Casanova, *La guerra de España. El Frente Popular abrió las puertas a Franco* (Barcelona: Editorial Fontamara, 1978) pp. 154, 156.

6. Rodríguez Miaja, *Testimonios y remembranzas*, p. 51.

7. Moradiellos, *Negrín*, p. 430; Negrín to Pascua, 9 February 1939, AHN, AMP, Caja 4, carpeta 2.

8. Miralles, *Juan Negrín*, p. 178.

9. Negrín to Prieto, 23 June 1939, *Epistolario Prieto y Negrín*, p. 38; Graham, *The Spanish Republic at War*, pp. 407–8.

10. Español Bouché, *Madrid 1939*, pp. 74–5, 134–7.

11. Negrín to De los Ríos, 10 March 1939, AHN, AMP, Caja 2, carpeta 11, Vayo declaration to Embassies 12 March 1939, Caja 1 (bis), carpeta 22; Negrín to Prieto, 23 June 1939, *Epistolario Prieto y Negrín*, pp. 49–50.

12. Bahamonde and Cervera, *Así terminó la guerra*, pp. 331–5.

13. Police telephone logs, AHN, FC-Causa General, Caja 1525, Exp. 10, pp. 1–7.

14. Bahamonde and Cervera, *Así terminó la guerra*, p. 387; Tagüeña, *Testimonio*, pp. 306–19.

15. Unpublished report by Eustaquio Cañas, 'Marzo de 1939. El último mes', in AFPI, ARLF-172-30, pp. 27–8; Ibárruri et al., *Guerra y revolución*, IV, pp. 305–17; Domínguez Aragón, *Los vencedores*, pp. 189–97; Viñas and Hernández Sánchez, *El desplome*, pp. 348–9, 352–3.

16. Bouthelier and López Mora, *Ocho días de revuelta comunista*, pp. 90–2; Bahamonde and Cervera, *Así terminó la guerra*, pp. 335, 399–400.

17. Rodríguez Miaja, *Testimonios y remembranzas*, pp. 55–8, 153–66; Domínguez Aragón, *Los vencedores*, p. 201, confuses Miguel Primo de Rivera with his sister Pilar; Jesús Hernández, 'Informe sobre el periodo de dominación de la Junta de Casado', documentary appendix to Viñas and Hernández Sánchez, *El desplome*, CD-ROM, p. 307.

18. Domínguez Aragón, *Los vencedores*, pp. 83–4.

19. Mera, *Guerra, exilio y cárcel*, pp. 209–12; Julián Vadillo Muñoz, *El movimiento obrero en Alcalá de Henares* (Madrid: Silente Académica, 2013) pp. 403–5; Casado, *Así cayó Madrid*, pp. 170–8; Pedro Alberto García Bilbao, Xulio García Bilbao and P. Carlos Paramio Roca, *La represión franquista en Guadalajara* (Guadalajara: Foro por la Memoria de Guadalajara/Ediciones Silente, 2010) p. 52.

20. Mera, *Guerra, exilio y cárcel*, p. 209.

21. Daniel Arasa, *Entre la cruz y la República. Vida y muerte del general Escobar* (Barcelona: Styria, 2008) pp. 415–20.

22. Domínguez Aragón, *Los vencedores*, p. 84; Francisco Alía Miranda, *La guerra civil en la retaguardia. Conflicto y revolución en la provincia de Ciudad Real (1936–1939)* (Ciudad Real: Diputación Provincial, 1994) pp. 360–5.

23. Rodríguez Vega, 'Notas autobiográficas', pp. 284–5.

24. Viñas and Hernández Sánchez, *El desplome*, pp. 333–41; Encinas Moral, ed., *Las causas de la derrota*, pp. 279–80; Ibárruri et al., *Guerra y revolución*, IV, pp. 317–24; Jesús Hernández, 'Informe sobre el periodo de dominación de la Junta de Casado', Francisco Ciutat, Informe al Comité Central sobre los acontecimientos durante el golpe de Casado, documentary appendix to

El desplome, CD-ROM, pp. 244, 304–7.

25. Viñas and Hernández Sánchez, *El desplome*, pp. 363–6.

26. Ciutat, Informe al Comité Central, documentary appendix to Viñas and Hernández Sánchez, *El desplome*, CD-ROM, pp. 243–4.

27. Wenceslao Carrillo, *El último episodio de la guerra civil española. Marzo de 1939* (Toulouse: Juventudes Socialistas Españoles, 1945) pp. 13–14; Bahamonde, *Madrid 1939*, pp. 185–7.

28. Ettore Vanni, *Io comunista in Russia* (Bologna: Capelli Editore, 1948) pp. 6–18; Pierre Broué and Emile Témime, *The Revolution and the Civil War in Spain* (London: Faber & Faber, 1972) p. 537; Romero, *El final*, p. 359.

29. Carrillo, *El último episodio*, pp. 14–15; Casado, *Así cayó Madrid*, pp. 179–81; Viñas and Hernández Sánchez, *El desplome*, p. 357.

30. Bahamonde, *Madrid 1939*, pp. 225–8.

31. Trial records of officers in AHN, FC-Causa General, Caja 1525, Exp. 8, those relevant to Barceló, pp. 15–18, 67–125; Rodríguez Vega, 'Notas autobiográficas', pp. 285–6; Cañas, 'Marzo de 1939', p. 29; Domínguez Aragón, *Los vencedores*, pp. 214–16; Carrillo, *El último episodio*, p. 15.

32. Graham, *Socialism and War*, pp. 240–3; Viñas, *El desplome*, p. 377.

33. Hernández Sánchez, *Guerra o revolución*, p. 440.

34. Bahamonde, *Palabras del Caudillo 19 abril 1937–7 diciembre 1942*, pp. 501–3.

35. On 18 and 27 February, Viñas and Hernández Sánchez, *El desplome*, pp. 116, 134, 252–4.

36. Bahamonde and Cervera, *Así terminó la guerra*, pp. 421–36.

37. Anderson, 'The Chetwode Commission', p. 252.

38. Bahamonde, *Madrid 1939*, p.12; Bahamonde and Cervera, *Así terminó la guerra*, p. 402; Secret report to Stalin on the events which ended the war, Viñas and Hernández Sánchez, *El desplome*, pp. 30, 47–63 and for the report itself, pp. 471–626.

39. Casado, *The Last Days*, p. 173; Casado, *Así cayó Madrid*, p. 178.

40. Aguilera Povedano, *Compañeros y camaradas*, pp. 333, 338.

41. Salas Larrazábal, *Historia del Ejército popular*, II, pp. 2318, 2340.

42. Domingo, *El ángel rojo*, pp. 267–8, and interview with Melchor's daughter Amapola (private communication to author by Alfonso Domingo); Cañas, 'Marzo de 1939', pp. 27–8, 30.

43. Rodríguez Vega, 'Notas autobiográficas', p. 285.

44. Casado, *Así cayó Madrid*, p. 183.

45. Martínez Bande, *El final*, pp. 296–9; Bahamonde, *Madrid 1939*, pp. 191–2.

46. The manuscript original of Casado's peace proposals drafted on 11 March, Centro Documental de la Memoria Histórica, Salamanca, FNFF, 19910, 19911, 19912. It is reprinted in *Documentos inéditos para la historia del Generalísimo Franco*, I, pp. 323–4. See also Casado, *Así cayó Madrid*, pp. 205–6; Casado, *The Last Days*, pp. 200–2; Carrillo, *El episodio final*, pp. 16–17; Martínez Bande, *El final*, pp. 296–301.

47. Gooden to Halifax, 12 March, 11 April 1939, TNA, FO 371/24153, W4257/2082/41, FO 371/24129, W6704/8/41.

48. Moradiellos, *La perfidia de Albión*, p. 358.

49. César M. Lorenzo, *Los anarquistas españoles y el poder* (Paris: Ruedo Ibérico, 1972) pp. 173–4, 264.

50. Peirats, *La CNT*, III, pp. 255, 272–3, 282, 288–9.

51. Lorenzo, *Los anarquistas*, pp. 173, 264–5; Iglesias, *La fase final*, pp. 118–20; García Pradas, *Cómo terminó la guerra*, p. 54.

52. Domínguez Aragón, *Los vencedores*, pp. 208–12; Rodríguez Vega, 'Notas autobiográficas', p. 283; Morla Lynch, *España sufre*, pp. 739, 751, 760, 764; Viñas and Hernández Sánchez, *El desplome*, pp. 303–4.

53. Bahamonde, *Palabras del Caudillo 19 abril 1937–7 diciembre 1942*, p. 509.

54. Bahamonde and Cervera Gil, *Así terminó la Guerra*, pp. 330–2.

55. Morla Lynch, *España sufre*, p. 765; Viñas and Hernández Sánchez, *El desplome*, p. 305.

56. Julián Besteiro, *Obras completas*, 3 vols (Madrid: Centro de Estudios Constitucionales, 1983) III, pp. 435–7. A facsimile of the manuscript of the document is reproduced by Arenillas de Chaves in *El proceso de Besteiro*, between pp. 288 and 289.

57. Rodríguez Vega, 'Notas autobiográficas', pp. 287–8.

58. Preston, *The Coming of the Spanish Civil War*, ch. 7.

59. Domínguez Aragón, *Los vencedores*, p. 250.

60. Eduardo Buil, '25 días de confusión y derrumbamiento', AFPI, AAVV, AEJM-83-9, pp. 2–4.

61. Cañas, 'Marzo de 1939', AFPI, ARLF-172-30, pp. 32–4, 36–7; Rodríguez Vega, 'Notas autobiográficas', p. 286.

62. García Bilbao, García Bilbao and Paramio Roca, *La represión franquista en Guadalajara*, pp. 53–4.

63. Ana Belén Rodríguez Patiño, *La guerra civil en Cuenca (1936–1939). II: La pugna ideológica y la revolución* (Madrid: Universidad Complutense, 2004) pp. 263–4

64. Alía Miranda, *Ciudad Real*, pp. 365–7.

65. Juan García Maturana, 'Informe sobre los últimos acontecimientos ocurridos en Almería', AHPCE, Documentos PCE, Organizaciones territoriales del PCE, Federación Comunista de Andalucía, Comités Provinciales; Ángel Aguillera Gómez, *La historia silenciada (1930–1989)* (Almería: Instituto de Estudios Almerienses, 1990) pp. 139–75; Sofía Rodríguez López, 'Vidas cruzadas. Las mujeres antifascistas y el exilio interior/ exterior', *Arenal: Revista de historia de mujeres*, vol. 19, no. 1, 2012, pp. 103–40; Rafael Quirosa-Cheyrouze y Muñoz, *Política y guerra civil en Almería* (Almería: Editorial Cajal, 1986) pp. 239–42.

66. Police telephone logs, AHN, FC-Causa General, Caja 1525, Exp. 11, p. 6.

67. Trial records of Eugenio Mesón Gómez, AHN, FC-Causa General, Caja 1525, Exp. 7, pp. 1–26. For trials of other Communists left in prison, see AHN, FC-Causa General, Caja 1525, Exp. 9, pp. 1–12; Francisco Moreno Gómez, *La guerra civil en Córdoba (1936–1939)* (Madrid: Editorial Alpuerto, 1985) pp. 686–8; Ibárruri et al., *Guerra y revolución*, IV, pp. 332–3; Vinas and Hernández Sánchez, *El desplome*, pp. 59, 149; Bahamonde and Cervera, *Así terminó la guerra*, p. 402.

68. Juan Ambou, *Los comunistas en la resistencia nacional republicana (La guerra en Asturias, el País Vasco y Santander)* (Madrid: Editorial Hispamerica, 1978) pp. 277–8.

69. Aurora Arnaiz, *Retrato hablado de Luisa Julián* (Madrid: Compañía Literaria, 1996) pp. 111–42, 158–9; Melquesidez Rodríguez Chaos, *24 años en la cárcel* (Paris: Colección Ebro, 1968) pp. 27–8, 73–5.

70. García Bilbao, García Bilbao and Paramio Roca, *La represión*

franquista en Guadalajara, pp. 42, 53–5.
71. Casado, *Asi cayó Madrid*, p. 178.
72. Vadillo Muñoz, *El movimiento obrero en Alcalá de Henares*, pp. 404–5.

Chapter 12: Casado Reaps the Whirlwind
1. Romero, *El final*, pp. 361–5; Mera, *Guerra, exilio y cárcel*, pp. 212–17.
2. Testimony of Julio Palacios in Arenillas de Chaves, *El proceso de Besteiro*, p. 436.
3. Police telephone logs, AHN, FC-Causa General, Caja 1525, Exp. 10, pp. 1–7, Exp. 11, p. 3.
4. García Pradas, *Cómo terminó la guerra*, pp. 117, 124–5.
5. Frank Mintz and Graham Kelsey, eds, *Consejo Nacional de Defensa* (Madrid: Cuadernos de la Guerra Civil, Fundación Salvador Seguí, 1989) pp. 101–5.
6. Peirats, *La CNT*, III, pp. 307–9.
7. Testimonio del procedimiento sumarísimo de urgencia seguido contra el Jefe del SIM, Ángel Pedrero García, AHN, FC-Causa General, Caja 1520-1, Exp. 1, pp. 77–8, 126–7.
8. Cañas, 'Marzo de 1939', AFPI, ARLF-172-30, pp. 29–30.
9. Manuel Valdés Larrañaga, *De la Falange al Movimiento (1936–1952)* (Madrid: Fundación Nacional Francisco Franco, 1994) pp. 90–2.
10. Luna said this to Father Alfonso Álvarez Bolado, SJ, at the time a theology student at Innsbruck. Luna's remark was included in a letter to the author from Dom Hilari Raguer, 7 July 1997, and later confirmed in conversation by Father Álvarez Bolado himself.
11. Besteiro, *Obras completas*, III, pp. 435–7.
12. Bullitt to Hull, 8 March 1939, *FRUS 1939*, II, pp. 760–3.
13. Viñas and Hernández Sánchez, *El desplome*, p. 289.

14. Rodríguez Vega, 'Notas autobiográficas', p. 287.
15. Halifax to Phipps (Paris) and Halifax to Henderson (Berlin) 15 March 1939, Halifax to Henderson 17 March 1939 *Documents on British Foreign Policy*, 3rd Series, vol. IV (London: HMSO, 1951) pp. 267, 271, 291; Hansard, HC Deb 31 March 1939, vol. 345, cols 2421–2; Anita J. Prazmowska, *Britain, Poland and the Eastern Front, 1939* (Cambridge: Cambridge University Press, 1987) pp. 57–61; Thomas, *The Spanish Civil War*, p. 911.
16. Regina García, *Yo he sido marxista. El cómo y porqué de una conversión*, 2nd edn (Madrid: Editora Nacional, 1952) pp. 330–1.
17. Romero, *El final*, pp. 264–5.
18. E. Jorge Moreno, 'Notas sobre los últimos días de la guerra civil española', AFPI, AAVV, AEJM-83-9, p. 2.
19. Gooden to Foreign Office, 26 March 1939, TNA, FO 371/24154, W5088/2082/41.
20. Eliseo Gómez Serrano, *Diarios de la guerra civil (1936–1939)* (Alicante: Universidad de Alicante, 2008) diary entries for 21 February, 12, 13, 14, 22, 26 March 1939, pp. 671–2, 684–6, 693, 695; transcript of Gómez Serrano's Consejo de Guerra, pp. 715–16. The book that distressed him was Antonio Bahamonde y Sánchez de Castro, *Un año con Queipo* (Barcelona: Ediciones Españolas, n.d. [1938]).
21. Casado, *The Last Days*, pp. 290–1; La Cierva, *1939*, p. 266; Ferrandiz Alborz, *La bestia*, p. 74.
22. Rodríguez Vega, 'Notas autobiográficas', p. 287; Domínguez Aragón, *Los vencedores*, pp. 212–13.
23. García Pradas, *Cómo terminó la guerra*, p. 131.
24. Mera, *Guerra, exilio y cárcel*, pp. 224–5.

25. José del Río, 'Besteiro, martir', *El Socialista*, 24 September 1959. See also Jackson, *The Spanish Republic*, p. 471, who speaks of 'the notion of vicarious sacrifice, the hope that his imprisonment and death might lighten the burden of reprisals against others'.

26. García Pradas, *Cómo terminó la guerra*, p. 131.

27. Martínez Bande, *Los cien últimos días*, pp. 227-35; Bahamonde, *Madrid 1939*, pp. 193-4.

28. Bahamonde and Cervera, *Así terminó la guerra*, pp. 453-7; Martínez Bande, *El final*, pp. 301-14.

29. Casado, *Así cayó Madrid*, pp. 221-6; Carrillo, *El último episodio*, pp. 17-18; Bahamonde, *Madrid 1939*, pp. 199-20.

30. Casado, *Así cayó Madrid*, pp. 226-35.

31. *Ibid.*, pp. 239-50; Bahamonde, *Madrid 1939*, pp. 196-7.

32. Vidal Zapater, 'Los Llanos (Albacete) 1939', pp. 9-15; Viñas and Hernández Sánchez, *El desplome*, pp. 290-4.

33. Paolo Spriano, *Storia del Partito comunista italiano. III: I fronti popolari, Stalin, la guerra* (Torino: Giulio Einaudi Editore, 1976) p. 272; Agosti, *Palmiro Togliatti*, p. 243; Hernández, *Yo fui un ministro de Stalin*, pp. 334-6; Jesús Hernández, *La grande trahison* (Paris: Fasquelle Editeurs, 1953) pp. 184-5; Howson, *Aircraft of the Spanish Civil War*, pp. 23-4, 107.

34. Martínez Bande, *El final*, pp. 328-30.

35. O. D. Gallagher, 'Five Waited for a City to Die', in Hanighen, ed., *Nothing but Danger*, pp. 228-40.

36. Martínez Bande, *El final*, pp. 330-3; Zugazagoitia, *Guerra y vicisitudes*, II, p. 242; Salas Larrazábal, *Historia del Ejército popular de la República*, II, pp. 2318-25.

37. Gooden to Foreign Office, 28 March 1939, TNA, FO 371/24154, W5244/2082/41; Rodríguez Miaja, *Testimonios y remembranzas*, pp. 11, 63-72, 101-19; Casado, *Así cayó Madrid*, pp. 254-5, 67. On the gift from Haile Selassie, see Romero, *El final*, p. 423. For the last interview, see the *Daily Express*, 27 March 1939.

38. Prieto to Negrín to, 3 July 1939, *Epistolario Prieto y Negrín*, p. 116; Lázaro Somoza Silva, *El general Miaja (biografía de un heroe)* (Mexico City: Editorial Tyris, 1944) pp. 273-8.

39. Guzmán, *La muerte*, pp. 197-9.

40. García Pradas, *Cómo terminó la guerra*, p. 132; Viñas and Sánchez Hernández, *El desplome*, p. 297.

41. *ABC* (Madrid), 28 March 1939; Casado, *The Last Days*, pp. 238-47; Mintz and Kelsey, *Consejo Nacional de Defensa*, pp. 123-4, following *Castilla Libre*, conflate the speeches of González Marín and Casado.

42. Guzmán, *La muerte*, pp. 200-7; García Pradas, *Cómo terminó la guerra*, pp. 124-7.

43. Procedimiento sumarísimo de urgencia contra Rafael Sánchez Guerra, AHN, FC-Causa General, Caja 1525, Exp. 14; Sánchez-Guerra, *Mis prisiones*, pp. 48-50; Casado, *Así cayó Madrid*, p. 287.

44. Guzmán, *La muerte*, pp. 213, 226.

45. Report of the International Delegation for Spanish Evacuation and Relief; Sir George Young, 'Agreed Account of Activities of the Delegation', Family Archive of Sir George and Lady Young.

46. Young, 'Agreed Account of Activities', p. 1; Domínguez Aragón, *Los vencedores*, pp. 256-78.

47. Laurin Zilliacus, 'The Last Days of Madrid', *New Statesman and Nation*, 23 December 1939, pp. 929-30. The claim by Casado to which Zilliacus refers, Casado, *The Last Days*, pp. 255-6.

48. André Ulmann, 'La Tragédie d'Alicante: 4.000 républicains, l'élite d'une nation amie, ont été livrés à l'assassinat et M. Bonnet en porte la responsabilité', *La Lumière*, 7 April 1939.

49. Guzmán, *La muerte*, pp. 251–7, 270–9, 303; Rodríguez Vega, 'Notas autobiográficas', p. 290; García Pradas, *Cómo terminó la guerra*, pp. 134–5.

50. Carrillo's telegram, Cañas, 'Marzo de 1939', AFPI, ARLF-172-30, pp. 42–4; E. Jorge Moreno, 'Notas sobre los últimos días de la guerra civil española', AFPI, AAVV, AEJM-83-9, p. 2; Eladi Mainer Cabanes, 'L'exili del coronel Casado amb el Consell de Defensa pel port de Gandia després de la cerca infructuosa d'una pau pactada', in José Miguel Santacreu Soler, ed., *Una presó amb vistes al mar. El drama del Port d'Alacant, Març de 1939* (Valencia: Tres i Quatre, 2008) pp. 138, 144.

51. Casado, *The Last Days*, pp. 262–3, 272–3; Español Bouché, *Madrid 1939*, pp. 67, 262.

52. García Pradas, *Cómo terminó la guerra de España*, pp. 140–1; Guzmán, *La muerte*, p. 303; Casado, *Así cayó Madrid*, p. 281.

53. Gooden to FO, 28 March, 29 March 1939, TNA, FO 371/24154, W5244/2082/41, W5263/2082/41; Tovey to Admiralty, TNA, FO 371/24154, W5263/2082/41; Mounsey to Butler, 29 March 1939, TNA, FO 371/24154, W5467/2082/41, W6012/2082/41, W6705/2082/41, W6795/2082/41.

54. Max Aub, *Campo de los almendros* (Madrid: Ediciones Alfaguara, 1981) p. 238.

55. Gooden to Halifax, 12 April 1939, TNA, FO 371/24154, W6705/2082/41.

56. Javier Juárez, *Comandante Durán. Leyenda y tragedia de un intelectual en armas* (Barcelona: Debate, 2008)

pp. 243–7; Aub, *Campo de los almendros*, pp. 238–40; Horacio Vázquez-Rial, *El soldado de porcelana* (Barcelona: Ediciones B, 1997) pp. 547–9.

57. Mainer Cabanes, 'L'exili del coronel Casado', pp. 145–6.

58. E. Jorge Moreno, 'Notas sobre los últimos días de la guerra civil española', AFPI, AAVV, AEJM-83-9, p. 3.

59. Mainer Cabanes, 'L'exili del coronel Casado', pp. 147–8.

60. TNA, FO 371/24154, W5263/2082/41, W5264/2082/41, W5943/2082/41; Mainer Cabanes, 'L'exili del coronel Casado', pp. 150–3; Eladi Mainar, José Miguel Santacreu and Robert Llopis, *Gandia i el seu port, març de 1939. El penúltim acte de la Segona República Espanyola* (Gandía: CEIC Alfons el Vell, 2010) pp. 136–40; Alpert, *La guerra civil española en el mar*, pp. 353, 360–2; Alpert, *The Republican Army in the Spanish Civil War*, pp. 284–5; Casado, *Así cayó Madrid*, pp. 269–84.

61. Casado, *Así cayó Madrid*, pp. 283, 287.

62. Gooden to FO, 26 March 1939, TNA, FO 371/24154, W5088/2082/41.

63. Juan Martínez Leal, 'El *Stanbrook*. Un barco mítico en la memoria de los exiliados españoles', *Pasado y Memoria. Revista de Historia Contemporánea*, vol. 4, 2005, pp. 66–7; Santiago Garcés, interview with Heleno Saña, 'Habla un ayudante de Negrín', *Índice*, 15 June 1974, p. 10.

64. Martínez Leal, 'El *Stanbrook*', pp. 67–81; José Miguel Santacreu Soler, 'El bloqueig naval franquista i la sort dels darrers vaixells de l'exili del port d'Alacant', in Santacreu Soler, ed., *Una presó amb visites al mar*, pp. 203–33; Francisco Escudero Galante, *Pasajero 2058. La odisea del*

Stanbrook (Alicante: Editorial Club Universitario, 2002) pp. 65–71.

65. AHN, FC-Causa General, Caja 1532, Exp. 30, p. 55; Rodríguez Vega, 'Notas autobiográficas', p. 293; Guzmán, *La muerte*, pp. 196ff; Laurin Zilliacus, letter to *New Statesman and Nation*, 23 December 1939; Domínguez Aragón, *Los vencedores*, p. 260; Rodriguez Chaos, *24 años en la carcel*, pp. 11–17; Manuel García Corachán, *Memorias de un presidiario (en las cárceles franquistas)* (Valencia: Publicacions de la Universitat de València, 2005) pp. 27–31; Alberto Rovighi and Filippo Stefani, *La partecipazione italiana alla guerra civile Spagnola*, 2 vols (Rome: Ufficio Storico dello Stato Maggiore dell'Esercito, 1992–3) II, i, pp. 427–30; Vicente Ramos, *La guerra civil (1936–1939) en la provincia de Alicante*, 3 vols (Alicante: Ediciones Biblioteca Alicantina, 1973) III, pp. 198–9.

66. Rodríguez Vega, 'Notas autobiográficas', pp. 291–5; M. Lafuente, 'Lo que ocurrio en el puerto de Alicante', AFPI, AAVV, AEJM-83-9) pp. 2–6; Eladi Mainer Cabanes, José Miguel Santacreu Soler and Ricard Camil Torres Fabra, 'El parany dels darrers dies de la guerra al port d'Alacant', in Santacreu Soler, ed., *Una presó amb vistes al mar*, pp. 157–95; Fraser, *Blood of Spain*, pp. 502–7.

67. Eduardo de Guzmán, *El año de la victoria* (Madrid: G. del Toro, 1974) pp. 19–23; Juan Caba Guijarro, *Mil gritos tuvo el dolor en el campo de 'Albatera'* (Ciudad Real: Imprenta Angama, 1983) pp. 3–9; Rodriguez Chaos, *24 años en la cárcel*, pp. 18–24; Tomasa Cuevas Gutiérrez, *Cárcel de mujeres (1939–1945)*, 2 vols (Barcelona: Sirocco Books, 1985) II, pp. 87–8.

68. Rodríguez Vega, 'Notas autobiográficas', pp. 295–6; Vicent Gabarda Cebellán, *Els afusellaments al Pais Valenciá (1938–1956)* (Valencia: Edicions Alfons el Magnànim, 1993) pp. 58–61; Guzmán, *La muerte*, pp. 387–94; Caba Guijarro, *Mil gritos*, pp. 9–13.

69. Guzmán, *El año de la victoria*, pp. 31, 43–6; García Corachán, *Memorias de un presidiario*, pp. 31–3; Javier Navarro Navarro, 'El terror com a epíleg a una guerra. La repressió franquista al País Valenciá: dos testimonis', in Pelai Pagès i Blanch, ed., *La repressió franquista al País Valencià. Primera trobada d'investigadors de la Comissió de la veritat* (Valencia: Tres i Quatre, 2009) pp. 307–17.

Epilogue: Repent at Leisure?

1. Sánchez-Guerra, *Mis prisiones*, pp. 53–60; Saborit, *Besteiro*, p. 300.

2. Besteiro, *Cartas*, p. 121.

3. Procedimiento sumarísimo de urgencia contra Rafael Sánchez Guerra, in Procedimientos sumarísimos seguidos por 'Tribunales Militares Nacionales' (Auditoría de Guerra del Ejército de Ocupación), AHN, FC-Causa General, Caja 1525, Exp. 14, pp. 201–20, 224, 235–8, 249, 266–9; Comandante Franco, *Diario de una bandera* (Madrid: Editorial Pueyo, 1922) p. 130.

4. Elías Díaz, *Los viejos maestros. La reconstrucción de la razón* (Madrid: Alianza, 1994) pp. 61–2.

5. Prieto, *Convulsiones*, III, pp. 334–7.

6. In Saborit, *Besteiro*, pp. 293–5.

7. On the imprisonment and death of Besteiro, see 'Notas de Dolores Cebrián', in Besteiro, *Cartas*, pp. 177–202; Saborit, *Besteiro*, pp. 301–15.

8. Zulueta, 'Introducción' to Besteiro, *Cartas*, p. 23.

9. Sánchez-Guerra, *Mis prisiones*, pp. 53–5.

10. Rodríguez Vega, 'Notas autobiográficas', pp. 329–30.

11. Domingo, *El ángel rojo*, pp. 29–31, 311–46; Raimundo Fernández Cuesta, *Testimonio, recuerdos y reflexiones* (Madrid: Ediciones Dyrsa, 1985) pp. 95–6; Leopoldo Huidobro, *Memorias de un finlandés* (Madrid: Ediciones Españolas, 1939) pp. 212–13. I am especially grateful to Alfonso Domingo for sharing with me his research on the trial.

12. Testimonio del procedimiento sumarísimo de urgencia seguido contra el Jefe del SIM, Ángel Pedrero García, AHN, FC-Causa General, Caja 1520, Exp. 2, pp. 153–4; Guzmán, *El año de la victoria*, pp. 102–3.

13. Emilio Majuelo, *La generación del sacrificio. Ricardo Zabalza 1898–1940* (Tafalla: Editorial Txalaparta, 2008) pp. 264–5, 276–82, 333–5.

14. Mera, *Guerra, exilio y cárcel*, pp. 228–67; Indalecio Prieto, *Palabras al viento*, 2nd edn (Mexico City: Ediciones Oasis, 1969) pp. 191–6.

15. Íñiguez, *Enciclopedia histórica del anarquismo español*, pp. 707–8, 775–6, 969–70, 1546, 1740.

16. Bahamonde, *Madrid 1939*, pp. 217–18; *Crónica de la guerra española. No apta para irreconciliables*, 5 vols (Buenos Aires: Editorial Codex, 1966) V, p. 388.

17. Procedimiento sumarísimo contra Diego Medina Garijo, AHN, FC-Causa General, Caja 1525, Exp. 14, pp. 299, 306, 314–53, 363–419.

18. Casado to Rafael Fernández de la Calzada, 26 March 1940, Archivo Rafael Fernández de la Calzada y Ferrer, Archivo General Militar de Ávila (henceforth AGMAV), C.1124, 1/1, 1/2, 1/3.

19. Bahamonde, *Madrid 1939*, pp. 218–20.

20. *Ibid.*, pp. 220–1; Rojo, *Vicente Rojo*, p. 409.

21. Pedro María Egea Bruno, 'Miguel Buiza Fernández-Palacios, Almirante habilitado', in García Fernández, ed., *25 militares de la República*, pp. 183–91; Fernández Díaz, *El exilio de los marinos republicanos*, pp. 150–4, 273–82; Antonio Vilanova, *Los olvidados. Los exilados españoles en la segunda guerra mundial* (Paris: Ruedo Ibérico, 1969) pp. 363–70; Evelyn Mesquida, *La Nueve. Los españoles que liberaron París* (Barcelona: Ediciones B, 2008) pp. 99–101, 120; Romain Durand, *De Giraud à de Gaulle. Le Corps franc d'Afrique* (Paris: Harmattan, 1999) p. 156. I am indebted to Dr Robert Coale for additional information about Buiza.

22. Eduardo Buil, '25 días de confusión y derrumbamiento', AFPI, AAVV, AEJM-83-9, p. 5.

23. Viñas, 'Playing with History and Hiding Treason: Colonel Casado's Untrustworthy Memoirs and the End of the Spanish Civil War', pp. 298–300. On the advance, see Luis Araquistain to Francisco Largo Caballero, 7 May 1939, Largo Caballero, *Obras completas*, XIII, pp. 5178–9.

24. The details of her failed marriage and subsequent divorce are taken from the *Singapore Free Press and Mercantile Advertiser*, 8 February 1939. Her translation of the letters of Antoine de Saint-Exupéry, *Wartime Writings 1939–1944* (New York: Harcourt, 1986).

25. Casado to Fernández de la Calzada, 15 June 1949, 8 June 1950, 15 November 1951, 3 December 1952, 3 November 1953, AGMAV, C.1124,1/45, 51, 58, 62, 67.

26. Viñas and Hernández Sánchez, *El desplome*, pp. 292–4.

27. Mera, *Guerra, exilio y cárcel*, p. 239.

28. Draft of Casado's letter reproduced in Viñas, 'Playing with History and Hiding Treason: Colonel Casado's

Untrustworthy Memoirs and the End of the Spanish Civil War', pp. 322–3.

29. Casado to Juan López 07-11-45, 05-12-45, AGRM, AJLS, JLS,998/1,167; JLS,998/1,172.

30. Casado to Juan López, 9 April 1941, AGRM, AJLS, JLS,998/1,60.

31. Casado to Juan López, 1 January 1947, AGRM, AJLS, JLS,998/1,192.

32. Casado to Fernández de la Calzada, Undated, May or June 1949, AGMAV, C.1124, 1/44.

33. Casado to Fernández de la Calzada, 23 March 1949, AGMAV, C.1124, 1/41–2.

34. Casado to Fernández de la Calzada, 15 June 1949, AGMAV, C.1124, 1/45. Casado's emphasis.

35. Casado to Fernández de la Calzada, 29 June 1949, AGMAV, C.1124, 1/43.

36. Casado to Fernández de la Calzada, 2 December 1954, 8 March, 21 August, 15 October 1956, 24 July 1959, AGMAV, C.1124, 1/73, 1/83, 1/87, 1/88, 1/108.

37. Casado to Fernández de la Calzada, 14 August 1954, 9, 19 May, 3 August 1955, 31 May 1956, 6 May, 20 August 1957, AGMAV, C.1124, 1/72, 1/75, 1/76, 1/79, 1/84–5, 1/90–1, 1/95.

38. Casado to Fernández de la Calzada, 2 December 1954, 14 June 1958, 29 January, 6 July, 20 September 1960, 9, 29 January, 4 May, 24 June 1961, AGMAV, C.1124, 1/76, 1/97, 1/116, 1/126, 1/132, 1/137–8, 1/146, 1/148–9; Ángel Viñas, 'Segismundo Casado López. Colonel', in García Fernández, ed., 25 militares de la República, pp. 239–42.

39. Casado to Fernández de la Calzada, 24 November 1962, 25 May 1964, 10 June 1965, AGMAV, C.1124, 1/174, 1/188, 1/190; Viñas, 'Segismundo Casado', pp. 243–5.

40. Casado to Fernández de la Calzada, 1 April, 5 June, 2 August 1967, Fernández de la Calzada to Casado, 27 July 1967, AGMAV, C.1124, 1/217, 1/226, 1/229–30, 1/231–2; Viñas, 'Segismundo Casado', pp. 246–53.

41. Minutes of Actas de la Diputación Permanente. Congreso de los Diputados, 31 de marzo de 1939, pp. 6, 7 and 13.

42. Bowers to Fischer, 18 February 1939, MC#024, Louis Fischer Papers, Seeley G. Mudd Manuscript Library, Princeton University.

43. Jackson, Juan Negrín, pp. 294–305.

44. Denis Smyth, 'The Politics of Asylum, Juan Negrín and the British Government in 1940', in Richard Langhorne, ed., Diplomacy and Intelligence during the Second World War (Cambridge: Cambridge University Press, 2003) pp. 126–46.

45. The complex story of Negrín's activities between the end of the Spanish Civil War and his death in 1956 is recounted fully in Moradiellos, Negrín, pp. 461–601.

46. Jackson, Juan Negrín, pp. 9–11, 30, 294.

47. Herbert L. Matthews, Half of Spain Died. A Reappraisal of the Spanish Civil War (New York: Charles Scribner's Sons, 1973) p. 231.

48. Vidarte, Todos fuimos culpables, p. 843.

ILLUSTRATION CREDITS

BIBLIOGRAPHY

PRIMARY SOURCES

(i) Unpublished Sources
Archivo General Militar de Ávila: Archivo Rafael Fernández de la Calzada y
   Ferrer
Archivo General Regional de Murcia: Archivo Juan López Sánchez
Archivo Histórico Nacional, Madrid:
   Causa General
   Archivo Marcelino Pascua
   Archivo General Rojo
Archivo Fundación Juan Negrín
Hoover Institution, Bolloten Collection, Miaja Papers
Archivo Histórico Fundación Pablo Iglesias
Archivo Histórico Partido Comunista de España
Papers of Sir George Young (Private Collection)
The National Archives (London):
   Cabinet Office Papers
   Foreign Office: FO 371 General Correspondence
   Foreign Office: FO 425 Confidential Prints
Hansard, *House of Commons Debates*, Fifth Series

(ii) Printed Collections of Official Documents and Speeches
Álvarez, Santiago, *Negrín, personalidad histórica. Documentos* (Madrid:
   Ediciones de la Torre, 1994)
Documentos inéditos para la historia del Generalísimo Franco, vol. I (Madrid:
   Fundación Nacional Francisco Franco, 1992)
Documents on British Foreign Policy 3rd Series, vol. IV (London: HMSO,
   1951)
Documents on German Foreign Policy, Series D, vol. III (London: HMSO,
   1951)
Foreign Relations of the United States 1939, vol. II (Washington: US
   Government Printing Office, 1956)

Franco Bahamonde, Francisco, *Palabras del Caudillo 19 abril 1937–7 diciembre 1942* (Madrid: Ediciones de la Vicesecretaría de Educación Popular, 1943)

Negrín, Juan, et al., *Documentos políticos para la historia de la Republica Española* (Mexico City: Coleccion Malaga, 1945)

Negrín, Juan, *Textos y discursos políticos*, ed. Enrique Moradiellos (Madrid: Centro de Estudios Políticos y Constitucionales & Fundación Juan Negrín, 2010)

(iii) Memoirs and Letters of Protagonists

Aguillera Gómez, Ángel, *La historia silenciada (1930–1989)* (Almería: Instituto de Estudios Almerienses, 1990)

Álvarez del Vayo, Julio, *Freedom's Battle* (London: Heinemann, 1940)

Álvarez del Vayo, Julio, *The Last Optimist* (London: Putnam, 1950)

Álvarez, Santiago, *Los Comisarios Políticos en el Ejército Popular de la República* (Sada-A Coruña: Ediciós do Castro, 1989)

Ansó, Mariano, *Yo fui ministro de Negrín* (Barcelona: Editorial Planeta, 1976)

Arenillas de Chaves, Ignacio, *El Proceso de Besteiro* (Madrid: Revista de Occidente, 1976)

Arnaiz, Aurora, *Retrato hablado de Luisa Julián* (Madrid: Compañía Literaria, 1996)

Azaña, Manuel, *Apuntes de memoria inéditos y cartas 1938–1939–1940*, ed. Enrique de Rivas, 2 vols (Valencia: Pre-Textos, 1990)

Azaña, Manuel, *Obras completas*, 4 vols (Mexico City: Ediciones Oasis, 1966–8)

Azaña, Manuel, *Obras completas*, ed. Santos Juliá, 7 vols (Madrid: Centro de Estudios Políticos y Constitucionales/Taurus, 2008)

Azcárate, Pablo de, *En defensa de la República. Con Negrín en el exilio* (Barcelona: Editorial Crítica, 2010)

Azcárate, Pablo de, *Mi embajada en Londres durante la guerra civil española* (Barcelona: Ariel, 1976)

Banac, Ivo, ed., *The Diary of Georgi Dimitrov* (New Haven: Yale University Press, 2003)

Besteiro, Julián, *Cartas desde la prisión* (Madrid: Alianza Editorial, 1988)

Besteiro, Julián, *Marxismo y anti-marxismo* (Madrid: Gráfica Socialista, 1935)

Besteiro, Julián, *Obras completas*, 3 vols (Madrid: Centro de Estudios Constitucionales, 1983)

Bouthelier, Antonio and López Mora, José, *Ocho días de revuelta comunista. Madrid 5–13 marzo 1939* (Madrid: Editora Nacional, 1940)

Bowers, Claude G., *My Mission to Spain* (London: Gollancz, 1954)

Cadogan, Sir Alexander, *The Diaries of Sir Alexander Cadogan 1938–1945*, ed. David Dilkes (London: Cassell, 1971)

Carrillo, Santiago, *Memorias*, 2nd edn (Barcelona: Editorial Planeta, 2006)

Carrillo, Wenceslao, *El último episodio de la guerra civil española. Marzo de 1939* (Toulouse: Juventudes Socialistas Españoles, 1945)

Casado, Colonel Segismundo, *The Last Days of Madrid. The End of the Spanish Republic* (London: Peter Davies, 1939)

Casado, Coronel Segismundo, *Así cayó Madrid. Último episodio de la guerra civil española* (Madrid: Guadiana de Publicaciones, 1968)

Casanova, Manuel, *La guerra de España. El Frente Popular abrió las puertas a Franco* (Barcelona: Editorial Fontamara, 1978)

Castro Delgado, Enrique, *Hombres made in Moscú* (Barcelona: Luis de Caralt, 1965)

Causa General, *La dominación roja en España* (Madrid: Ministerio de Justicia, 1945)

Cervera Valderrama, Almirante Juan, *Memorias de Guerra (1936–1939)* (Madrid: Editora Nacional, 1968)

Cordón, Antonio, *Trayectoria (Recuerdos de un artillero)* (Paris: Colección Ebro, 1971)

Cordón, Antonio, *Trayectoria (Recuerdos de un artillero)*, ed. Ángel Viñas (Seville: Espuela de Plata, 2008)

Dallin, Alexander and Firsov, Fridrikh Igorevich, eds, *Dimitrov and Stalin, 1934–1943. Letters from the Soviet Archives (Annals of Communism)* (New Haven: Yale University Press, 2000)

Domínguez Aragonés, Edmundo, *Los vencedores de Negrín*, 2nd edn (Mexico City: Ediciones Roca, 1976)

Encinas Moral, Ángel L., ed., *Las causas de la derrota de la República española. Informe elaborado por Stoyán Mínev (Stepanov), Delegado en España de la Komintern (1937–1939)* (Madrid: Miraguano Ediciones, 2003)

Estado Español, Ministerio de la Gobernación, *Dictamen de la comisión sobre ilegitimidad de poderes actuantes en 18 de julio de 1936* (Barcelona: Editora Nacional, 1939)

Falcón, Irene, *Asalto a los cielos. Mi vida junto a Pasionaria* (Madrid: Temas de Hoy, 1996)

Fernsworth, Lawrence, *Spain's Struggle for Freedom* (Boston: Beacon Press, 1957)

Ferrandiz Alborz, F., *La bestia contra España. Reportaje de los últimos días de la guerra española y los primeros de la bestia triunfante* (Montevideo: CISA, 1951)

Fischer, Louis, *Men and Politics. An Autobiography* (London: Jonathan Cape, 1941)

Franco, Comandante, *Diario de una bandera* (Madrid: Editorial Pueyo, 1922)

García, Regina, *Yo he sido marxista. El cómo y porqué de una conversión*, 2nd edn (Madrid: Editora Nacional, 1952)

García Pradas, José, *Cómo terminó la guerra de España* (Buenos Aires: Ediciones Imán, 1940)

García Pradas, José, *Rusia y España* (Paris: Ediciones Tierra y Libertad, 1948)

García Pradas, José, *¡Teníamos que perder!* (Madrid: G. del Toro, 1974)

Gómez Serrano, Eliseo, *Diarios de la guerra civil (1936–1939)* (Alicante: Universidad de Alicante, 2008)

Guzmán, Eduardo de, *El año de la victoria* (Madrid: G. del Toro, 1974)

Guzmán, Eduardo de, *La muerte de la esperanza* (Madrid: G. del Toro, 1973)

Guzmán, Eduardo de, *Nosotros, los asesinos (Memorias de la guerra de España* (Madrid: G. del Toro, 1976)

Hanighen, Frank C., ed., *Nothing but Danger* (New York: National Travel Club, 1939)

Hernández, Jesús, *La grande trahison* (Paris: Fasquelle Editeurs, 1953)

Hernández, Jesús, *Yo fui un ministro de Stalin* (Madrid: G. del Toro, 1974)

Hidalgo de Cisneros, Ignacio, *Cambio de rumbo (Memorias)*, 2 vols (Bucharest: Colección Ebro, 1964)

Hodgson, Sir Robert, *Spain Resurgent* (London: Hutchinson, 1953)

Huidobro, Leopoldo, *Memorias de un finlandés* (Madrid: Ediciones Españolas, 1939)

Ibárruri, Dolores, *El único camino* (Madrid: Editorial Castalia, 1992)

Ibárruri, Dolores, *En la lucha. Palabras y hechos 1936–1939* (Moscow: Editorial Progreso, 1968)

Ibárruri, Dolores, et al., *Guerra y revolución en España 1936–39*, 4 vols (Moscow: Editorial Progreso, 1966–77)

Lamoneda, Ramón, *Posiciones políticas-documentos-correspondencia* (Mexico City: Roca, 1976)

Largo Caballero, Francisco, *Mis recuerdos. Cartas a un amigo* (Mexico City: Editores Unidos, 1954)

Largo Caballero, Francisco, *Obras completas*, 16 vols (Madrid and Barcelona: Fundación Largo Caballero/Instituto Monsa, 2003–9)

Líster, Enrique, *¡Basta! Una aportación a la lucha por la recuperación del Partido*, 2nd edn (Madrid: G. del Toro, 1978)

Líster, Enrique, *Nuestra guerra* (Paris: Colección Ebro, 1966)

López, Juan, *Una misión sin importancia (memorias de un sindicalista)* (Madrid: Editora Nacional, 1972)

Martínez Barrio, Diego, *Memorias* (Barcelona: Editorial Planeta, 1983)

Martínez Paricio, Jesús I., ed., *Los papeles del general Vicente Rojo. Un militar de la generación rota* (Madrid: Espasa Calpe, 1989)

Méndez, Rafael, *Caminos inversos. Vivencias de ciencia y guerra* (Mexico City: Fondo de Cultura Económica, 1987)

Mera, Cipriano, *Guerra, exilio y cárcel de un anarcosindicalista* (Paris: Ruedo Ibérico, 1976)

Modesto, Juan, *Soy del Quinto Regimiento (Notas de la guerra española)* (Paris: Colección Ebro, 1969)

Morla Lynch, Carlos, *España sufre. Diarios de guerra en el Madrid republicano* (Seville: Editorial Renacimiento, 2008)

Perea Capulino, Juan, *Los culpables. Recuerdos de la guerra civil 1936–1939* (Barcelona: Ediciones Flor del Viento, 2007)

Pérez Salas, Coronel Jesús, *Guerra en España (1936 a 1939)* (Mexico City: Imprenta Grafos, 1947)

Prieto, Indalecio, *Cómo y por qué salí del Ministerio de Defensa Nacional. Intrigas de los rusos en España (Texto taquigráfico del informe pronunciado el 9 de agosto de 1938 ante el Comité Nacional del Partido Socialista Obrero Español)* (Mexico City: Impresos y Papeles, S. de R.L., 1940)

Prieto, Indalecio, *Convulsiones de España. Pequeños detalles de grandes sucesos*, 3 vols (Mexico City: Oasis, 1967–9)

Prieto, Indalecio, *Palabras al viento*, 2nd edn (Mexico City: Ediciones Oasis, 1969)

Prieto, Indalecio and Negrín, Juan, *Epistolario Prieto y Negrín. Puntos de vista sobre el desarrollo y consecuencias de la guerra civil española* (Paris: Imprimerie Nouvelle, 1939)

Rivas Cherif, Cipriano de, *Retrato de un desconocido. Vida de Manuel Azaña* (Barcelona: Ediciones Grijalbo, 1980)

Rodríguez Miaja, Fernando, *Testimonios y remembranzas. Mis recuerdos de los últimos meses de la guerra de España* (Mexico City: Imprenta de Juan Pablos, 1997)

Rodríguez Vega, José, 'Notas autobiográficas', *Estudios de Historia Social* (Madrid), no. 30, July–September 1984, pp. 267–346

Rojo, General Vicente, *¡Alerta los pueblos! Estudio político-militar del período final de la guerra española*, 2nd edn (Barcelona: Ariel, 1974)

Rojo, General Vicente, *Así fue la defensa de Madrid* (Mexico City: Ediciones Era, 1967)

Rojo, General Vicente, *España heroica. Diez bocetos de la guerra española*, 3rd edn (Barcelona: Ariel, 1975)

Rojo, Vicente, *Historia de la guerra civil española* (Barcelona: RBA Libros, 2010)

Sánchez Guerra, Rafael, *Mis prisiones. Memorias de un condenado por Franco* (Buenos Aires: Editorial Claridad, 1946)

Sanz, Ricardo, *Los que fuimos a Madrid. Columna Durruti 26 División* (Toulouse: Imprimerie Dulaurier, 1969)

Tagüeña Lacorte, Manuel, *Testimonio de dos guerras* (Mexico City: Ediciones Oasis, 1973)

Tierno Galván, Enrique, *Cabos sueltos* (Barcelona: Bruguera, 1981)

Togliatti, Palmiro, *Escritos sobre la guerra de España* (Barcelona: Editorial Crítica, 1980)

Togliatti, Palmiro, *Opere IV: 1935–1944* (Rome: Editori Riuniti, 1979)

Valdés Larrañaga, Manuel, *De la Falange al Movimiento (1936–1952)* (Madrid: Fundación Nacional Francisco Franco, 1994)

Vanni, Ettore, *Io comunista in Russia* (Bologna: Capelli Editore, 1948)

Vanni, Ettore, *Yo comunista en Rusia* (Madrid: Ediciones Destino, 1950)

Vaupshasov, Stanislav, *Na trevozhnykh perelrestkakh: zapiski chekista* (Moskva: Voenizdat, 1988) [http://militera.lib.ru/memo/russian/vaupshasov/19. html]

Vázquez Ocaña, Fernando, *Pasión y muerte de la Segunda República española*, 2nd edn (Madrid: Biblioteca de la Cátedra del Exilio/Fondo de Cultura Económica de España, 2007)

Vega Díaz, Francisco, 'El último día de Negrín en España', *Claves de la Razón Práctica*, no. 22, May 1992, pp. 60–3

Vidarte, Juan-Simeón, *Todos fuimos culpables* (Mexico City: Fondo de Cultura Económica, 1973)

Zugazagoitia, Julian, *Guerra y vicisitudes de los españoles*, 2nd edn, 2 vols (Paris: Librería Española, 1968)

SECONDARY WORKS

Agosti, Aldo, *Palmiro Togliatti* (Torino: UTET, 1996)

Aguilera Povedano, Manuel, *Compañeros y camaradas. Las luchas entre antifascistas en la Guerra Civil española* (Madrid: Actas Editorial, 2012)

Alcofar Nassaes, José Luis, *Los asesores soviéticos en la guerra civil española: los mejicanos* (Barcelona: Dopesa, 1971)

Alía Miranda, Francisco, *La guerra civil en la retaguardia. Conflicto y revolución en la provincia de Ciudad Real (1936–1939)* (Ciudad Real: Diputación Provincial, 1994)

Alonso, Bruno, *La flota republicana y la guerra civil de España (Memorias de su comisario general)* (Seville: Espuela de Plata, 2006)

Alpert, Michael, *La guerra civil española en el mar* (Madrid: Siglo XX, 1987)

Alpert, Michael, *The Republican Army in the Spanish Civil War 1936–1939* (Cambridge: Cambridge University Press, 2013)

Álvarez, Santiago, *Negrín, personalidad histórica. Biografía*, 2 vols (Madrid: Ediciones de la Torre, 1994)

Álvarez, Santiago, *Osorio-Tafall. Su personalidad, su aportación, su historia* (Sada-A Coruña: Ediciós do Castro, 1992)

Álvaro Dueñas, Manuel, *'Por ministerio de la ley y voluntad del Caudillo'. La Juridicción Especial de Responsabilidades Políticas (1939–1945)* (Madrid: Centro de Estudios Políticos y Constitucionales, 2006)

Ambou, Juan, *Los comunistas en la resistencia nacional republicana (La guerra en Asturias, el País Vasco y Santander)* (Madrid: Editorial Hispamerica, 1978)

Anderson, Peter, 'The Chetwode Commission for Prisoner Exchange and British Diplomatic Responses to Violence behind the Lines during the

Spanish Civil War', *European History Quarterly*, vol. 42, no. 2, 2012, pp. 235–60

Anuario Militar de España (Madrid: Ministerio de la Guerra, 1936)

Araquistain, Luis, *Sobre la guerra civil y en la emigración* (Madrid: Espasa Calpe, 1983)

Arasa, Daniel, *Entre la cruz y la República. Vida y muerte del general Escobar* (Barcelona: Styria, 2008)

Aróstegui, Julio, *Largo Caballero. El tesón y la quimera* (Barcelona: Debate, 2013)

Aróstegui, Julio and Martínez, Jesús, *La Junta de Defensa de Madrid* (Madrid: Comunidad de Madrid, 1984)

Aub, Max, *Campo de los almendros* (Madrid: Ediciones Alfaguara, 1981)

Aznar, Manuel, *Historia militar de la guerra de España (1936–1939)* (Madrid: Ediciones Idea, 1940)

Bahamonde Magro, Ángel, *Madrid 1939. La conjura del coronel Casado* (Madrid: Ediciones Cátedra, 2014)

Bahamonde Magro, Ángel and Cervera Gil, Javier, *Así terminó la Guerra de España* (Madrid: Marcial Pons, 1999)

Benavides, Manuel D., *La escuadra la mandan los cabos*, 2nd edn (Mexico City: Ediciones Roca, 1976)

Blanco Escolá, Carlos, *Vicente Rojo, el general que humilló a Franco* (Barcelona: Editorial Planeta, 2003)

Blas Zabaleta, Patricio de and Blas Martín-Merás, Eva, *Julián Besteiro. Nadar contra corriente* (Madrid: Algaba Ediciones, 2002)

Bolloten, Burnett, *The Spanish Civil War. Revolution and Counterrevolution* (Hemel Hempstead: Harvester Wheatsheaf, 1991)

Broué, Pierre and Témime, Emile, *The Revolution and the Civil War in Spain* (London: Faber & Faber, 1972)

Caba Guijarro, Juan, *Mil gritos tuvo el dolor en el campo de 'Albatera'* (Ciudad Real: Imprenta Angama, 1983)

Campanario, Juan Miguel, 'Los ascensos y nombramientos de militares comunistas en marzo de 1939, la sublevación del coronel Segismundo Casado y el hallazgo del Diario Oficial del Ministerio de Defensa Nacional del día 5 de marzo cuya existencia se desconocía', Ponencia presentada en el X Congreso de la Asociación de Historia Contemporánea, que se celebró en Santander el 16–17 de septiembre de 2010

Campanario, Juan Miguel, Díez Hernando, Carlos and Cervera Gil, Javier, 'El enigma del general republicano Manuel Matallana Gómez, Jefe del Estado Mayor de Miaja: ¿Fue un miembro activo de la Quinta Columna?', paper delivered at the Conference 'La Guerra Civil Española, 1936–1939', Madrid, 28 November 2006

Cervera, Javier, *Madrid en guerra. La ciudad clandestina 1936–1939*, 2nd edn (Madrid: Alianza Editorial, 2006)

Cierva, Ricardo de la, *1939. Agonía y victoria (El protocolo 277)* (Barcelona: Editorial Planeta, 1989)

Cierva, Ricardo de la, *La victoria y el caos. A los sesenta años del 1 de abril de 1939* (Madrid: Editorial Fénix, 1999)

Corral, Pedro, *Desertores. La guerra civil que nadie quiere contar* (Barcelona: Debate, 2006)

Crónica de la guerra española. No apta para irreconciliables, 5 vols (Buenos Aires: Editorial Codex, 1966)

Cruanyes, Josep, *El papers de Salamanca. L'espoliació del patrimoni documental de Catalunya* (Barcelona: Edicions 62, 2003)

Cuevas Gutiérrez, Tomasa, *Cárcel de mujeres (1939–1945)*, 2 vols (Barcelona: Sirocco Books, 1985)

Díaz, Elías, *Los viejos maestros. La reconstrucción de la razón* (Madrid: Alianza, 1994)

Domingo, Alfonso, *El ángel rojo. La historia de Melchor Rodríguez, el anarquista que detuvo la represión en el Madrid republicano* (Cordoba: Editorial Almuzara, 2009)

Dunthorn, David J., *Britain and the Spanish Anti-Franco Opposition, 1940–1950* (London: Palgrave, 2000)

Durand, Romain, *De Giraud à de Gaulle. Le Corps franc d'Afrique* (Paris: Harmattan, 1999)

Elorza, Antonio and Bizcarrondo, Marta, *Queridos Camaradas. La Internacional Comunista y España, 1919–1939* (Barcelona: Editorial Planeta, 1999)

Escudero Galante, Francisco, *Pasajero 2058. La odisea del Stanbrook* (Alicante: Editorial Club Universitario, 2002)

Español Bouché, Luis, *Madrid 1939. Del golpe de Casado al final de la guerra civil* (Madrid: Almena Ediciones, 2004)

Fernández Cuesta, Raimundo, *Testimonio, recuerdos y reflexiones* (Madrid: Ediciones Dyrsa, 1985)

Fernández Díaz, Victoria, *El exilio de los marinos republicanos* (Valencia: Universitat de València, 2009)

Fraser, Ronald, *Blood of Spain. The Experience of Civil War 1936–1939* (London: Allen Lane, 1979)

Fraser, Ronald, *Las dos guerras de España* (Barcelona: Editorial Crítica, 2012)

Gabarda Cebellán, Vicent, *Els afusellaments al Pais Valenciá (1938–1956)* (Valencia: Edicions Alfons el Magnànim, 1993)

Gabriel, Pere, *Historia de la UGT. Un sindicalismo de guerra* (Madrid: Siglo XXI, 2011)

Gallego, Gregorio, 'La CNT acuerda sublevarse contra el doctor Negrín', *Historia y Vida*, special issue, 4, 1974

Gallego, Gregorio, *Madrid, corazón que se desangra* (Madrid: G. del Toro, 1976)

García Bilbao, Pedro Alberto, García Bilbao, Xulio and Paramio Roca, P. Carlos, *La represión franquista en Guadalajara* (Guadalajara: Foro por la Memoria de Guadalajara/Ediciones Silente, 2010)

García Corachán, Manuel, *Memorias de un presidiario (en las cárceles franquistas)* (València: Publicacions de la Universitat de València, 2005)

García Fernández, Javier, ed., *25 militares de la República* (Madrid: Ministerio de la Defensa, 2011)

García Oliver, Juan, *El eco de los pasos* (Barcelona: Ruedo Ibérico, 1978)

Gordon, Richard Alan, 'France and the Spanish Civil War', unpublished doctoral thesis (Columbia University, New York, 1971)

Graham, Helen, 'Casado's Ghosts: Demythologizing the End of the Spanish Republic', *Bulletin of Spanish Studies: Hispanic Studies and Researches on Spain, Portugal and Latin America*, vol. 89, nos 7–8, 2012, pp. 255–78

Graham, Helen, *Socialism and War. The Spanish Socialist Party in Power and Crisis, 1936–1939* (Cambridge: Cambridge University Press, 1991)

Graham, Helen, *The Spanish Civil War. A Very Short Introduction* (Oxford: Oxford University Press, 2005)

Graham, Helen, *The Spanish Republic at War 1936–1939* (Cambridge: Cambridge University Press, 2002)

Graham, Helen, *The War and its Shadow. Spain's Long Civil War in Europe's Long Twentieth Century* (Brighton: Sussex Academic Press/Cañada Blanch, 2012)

Grisoni, Dominique and Herzog, Gilles, *Les Brigades de la mer* (Paris: Grasset, 1979)

Hemingway, Ernest, 'Preface', in Gustav Regler, *The Great Crusade* (New York: Longmans Green, 1940)

Hernández Sánchez, Fernando, *Guerra o revolución. El Partido Comunista de España en la guerra civil* (Barcelona: Editorial Crítica, 2010)

Howson, Gerald, *Aircraft of the Spanish Civil War 1936–1939* (London: Putnam, 1990)

Howson, Gerald, *Arms for Spain. The Untold Story of the Spanish Civil War*, 2nd edn (New York: St Martin's Press, 1999)

Iglesias, Ignacio, *La fase final de la guerra civil (De la caída de Barcelona al derrumbamiento de Madrid* (Barcelona: Editorial Planeta, 1977)

Íñiguez, Miguel, *Enciclopedia histórica del anarquismo español*, 3 vols (Vitoria: Asociación Isaac Puente, 2008)

Jackson, Gabriel, *Juan Negrín. Spanish Republican War Leader* (Brighton: Sussex Academic Press, 2010)

Jackson, Gabriel, *The Spanish Republic and the Civil War* (Princeton, NJ: Princeton University Press, 1965)

Jackson, Gabriel and Alba, Víctor, *Juan Negrín* (Barcelona: Ediciones B., 2004)

Juárez, Javier, *Comandante Durán. Leyenda y tragedia de un intelectual en armas* (Barcelona: Debate, 2008)

Juliá, Santos, *Vida y tiempo de Manuel Azaña 1880-1940* (Madrid: Taurus, 2008)

Lacruz, Francisco, *El alzamiento, la revolución y el terror en Barcelona* (Barcelona: Librería Arysel, 1943)

Lamo de Espinosa, Emilio and Contreras, Manuel, *Filosofía y política en Julián Besteiro*, 2nd edn (Madrid: Editorial Sistema, 1990)

Langhorne, Richard, ed., *Diplomacy and Intelligence during the Second World War* (Cambridge: Cambridge University Press, 2003)

Llarch, Joan, *Cipriano Mera. Un anarquista en la guerra civil española* (Barcelona: Producciones Editoriales, 1977)

Llarch, Joan, *Negrín ¡Resistir es vencer!* (Barcelona: Editorial Planeta, 1985)

López Fernández, Antonio, *El general Miaja, defensor de Madrid* (Madrid: G. del Toro, 1975)

Lorenzo, César M., *Los anarquistas españoles y el poder* (Paris: Ruedo Ibérico, 1972)

Mainar, Eladi, Santacreu, José Miguel and Llopis, Robert, *Gandia i el seu port, març de 1939. El penúltim acte de la Segona República Espanyola* (Gandía: CEIC Alfons el Vell, 2010)

Mainar, Eladi, Santacreu, José Miguel and Llopis, Robert, *La agonia de la II República* (Valencia: La Xara, 2014)

Mainer Cabanes, Eladi, 'L'exili del coronel Casado amb el Consell de Defensa pel port de Gandía després de la cerca infructuosa d'una pau pactada', in José Miguel Santacreu Soler, ed., *Una presó amb vistes al mar. El drama del Port d'Alacant, Març de 1939* (Valencia: Tres i Quatre, 2008) pp. 115–56

Mainer Cabanes, Eladi, Santacreu Soler, José Miguel and Torres Fabra, Ricard Camil, 'El parany dels darrers dies de la guerra al port d'Alacant', in Santacreu Soler, ed., *Una presó amb vistes al mar*, pp. 157–95

Majuelo, Emilio, *La generación del sacrificio. Ricardo Zabalza 1898-1940* (Tafalla: Editorial Txalaparta, 2008)

Mario de Coca, Gabriel, *Anti-Caballero. Una crítica marxista de la bolchevización del Partido Socialista Obrero Español* (Madrid: Ediciones Engels, 1936)

Martín Nieto, Isaac, 'Anarcosindicalismo, resistencia y grupos de afinidad. La comisión de propaganda confederal y anarquista (1937–1939)', *El Futuro del Pasado*, no. 1, 2010, pp. 597–611

Martínez Bande, José Manuel, *El final de la guerra civil* (Madrid: Editorial San Martín, 1985)

Martínez Bande, José Manuel, *La batalla del Ebro*, 2nd edn (Madrid: Editorial San Martín, 1988)

Martínez Bande, José Manuel, *La campaña de Cataluña* (Madrid: Editorial San Martín, 1979)

Martínez Bande, José Manuel, *Los cien últimos días de la República* (Barcelona: Luis de Caralt, 1973)

Martínez Leal, Juan, 'El *Stanbrook*. Un barco mítico en la memoria de los exiliados españoles', *Pasado y Memoria. Revista de Historia Contemporánea*, vol. 4, 2005, pp. 65–81

Martínez Leal, Juan, *República y guerra civil en Cartagena (1931–1939)* (Murcia: Universidad de Murcia/Ayuntamiento de Cartagena, 1993)

Matthews, Herbert L., *The Education of a Correspondent* (New York: Harcourt Brace, 1946)

Matthews, Herbert L., *Half of Spain Died. A Reappraisal of the Spanish Civil War* (New York: Charles Scribner's Sons, 1973)

Matthews, Herbert L., *A World in Revolution. A Newspaperman's Memoir* (New York: Charles Scribner's Sons, 1971)

Matthews, James, *Reluctant Warriors. Republican Popular Army and Nationalist Army Conscripts in the Spanish Civil War, 1936–1939* (Oxford: Oxford University Press, 2012)

Matthews, James, '"The Vanguard of Sacrifice"? Political Commissars in the Republican Popular Army during the Spanish Civil War, 1936–1939', *War in History*, vol. 21, no. 82, 2014, pp. 82–101

Mesquida, Evelyn, *La Nueve. Los españoles que liberaron París* (Barcelona: Ediciones B, 2008)

Míguez, Alberto, *El pensamiento filosófico de Julián Besteiro* (Madrid: Taurus, 1971)

Millares Cantero, Sergio, ed., *Juan Negrín el estadista. La tranquila energía de un hombre de Estado* (Las Palmas: Fundación Juan Negrín, 2005)

Mintz, Frank and Kelsey, Graham, eds, *Consejo Nacional de Defensa* (Madrid: Cuadernos de la Guerra Civil, Fundación Salvador Seguí, 1989)

Miralles, Ricardo, *Juan Negrín. La República en guerra* (Madrid: Ediciones Temas de Hoy, 2003)

Montiel, Francisco-Félix, *Un coronel llamado Segismundo. Mentiras y misterios de la guerra de Stalin en España* (Madrid: Editorial Criterio-Libros, 1998)

Moorehead, Caroline, *Martha Gellhorn. A Life* (London: Chatto & Windus, 2003)

Moorehead, Caroline, ed., *Selected Letters of Martha Gellhorn* (London: Chatto & Windus, 2006)

Mora, Constancia de la, *In Place of Splendor* (New York: Harcourt, Brace, 1939)

Moradiellos, Enrique, *Don Juan Negrín López* (Barcelona: Ediciones Península, 2006)

Moradiellos, Enrique, *El reñidero de Europa. Las dimensiones internacionales de la guerra civil española* (Barcelona: Ediciones Península, 2001)

Moradiellos, Enrique, *Juan Negrín López 1892–1956* (Santa Cruz de Tenerife: Parlamento de Canarias, 2005)

Moradiellos, Enrique, *La guerra de España (1936–1939)* (Barcelona: RBA Libros, 2012)

Moradiellos, Enrique, *La perfidia de Albión. El Gobierno británico y la guerra civil española* (Madrid: Siglo XXI, 1996)

Moradiellos, Enrique, *Neutralidad benévola. El Gobierno británico y la insurrección militar española de 1936* (Oviedo: Pentalfa Ediciones, 1990)

Moreno de Alborán y de Reyna, Fernando and Moreno de Alborán y de Reyna, Salvador, *La guerra silenciosa y silenciada. Historia de la campaña naval durante la guerra de 1936–39*, 4 vols (Madrid: Gráficas Lormo, 1998)

Moreno Gómez, Francisco, *La guerra civil en Córdoba (1936–1939)* (Madrid: Editorial Alpuerto, 1985)

Morón, Gabriel, *Política de ayer y política de mañana. Los socialistas ante el problema español* (Mexico City: Talleres Numancia, 1942)

Pagès i Blanch, Pelai, ed., *La repressió franquista al País Valencià. Primera trobada d'investigadors de la Comissió de la veritat* (Valencia: Tres i Quatre, 2009)

Partido Socialista Obrero Español, *Convocatoria y orden del día para el XIII Congreso ordinario* (Madrid: Gráfica Socialista, 1932)

Peirats, José, *La CNT en la revolución española*, 2nd edn, 3 vols (Paris: Ediciones Ruedo Ibérico, 1971)

Peñafiel, Jaime, *El General y su tropa. Mis recuerdos de la familia Franco* (Madrid: Temas de Hoy, 1992)

Pérez Adán, Luis Miguel, 'El hundimiento del Castillo de Olite', *Revista Cartagena histórica*, no. 2, January 2003, pp. 5–13

Pernau, Josep, *Diario de la caida de Cataluña* (Barcelona: Ediciones B, 1989)

Pi Sunyer, Carles, *La República y la guerra. Memorias de un político catalán* (Mexico City: Ediciones Oasis, 1975)

Pike, David Wingeate, *France Divided. The French and the Civil War in Spain* (Brighton, Portland and Toronto: Sussex Academic Press/Cañada Blanch, 2011)

Pike, David Wingeate, *Vae Victis! Los republicanos españoles refugiados en Francia 1939–1944* (Paris: Ruedo Ibérico, 1969)

Portela Valladares, Manuel, *Dietario de dos guerras (1936–1950). Notas, polémicas y correspondencia de un centrista español* (Sada-A Coruña: Ediciós do Castro, 1988)

Prazmowska, Anita J., *Britain, Poland and the Eastern Front, 1939* (Cambridge: Cambridge University Press, 1987)

Preston, Paul, *Botxins i repressors. Els crims de Franco i dels franquistes* (Barcelona: Editorial Base, 2006)

Preston, Paul, *The Coming of the Spanish Civil War. Reform, Reaction and Revolution in the Spanish Republic*, 2nd edn (London: Routledge, 1994)

Preston, Paul, *¡Comrades! Portraits from the Spanish Civil War* (London: HarperCollins, 1999)

Preston, Paul, *The Spanish Civil War. Reaction, Revolution, Revenge* (London: HarperCollins, 2006)

Preston, Paul, *The Spanish Holocaust. Inquisition and Extermination in Twentieth Century Spain* (London: HarperCollins; New York: W. W. Norton, 2012)

Preston, Paul, *We Saw Spain Die. Foreign Correspondents in the Spanish Civil War* (London: Constable, 2008)

Puell de la Villa, Fernando, *Gutiérrez Mellado. Un militar del siglo XX (1912–1995)* (Madrid: Biblioteca Nueva, 1997)

Quirosa-Cheyrouze y Muñoz, Rafael, *Política y guerra civil en Almería* (Almería: Editorial Cajal, 1986)

Ramos, Vicente, *La guerra civil (1936–1939) en la provincia de Alicante*, 3 vols (Alicante: Ediciones Biblioteca Alicantina, 1973)

Richards, Michael, *A Time of Silence: Civil War and the Culture of Repression in Franco's Spain, 1936–1945* (Cambridge: Cambridge University Press, 1998)

Rodríguez Barreira, Óscar J., *Migas con miedo. Prácticas de resistencia al primer franquismo. Almería, 1939–1953* (Almería: Editorial Universidad de Almería, 2008)

Rodríguez Chaos, Melquesidez, *24 años en la cárcel* (Paris: Colección Ebro, 1968)

Rodríguez Gutiérrez, Cristina Elia, 'Julio Álvarez Del Vayo y Olloqui: Biografía Política de un Socialista Heterodoxo', unpublished doctoral thesis (Universidad Nacional de Educación a Distancia, Madrid, 2013)

Rodríguez López, Sofía, 'Vidas cruzadas. Las mujeres antifascistas y el exilio interior/exterior', *Arenal: Revista de historia de mujeres*, vol. 19, no. 1, 2012, pp. 103–40

Rodríguez Patiño, Ana Belén, *La guerra civil en Cuenca (1936–1939). II: La pugna ideológica y la revolución* (Madrid: Universidad Complutense, 2004)

Rojo, José Andrés, *Vicente Rojo. Retrato de un general republicano* (Barcelona: Tusquets Editores, 2006)

Romero, Luis, *El final de la guerra* (Barcelona: Ariel, 1976)

Rosal, Amaro del, *El oro del Banco de España y la historia del Vita* (Barcelona: Grijalbo, 1977)

Rosal, Amaro del, 'El Tesoro del Vita', *Historia 16*, no. 95, 1984, pp. 11–23

Rosal, Amaro del, *Historia de la UGT de España 1901–1939*, 2 vols (Barcelona: Grijalbo, 1977)

Rovighi, Alberto and Stefani, Filippo, *La partecipazione italiana alla guerra civile Spagnola*, 2 vols (Rome: Ufficio Storico dello Stato Maggiore dell'Esercito, 1992–3)

Saborit, Andrés, *El pensamiento político de Julián Besteiro* (Madrid: Seminarios y Ediciones, 1974)

Saborit, Andrés, *Julián Besteiro* (Buenos Aires: Losada, 1967)

Salas Larrazábal, Ramón, *Historia del Ejército popular de la República*, 4 vols (Madrid: Editora Nacional, 1973)

Sánchez Recio, Glicerio et al., *Guerra civil y franquismo en Alicante* (Alicante: Instituto de Cultura Juan Gil-Albert, 1991)

Santacreu Soler, José Miguel, ed., *Una presó amb vistes al mar. El drama del Port d'Alacant, Març de 1939* (Valencia: Tres i Quatre, 2008)

Sevilla Andrés, Diego, *Historia política de la zona roja* (Madrid: Editora Nacional, 1954)

Somoza Silva, Lázaro, *El general Miaja (biografía de un heroe)* (Mexico City: Editorial Tyris, 1944)

Spriano, Paolo, *Storia del Partito comunista italiano. III: I fronti popolari, Stalin, la guerra* (Torino: Giulio Einaudi Editore, 1976)

Starinov, A. K., *Behind Fascist Lines. A First-hand Account of Guerrilla Warfare during the Spanish Revolution* (New York: Ballantine Books, 2001)

Tarín-Iglesias, Manuel, *Los años rojos* (Barcelona: Editorial Planeta, 1985)

Thomas, Hugh, *The Spanish Civil War*, 3rd edn (London: Hamish Hamilton, 1977)

Tuñón de Lara, Manuel, *La España del siglo XX*, 2nd edn (Paris: Librería Española, 1973)

Tuñón de Lara, Manuel, Miralles, Ricardo and Díaz Chico, Bonifacio N., *Juan Negrín López. El hombre necesario* (Las Palmas: Gobierno de Canarias, 1996)

Vadillo Muñoz, Julián, *El movimiento obrero en Alcalá de Henares* (Madrid: Silente Académica, 2013)

Vadillo Muñoz, Julián, *Mauro Bajatierra. Anarquista y periodista de acción* (Madrid: La Malatesta Editorial, 2011)

Valero Escandell, José Ramón, 'El final de la II República: La Posición Yuste', *Tiempo de historia*, Año VII, no. 83 (1 Oct. 1981) pp. 36–49

Valero Escandell, José Ramón, *El territorio de la derrota. Los últimos días del Gobierno de la II República en el Vinalopó* (Petrer: Centre d´Estudis Locals del Vinalopó, 2004)

Vázquez-Rial, Horacio, *El soldado de porcelana* (Barcelona: Ediciones B, 1997)

Vidal Zapater, José Manuel, 'Los Llanos (Albacete) 1939', unpublished manuscript (Madrid, 1994)

Vilanova, Antonio, *Los olvidados. Los exilados españoles en la segunda guerra mundial* (Paris: Ruedo Ibérico, 1969)

Villamea, Luis F., *Gutiérrez Mellado. Así se entrega una victoria* (Madrid: Fuerza Nueva Editorial, 1996)

Villarroya i Font, Joan, *Els bombardeigs de Barcelona durant la guerra civil (1936–1939)*, 2nd edn (Barcelona: Publicacions de L'Abadia de Montserrat, 1999)

Viñas, Ángel, *El honor de la República. Entre el acoso fascista, la hostilidad británica y la política de Stalin* (Barcelona: Editorial Crítica, 2009)

Viñas, Ángel, 'Playing with History and Hiding Treason: Colonel Casado's Untrustworthy Memoirs and the End of the Spanish Civil War', *Bulletin of*

Spanish Studies: Hispanic Studies and Researches on Spain, Portugal and Latin America, vol. 91, nos 1–2, 2014, pp. 295–323

Viñas, Ángel and Hernández Sánchez, Fernando, *El desplome de la República* (Barcelona: Editorial Crítica, 2009)

Volodarsky, Boris, 'Soviet Intelligence Services in the Spanish Civil War, 1936–1939', unpublished doctoral thesis (London School of Economics, 2010)

INDEX

ABC 130, 164
Acción Nacionalista Vasca 45
Acedo Colunga, Felipe 300–1
Afrika Korps 308
Aguilera Povedano, Manuel 250
Aguirre, José Antonio 54
Agrupación Socialista Madrileña
   (ASM) 141, 164, 179, 213, 248,
   255
Air France 63, 163, 296
Aizpuru Maristany, Gabriel 226
Alba y de Berwick-on-Tweed, Duque
   de 146, 253
Alcalá Zamora, Niceto 4–5, 284
Alfonso XIII 80
Alianza Nacional de Fuerzas
   Democráticas 312
Allen, Jay 4
Alonso, Bruno 95, 96–7, 144, 179,
   183, 184, 188, 189–90, 191, 196,
   198, 201
Alonso Vega, Camilo 308
Álvarez, Santiago 82
Álvarez del Vayo, Julio 20, 51, 52, 53,
   57, 58–9, 61, 62, 63, 73, 89, 91, 96,
   97, 98, 110, 111, 118, 123, 156, 164,
   173, 199, 205–6, 220, 226, 230,
   233–5, 255, 270, 281
Álvarez Quintero, brothers 304
Amil, Manuel 69–70, 134, 135, 137,
   282
Ansó, Mariano 74, 110
Anti-Comintern Pact, 1937 256
Antón, Francisco 82

Antona, David 243, 259
Aranguren Roldán, General 226
Arenillas de Chaves, Ignacio 304
Armentia, Gerardo 191–3
Army Group of the Centre (GEZC)
   47, 93, 95, 113, 176, 208; *see also*
   Army of the Centre
Army of Africa 8, 10
Army of Andalusía 5, 17, 24, 49, 95,
   109, 155–6, 177, 202, 203, 245
Army of Catalonia 33, 39, 49, 74, 93
Army of Extremadura 49, 95, 109,
   177, 243, 263, 279
Army of Madrid 122
Army of the Centre 1, 5, 17, 24, 30–1,
   32, 33, 34, 43, 47, 49, 92, 93, 94–5,
   101, 102, 103, 105, 109, 117, 123,
   126, 127, 128, 130, 137, 139, 143,
   151, 157, 169, 170, 171, 175, 176,
   177, 180, 205, 208, 211, 220, 226,
   237, 241, 250, 263, 264; *see also*
   Army Group of the Centre
Army of the East 37, 73, 74, 180
Army of the Levante 17, 47, 109, 132,
   143, 154, 155–6, 176, 177, 207, 220,
   223–4, 244, 285, 291
Arnaiz, Aurora 260–1
Ascanio, Guillermo 241, 260
Asensio Torrado, General José 74
Attlee, Clement 145, 146–7
Aub, Max 291
Azaña, Manuel 5, 11, 24, 30, 31, 36–7,
   43, 44, 47, 51–4, 58, 62–3, 65, 70,
   72–3, 78, 83–5, 90, 103, 112, 113,

Azaña, Manuel *cont* ...
119, 121, 122, 123, 132, 141, 142,
147–50, 154, 158, 159, 160, 163,
164, 170, 172, 182, 204, 255, 301
Azcárate, Pablo de 80, 105, 106–7,
108, 146, 149, 161
Aznar, Manuel 249, 255

Badajoz, massacre of 8
Bahamonde, Ángel 66, 250
Bahamonde, Antonio 272
Ballesteros, Clotilde 260–1
Barceló Jover, Luis 172, 241, 248
Barrionuevo, Rafael 193, 198, 199,
200, 202
Barrios, Jacinto 250
Barrón y Ortiz, Fernando 46, 101, 310
Batista, Fulgencio 281
Baztán, Melchor 137
BBC World Service 310
Bérard, Léon 57–8, 107
Bernal García, Carlos 109, 110, 111,
157, 182–5, 188, 189, 190, 191
Bertoloty Ramírez, Dr Ricardo 31, 46,
124
Besteiro, Julián:
culpable naivety in loss of thousands
of lives 1, 219–20, 302–3
motivations for joining Casado coup
23, 25–30, 172–3, 257, 302–3
announcement of National Defence
Junta (Consejo Nacional de
Defensa) and 23, 211, 213–14, 215,
220
Fifth Column links 23, 30, 32, 44,
46, 134, 180
Professor of Logic, University of
Madrid 23, 26, 27, 30
misplaced optimism about Franco
26, 44, 219–20, 267–70, 303
councillor of the Ayuntamiento de
Madrid 26, 27
commitment to a peace settlement
during Spanish Civil War 26, 27–8,
43–4, 45, 300

anti-Communism 28, 29, 30, 42–3,
128, 257
hostility towards Negrín 27, 29, 43,
142, 212, 225, 257
critic of Republican government 27,
28, 30
trial at hands of Francoists 30,
300–2, 304
early meetings with Casado 32,
43–4, 45–6, 48, 121
PSOE executive committee meeting
speech, 15 November 1938 42–3
birth and planning of Casado coup
and 32, 43–4, 45–6, 48, 50, 102–3,
121, 122, 123, 128, 141, 142, 150,
151–2, 164, 168–9, 172–3, 174, 180,
204
refusal to allow government
resources to pay for passage of
those who wish to flee Spain 91, 294
formation of government of
surrender, discusses possibility of
121, 122, 123
Casado dismisses rumours over
contact with 150
Franco rejects request to negotiate
in person with 151–2
role in launch of Casado coup
211–15, 220
accepts dual post of Vice-President
and Minister of Foreign Affairs
211, 215, 218
poor health 219, 239, 243, 267, 273,
274
seeming ignorance of Francoist
repression 219–20
role in encouraging Casado to reject
transfer of powers 225, 232, 233,
294
document of guidance to press
drawn up by 256–7
revenge as motivation for 257,
302–3
stays on in Madrid 271, 273–4, 284,
299

sentenced to thirty years in prison 293, 301–2
optimism while in prison 299–300
plea of mitigation during trial 301–2
death 302, 303
Betancourt González, Antenor 306–7
Bilbao Hospitalet, Tomás 45, 183, 188
Blanco, Segundo 70, 183, 188, 225, 254
Blum, Léon 8
Boadilla, battle of, 1936 11
Bolloten, Burnett 82, 90, 115, 177
Bonel Huici, Francisco 151
Bonnet, Georges 53, 57, 59, 107, 319
Bouthelier España, Antonio 7, 31, 36, 68, 130–1, 136, 241–2, 255, 307, 308
Bowers, Claude 59, 319
British Committee for Refugees from Spain 310
British Intelligence 4
Brunete, battle of, 1937 3, 5, 13, 33, 34–5, 88
Bueno, Emilio 170, 172, 241, 248
Bugeda, Jerónimo 80
Buil Navarro, Eduardo 257–8, 309–10
Buiza Fernández-Palacios, Miguel 34, 49, 74–5, 94, 95–7, 98, 101, 105, 109, 110, 111, 132, 133, 144, 156–7, 172, 175, 182, 183, 184–5, 188, 189–90, 191, 192, 193, 194, 196, 198, 200–1, 206, 229, 246, 308, 309
Bullitt, William 59, 269–70
Burillo Stohle, Ricardo 188, 226, 233, 236, 244, 258, 295–6

Cabo Giorla, Luis 93
Cabrera Sánchez, Blas 162
Cadogan, Sir Alexander 145, 149, 271
Camacho Benítez, Antonio 49, 94, 109, 110–11, 132–3, 229, 230, 234, 277
Cañas, Eustaquio 183–4, 195, 199, 202, 226, 227, 235–6, 248, 250–1, 258, 267, 288
Carrillo, Santiago 40, 42, 68, 82

Carrillo, Wenceslao 23, 40, 68, 127, 141–2, 164, 179, 211, 212, 213, 218, 226, 227, 233, 236, 240, 241, 243–4, 245, 248, 250, 252, 255, 257, 258, 259, 260, 272, 275, 276, 288, 292, 295–6
Casado Junta 215–27, 230, 231, 232, 236, 237, 239, 240, 245, 246, 248, 254, 257, 259, 263, 267, 269, 271, 280, 282, 283, 288, 300–4
Casado López, César 31, 307
Casado López, Segismundo:
launches military coup against government of Negrín 1, 3, 172–3, 174, 199–201, 205–8, 211–15, 216, 217, 218, 219
claims coup launched to prevent Moscow-inspired Communist dictatorship 1–2, 23, 60, 61, 157–8, 175, 176, 177, 178, 179, 190, 211, 317
claims coup launched to put a stop to slaughter and to secure clemency from Franco for all but Communists 3, 151, 165
negotiations with Franco 3, 24, 101–4, 121, 124–6, 133, 151, 152, 251–4, 255, 263, 264, 266–7, 268, 269–70, 272–8, 286, 290, 293–4, 300, 303, 308
British influence on efforts to end war 4, 32, 44, 121–2, 150–1, 253–4, 290, 291, 292, 293, 310, 311, 314–15
appointed head of the Army of Andalusia 5, 24
appointed head of the Army of the Centre 5, 24–5
stomach ulcers 5–6, 40, 48, 211–12, 216
doubts over character of 5–7
self-serving arrogance 6, 102, 133
memoirs 6, 94, 98, 100–1, 122, 182, 250, 251, 252, 284, 293, 310, 316–17

Casado López, Segismundo *cont* ...
'Pasionaria' on 6–7, 88, 93
Fifth Column and 23, 41, 95, 100,
101, 143, 164, 180, 214, 254, 317
denounces Negrín's commitment to
continued resistance 23–4
anti-Communism 24–5, 31, 87–8,
127–8, 129, 141, 218, 248–9, 250–1,
254, 264, 316
Besteiro's position converges with
30–1
protects pro-Francoist officers 31–2
SIM and 31, 127, 180, 267, 307
SIPM and 32, 45, 81, 94, 102, 123–4,
126, 149–50, 151, 152, 310
defeatism and command of Army of
the Centre 32–3, 34, 36
early meetings with Besteiro 43–4,
45, 46–7
Negrín receives warnings about
motives of 45, 94, 126, 142
guarantees offered to professional
Republican soldiers and 45–6,
124–6, 151, 178, 252
Valencia lunch with Generals
Matallana, Miaja and Menéndez (2
or 3 February 1939) and
conspiracy with 47–8, 63, 69, 94,
110, 132
Los Llanos meeting (7 or 8 February
1939) and 48–9, 94, 95, 132–3
anarchists participation in coup of
60–1, 67–70, 94–5, 127, 128–39,
141, 155, 156, 164, 171, 177, 179,
211–13, 225, 226, 254–5, 263, 282,
303–4
attempts to recruit Mera 94–5, 127,
128, 133, 134, 138–40
Buiza's statement on morale of fleet
to Negrín and 97, 98
meeting with Negrín, 12 February
1939 98–101
convinced that end of war would be
negotiated between himself and
Franco 102–4, 133

blocks or delays communications
between Negrín and embassies in
London and Paris 107, 118, 161–2
Los Llanos meeting of high
command of armed forces, 16
February 1939 and 109–11, 123–4
promotion to general 121, 170–1
Centaño and Guitián press not to
delay coup 123–6, 149–50
document containing Franco's offer
of concessions and 124–6, 151
ignores order to dismiss Pedrero
127
hostility to Communists to
ingratiate himself with Franco 127
prepared to pay for Franco's
clemency in Communist blood
134, 151, 165, 238
ASM and 141–2
plan to imprison Negrín 143
Cordón meeting with, 24 February
1939 149–50, 151, 178
Negrín meeting with, 2 March 1939
156, 183
proposal for Modesto to replace as
head of the Army of the Centre
157, 169, 170
failure to see responsibility for
Republicans unable to escape 165
Tagüeña suggests pre-empting coup
by arresting 171–2
failure of Negrín to react decisively
to machinations of 172, 179, 180,
220
postings and promotions, 3 March
1939 and 175, 176, 177, 178–9, 182
aborted meetings with Negrín, 3 and
4 March 1939 181–2
plan to use departure of fleet to
blackmail government into
resigning 96, 97, 110, 156, 184, 185,
188, 190, 191–2, 193, 194, 195, 197,
198, 199–201
refuses presidency and offers to
Miaja 211, 215, 216

civil war of/armed resistance to coup of 217, 237–61

phone conversations between headquarters following broadcasts announcing coup 220–8

Negrín's offer of transfer of powers and 221–2, 223, 224, 225, 229, 231–3, 234, 235, 294

claims 30,000 prisoners taken in fighting with Communists 250

blindness to weakening of Republic by coup and elimination of Communists 251

negotiations with Franco's headquarters over surrender and evacuation 251–4, 255, 264, 270, 272–3, 274–8, 290, 293–4, 308

victory over Communists exposes contradictions in aims of FAI and 263–7

flight from Spain 283, 284, 286–93, 305

flimsiness of claims regarding evacuation as a priority 286–7, 290–2, 293

British help to flee Spain and influence life in exile 290, 291, 292, 293, 310, 311, 314–15

shows no remorse for his actions 309, 310, 311

exile from Spain 311–16, 317

relationship with Norah Purcell 310–11

Columbia and Venezuela, life in 311, 315–16

confidence in actions and in his importance 311–12

optimism about removal of Franco and readiness to return to Spain as part of government 311, 312–13

anti-Semitism 315–16

sentenced in absence for being a freemason 316

application for military pension leads to investigation of, 1962–5 316

return to Spain, health deteriorates, death 316–17

Casado Santodomingo, Segismundo 307

Casado Segismundo, María del Carmen 289, 307

Casanova, Manuel 238

Cascón Briega, Manuel 234, 277–8, 311

Castilla Libre 135, 264, 283

Castro Delgado, Enrique 33, 34–5, 80–1, 168, 171, 174

Catalá, Sigfrido (Lohengrin) 312

Cazorla, José 68, 93, 94, 242, 258, 260, 261

Cebrián, Dolores 302

Centaño de la Paz, José 31–2, 45, 113, 123, 150, 178, 274

Cervera, Javier 250

Cervera, Pascual 201

Chamberlain, Neville 15, 105–6, 107, 121, 145–9, 150, 249, 271, 319

Checa, Pedro 90, 171, 174, 183, 189, 231, 235, 237, 244, 246, 278

Chetwode Commission 4, 121

Churchill, Winston 75, 146, 283

Cierva, Ricardo de la 171

Ciutat de Miguel, Francisco 66, 154, 176, 220–1, 224, 225, 244, 291

Claridad 255–6

Claudín, Fernando 235, 244

Clemenceau, Georges 2

CNT (periodical) 26, 129–30

CNT-FAI 67–70, 77, 127, 128, 129–31, 132, 137, 164, 238

Comintern 25, 35, 39, 66, 88, 118, 128, 171, 179, 235, 255, 256

Comité Internacional de Coordination et d'Information pour l'Aide à l'Espagne Republicane 285, 295

Comité Provincial de Investigación Pública 137

Comité Regional de Defensa (CRD) 128–30, 134–5, 137, 138, 214, 285

Companys, Lluís 54
Condado y Condado, María de las
 Mercedes 31, 307
Condor Legion 12, 15
Conesa Arteaga, José 248
Confederación Nacional del Trabajo
 (CNT) 26, 31, 40, 41–2, 65, 67–70,
 127, 129–30, 131, 132, 134, 135,
 163, 172, 187, 190, 212, 214, 218,
 254, 259, 305, 312
Consejo Nacional de Defensa 23, 48,
 91, 94, 134, 141, 157, 165, 170, 173,
 179, 211, 212, 214–15, 229, 232,
 235, 239, 240, 242, 243, 244, 246,
 247, 248, 251, 253, 256, 257, 264,
 266, 272, 275, 276, 279, 280, 281,
 282, 287–9, 291, 293, 309
Cordón, Antonio 24, 33, 66–7, 81,
 82–3, 84, 90, 91, 92–3, 94, 120, 121,
 122, 124, 126, 142, 149–50, 151,
 154, 162, 170, 175, 176, 177, 178,
 189, 204, 206–9, 216, 220, 221,
 222–9, 230, 234–5, 260
Corps Franc D'Afrique (CFA) 308–9
Cowan, Denys 4, 121–2, 127, 150,
 249–50, 310
Cruz, Hilario de la 164

Daily Express 279
Daily Herald 55–6
Daladier, Édouard 14, 145
David (codename for PCE) 171
Delgado, Álvaro 41
Díaz, Pepe 85
Díaz Tendero Merchán, Eleuterio 73
Dickson, Archibald 295
Diéguez, Isidoro 238, 241, 278
Dimitrov, Georgi 39
Domínguez Aragonés, Edmundo 5–6,
 34, 88, 101, 126–8, 142, 154, 170,
 172, 180, 211, 212–13, 216, 217,
 220, 221, 225, 233, 237, 242, 248,
 257, 295
Durán, Gustavo 245, 291
Durruti, Buenaventura 129

Ebro, battle of 15–16, 17–18, 19, 28,
 33, 25, 27, 79–80, 82, 102, 131, 237,
 254, 270, 308, 309
Escobar Huertas, Antonio 49, 109,
 240–1, 243
Esquerra Republicana de Catalunya 45

Falange Española 46, 260, 299, 304,
 307, 308, 314
Falcon, Irene 117, 230, 233, 235
Faringdon, Lord 285
Federación Anarquista Ibérica (FAI)
 27, 68–9, 129, 131, 135, 136, 138,
 164, 254, 263
Federación de Juventudes Libertarias
 69, 129
Federación Nacional de Trabajadores
 de la Tierra 142
Fernández Cuesta, Raimundo 304
Fernández de la Calzada, Rafael 311,
 312, 314, 317
Fernández Osorio y Tafall, Bibiano
 90–1, 189, 191, 196–7, 199
Fernsworth, Lawrence 60
Fiedelmann, Marie 320
Fischer, Louis 4, 89, 173, 319
Forcinal, Albert 285, 291
Foreign Legion 8
Foreign Office 106, 140, 145, 149,
 150, 249, 253–4, 290, 310, 311
Franco, Francisco 16
 Casado claims coup launched to
  secure clemency for all but
  Communists 3, 23, 151, 165
 Casado negotiations with 3, 24,
  101–3, 121, 124–6, 151, 152, 251–4,
  255, 263, 264, 266–7, 268, 269–70,
  272–8, 286, 290, 293–4, 300, 303,
  308
 Republican capture of Teruel and 13
 offensive through Aragon and
  Castellon 13, 155
 favours total destruction of
  Republican forces 14, 15–16, 17,
  50, 309

Valencia attack, July 1938 14, 15
Gandesa battle and 15–16, 17
Ebro counter-offensive, October
  1938 and 17
unconditional surrender demanded
  by 17, 18, 51, 104, 151, 169, 274–7,
  286
Catalonia offensive, 1938–9 and
  19–20, 33, 36, 47, 66
Burgos headquarters 23, 30, 32, 34,
  45, 46, 57–8, 60, 100, 102, 107, 123,
  126, 140, 144, 146, 151, 152, 156,
  158, 176, 190, 197, 253, 263, 274,
  275, 277, 281, 284, 293, 308
guarantees to professional
  Republican soldiers and 45, 46, 50,
  124
Law of Political Responsibilities
  49–50, 173, 269, 309
Negrín attempts to negotiate peace
  with 51, 52, 53, 55, 56, 57–61,
  72–3, 76, 79, 85, 87, 91, 100, 101,
  104–9, 119–20, 173, 249, 279
British and French governments and
  peace negotiations with 57–61, 63,
  91, 92, 95, 100, 105, 122, 144–9,
  150–1
Britain and France recognition of
  85, 100, 105–8, 144–9, 150, 158,
  159, 160, 163, 167, 182, 206, 235,
  253, 271
document containing offer of
  concessions from 124–6, 151
Casado trusts with culpable naivety
  133, 150, 266–7
Casado prepared to pay for
  clemency of in Communist blood
  134, 151, 165, 238
orders a de facto ceasefire in
  anticipation of Casado coup 241
clarifies plans for defeated, 31
  December 1938 248–9, 255
British refuse to evacuate refugees
  without permission of 249–50,
  253–4, 296

Consejo Nacional de Defensa
  negotiations with 251–4, 263,
  266–7, 268, 269–70, 273–7, 286,
  300, 303
Besteiro's naivety about 268, 269–70,
  273–4, 300, 303
Madrid offensive, 27 March 1939
  279, 280, 281–2
evacuation of Republicans from
  Madrid and 286–7, 288, 289,
  290–1, 293, 296
Casado flight from Spain and 286–7,
  288, 289, 290–1, 293
trial of Republican officers and 306,
  308
aim to eradicate the ideals and
  hopes stimulated by the Republic
  309–10
Casado exile and 311, 312–16, 317
Franco Salgado-Araujo, Francisco
  113
Fraser, Ronald 41
French Foreign Legion 201, 308
Frente Libertario 68, 129–30, 135

Galán Rodríguez, Fermín 185
Galán Rodríguez, Francisco 157, 175,
  176, 182, 185, 188–98, 200
Gallagher, O'Dowd 279, 280
Gallego, Gregorio 129, 135, 196–7
Gambara, Gastone 295
Gamir Ulíbarri, General Mariano 74
Garcés Arroyo, Santiago 63, 94, 127,
  152, 180, 206, 220, 225, 226, 230,
  234
García, Claudina 217
García, Regina 271
García Barreiro, José 184, 198, 199
García Oliver, Juan 70, 129
García Pradas, José 1, 68, 127–8,
  129–30, 131, 135, 136, 137, 138,
  143, 155, 163, 164–5, 177, 187, 203,
  211, 212, 214, 215, 220, 251, 254,
  263–4, 273, 274, 284–5, 287, 288,
  289, 290, 291, 292, 306

García Viñals, Francisco 33
Garijo Hernández, Antonio 35, 113, 123, 176, 274, 277, 307–8
Gellhorn, Martha 71
George IV, King of England 26
Giner de los Ríos, Francisco 222, 225
Giral, José 7, 8, 9, 103, 113
Girauta, Vicente 117, 139, 250–1
Girón, Domingo 171, 205, 238, 246, 260
Gómez, Sócrates 250
Gómez, Trifón 63, 91–2, 155, 179–80, 225, 233, 250, 251, 294
Gómez Egido, Juan 164
Gómez, Osorio, José 183, 250, 296
Gómez Sáenz, Paulino 118–19, 183–4, 187, 222, 225, 229
Gómez Serrano, Eliseo 272–3
Gómez-Jordana, Francisco 58, 107–8, 144–5, 146, 148–9, 253
González, Liberino 242
González, Valentín, 'El Campesino' 177, 245
González Marín, Manuel 130, 137, 139, 211, 212, 218, 251, 264, 282, 283, 289, 290, 292, 306
González Montoliú, José 242
González Peña, Ramón 85, 118, 168, 183, 188, 206, 217
González Ubieta, Luis 74, 75
Gooden, Abbington 139–40, 149, 150, 253, 272, 280, 290, 291, 294
Guadalajara, battle of 11, 12, 309
Güemes, Ernesto 245
Guitián, Manuel 113, 123, 124, 126, 149–50, 178, 274
Guzmán, Eduardo de 283, 284–5, 287–9
Guerrilla Army 154, 155, 245

Haile Selassie 281
Halifax, Lord 105, 106–7, 108, 121, 149, 150, 253, 271
Hay, Colonel 294
Hemingway, Ernest 3

Henche, Rafael 233, 296, 303, 312
Henderson, Nevile 271
Henry, Jules 14, 57, 58
Hernández, Jesús 33–5, 48–9, 92, 93, 94, 111, 132–3, 176, 204–5, 206–7, 244, 245, 278
Hernández Saravia, Juan, General 62, 74, 77, 132
Hervás Soler, Juan 93
Hidalgo de Cisneros, Ignacio 13, 67, 81, 82, 83–4, 122, 124–5, 162, 170, 178, 182, 220, 222, 229, 230, 235
Higher War College 93
Hillgarth, Alan 75
Hitler, Adolf 9–10, 11, 15, 16, 61, 255, 271
Hoare, Sir Samuel 121
Hodgson, Robert 58, 107, 140, 144–6, 148
Huidobro Pardo, Leopoldo 304

Ibárruri, Dolores, La Pasionaria 6–7, 85, 88, 93, 117, 230, 233, 234, 278, 309
International Brigades 2, 10, 14, 15, 35
Irujo, Manuel 45, 54, 312

Jarama, battle of 3, 11, 12
Jato, David 41
Jiménez, Hernández, Gerardo 291–2
Jordana, conde de 58, 107–8, 144–5, 146, 148, 149, 253
Juan de Borbón 315
Junta de Defensa de Madrid 68
Jurado, Enrique 74, 76, 77, 82–3, 84, 111–12, 120–1
Juventudes Libertarias 69, 129, 131, 135
Juventudes Socialistas 42, 141–2
Juventudes Socialistas Unificadas (JSU) 40, 41, 42, 243, 248, 259, 260, 284

Kalmanovitch, Jacob Maurice 285

Labour Party, British 145
Labrador, Orencio 141
Laín Entralgo, José 259
Largo Caballero, Francisco 5, 9, 10, 25, 26, 27, 28, 29–30, 40, 56, 68, 69, 87–8, 141, 142, 164, 165, 248, 255, 257, 301
Larios, Marqués de 48
Larrañaga, Jesús 244
Law of Political Responsibilities 50, 173, 269–70, 275, 288, 306, 309
Leclerc, Philippe 309
Lenin, Vladimir Ilich Ulianov 2, 248
Left Republican 67, 90
Líneas Aéreas Postales de Españolas 162–3
Líster, Enrique 20, 33, 81–2, 89, 143, 153, 154, 167, 168, 171, 174–5, 177, 178–9, 199–200, 230, 233, 234, 235, 247
Llarch, Joan 119–20
López, Feliciana 320
López, Juan 69–70, 77, 264–5, 306, 312–13, 315
López de Letona, Antonio 68
López Mora, José 36
López Otero, José 44, 93–4, 127
López Palazón, José 30, 35
López Sánchez, Juan 69, 306
Losas, Eduardo 279
Luca de Tena, Marqués de 164
Luna García, Antonio 30, 42, 44, 45, 219, 268, 299
Luque, Ángel 299

Madariaga, Salvador de 305, 315
Madrid, city of 3, 4, 6, 8, 10, 11, 12, 13, 24, 25, 36, 39, 40, 41, 42, 44, 60
Madrid Radio 282
Mancebo, Benigno 137, 138
Mantecón, Juan Ignacio 155, 176, 291
Martínez, Cayetano 259
Martínez Barrio, Diego 36–7, 51, 54, 73, 85, 158, 159, 160–3, 164, 173, 224

Martínez Cabrera, Toribio 172
Martínez Cartón, Pedro 177, 243, 244
Martínez Santa Olalla, Julio 30
Masquelet, Carlos 74
Matallana, Alberto 35
Matallana Gómez, Manuel 17, 33, 34–6, 44, 47, 49, 63, 76, 84, 89, 92, 93, 94, 95, 96, 97, 98, 101, 109, 110, 111, 112–13, 132–3, 138, 139, 143, 151, 152, 156, 157, 161, 171, 172, 175, 176, 181, 183, 184, 190, 191, 192, 193, 194–5, 197, 198, 200, 206–8, 215, 220, 221, 224, 225, 227–9, 241–2, 245, 263, 274, 306, 307–8
Matthews, Herbert 1–2, 20–1, 36, 55, 56–7, 320
Maupoil, Bernard 285
Mayalde, José Finat Escrivá de Romaní, conde de 310
Medina, Diego 6, 31, 46, 103, 113, 306–7, 308
Medrano Ezquerra, Carmelo 274
Mella, Ricardo 236
Méndez Aspe, Francisco 12, 62, 63, 64, 72, 80, 103, 111, 118, 180–1, 251
Méndez Martínez, Rafael 4, 19, 61, 73, 76, 77, 80, 82, 159, 202
Menéndez, Leopoldo 47–8, 109, 132, 143, 177, 207–8, 220, 223–4, 240, 244–5, 274, 285–6, 291, 304
Mera, Cipriano 23, 68, 94–5, 98, 127, 128, 133, 134–5, 136, 138, 139, 141, 143–4, 163, 164, 172, 177, 205, 211, 215, 220, 238, 241, 242, 243, 254, 258, 260, 261, 263–4, 273, 280, 288, 305, 311–12
Mesón, Gómez, Eugenio 260
MI6 310
Miaja, José 6, 7, 10, 17, 23, 33, 34, 35, 36, 37, 44, 47–8, 49, 62–3, 69, 75, 88, 92, 93, 94, 95, 96, 97, 98, 101, 102, 109, 110, 112, 132, 133, 139, 143, 156, 157, 161, 169, 174, 175,

Miaja, José *cont* …
  176, 177, 180, 181, 183, 184, 188,
  192, 195, 208–9, 211, 215–17, 218,
  232, 233, 238, 242, 280, 281, 283,
  294, 320
Mije, Antonio 82
Milanes, Senior 139–40, 150
Miller, James 44
Minev, Stoyan (Boris Stepanov) 88,
  118, 171; *see also* Stepanov, Boris
Modesto Guillote, Juan 33–4, 81, 93,
  101, 157, 169, 170, 171, 174, 175,
  177, 182, 230, 233
Moix Regas, José 89, 118, 222, 230
Mola, Emilio 1, 8, 12
Molina, Calixto 192
Molotov-Ribbentrop Pact 61
Montagnana, Rita 247
Montiel, Francisco-Félix 4, 5, 24, 238,
  241
Monzón Reparaz, Jesús 93, 94, 234
Morel, Henri 109
Moreno, Evaristo Jorge 272, 288
Moriones Larraga, Domingo 49, 109,
  202, 225, 240–1
Morla Lynch, Carlos 172
Movimiento Libertario Español
  (MLE) 131, 134, 138, 254, 264–6
Muedra Miñon, Félix 35, 92, 176, 208,
  308
Muirhead-Gould, Gerald 75, 76
Mujeres Antifascistas 259
Mundo Obrero 88
Munich Agreement 15, 16, 17, 18, 19,
  20, 61, 258, 270, 271
Muñoz Grandes, Agustín 304
Mussolini, Benito 9–10, 11, 255

Negrín López, Juan:
  Casado launches coup against
    government of 1, 123–4, 172–5,
    211, 212, 213, 214, 215, 217, 218,
    220
  government accused of being
    puppet of PCE and leading a

  Communist coup 1–2, 88–9, 90,
    93, 134, 158, 169–70, 176–7, 178–9
  belief in continued resistance to
    achieve a peace settlement 3, 19,
    20–1, 23–4, 27, 40, 41, 51, 52, 53,
    55, 57, 71, 79, 90–1, 104–5, 163,
    172–4
  Minister of Finance 11, 12–13, 26
  government under premiership of
    12, 13, 26
  refuses to acknowledge the
    possibility of defeat 13–14
  Munich Agreement and 15, 18,
    270–1
  centralised war effort, creation of 16,
    26–7
  efforts to secure military supplies
    from Russia 16–17
  minimal conditions for negotiations
    with Franco 18–19
  appoints Casado commander of the
    Army of the Centre 5, 24–5
  Besteiro's hostility towards 27, 29,
    43, 142, 212, 225, 257
  relations with Azaña 36–7, 51–2
  loss of Catalonia and 38
  popular sense that government had
    abandoned centre 41
  declaration of martial law, 23
    January 1939 47
  sense of responsibility towards
    Republican population 50–1
  Azaña's departure for France and
    51–2, 54, 72–3, 84, 85
  reaches Paris after Casado coup 52
  government in Figueras 54, 55
  speaks to meeting of Republican
    Cortes, 1 February 1939 55–7
  British and French governments
    press to agree to cessation of
    hostilities 57, 58–61
  crosses into France, 9 February 1939
    61–2
  returns to Spain in hope of
    negotiating settlement 62–3, 65

evacuation of Republicans from
Spain and 63, 70, 72, 78, 79, 80, 91,
97, 98, 104, 121, 128, 163, 164, 173,
175, 176, 177, 180, 182, 187, 188,
194, 196, 199, 206, 208, 229, 234,
239, 240, 249–50, 266
stress endured by and effect upon
health 65–6, 90–1, 117–20, 171–2
anarchists opposition to 70, 94,
133–6, 254, 255, 266
Martha Gellhorn on 71
Rojo criticisms of 71–2
Rojo's decision not to return to
Spain and 76, 77, 78, 79, 80–1, 82,
83, 84, 111–15, 120–1
establishment of SERE and 80,
319–20
suffers from indecision following
return to Spain 90–1
meeting with Casado, February 1939
98–102
announces Madrid as seat of
government 103
broadcast, 13 February 1939 103–4
British government and efforts to
negotiate peace 106, 107, 108, 109,
144, 147–8, 149, 150
optimism that Republic could hold
out 109
meeting of high command of three
branches of armed forces, Los
Llanos, 16 February 1939 and
109–12, 117, 119, 123–4, 126, 141,
142, 144
promotions of Rojo, Jurado and
Casado 120–1
learns of extent of Casado's
conspiracy against 126–7, 142–3,
154–5
anarchists collaboration in Casado
coup and 131, 133, 134, 135–6.
137–8
Mera meeting, 23/24 February 1939
143–4
establishes base at El Poblet 152–6

meeting with Miaja, Matallana,
Casado and Buiza, 2 March 1939
156–8
urges Azaña to return to Spain 158,
159
Azaña's resignation and 159–60,
163
Anglo-French recognition of Franco
and 159, 163, 167
Barrio's appointment as interim
president and 160–3
Togliatti's proposals for stiffening
war effort and dealing with Casado
coup and 169–70
Casado's promotion to general and
169–70
postings and promotions, 3 March
1939 and 175–80
fate of naval base at Cartagena and
plans for evacuation 182–5, 87,
188–9, 190, 191, 192–6, 197, 199,
201, 202–3, 204, 206, 207
conversation with Casado informing
of coup 221–2
offer of hand over of power 221–2,
223, 224, 225, 229, 231–3, 294
decision to abandon Spain 228,
229–31, 233–4, 235, 237, 239
conciliatory declaration to Casado
231–3, 234
uses government resources to keep
centre zone supplied 238–9
reprimands de los Ríos for public
declaration recognizing Consejo
Nacional de Defensa 240
troops stay loyal to after exile to
Paris 242, 243, 245, 261
Socialist press criticism of 255–6
Casado attempts to freeze bank
accounts held outside Spain by
367
cordial relations with Miaja in Paris
281
charters ships from Mid-Atlantic
Shipping Company 294, 295

Negrín López, Juan *cont ...*
  addresses standing committee of
    Republican Cortes in Paris 317–19
  post-war life 320–1
  Orwell and 320–1
Nelken, Margarita 73
New York Times, The 36
Núñez Maza, Carlos 67
Núñez Rodríguez, José 198, 200

Olivia Llamusí, Fernando 191
'Organización Antonio' 30, 31–2, 35,
    45, 102–3
Orgaz, Luis 113
Ortega, Antonio 172
Ortega, Daniel 174, 205, 260
Ortega, Francisco 176
Ortega Nieto, Leopoldo 274–6, 277,
    293
Orwell, George 11, 320–1
Osorio y Tafall *see* Fernández Osorio
  y Tafall, Bibiano
Ossorio y Gallardo, Ángel 52, 54

Palacios, Julio 30, 45, 46, 101–2, 130,
    255, 283, 307
Palau, José 244, 245
Páramo, Mario 217
Partido Comunista de España (PCE)
    1, 5, 28–9, 35, 39, 40, 43, 61, 76, 82,
    87, 88–9, 90, 93, 115, 118, 128, 131,
    134, 135, 141, 152, 154, 169, 170,
    171, 172, 176–7, 179, 183, 189, 205,
    218–19, 233, 235, 237, 238, 241,
    242, 243, 244, 245, 246, 247, 249,
    258–61, 278
Partido Communista Français (PCF)
    39
Partido Obrero de Unificación
    Marxista (POUM) 27, 118–19, 238
Partido Socialista Obrero Español
    (PSOE) 3, 18, 25, 26, 27, 28, 40, 41,
    42, 68, 118, 141, 173, 212–13, 218,
    236, 248, 256–7, 259, 296, 305, 320,
    321

Pascua, Marcelino 2, 52–3, 72–3, 74,
    77, 79, 84, 91, 105, 113, 158, 159,
    236
Pedrero García Ángel 31, 32, 43, 46,
    93, 94, 117, 119, 127, 130, 138, 141,
    172, 216, 226, 244, 266–7, 281,
    304–5
Peirats, José 69, 254
Perea Capulino, Juan 33
Pérez García, Antonio 239–40, 248,
    272, 294
Pérez Martínez, José 216–17
Pérez Salas, Joaquín 202, 258
Pertegás, Vicente 238, 241
Pi Sunyer, Carles 79
Piñol, Joaquín 260
Portela Valladares, Manuel 219
Pozas, Sebastián 73, 74
Prada, Manuel 264, 279
Prada Vaquero, Adolfo 279
Prat, José 80
Precioso, Artemio 189, 190–1, 192,
    195, 197, 199, 202
Prieto, Indalecio 11, 13, 24, 28, 30, 61,
    80, 91, 118, 173–4, 179–80, 239,
    240, 257, 281, 315, 319, 320
Primo de Rivera, Miguel 25, 242, 268
Puche Álvarez, José 202–4
Pueblo 317
Purcell, Norah 310–11
Purcell, Victor 311

Quaker International Commission
  for the Assistance of Child
  Refugees 40
Queipo de Llano, Gonzalo 272, 300
Quinta Columna de Madrid 6, 7, 23,
    30, 31, 35, 39–40, 41, 44, 46, 50,
    67–9, 75, 95, 100, 101–2, 108, 112,
    113, 130, 133, 134, 135, 137, 138,
    143, 161–2, 164, 171, 179, 180, 182,
    183, 193–4, 214, 229, 254–5, 258,
    264, 266, 268, 274, 276, 279, 289,
    293, 299, 303, 305, 306, 307, 308,
    317

Quiñones de León, José María 59,
    269–70

Radio España 211
Radio Flota Republicana 193
Ramírez Togores, Vicente 182, 184,
    191, 192, 194, 196, 198, 199
Ramón y Cajal, Santiago 117
Raposo, Juan 260–1
Río, José del 218, 273–4, 317
Ríos, Fernando de los 91, 240
Riquelme y López Bago, General José
    74
Rivas Cherif, Cipriano 52, 53
Rivas Cherif, Dolores 54
Rodríguez, Benigno 64, 152, 162, 230,
    231
Rodríguez, Joaquín 195, 199, 201–2
Rodríguez García, Melchor 138–40,
    156, 250, 279
Rodríguez Madariaga, Eduardo 274
Rodríguez Miaja, Fernando 6, 48,
    238, 280
Rodríguez Olazábal, José 288, 289,
    291
Rodríguez Vega, José 142, 154, 155,
    156, 203, 212, 213, 215, 217, 220,
    232, 233, 244, 257, 270, 263, 288,
    296
Rojo, Vicente 5, 6, 10, 13, 14, 16, 17,
    24, 28–9, 32, 33, 34, 35, 36, 47, 61,
    62, 63–4, 65, 70, 71–2, 74, 76–81,
    82–4, 89, 102, 111–12, 113–15,
    120–1, 143, 158, 159, 162, 176, 207,
    237, 308, 316, 320
Romero Marín, Francisco 82, 233,
    234
Rommel, Erwin 308
Roosevelt, Eleanor 71
Roosevelt, Franklin D. 319
Royal Navy 249, 253–4
Rubiera, Carlos 141, 296
Ruiz, Antonio 189, 195, 197, 198,
    199
Ruiz Fornells, Colonel 151–2

Sagardía Ramos, Antonio 261
Saint-Exupéry, Antoine de 311
Salas Larrazábal, Ramón 250
Salgado Moreira, Manuel 31, 68, 129,
    130–1, 134–9, 163, 164, 211, 251,
    254–5, 263, 264, 283, 284–5, 287,
    288, 289, 290, 292, 306
Samitiel, José 182
San Andrés Castro, Miguel 214, 218,
    220, 239–40, 272
Sánchez, Serafin 291
Sánchez Arcas, Manuel 152, 230
Sánchez García, Alfonso 139
Sánchez Guerra, Rafael 138–9, 283–4,
    299, 300
Sánchez Román, Felipe 18–19
Santiago, Lucio 245
Santodomingo de Vega, Carmen 289,
    310, 311
Sanz, Ricardo 129
Sarrault, Albert 80
Sartorius, Fernando 75–6
Sayagués, Prudencio 235
Servicio de Evacuación de los
    Refugiados Españoles (SERE) 80,
    319
Servicio de Información Militar
    (SIM) 18, 31, 42, 93, 94, 127, 152,
    180, 226, 235, 267, 295, 307
Servicio de Información y Policía
    Militar (SIPM) 31–2, 33, 45, 81,
    84, 94, 102, 112, 113, 123, 124,
    149, 151, 152, 241–2, 306, 308,
    310
Servicio de Investigación Militar for
    the Army of the Centre 31, 43, 117,
    127, 226
Servicios Secretos de Guerra 68
Shumilov, Mijail Stepanovich (alias
    Shilov) 234
Sindicato de Espectáculos Públicos
    135
Socialista, El 43, 256
Socorro Rojo Internacional 41, 167,
    260

Soley Conde, Julián 143–4, 152
Sosa y Pérez, Luis de 30
Soviet Military Intelligence (GRU) 155
Stalin, Josef V. D. 9, 15, 20, 21, 27, 179, 238, 247, 256
Stepanov, Boris (Stoyan Minev) 88, 90, 118, 119–20, 161, 171, 172, 230; *see also* Minev, Stoyan
Stevenson, Ralph Skrine 4, 32, 44, 54–5, 57, 58–9, 140
Suárez, Julián 113

Tagüeña, Manuel 20, 73, 81, 82, 84, 167, 168–9, 170–2, 174, 175, 176–7, 182, 205, 229, 231, 233, 235
Thorez, Maurice 39
Thurston, Walter 59
Tierno Galván, Enrique 219
Tillon, Charles 285, 287
Times, The 60, 218, 269
Togliatti, Palmiro 35, 36, 66, 67, 76, 88, 89–90, 103, 169–70, 171, 172, 174, 179, 226, 230–1, 235, 244, 246, 247, 278
Tomás, Pascual 236, 296
Torrecilla Guijarro, Ramón 260
Tovey, John 290, 292

Ulimann, André 285, 287
Ungría, Domingo 154, 155, 245
Ungría Jiménez, José 31, 45, 50, 102, 123, 274–6, 277, 293–4, 310
Unión General de Trabajadores (UGT) 5, 25, 28, 41, 139, 142, 155, 212, 213, 217, 218, 220, 232, 233, 237, 244, 248, 257, 259, 267, 294, 296
Unión Radio 138, 211, 265
United Press 44, 50, 82
Uribe, Vicente 14, 47, 63, 69, 76–7, 83, 85, 88, 89–90, 98, 111, 117, 118, 143, 153, 154, 168, 175, 179, 184, 206, 220, 222, 226, 230, 233, 255, 259, 278

Val Bescós, Eduardo 69–70, 127–9, 130, 131, 134–5, 137–8, 139, 163, 164, 211, 212, 218, 238, 251, 254–5, 263–4, 283, 284–5, 287, 288, 289, 290, 292, 306
Valdés Larrañaga, Manuel 258, 267, 307
Vanni, Ettore 247
Varela, José Enrique 8–9
Vaupshasov, Stanislav 154, 155, 169, 234
Vázquez, Mariano 70, 254
Vega, Etelvino 175, 176–7, 182, 226, 233
Vega Díaz, Francisco 202–3, 206, 220, 229, 230, 234
Velao, Antonio 183
Verardini Díez de Ferreti, Antonio 68, 263
Verdad, La 247
Victoria, Luis Gonzalo 274–7, 293–4
Vidal de Cubas, Federico 183, 198–9
Vidal Zapater, José Manuel 48–9, 95, 229–30, 234
Vidarte, Juan-Simeón 3, 18, 51, 60, 68, 321
Vigón, Juan 152
Viñas, Ángel x, 310
Voz, La 271

Wood, Barbara 285

Yagüe Blanco, Juan 279, 310
Young, Sir George 285, 291

Zabalza, Ricardo 142, 305
Zapiráin, Sebastián 244
Zilliacus, Laurin 'Konni' 285–7, 295, 313
Zorita, Antonio 73
Zugazagoitia, Julián 29, 43, 54, 55, 56, 60, 64, 74, 76, 77, 79, 84, 90, 111–12, 118, 119, 157, 158, 159, 163, 168, 170, 220–1